PERILOUS BEASTS

Diálogos Series

KRIS LANE, Series Editor

Understanding Latin America demands dialogue, deep exploration, and frank discussion of key topics. Founded by Lyman L. Johnson in 1992 and edited since 2013 by Kris Lane, the Diálogos Series focuses on innovative scholarship in Latin American history and related fields. The series, the most successful of its type, includes specialist works accessible to a wide readership and a variety of thematic titles, all ideally suited for classroom adoption by university and college teachers.

Also available in the Diálogos Series:

Understanding Latin America's Economy in the Twenty-First Century by Jeff Dayton-Johnson
Armed Frontier: Warfare and Military Culture in the Texas–Northeastern Mexico Borderlands, 1686–1845 by Luis Alberto García-García
Driving Terror: Labor, Violence, and Justice in Cold War Argentina by Karen Robert
Frontier Justice: State, Law, and Society in Patagonia, 1880–1940 by Javier Cikota
Anti-Catholicism in the Mexican Revolution, 1913–1940 edited by Jürgen Buchenau and David S. Dalton
The Struggle for Natural Resources: Findings from Bolivian History edited by Carmen Soliz and Rossana Barragán
Viceroy Güemes's Mexico: Rituals, Religion, and Revenue by Christoph Rosenmüller
At the Heart of the Borderlands: Africans and Afro-Descendants on the Edges of Colonial Spanish America edited by Cameron D. Jones and Jay T. Harrison
The Age of Dissent: Revolution and the Power of Communication in Chile, 1780–1833 by Martín Bowen

For additional titles in the Diálogos Series, please visit unmpress.com.

STEPHEN B. NEUFELD

PERILOUS BEASTS

MEXICAN NECROPOLITICS,
ANIMAL DEATHS, AND
BLOOD SPORTS, 1870–1920

UNIVERSITY OF NEW MEXICO PRESS
ALBUQUERQUE

© 2026 by the University of New Mexico Press
All rights reserved. Published 2026
Printed in the United States of America

Library of Congress Cataloging-in-Publication Data
Names: Neufeld, Stephen author
Title: Perilous beasts : Mexican necropolitics, animal deaths, and blood sports, 1870–1920 / Stephen B. Neufeld.
Description: Albuquerque : University of New Mexico Press, 2025. | Series: Diálogos series | Includes bibliographical references and index.
Identifiers: LCCN 2025035009 (print) | LCCN 2025035010 (ebook) | ISBN 9780826369093 hardback | ISBN 9780826369109 paperback | ISBN 9780826369116 epub
Subjects: LCSH: Animal welfare—Mexico—History | Human-animal relationships—Mexico—History | Bullfights—Social aspects—Mexico—History | Hunting—Social aspects—Mexico—History
Classification: LCC HV4771.A3 N48 2025 (print) | LCC HV4771.A3 (ebook)
LC record available at https://lccn.loc.gov/2025035009
LC ebook record available at https://lccn.loc.gov/2025035010

Founded in 1889, the University of New Mexico sits on the traditional homelands of the Pueblo of Sandia. The original peoples of New Mexico—Pueblo, Navajo, and Apache—since time immemorial have deep connections to the land and have made significant contributions to the broader community statewide. We honor the land itself and those who remain stewards of this land throughout the generations and also acknowledge our committed relationship to Indigenous peoples. We gratefully recognize our history.

Cover illustration: "Lolita Rejoneando," *El Toreo,* Mar. 7, 1898, 3. Sketch.
Designed by Isaac Morris
Composed in Adorn and Baskerville 10.25 | 14.5

CONTENTS

List of Illustrations ~ vii

Acknowledgments ~ ix

Introduction ~ 1

Part I. In the Cities

Chapter One.
The Sad Repugnant Spectacle:
Street Dogs and Public Health in the Killer City ~ 19

Chapter Two.
Lurking in the Outskirts:
Great Separations and Visible Death ~ 54

Part II. In the Arena

Chapter Three.
Birth of the *Fanático*:
Cultural Takes on the Bullfight Audience ~ 87

Chapter Four.
Owners and Haters:
Capitalism and Activism in the Bullring Business ~ 121

Chapter Five.
Dancing with Bulls:
Gender and the Porfirian Bullfighter ~ 152

Part III. In the Wilds

Chapter Six.
Stalking the Modern:
Sportsmen, Wild Beasts, and Conservation in Mexico ~ 185

Chapter Seven.
Imperial Huntsmen and Missionaries of Death:
Colonizing Practices, Indigenous Ways, and Symbolic Big Game ~ 213

Epilogue ~ 239

Postscript ~ 245

Appendix.
Theoretical Interventions ~ 246

Notes ~ 253

Bibliography ~ 290

Index ~ 311

ILLUSTRATIONS

FIGURE 1.1. Vultures around the meat market, the scavengers of Vera Cruz, Mexico, 1901. ~ 22
FIGURE 1.2. "Tela á prueba de balas," 1897, 1. ~ 32
FIGURE 1.3. H. C. White, "Shoe stalls in the mercado volador (thieves' market), Mexico City," 1908. ~ 37
FIGURE 1.4. J. M. Villasana, "Pauperismo y Plutocracia, la limosna de Año Nuevo," 1897. ~ 47
FIGURE 1.5. José Guadalupe Posada, "Décimas: La perra brava," 1910. ~ 49
FIGURE 1.6. J. M. Villasana, "Los desheredados," 1897. ~ 51
FIGURE 2.1. Casimiro Castro, "La Ciudad de México desde un Globo," 1869. ~ 58
FIGURE 2.2. H. C. White, "Viga Canal and 'Floating Gardens' Santa Anita," 1908. ~ 66
FIGURE 2.3. Hendrik Hondius and Antonio Tempesta, "Two Roosters Fighting," 1610. ~ 71
FIGURE 2.4. Unknown, "Mexico. Cock fight," ca. 1919–1920. ~ 74
FIGURE 3.1. José Guadalupe Posada, "Corrido don chepito mariguano," 1902. ~ 111
FIGURE 3.2. "Bronca al 'Sanluqueño," 1896. ~ 113
FIGURE 3.3. José Guadalupe Posada, "Terrible incendiado de la plaza de toros de Puebla," 1902. ~ 115
FIGURE 3.4. "Por tantiar salir tantiado," 1895. ~ 117
FIGURE 4.1. José Guadalupe Posada, "Desde la Barrera," 1904. ~ 128
FIGURE 4.2. "Tepeyahualco bull," 1896. ~ 137
FIGURE 5.1. José Guadalupe Posada, "Cogida de Rodolfo Gaona en la plaza de toros de Puebla, el 13 de Diciembre de 1908," 1908. ~ 155
FIGURE 5.2. Rodolfo Gaona, mugshot, Juzgado Quinto de Instrucción, Dec. 5, 1909. ~ 161
FIGURE 5.3. José Guadalupe Posada, "Sufrimientos, Reflexiones y Consejos de la Suicida María Luisa Noeker: en la Otra Vida," 1908. ~ 164

FIGURE 5.4. José Guadalupe Posada, "Cogida y muerte de Timoteo Rodríguez," 1895. ~ 168

FIGURE 6.1. "El de la Presa," 1902. ~ 193

FIGURE 6.2. El Buen Tono, advertisement for cigarettes, 1904. ~ 195

FIGURE 6.3. "Arturo Imaz con un jabalí," 1949. ~ 200

FIGURE 7.1. "Interior de Federico Lamin," 1911. ~ 227

FIGURE 7.2. Porfirio Díaz Jr., "President Diaz Hunting in the Mountains," 1908. ~ 231

FIGURE 7.3. Porfirio Díaz Jr., "President Diaz Stands on the Right," 1908. ~ 233

FIGURE 7.4. Porfirio Díaz Jr., "President Diaz Dining with His Hunting Companions," 1908. ~ 234

FIGURE 7.5. "En Chapultepec," 1898. ~ 236

ACKNOWLEDGMENTS

This beast has been long in emerging, and I find myself indebted to many without whom it would never have been finished. Some obvious culprits would include those at California State University, Fullerton. The Dean's Office coughed up moneys to support my research in Mexico with an award, a summer stipend, and two international travel grants. From my department I received research support from the Bellot grant, and invaluable commentary and support from my colleagues who have endured my rantings both at brownbag symposia and in passing over these years. Thank you, all.

Additionally, all my students inspire me and my work, and they asked the many questions that helped me make this all come together. Two master's graduates in particular warrant note as my research assistants in early phases of the project as they pored over miles of newspapers looking for my animals—my thanks to John Bradshaw and Lindsay Weiler-Leon for their efforts.

In Mexico, staff and archivists at the Archivo Histórico del Distrito Federal were delightful to work with, as were the helpful staff at the Instituto Mora, and the Archivo General de la Nación generally did its best.

Community, especially at meetings of the Rocky Mountain Conference of Latin American Studies, also contributed to this book since many of the ideas emerged first in conference presentations. A number of scholars whose commentary really stood out and whose suggestions I readily adopted included Jeffrey Shumway, Virginia Girard, Linda Curcio-Nagy, Donald Stevens, Kathryn Sloan, and Sonia Lipsett-Rivera. It is absolutely essential to have feedback from such great thinkers—thank you.

On particular topics Robert Fehr, Amanda Lopez, and John Klingemann offered me some much needed nuance, and my frequent discussions with Robert Scott led to crucial ideas (as with considering taxidermy). Within animal studies broadly, I would like to acknowledge the influence of Zeb Tortorici, Martha Few, Marcy Norton, and Emily Wakild, who have all built this field into what it is today.

At the press level, my gratitude to University of New Mexico's editors and staff for all that they do. I deeply appreciated the useful and considerable feedback from Steven Bunker and Kris Lane on how to make this a better and more coherent book. I must also shamefacedly thank anonymous reviewers at the *Estudios Mexicanos* journal for comments (now incorporated here) on an article that I never managed to revise and resubmit. Your efforts were, I hope, not in vain.

At more personal levels, I want to add deepest gratitude for a few people. Thanks so much to Bill French for taking the time to read my whole manuscript and reining me in and calling me out when my theoretical enthusiasms overcame my good sense. To be fair, I learned that propensity from him. Michael Matthews was damn near a coauthor on this one with his in-depth commentary, feedback, ideas, and even providing an abundance of sources that I could not obtain myself. Thank you deeply, my brother, for without all your help this book would not be.

And, finally, thanks to Carrie for all the other stuff—life, love, perspective, and helpful things like that.

Introduction

Imagine the view from a great buzzard lazily wheeling over turn-of-the-century Mexico City. Below sweeps a mixed city of colonial and modern buildings, a blend of cityscape and countryside, rapidly expanding but still unclear around its edges. Green swaths and concrete dapple the landscape. Far below, industrial workshops, massive abattoirs, and shiny new department stores vie for every inch of space against parks and streets. It flows from the east, from Peralvillo, to San Lázaro, to new hospitals and the grand penitentiary at Lecumberri, to the palaces and cathedral of the center, and out to the great forests surrounding Chapultepec and its imposing castle high atop.

Movement catches the eye as far below abound creatures in huge numbers. Rats and possums scamper across shadow etched streets. Two-legged animals, too, always scurrying about, mostly blind or indifferent to the other creatures. Seas of sombreros and top hats part reluctantly for the inexorable and ponderous grind of trolley cars. The hum of electric lines is barely drowned out by screams of anger and delight at the *palenques* (arenas), where roosters maim and men gamble. Dogs roam, some privileged as pampered pets, others in packs on streets struggling to survive, often sick, and murdered at a whim.

On these busy shared streets also rises the noisy squeals from herds of openly smuggled hogs destined for private backyard slaughter. On either side of the mucky passages and freshly paved streets, and in innumerable alleys, vagrants loiter. Some creatures have fur, or hooves, whereas others wore white cotton pants.

Avoiding the enormity of a slow-gliding blimp, whose paint matches thousands of banners and advertising posters below, emerges the sight of one of the many huge new arenas recently rising from the empty lots. Within and to the roaring approval of thousands, a bloodied bull falls dead.

Nearer to the train stations of the east, heavily armed trophy hunters saunter off to begin expeditions and adventures into the unconquered wild places of the nation. There they would pit their skills against creatures fierce or unwary. Others of these returned to the city triumphant, with their porters hauling perfect cadavers to the shops of taxidermists for reanimation. In a side street shadowed by the market at La Bolsa, the hungry buzzard alights by the rotting carcass of a mule and dines.

If the circling buzzard could not tell who ruled, who was prey, or whose deaths should warrant applause, an emerging modern society made this clear within their own human ranks. Enormous contrasts between modern life and unnecessary animal deaths reflected profound contradictions in fin-de-siècle Mexico.

Our relationship with animals forms a big part of what makes us who we are. To be inured to, to seek out, or even to cheer for animal deaths speaks to the complexity of our cultures as a human animal. We tell stories about ourselves, to ourselves, that help to define us. We speak of nation, religion, family, and traumas of all kinds. These stories spoke, too, of the animal lives around them and at times justified how these creatures died.

Some beasts died to the cheers and jeers of the crowd, in ways legal or not; others perished in furtive markets or distant wilds, and this had implications for Mexican society. The dark side of the modern liberal-capitalist state developed ways of killing and directed these against Others—in this book—against animals of many sorts. The cultural norms shared by communities and their expectations overcame public reprehensions or disgust. The creatures killed for science or entertainment make these choices and values evident.

For animals, the modernizing nation presented myriad dangers and opportunities. Human animals reacted to their deaths in contradictory ways. Many proved indifferent, or even, actively cruel.[1] Foreign travelers frequently remarked on this, claiming that the "cruelty of those who had to do with animals in this country is shocking," and that even human life garnered little respect.[2] One noted, "I am too overheated to talk on subject of animal cruelty."[3] He went on to admit that

> most Mexicans were fond of animals, and had more pets than in any other country (including sheep, pigs, chickens, ranch dogs)—the pets are played with but never fed—the national love of grace and beauty renders [Mexicans] sensitive to the beauty and grace of animals, but

to their comforts, even their necessities, they are blind and therefore indifferent.⁴

Mexicans themselves remarked with frequency on various spectacles they labeled as "sad," "painful," and (most often) "repugnant." Yet proclaiming this did not address the problem. In practice, animals continued to die in astounding numbers, and cultural frames continued to encourage it.

The Big Questions

Several questions inform this inquiry. How did different groups in Mexico construct a culture that reconciled the psychosocial cost of killing? Who had the privilege or responsibility to kill? How did people frame ideological rationales about animal deaths that had little or no connection to necessity? How did the resulting set of ideas evolve and transform to account for the emergence of a new type of society that took the form of a modern capitalist secular state?

In the broad sense that it is used here, *culture* as a framework for understanding and expressing social meanings fulfilled multiple purposes. Culture facilitated the processing of trauma (even at low levels) and reconciled contradictions between beliefs and practices. In other words, participating in violence toward animals required those involved to excuse themselves using justifications built on notions of science, leisure, and identity. The stories they told established rationales and did not appear out of nothing, but rather they emerged in the context of new types of consumerism, public discourses (e.g., health and hygiene), and conservationism. Animals embodied symbols of capital and normativity, and the capacity of animal life to be taken, both literally and figuratively, empowered a tangle of biopolitical relations.⁵ The animal became an "Other, as a subject of a difference that is almost the same, but not quite," and the victim of routine "non-criminal putting to death" and the euthanasia of the unwanted.⁶ These cultural contexts, among their other facets, marked a liberal state that relied increasingly on non-traditional forms of authority (eschewing monarchs or religion), surveillance, and power relations.⁷

The period of the study encompasses the great changes in Mexican life from about the 1870s to 1920s. This half century witnessed basic changes to where people found food and found work. Governments in this time passed the most comprehensive laws regarding animals.[8] Transnational influences pushed Mexico into building parks and starting societies to protect against animal cruelty. This time period captures the rise of industry in entertainment, in food sourcing, and in daily life. The nation underwent rapid urbanization. A wider view encompasses both the hangovers from colonial or French influences (from 1862 to 1867), the consolidation of the liberal oligarchic regimes, and it takes in some of the efforts to reform from the Revolution between 1910 and 1920. Crucially, the national regime itself does not really matter as much as that of local cultural productions and the continuities of tradition. That said, the book focuses most on the Porfirian era (1876–1911) as the time of most pronounced and dramatic changes in animal-human relations.

This study hinges on certain premises: humans have little stomach for killing animals unnecessarily; cultural constructions predicate our view of the animal world; these constructs intervene and allow us to kill animals in unusual circumstances.[9] Few would reject the need to kill in self-defense, for mercy, for food (until later in the twentieth century), or even for clothing.[10] A consensus that broad has little to teach, perhaps. But kills also occur at the fringes of rationality and acceptability. People applied illogical moral heuristics to their behaviors.[11] Dogs could be killed on suspicion or for notions of urban hygiene, bulls and roosters for the pleasure of spectacle, wild game for reasons masculine and imperial.

Many types of killing, of course, are left out of analysis. Primarily, this study follows larger, arguably more charismatic, creatures. We are more deeply connected to certain animals, and more likely to see their fates as tied to our morality and selves.[12] Rats are on their own. Few people contest the killing of insects, or certain reptiles, and so on. Whales and dolphins are beyond my scope, as are the deaths of laboring animals. The abattoir has its own literature. At the heart of the slaughter emerged a new communal understanding of nature.

What I argue is that many Mexicans in a time of changing social expectations adapted certain practices (like blood sports) in a "modern" age marked by the adoption of *necropolitics*.[13] While hunting, blood sports, and animal control can hardly be seen as new to the era, the systemic context of animal death in regulations, consumption, commerce, legislation, and scientific discourse represented novel features.

(For readers inclined to the theoretical, please turn at this point to the Appendix, "Theoretical Interventions," on page 000 for a more in-depth discussion;

consider this your intellectual Choose-Your-Own-Adventure option. For those otherwise inclined, the next few pages provide an overview of the key conceptual interventions.)

Best described in the work of Achille Mbembe, necropolitics is the deployment of systems of power and the means to exploit populations in ways that require the use of violence and extermination against marginalized groups.[14] That these systems worked to wipe out populations is again not a new concept in understanding colonial power. As an excellent example, consider the indigenous bison-hunting world in the early United States. There, colonists destroyed various populations in tandem and as part and parcel of dispossession and colonizing. Eradicating the great bison herds in industrial fashion functioned to destroy indigenous resistance in the plains and opened territory for colonizers to settle. These combined deaths, made possible by industrial technologies, many officials justified in scientific terms and as entertainment, and as serving the cause of Manifest Destiny.

In *Perilous Beasts* this impulse is shown to apply to neocolonial peoples and animals, too, offering new insights into how the processes of subjugating indigenous peoples also worked against animals. In the buffalo extermination, and the concurrent destruction of the Plains peoples, came an object lesson that I apply to Mexico in the late nineteenth century. More broadly, I show a process that represented a part of the global changes that capitalism and liberal society employed to build hegemony over all life within the nation-state.

The transformative and necropolitical process brought together myriad places and re-created social communities. Urbanization saw the complex city itself become a scientifically empowered killer in other ways. This all related to how people saw nature more broadly. Reformists, conservationists, activists, and hygienists mustered their energies to impose a new alien vision for animal deaths. Fight fans, ambitious entrepreneurs, indigenous hunters, and varied communities worked to maintain their understood set of norms, reciprocities, and relations to nature, including notions of animality and the right to kill. They expressed these vociferously where they could and acted clandestinely where they could not. These ideas of community expectations toward the natural world, a moral ecology, they set against the foil of structured legalistic and scientific ideas imposed from without by a necropolitical ecology (for more on moral ecology, see the appendix).

These ecologies comprised systems of discourse and practice connected to collective relationships with nature. They formed a specific lethal set within what

Marcy Norton calls modes of interaction; the "entrenched customs, patterns of behavior, institutions, and above all, quotidian techniques that people used to observe, listen to, capture, nurture, kill, eat, tan, breed, herd, train, communicate with, feed, or heal other beings."[15] If these other beings mattered to people, if they had worth, then how then to account for killing them nonchalantly?

I argue that an enthusiastic acceptance of animal deaths for science or entertainment represented a necessary feature of the modern liberal-capitalist society. A change occurred at the end of the nineteenth century, framed as modern, with the advent of new governance. The government and society stripped animal subjectivity or selfhood, making creatures into expendable fetish objects. The creatures they selected as sacrifices died for science and entertainment, with their demise permitted by the inculcated cultural indifference of the broader populace. This applied, too, to marginalized humanity. Broader identities formed around an acceptance of death—the blood sports fan, the trophy hunter, the celebrity matador, and perhaps even, the average Mexican. Their ideas became baked into laws, customs, stereotypes, literature, and mythologies. Social relations inscribed necropolitical power onto animal bodies.

Another conceptual thread ties this work together. Moral ecology, in this case, is narrowed down from relations to nature in general to the ways that people related to an extreme case of the deaths of animals outside the usual justifications of food or survival. As a mode of interaction that defined a community with common ideas, it may be seen as akin to *mentalité* or perhaps as a subculture, but with a focus on how people interact with animality. While many acknowledged some kinship to animals, this also entailed a dynamic relationship that increasingly set animals apart by removing their subject status to treat them more often as objects over time. In this limited sense, the social impulse by the end of century increasingly set the animal world as Other to a human ascendency, and in new ways.

These sets of traditions, expectations, and practices changed slowly and in the context of political ecological structures. These forces sometimes set outside norms into conflict with what may be considered the ordinary and local ways of seeing animal death. This opposing strain of thought informed political actions and measures to regulate how the casual killing of animals could occur.

The political ecology was, moreover, infused and shaped by the necropolitical drive that became increasingly powerful during the late nineteenth century in Mexico.

As the nation consolidated around the form of the liberal-capitalist state, lethal logics defined subjectivity and determined who mattered in the country, and who (or what) would face erasure as they became the Other. This ties together animal deaths as a feature of the new modernizing state, and in this study, it ranged in practices from population controls to blood sports to trophy hunting. City official, medical hygienist, spectacle promoter, and game warden all acted as accomplices to the sanguinary society. Throughout these interplays of moral ecological norms and necropolitical ecologies, people expressed their relations to nature and to killings through subcultures of sport, hygiene, and conservation. The resulting cultural justifications reinforced and perpetuated these ideas and mores. By examining the reasoning and clashes around this macabre topic, we can understand the place of animals as a class in society and the contradictions of modern subjectivity.

Ultimately, how Mexicans made sense of and permitted or encouraged the killing of animals for reasons beyond necessity had cultural roots. These cultural choices described a broad sense of identity as Mexico entered the century, with both elements of cruelty and hope for progress.[16] Animals' experiences provided a lens and litmus test to change as they bore witness to and paid the price for a new society.

This work examines the place of animals in the world of human society. This includes a wide array of activities from blood sports like cockfights, bullfights, and trophy hunting to the scientifically approved elimination of stray animals. Creatures and their treatment thus serve as a proxy for certain world views and as a means to see a projection of humanity.[17] In this narrowed moral ecology, where a relation to nature focuses only on the killing animals, it reveals literal embodiments of power. It is a history not simply or rudely of power and cruelty, but one that takes into account the majority of the populace that held and voiced misgivings about the treatment of animal companions.

The relationship that people have with animals, whether wild or domestic, is part of a set of normative values that includes elements of what people believe they are. The treatment of animals becomes part of gender roles, masculinity, racial expectations, social class performance, and sacred or religious dogma.[18] Animal status also called into question the definition of city, and of indigeneity. In other words, relations with animal death represented the moral and the necropolitical ecology. Relations to nature shaped social practice.

Methods and Situation in Literature

The conceptual framework of ideological "nature" reflected more about those who sought to define it rather than some reality of the geography. As William Cronon argues, *nature* is the human notion of the difference between the civilization and the other, the "natural," and is in his words "the mirror of unexamined longings and desires."[19] The different versions of what *nature* meant become rhetoric and discourses that jostled for preeminence in broader political battles. Boundaries between the wilds and the human-controlled become blurry when closely examined, and even the urban-rural edges can sometimes fade from sight. The addition of animals and animal-human relationships to this complexity, especially within the context of a modernizing nation-state, affords additional insights into the fundamental historical tensions of society. Of course, simply analyzing "relations to nature" itself poses other challenges given the romantic and problematic artifice underlying the concept of "nature," as many have argued elsewhere.[20] One element of this rises in animal history.

By taking our species as merely another animal in the workings of history, it brings out a wealth of understudied economic and cultural aspects of daily life in Latin America and Mexico. This becomes best evident in the nineteenth and early twentieth centuries as technological change, rampant urbanization, and global capitalism rapidly reconfigured Latin America.[21] Animals' places in society changed more dramatically in these years than in centuries preceding, or the century after. How humans understood themselves relative to animals also shifted, and categories like "man" (discursively excluding women, indigenous, and the poor) faced challenges—so, too, the definition of human as simply "animal-plus" or "not-animal" became less assumed.[22] Generally, animals have appeared in the history in rather limited ways: as objects and categories of economic study; as elements of environmental and conservationist concerns; as aspects of public health, diet, and disease; and as carriers of cultural freight in areas like art, symbolism, ideology, religion, and lifestyles.[23] Rarely do they appear as historical subjects in their own rights. Nonetheless, animals' and humans' entanglements created history.[24]

Animals in general represented historical beings in Mexico embedded in labor regimes, land use, and even in perceptions of backwardness. As has been shown elsewhere, changes in the nineteenth century saw a shift in the foundations of wealth and production that left animals behind in favor of the mechanical. Animal labor, and even their mere presence in human places, became signs of the "uncivilized" past. Human perspectives of non-human creatures inexorably turned toward seeing them as fundamentally Other and expendable.[25]

How people used and interacted with animals led to new social relations and altered the fundamental definitions of people, for example, with categories like indigeneity and the "sportsman" hunter (an ideal of considerable cultural import).[26] Animals changed, too, as creatures adapted with history, for instance, a wolf in fifteenth-century Mexico had different relations to humans, to climate, and to food. It became a fundamentally different wolf in time.[27] Interactions with animals also shaped the ways societies worked to understand themselves and how they experienced forms of self-colonization, neocolonialism, and settler colonialism. Human society, a highly invasive species, certainly treated animals in ways reminiscent to how elite groups had exerted power over minority (human) Others historically. Whether in exploitation, casual massacre, or discursive displacement to subaltern status, the similar patterns that theorists attributed to the colonial consolidation of power apply here too.[28] Animals played a role in this culturally as embodiments of national or local symbols, but also in broader shifts in labor, commodities, capital, and other economic areas. Beyond the rapidly exploding cityscapes and domestic realms, animals proved key to defining rural and frontier identities as societies evaluated nature, wilderness, and progress.[29] The population question, whether of animal or human, and the issues of extinction or conservation fundamentally underpinned policies set into medical and eugenic practice.

As Mexican elites sought to create their version of the modern nation, they did so in the context of changing ideas about nature, race, and progress. Nevertheless, few scholars have addressed the animal-human relationships that played a role in this development, or they have focused more particularly on conservation efforts such as the later creation of national parks.[30] For Latin America generally, the most important work was *Centering Animals in Latin American History*, which as an edited volume covered a large span of time and many disparate places with only one chapter covering Yucatecan vermin for the modern era of Mexico.[31] A solid work on the Mexican sausage industry made alluring hints, but offered little meat for cultural analyses.[32]

Scholars have written surprisingly little on strays, blood sports, or hunting in modern Mexico, but those that have contributed greatly to this book. A few anthropological studies tackled indigenous hunting, some colonial-era studies have touched on street dogs and bullfighting for their periods, and the more modern story of bullfighter Rodolfo Gaona has received thoughtful analysis.[33] Adrian Schubert provided a great social history of the bullfight in Spain (with some coverage for Mexico and Latin America).[34] Mauricio Tenorio-Trilllo's excellent *I Speak of the City* touched on some matters of urban animals and pests.[35] Marcy Norton has recently tackled a long history of animal subjectivity in the Atlantic World.[36] But, generally, much remains for historical exploration.

Perilous Beasts carries the theme of culturally constructed animal deaths from the city streets to the leafy suburbs and outward to the wide wildernesses and back again. It extends the logic of necropolitics from colonialism to animal relations. It plays with a human subjectivity caught in the maelstrom of becoming a modern nation, demonstrating how people expressed identities through the macabre extremes of human practices.

This study comes from an initial chance encounter with the tale of a rabid pig gunned down in the middle of a Mexico City street. The questions this raised, about weapons, rabies, city life, animal control and presences, and so on, drew me in. Observations about cruelty to animals, some apparently evident in the continued realm of blood sports, made little sense given my experience of Mexican compassion and conscience.

Death had particular meanings in Mexico, as authors like Claudio Lomnitz show, but this did not explain the rift.[37] A resulting cognitive dissonance between people's cruelty and grace, and given my rural upbringing perhaps an odd reaction, made me recognize that I could not explain this aspect of animal treatment in Mexican society.[38] As Robert Darnton suggests, a good cultural history should begin with the "joke that you do not get" or, in this case, an emotional response not fully understood.[39]

This work is therefore inspired from that point of view. A broad reading of the literature sets the stage and provides a frame for this examination. For primary sources, the research draws from multiple archives: travelers' accounts, contemporary newspapers, folk music, broadsheet artwork, oral histories, and published memoirs. These afforded voices from all sides and multiple classes and helped express how Mexicans experienced and thought about the many "repugnant spectacles" they witnessed. They provide the traces and tracks of animal life and death that the researcher stalks.⁴⁰ Close reading and interpretation "against the grain" bring the material together.

Cultural in approach and social in bias, this book builds on the theoretical ideas of the necropolitical and the moral ecology (itself a derivative of "moral economies," and hence, of Marxist ideas), yet it stops short of fully embracing the "non-human turn."⁴¹ Against this completely animal-oriented history, humans remain my focus and questions of animal agency are left largely aside. The meaning of the choice to kill animals for ideology, leisure, or precaution takes preeminence here. I also avoid the (fortunately) rare and deviant killing of creatures for reasons psychotic or sexual or both. This may mean the study goes too far for some political or economic-minded scholars, and that it goes not far enough for those more environmental or ecocritical in mindset. Rather, I hope this finds a happier middle ground where culture, power, and nature are all shaped in relation to one another.

This book therefore addresses the deaths of animals in particularly limited venues and rationales. Scientific reasonings, urban collateral damage, ideologies of the hunt, leisure complexes, and capitalist entertainment, and even the effort to otherwise hide deaths (as in clandestine meat markets) all belong to the human animal. They are perilous beasts.

Perilous Beasts on a Map

Overall, this study moves from the city to the suburbs and then out to the wider wilderness in Mexico.⁴² The two chapters in part 1 explore animals in the streets and suburbs. Part 2 works through a social history of the bullfight in three chapters. Two chapters on hunting form part 3.

Chapter 1, "The Sad Repugnant Spectacle: Street Dogs and Public Health in the Killer City," examines the rising power of public health discourses to manage perceived problems of the unhygienic city and its various animalities. It reveals a necropolitical ecology of great persuasion through the various battles that took place between elite actors and governments against the less fortunate denizens of the urban streets in Mexico. The ongoing efforts of officials to combat rabies through hygiene and veterinary sciences meant implementing dangerous and controversial forms of animal control such as mass poisonings with strychnine.

The presence of stray dogs in the city also furthered an image of squalor in a city of sensory experiences. I connect this through the phrase "perros callejeros" to the ways in which elite often included the urban poor into this schema. "Street dogs" became the euphemism for members of the lower social classes who, like their canine counterparts, lost their place in city spaces and faced harsh conditions for their "unnatural" appearance amid the modern world. The treatment of animals, from massacre to pity to hygiene to imprisonment, also reflected the tragic reality of many human animals.

The second chapter, "Lurking in the Outskirts: Great Separations and Visible Death," broadens the city to include neighboring municipalities. In the Mexican case the drive to control the countryside and reshape populations hinged on relationships between humans and fetishized animals, and these often played out first in the urban outskirts. In this context various necropolitical regimes enacted laws targeting poor Mexicans. Laws criminalized the gathering of food from roadkill and urban hunting, and with increasing vigor sought to remove all livestock from within the city. Officials displaced all visible animal deaths, in particular the slaughterhouse, from open city spaces. These measures proved difficult to enforce, and clandestine meat smugglers thrived and traded from suburban bases.

And while, on one hand, officials attempted to make killing invisible, at the suburban level cockfighting remained ubiquitous. This pageantry of death, the *pelea de gallo* (cockfight), represented a powerful and persistent expression of the moral ecology. An examination of the sport, its history, and its meanings reveals the conflicts between vehement supporters and cosmopolitan reformers. While the meat markets fought toward a sterile vision of a nation without visible slaughter, Sundays were for strapping knives on to your murderous rooster.

The cockfight aside, the truly big spectator sport of Mexico, in city and suburbs alike, competed at the Sunday afternoon bullfight. Chapter 3, "Birth of the *Fanático*: Cultural Takes on the Bullfight Audience," examines the cultural creation of the modern sports fandom. By the end of the nineteenth century, tens of thousands gathered at multiple *plazas* every week in the winter months. Complete with targeted merchandise, modern venues, and new media, the sport and its proprietors built a new kind of fan and a world for them. Specialty papers and folksongs facilitated a novel relationship with the sport. Audiences made their expectations clear with their wallets and with participation in the event. When bulls or fighters disappointed them, the entitled fans criticized with everything from whistles and thrown cushions to full-blown rioting and arson. Ultimately, a modernizing fan culture and consumerism emerged to watch the death of animals as pure spectacle.

Chapter 4, "Owners and Haters: Capitalism and Activism in the Bullring Business," develops the multiple and contending political forces around the bullfight. The years between 1887 to 1910 represented a golden age for the bullfight industry. During this time promoters built numerous new plazas and on a greater architectural scale than had ever been possible. Allied with their mass spectator class they changed the sport. Cattlemen (*ganaderos*) bred better and meaner fighting bulls to vie with expensive matadors. Activists including the Society for the Protection and Care for Animals (SPCMA) fiercely resisted the bullfight and sought to reinstate bans on the practice. Foreign witnesses wrote harsh tirades. Humanitarian and foreign ideologies competed poorly against an alliance of moral ecological traditions and capitalist profitability. The audiences continued attending, the empresarios cultivated lawmakers, and the abolitionist activists failed.

Chapter 5, "Dancing with Bulls: Gender and the Porfirian Bullfighter," contrasts fan expectations and societal expectations in the world of the bullfighter elite. It delves into the gender and social roles of the *diestro* (expert), the *matador del toros*, who acted as the celebrity front man for a team of *torero* bullfighters. He (usually) embodied generational fantasies, class identities, overt masculinity, and even at times transcended racial prejudices. The legal limits to managing and promoting this kind of celebrity became evident in the case of Rodolfo Gaona and his involvement with a teenaged girl. Gendered elements to the constructed celebrity also extended to behaviors of fans, and to the rare spectacle of the female torera bullfighter. In all cases, the celebrity animal killer became and remained iconic in Mexican cultural production and in broad views of natural animality.

Other places, far from the city, experienced different cultural clashes. Chapter 6, "Stalking the Modern: Sportsmen, Wild Beasts, and Conservation in Mexico," examines the role of Mexican game hunters in the formation of ideas about wildlife and conservation laws. What might have been considered a limited perspectives of a few hunter-authors entwined with legal and scientific discourses of the "nature state." The government legislated and regulated, and in time, seized control over natural resources to impose a singular political ecology that excluded alternatives. Naturalist hunters wielded enormous influence over changing discourses on the hunt.

These self-professed "sportsmen" told tales of hardship, danger, and reward. They built a customary social practice around performed masculinity. Their experiences defined the "good hunter." Legislators responded with necropolitical laws to protect and conserve certain species for the *riqueza pública* (public wealth). For many creatures this failed; grizzlies and wolves disappeared, and dispossessed indigenous hunters became poachers and pirates.

Chapter 7, "Imperial Huntsmen and Missionaries of Death: Colonizing Practices, Indigenous Ways, and Symbolic Big Game," analyzes indigenous, foreign, and elite hunters. After briefly considering the anthropological accounts of native hunting, and the moral ecology this represents, it primarily focuses on performances by the elite of the elite hunters. Most did not eat their kills, but stalked prey for the sake of the ritual, the fun, the show of power, and the demonstration of their distance from the poor. It brings the book full circle, as it returns to a form of blood sport and leisure that no poor people or those derogatorily termed "perros callejeros" (street dogs) could afford. Even the accompanying hounds received kinder treatment than some indigenous porters. The ceremonial aspects and traditions of the elite hunt worked as a show of "imperial reach" and a postcolonial perspective that illustrates the normative assumptions of participants. Trophies and taxidermy made the fetishized kill permanently visible, in sharp contrast to the vanished dogs of the city. The development of this political ecology also showed in the transnational influences of foreign hunter-tourists who brought a neocolonial spin to the wilds. These outsiders urged Mexicans to establish a national stewardship over nature to preserve exotic creatures for the best future safari hunts. Nature became a national property, an international commodity, and an export good. In this world, animals' value became sharply delineated and a symbolic fetish.

Perilous Beasts explains the changing dynamics of the human and animal coexistence in a historical era when Mexican society dramatically lurched toward the capitalist modern default. It adds a new element to understanding complexities of power and class identities.

This study reaches beyond Mexico to add to our comprehending of the darker side of the liberal-capitalist state, of ways of colonization, and of animals' places in the modernizing world. By industrializing murder, the intimacy of killing became something colder as animals became fetishized objects and the value of life shifted to the marketplace. A new society included a built-in indifference to genocide, whether of animals or anyone else. It challenges our assumptions of benign governance by reading animals deaths in the shadow of modernization, not as inadvertent or collateral damage, but rather as a necessary facet of a new kind of power over populations. This capacity tied to collective expectations in the wider population. Deaths became normal and acceptable. A postmodern and postcolonial history of the animal in a society where they lost selfhood speaks to processes of commodification and environmental discourses, and it tells a tale of the dispossession and violence inherent to global capitalism. It also changed the performance of a human-animal identity to one formed around animal meanings. In this way, an explanation of blood sports, wildlife conservation, and animal control—as cultural phenomena—explains deeper global processes of identity and Othering.

This book explores a changing society with identities in flux, where violence and cruelty represented both the new face of Mexico and a deliberate invocation of long historical practices. No one acted cruelly, of course, in their own eyes. Cultural excuses dismissed animal discomforts as unreal (as with cocks, who could not feel pain), necessary (as with possibly sick dogs), or artistic (as with the fighting bull). Modern trappings and accessories made long-standing practices more immune to criticism since any small evidence of advances suggested progress. Science, particularly medicine, offered utilitarian excuses for animal testing and culling. Game hunters argued that they preserved natural balances and served conservation. They asserted, too, that the hunt provided men with the only antidote against the poisonous effects of urban industrial living and the "iron cage of modernity." It re-created them.

At the levels of day-to-day life, Mexicans of all classes interacted with animal deaths in the arenas of leisure, foodways, and performance. Animals remained an integral part of how people enjoyed life and re-created themselves. Sports and food worked as a part of self-expression and of the creation of taste, class, and ethnicity. A performance of identity could be found on dinner plates as well as in choices about entertainment. Not all, of course, followed the herd into watching blood sports. Sports like baseball, soccer, and bicycling had a great appeal for a reason. But for many the appeal of things like the bullfight pulled them in and gave them a reason to feel pride in their nationalism, their tough demeanors, and their sense of power.

Modern nation-states inscribed power on bodies to, alongside surveillance and discipline, control how the governed behaved.[43] Sciences, medicine, laws, institutions like the military or schools, and other discourses and structures functioned to shape a modern subject. This certainly proved true for many animals in fin-de-siècle Mexico. Animals literally and figuratively faced inscription. Some became permanent story prompts through taxidermy that re-created their dead bodies with wire, stuffing, and cured hides. Some became the topics of songs, poems, and art, and figuratively gained an immortal place in culture. The cultural work that people did around animal death wove tapestries of interwoven meanings and intimacies.[44] This power allowed Mexicans to create themselves with ideas about taste, ethnicity, and the nation. Animal presences and absences shine light on cultural variations and conflicts during an age of changes. They shaped imaginations.

The necropolitical ecology, infused by imaginings that extended biopower into the realms of animal death, ordered the demise of those deemed lesser. Those categorized as having "bare life" and not counted fully as subjects became necessarily relegated to extermination, or at least, expendable in the agenda of power, capital, and civilizing.[45] Democracy, liberalism, and even humanism did not structure this as an aberration or "state of exception," but rather as a feature of the colonizing process. Power exerted statistically against populations, biopower, extended its reach (and that of elite agents) over categorical Others—in this case, against non-human animals. In other words, the rampant killing of less useful populations had, by this era, become a requisite feature of the liberal governance. This power shaped popular assumptions and expectations and articulated with broader cultures.

The place of creatures in culture tapped into deep ideas of religion and fantasy. Animal nature occasioned art and fashioned Romantic ideals. Artists often portrayed the deer as holy, sacred, and an object of innocent beauty. The bull appeared as sacrifice and a metaphor for bravery. The dog became the hero of every hunting tale. Catholics venerated saints like Francis or Eustace for their connection to beasts.[46] Indigenous peoples held to nature as a spiritual wellspring and a political basis for resistance.[47] Modernists dreamed that the trolley and the railway would liberate the laboring horses and burros. Yet, even with all this cultural freight, the animals continued to die needless deaths. The paradoxes and the complexity of these cultural norms presented a complicated and contradictory world.

In both intimate and public sites, Mexicans treated with their animal compatriots. Indifference toward death, any death, is a cultural construction.[48] As such, the tenuous place of animals among us proves integral to the human condition and to understandings of modern life and constructions of nature. The animals' lives and deaths reflected both the best and the worst of our human essence in their myriad roles within the city and in wilds.

PART I

In the Cities

CHAPTER ONE

The Sad Repugnant Spectacle

Street Dogs and Public Health in the Killer City

The idea of a neutral science is a fiction, and an interested fiction[1]

In an aversion to animals, the predominant feeling is fear of being recognized by them through contact. The horror that stirs deep in man is an obscure awareness that something living within him is so akin to the animal that it might be recognized. . . . He may not deny his bestial relationship with the creature, the invocation of which revolts him: he must make himself its master.[2]

Gunshots cracked in the leafy spaces of late nineteenth-century Mexico City—a city where wilderness continued to infringe to the doorsteps of the urbanites and where the shooting of animals marked ambiguities of country, town, and wilds. Near the end of the nineteenth century, this was not an isolated or rare occurrence, nor was shooting the domain of police and criminals, nor accidents and target practice. The edges of the city blurred into a countryside that remained untamed or wild. Rapid modernization had seen the city change with some pavement, bathed in electric lights, and tied together with steel rails and telephone wires. The nation itself remained more than 88 percent rural in populace, and perhaps more so, as even in the most modern of cities daily life and behaviors could not be well distinguished from rural ways.[3] So, where, in this city on the fringe of modern, on the edge of wilds, did the gunfire come from?

The answer lay in the complex relationships people had with the animals in their lives. Animals adapted to city or wandering feral (synanthropes) or wild (antathropes), as well as the urban-domesticated, inhabited all city spaces top to bottom. There they fed, foraged, hid, bred, and, in huge numbers, died. As the compelling work of Nigel Thrift asserts, the city became a massively efficient killer.[4] The urban terrain killed some, competing animals took others, and many more creatures fell prey to humans who exterminated, "controlled," overworked, and, at times, ate them.

In late nineteenth-century Mexico City, the culling of street animals pointed to an evolving society where the death of the less-than-human could be justified in the grand context of civilizing in the name of "progress and order." It also called into question the definition of city, and of indigeneity. At the extreme of animal-human relationships, the kill thus represented an extension of the long and dramatic hunt for a modern nation. This struggle over the moral and political ecology would be played out in state efforts to legislate attempts to make the streets safe, and in the establishment of new governance over the poor—whether this be animal or not. Ultimately, higher society subjected the vermin of city streets and the humans that lived with them to the same modernizing strains.[5] This necropolitical agenda shaped and organized efforts to control modern urban life.

The dominion of the liberal-capitalist state over all life, as biopolitics, extended into a necropolitics that selected statistically and clinically which lives in the nation mattered or, often, those who did not. This affected the poor and the street dog in ways uncannily similar in rhetoric and science. Biopolitics—the political administration and regulation of the life of species and a locality's populations—extended to necropolitics that relegated some marginal creatures to death. This entails a slippery slope, since many assumed the benign nature of a biopolitical agenda. Yet as Walter Benjamin points out: "pernicious too, is the law preserving 'administrative' violence that serves [the state]."[6] In this system, the killing impulses represented not a side effect or bug but a feature that allowed the new kinds of authority to prevail. The drive to a sovereign and utilitarian liberal state, one enjoying what Foucault terms *security*, cannot succeed without the creation of the Other and the means to combat them.

Scientists backed by political power rose in prominence (and with increased scale and scope) to drive notions of public health that openly worked against animals' welfare. Discourses became institutionalized by experts who inveighed on water, architecture, food, medicine, alcohol, and sexuality. And with coercive state supports they had armed force and legality backing their orders.[7] Among the many plans and programs came "modern" ways to combat zoonotic diseases, to massacre possible vermin, to combat rabies, to medically experiment on critters, and to dictate the disposal of corpses. They sought to perfect Mexican life and death—achieving order and progress—and in their wake left a host of dead animals.[8]

To be sure, this was not a task to which the Porfirian (1876–1910) and Revolutionary regimes (1911–1920) found themselves well suited. At the local levels, people involved in areas like animal control resisted laws for pragmatic reasons. Generally, the slippage between elite practice and their requirements for plebeians did not go unnoticed. And where the wilds met the city, where animals met their end, the agents of the nature state struggled to implement changes.

The city represented a sensory experience of animality and nature, where sentiments and sciences clashed. Here, the success of a cultural construction that forgave killing and erasing worked in the name of the social good promised by medical advances.[9] In Mexico this proved to be a project of modernization that necessarily tackled vermin and human life simultaneously, unable to separate the two in the changing city.

This chapter explores the context of urban nature as a killer of animals. I evaluate the perils of the street as a wild and sensory place where dangerous beasts roamed and challenged public health and tranquility. I argue that, ultimately, the elite subjected the canine vermin of city streets and the humans that lived with them to evolving powers. Some creatures, of course, did better than others. It has been noted that horses proved better at adapting to urbanization than did most humans.[10] Nonetheless, the killer city, the stray hounds, and the well-intentioned scientists demonstrated the workings of necropolitics in the new political ecology.

Necropolitics manifested as systemic indifference to the "bare life" of former subjects who became objects subject to public hygiene. Dogs of any species did not "count" as they transformed into the natural enemy of city living and modern aesthetics. Public health measures, clearly well-intended and benign, also represented the outgrowth of the liberal state, that found it easy enough to justify canine surveillance, experimentation, and even massacres.[11] This fit a framework that informed the political ecology and it reformed the place of dogs in Mexico City.[12] The logic created hierarchies with those who mattered to society receiving biopolitical advantages, funding, efforts, and status. Meanwhile the non-productive became labeled as pests, parasites, and vermin subject to destruction. The system aimed for the ascendence, civilizing, and prosperity of a new society, one enjoying security and perpetuity, through policy, legislation, and discourses about worth and progress. Animals that did not meet this agenda become an Other. By being rationally set aside, the discarded reinforced the success, security, and cohesion of a dominant social ideology. Therefore, extermination logically leads to a specific and orchestrated image of a nation that serves all the citizens (who count), and this guaranteed their security. The necropolitics demanded the demise of the marginal for the success of the majority, who may then become subjects within a biopolitical schema. The clash took place in a complex venue.

The Urban Ecology as a Sensory Experience

When, exactly, does a cluster of homes and businesses become a city? Mexico City (sometimes hereafter "DF") had been the largest in the Western Hemisphere in 1500, 1600, 1700, and 1800—losing this status by 1900—and regaining it, arguably, by 2000.[13] Yet even with some 3–400,000 inhabitants as a city in 1910 it may not have been easily recognized as such by us.[14] For one thing, livestock represented a common feature and many households, particularly (but not solely) recently urbanized and lower classes, kept everything from swine to goats to turkeys.[15] Flocks of turkeys, a hundred strong, strutted down San Francisco street in DF to the surprise of foreigners.[16] Certain barrios remained semi-rural well into the next century, including those on the fringes of the city, like Tacuba, and nearby towns like Xochimilco. Coyoacán retained large numbers of its namesake coyotes around its farmland edges and through its city streets. In the mixed urban centers of the capital, eastern neighborhoods like Peralvillo with its stockyards and markets thronged with animal life.[17] Travelers and residents commented on Mexico City's packs of dogs and traffic of burros; they nonetheless compared it favorably with Vera Cruz when it came to skylines rimmed by swarming vultures.[18] There, the city protected them as "useful birds" that cleared out unwanted refuse despite creating a "repugnant spectacle."[19] The city represented a sensory experience.

Urban life flourished amid great filth and uneven prosperities. Rapid urbanization brought in rural migrants with less resources and less education. The official literacy rate dropped from 62 percent in 1895 to about 50 percent by 1919.[20] While city officials did their best to instill hygienic measures, clean streets, and update

FIGURE 1.1. Vultures around the meat market, the scavengers of Vera Cruz, Mexico. Veracruz Llave Mexico, 1901. Photograph. Underwood & Underwood, Publisher. www.loc.gov/item/2021637513/.

regulations, nonetheless, insects and dogs swarmed, and people suffered bites from scorpions and the odd snakes as well.[21] As in the countryside, mosquitoes and bugs proved a constant irritation.[22] Open sewers and overflowing or blocked gutters turned streets into morasses.[23] Frequent periods of heavy rain made passages impossible with muck. The many animal pens and attendant feces drove some thirty to forty residents in 1910 to call for better urbanization to combat the "nauseating stench" that they endured.[24]

The city also faced calls for assistance in "saneamiento" (making healthy) from its suburban neighbors. Residents in Peralvillo pointed out issues with bad hygiene, poor drainage, piled feces, and uncollected garbage that, along with frequent floods, created "evil conditions" and a deplorable state that mired wagons among the "many streams." In this case, the city rejected their pleas as Peralvillo was not their responsibility.[25] This was also the case within the city where residents complained about the "putrefaction of hog pens" that plagued them.[26] The possibility of this turning into public health outbreaks spurred efforts to remedy things. Residents (*vecinos*) living near a set of sties in 1892 sent a petition with twenty-six signatures demanding changes and claimed that they had suffered a typhus outbreak due to the bad hygiene. Whether this claim had scientific merit or not, the city moved the pens to a new site, and brought in better lighting, drains, pavement, and a water source.[27]

Feces and water issues continued to plague many areas. Army buildings like the artillery facilities at Chapultepec did fall under municipal authority, and when officers complained in 1908 about the lack of water (they only had rain barrels) the city paid attention. They feared that the situation "envenomed the atmosphere and made anti-hygienic foci of infection and bad health," and worse, that this would contaminate downstream water sources.[28] It proved a near impossible and expensive problem to remedy. Animal waste in the streets cost the City 15,000 pesos a month, 180,000 pesos annually, to clear in the 1880s.[29] Officials struggled with issues of refuse and streets that could only be considered somewhat clean during periods of heavy rain and flooding (if then).[30] The urban world assaulted convenience and the human senses.

The city had its own sensory world. Raucous by day, outsiders noted that the streets seemed eerily quiet in the nighttime hours.[31] In an odd contrast to modern sensibilities, other foreigners claimed that the countryside seemed "excessively noisy with the noise of animals, bells, and human beings."[32] Another complained of the rural cacophony of wild fowls.³³ Pitch black city nights kept residents off the mucky streets even as electrification arrived slowly to replace the often-faulty gas lighting.³⁴

Artificial urban lighting began to transform Mexico City spaces in the late nineteenth century but did not arrive easily. For elite classes lighting seemed an obvious boon that would make streets modern and safe.³⁵ Couched as a public health concern, lights permitted the safe transit of doctors and priests to attend nighttime emergencies. Even scattered patches of lamplight might ward away crime and violence. Proponents argued that light could produce order, because in the darkness "night is chaos."³⁶

Less convinced, some of the poorer inhabitants did not see increased lighting as "seguridad" (security).³⁷ Rather, to them, illumination clearly marked the intrusion of policing, of state surveillance, and of unasked-for authorities.³⁸ Patrols with lamps in Mexico City had policed the poor in Bourbon eras, and gendarmes continued the practice (and its selective targets) into the twentieth century.³⁹ The notion of using dogs to assist these patrols seems to have been largely dismissed, and in 1897 mentioned as a novelty taking place in London.⁴⁰ The absence of vigilant patrols and revealing light suited some just fine.

Many animals thrived in the darkness and a nocturnal life.⁴¹ Flickering shadows and inconstant lighting camouflaged, protected, and empowered them. Their world in the darkness of the city streets represented a sensorial chasm full of secrets kept from humanity's limited perspective.⁴² Human sensory limitations leave urban spaces an open habitat for the broadly gifted creatures adapted for the night.⁴³ Humans tried to bring light to the city for many reasons, not least cultural ones reacting to ideas about fear, sins, and the supernatural.⁴⁴ After all, in the dark of Europe roamed will-o-the-wisps and goblins, and in Mexico, *duendes*.⁴⁵ Animals lived there too, in a world beyond our full comprehension. For city officials, the darkness meant wildness, it meant rurality and indigeneity, and it created an illegible place of myriad dangers. True animal nature emerged. Officials therefore sought to expunge threats under whatever lights they could muster, whether the perils were rats or *rateros* (thieves). Notably, the same lantern-bearing patrols that sought burglars and harassed vagrants also caught stray dogs. Beyond policing, the urban spaces became lethal with time.

Cities arriving at the twentieth century became efficient dealers in death for all sorts of animals. New trolleys killed so many of the unwary that newspaper cartoons joked darkly about their collusion with mortuaries and nicknamed them *mataristas* (killers) as a play on *motoristas* (motorists). Market hygiene seemed relatively rare, sick beggars common, and criminality ubiquitous. That said, Mexico City appeared all in all quite the match for New York or London for its improving infrastructure and apparent modernity.[46] Foreigners' accounts support this notion.[47] Large building projects and public works started to change the face of the city with a modern facade, behind which denizens dealt with challenges of everyday urban existence. Humans took precedence everywhere.

Other large international cities forged their ways toward some idea of the modern, too, and they did so at the expense of changing or obliterating animal worlds. Obvious death became something of a taboo: officials moved cemeteries out of cities, they discreetly disposed of dead animals of all sorts, regulations moved slaughter to institutionalized abattoirs, and even human executions became semi-private affairs. At the same time, they tried to erase evidence of living animals, in particular the dung and feces that had become such an issue for quality of life that it required enormous expense to clear away. Exterminator businesses boomed as well. Abattoirs abounded. Non-animal transportation prevailed.[48] Like their international rivals, officials in Mexico City also adapted and changed human inhabitants' relationships with urban animals, and they altered what it meant to live in an urban center. Their city remained, nevertheless, full of nature.

Certainly, the city provided risky habitat for the deer, but for the rat it was a home with fewer risks than the farm field or snake-infested woods. From an animal's perspective, the city represents an ecological niche of great opportunity and great dangers—much the same as for recent human arrivals from the countryside. On the whole, one cannot find many genuine divisions between an artificial city and a natural wilderness when the urban landscape blurred into rural outskirts, and where animals and people flowed fluidly between the other. In fact, one of the few areas of difference might be the experience of the killer city, as it became a place of greatly increased mortality and ways for animals to die. The perils increased with the advance of sciences.

Of Vermin, Pets, and Public Health in the Streets

The drive for better public health and hygiene was clearly not a new movement in Mexico, nor unique in its application of science to political aims. Nor did this era represent the first time that Salubridad (Public Health) enjoyed government support. Yet by the late nineteenth century, this had clearly become more intrusive, more capable, and more assumed to be the default for governance. The public health system, it must be emphasized, does not represent the villain in this narrative, and the motives of these doctors and other professionals stand beyond reproach. They sought to better and to save lives. That said, when the underlying logics of necropolitics influences otherwise benign policies and institutions, governance necessarily includes the selection of some creatures over others in ways that can seem dire. Humans came first. Certain animals, at the bottom of the chain, lost any semblance of subjectivity and became an enemy to a society that exiled, caged, and killed them, and increasingly, viewed this not as tragic but as signs of progress. Rather than cruel necessity, the killing (regardless of any other options) became laudable and inevitable. Yet as Max Horkheimer relates (in discussing the French Comité de Salut Publique), "The individual has to learn that the life of the whole is the necessary precondition of his own."[49] The science of the public health profession became an accomplice in a changing political ecology despite any good intentions they might have professed.

The discourse of public health and hygiene became newly empowered in late nineteenth-century Mexico as officials brought all tools to bear against disease and infection.[50] At times they targeted the poor and the indigenous, seen as inherently dirty or diseased with a proper hygiene that might remedy racial "lacking."[51] Food and animals intertwined with ideas like race and modernity and hygiene under the auspices of the regime's public health officials. At times this seemed harmless, as in an edict to prevent stray bits of animal brain from getting mixed in with the milk that people drank.[52] More often, the officials intervened in daily affairs but with an eye to solving the greater epidemiological issues of the nation. While well-intentioned, their efforts to add science to the city life presented an "arrythmia of production and appropriation of knowledge" that selectively targeted the poor and, I argue, dogs.[53] It established a necropolitics that relegated animals from subjects to objects and insisted on the harshest measures to eradicate them as a "problem." According to a scientific conference in 1895, public health represented the essence of the riqueza pública.[54] How then to solve the challenge of rabies that threatened this wealth?

Man's designated bounds of park, street, and home meant nothing to animals driven mad from the disease and whose bite, in that era, and novel treatments notwithstanding, meant almost certain death.[55] Attempts to ban animals from urban households came as the first, simplest, prophylaxis. Laws addressed animals specifically at times, for instance in the Sanitary Code of 1902.[56] Doctor Bernáldez, the Sanitary inspector of the sixth cuartel, dictated that no animals be kept in households.[57] Future officials also attempted to make this happen. In 1915 the Interior Ministry declared that no one should keep pigeons, hens, dogs, or other animals in their house.[58] It should come as no surprise that these and similar edicts had no effect until (perhaps) late in the twentieth century. And some animals enjoyed a safer status.

Pets fell into a different category.[59] No less then than for us now, people see their pets as something more than mere beasts.[60] Birds, cats, and non-working dogs feature in paintings and daily life from early in the colonial period, but we know, too, that the Mexica Aztecs previously kept dogs (like the *xoloitzcuintli*) both as food and companionship.[61] Pets had their own place.[62]

This seemed so even in the illustrative case of the US Consul General, David Strother, who adopted a stray mongrel that he and his wife could not bear putting out.[63] Shortly after losing his pet songbird, a "mongrel" came to his door begging for food. Steeling himself, he ordered the little dog "into Exile" out into the street, but it barked and wailed all night. In the morning it snuck in, jumped into his bed, and nestled in. In an attempt to maintain proper masculine lack of sentimentality, Strother claims that it was "Madame [who] had no heart to put it out" and so they kept the dog.[64] This seems a little out of keeping, nonetheless, with his continued and affectionate mentions of feeding the dog bread and milk, of how a rat scared the dog, or of walking him around the Alameda Park.[65] At least in this case the canine successfully colonized a new space for himself, complete with food and care, as a pet rather than as an animal.

His tales provided not an indication of normal Mexican reality but merely offered something of a baseline for sentiments about dogs. Mexican sources suggest similarities, though foreigners' pets often appear since their owners seem to have been quite vocal. For instance, in the 1860s Princess Agnes Salm-Salm brought her lapdog Louis to her interview where she pleaded for President Benito Juárez to spare

Emperor Maximilian from the firing squad. A misjudgment, perhaps, if she hoped Louis would rule in her favor. The execution went forward. Most peoples' dogs garnered less historical blame but many rules.

In theory, owners relegated pets to the home, and police regulations clearly demanded at least a nighttime curfew or even perpetual indoors isolation.[66] Equally clearly, few paid heed to this law, and numerous memoirs reported using city parks for the family dog's amusement off leash.[67] Some even had their dogs pull a cart "in the English style" for cruising down the Paseo de la Reforma.[68] Closing one's main doors during the daylight hours was, moreover, socially unacceptable particularly for women alone at home (since any sort of scandal might take place inside with excessive privacy). This certainly suggests a difficulty in restraining the bounds between the house and the street to people, let alone to animals. Yet it does draw attention to a rhetorical line being drawn—if nowhere else, the ideal home was domesticated and un-wilded. The family dog and its offspring did not always remain so tamed.

Failing to sterilize homes, efforts turned to securing the streets. Experts trained in Europe would wage the professional war against rabies in Mexico City. First opened in 1888, the Anti-Rabies Institute (Instituto Anti-Rábico Mexicano) connected the finest doctors educated in Paris and Mexico City.[69] Dr. Eduardo Licéaga studied the Pasteur method at the Pasteur Institute from 1887 to 1888 and returned to Mexico prepared to work.[70] The method of the day required the infection of rabbits with rabies, whose brains they then extracted to make a serum, and painfully injected this into the possibly infected human some 23–37 times until their symptoms cleared.[71] Or they died, or they fled. Following very specific instructions at each step, the treatment generally worked for those who endured all the shots. In 1890 they fully treated 414 human cases with only one failure.[72] Some of the advice that accompanied the treatment seemed more anecdotally based than scientific, for example, that alcohol or saunas (*baños rusos*) were curative. Since both treatments dehydrated the patient, this seems dangerous advice at best. Public Health had more success tackling the disease as new actors appeared.

Depending on his anti-rabies laurels, Eduardo Licéaga became one of the key figures in Public Health in Mexico.[73] In later scientific reports, he expounded on proper use (rather than disposal) of human cadavers and the dangers of burial for water contamination. Newspapers covered his work in the city carefully.[74] He also, again with dubious sciences, claimed that mental illnesses like fetal alcohol syndrome (which he refers to obliquely, as the *tipos degenerados* parented by alcoholics) could be solved by having better quality controls on booze. He also spoke more of yellow fever in this tract than of rabies—once a rabies cure became feasible, the focus had shifted.[75] Institutional changes encompassed all.

Public health took a great leap forward institutionally with the establishment in November 15, 1894, of the Superior Health Council, whose policies largely enforced the 1891 Código Sanitario (Sanitary Code). This organization consisted of eleven core members: five civilian doctors, the director of the Military Hospital, the professor of hygiene at the national medical school, a veterinarian, a pharmacist, a lawyer, and an engineer. To this they added working staff—eight medical inspectors (for neighborhoods), six for *foraneos* (outskirts), four chemists to test food, one bacteriological lab technician, one vaccinator with two aides, four agents and eight inspectors for the city, and one chief of the disinfection service. For farther out they added two inspectors each for Tepic, Baja, and the border zones, as well as a sanitary agent and a veterinarian at Ciudad Juárez, Ciudad Porfirio Díaz, and Laredo. In all, they mustered sixty people.[76] They later specialized even further, adding the twelfth division to inspect meat, butchers, and "all other subjects of sanitary policy with relation to animals," many of these latter quite separate from markets.[77] A Commission of Veterinary Subjects also inspected stables, abattoirs, waste meat, and dealt with epizootics.[78] They also assigned one member of the main board to focus specifically on anti-rabies vaccines.[79] Their campaigns continued into Mexico's Revolutionary era.

Another of the public health pioneers was Juan Olivera López, who joined the Medical Institute of Toluca in 1908 and rose to leading the Servicio Sanitario (Sanitary Service) by 1925. Unlike his predecessors (Eduardo Navarro to 1886, Juan Campos to 1891, Juan Rodríguez to 1900, and Fernando Moreno to 1915), he sought to professionalize the service. They only hired actual doctors with degrees now, and no longer trusted *curanderos* or folk healers. Among his greatest accomplishments, the creation of a federal Department of Salubridad in 1917, with a personal stamp of hygiene for dairies and *pulquerías* that read simply "Juan sin miedo" (Juan without fear), and a clean hands campaign that included a public musical on how to wash up.[80]

Other public health officials combined medicinal knowledge with animals. Dr. Pedro Pérez Grovas went to medical school in 1905, trained by Dr. Aureliano Urrutia (at later times the director of Salubridad, Secretary of Government, and surgeon to the matador Rodolfo Gaono). Comfortable in his upper-class status, Grovas met with President Díaz and his wife Carmen, ate ice cream with them, and in later years declared himself a "porfirista." He recalled how they had trained in surgery using dogs, especially practicing with chloroform as anesthesia—and that this was difficult because "the dog is very sensitive" given that they "had the same defects as all of us, and the same cruelty." Although this cruelty bit seems like projection, the use of dogs in medical training had a long history, too, as mentioned in the *Periquillo Sarniento* of José de Lizardi back in the late days of the colony. Grovas also recalled the difficult years of the Revolution in Mexico, as September 1915 saw famine in the city, 1916–1917 an outbreak of typhus, hemorrhagic fever, and *tabardilla* (typhus variant) in city and countryside, and many cases of rabies. He made no mention of the impending Spanish flu, but clearly the country had a terrible time even without it. During World War I, they again sent a bacteriologist, Octaviano González Fabla, to the Pasteur Institute in Paris to get a new rabies vaccine to bring to Mexican rabbits. For Grovas, the greater health concerns he faced rose not from rabies but from typhus and fleas.[81] Testing on dogs and other animals presented another face to the conflict.

Dogs became the test animal of choice in other dubious or pseudoscientific experiments. In 1881 a Dr. Lacerdo tested potassium permanganate as an antivenom against cobra bites on a number of dogs in Mexico City.[82] It horribly did not work. Others used dogs as targets in testing bulletproof vests.[83] The papers also remarked curiously on experiments done in New York and London using electricity to execute stray dogs. They reported, impressed, that the English managed to kill some fifty dogs each hour.[84] More genuine scientific testing did play an important role in Mexico.

Animals played a different role in the war against typhus.[85] By the early twentieth century, science methodically used animals as test subjects for medical experimentation.[86] In Mexico, the Pathology Institute ran tests on a variety of animals including monkeys, calves, rabbits, and dogs. In addition to their twelve monkeys, their budget for food and cages and replacements suggests a significant number of creatures in their care, if only briefly. Just for dogs, they spent 75 pesos a month on food. Monkeys cost 350 pesos each, plus another 150 pesos for cages, and so on, while the other animals cost about 400 pesos in overhead. Five years later, the chief scientist, Manuel Fonssament, asked Secretary of Public Instruction Justo Sierro for 1,200 pesos a month, and additional animals and a *mozo* (servant) to continue his experiments.[87] Science notwithstanding, the old problem continued to plague Mexican cities and officials would resort to the mass "canicide" of stray animals.[88]

FIGURE 1.2. "Tela á prueba de balas," sketch, *El Imparcial*, July 23, 1897, 1.

The Street Dog

The new scale of urban animal death required the facilitation of technology and the approval of scientists. Modern means of extermination slowly improved or became mechanistic. For instance, the work of cats and terriers still surpassed traps for mice and rats. Local officials contracted garbage collectors like Ramón Perez to collect dead and poisoned animals, and pick up horses and mules (plus garbage).[89] Yet with few measures for proper trash removal, with urban livestock adding to the noise, smells, and messes, and with houses far from impermeable, the vermin thrived. Enormous issues with rats plagued Mexico City.[90] Rats adapt incredibly well to human cities, and if they clean up some unwanted things (like cockroaches) they posed a considerable vector for zoonotic diseases ranging from hantavirus to bubonic plague.[91] In other great cities of the age like London and New York likewise overrun, officials worked systematically to control the population through poisonings and setting bounties for tails. I have found little evidence for this in Mexico City before 1912.[92] It is likely that extermination duties largely fell to private hands who took care of it quietly, but this did not satisfactorily expunge the rats who could (and would) simply lay low next door until the dangers had passed. Much more successful in Mexico City were efforts to eliminate stray dogs—so institutional and effective, in fact, that they warranted their own volumes in the City Archives labeled, chillingly, "Dog Massacres."

This peril of strays became an increasing priority for the growing police presence in Mexico City and around the nation. At least in theory, animal control had been high on the list in police regulations for decades prior and appeared as the second or third duty in numerous cities.[93] Rabies made this necessary.[94] From very early on, we have reports of numerous stray dogs and their rabid infections—or *hidrofobios* as it was still widely termed by the 1890s.[95] By 1888 the rabies vaccine had begun to be standard, thanks to great efforts by officials, but, for many of the bitten, rabies remained the cause of a probable and painful death.[96] Psychologically, the powerful underlying fear of rabies extended to the way that the disease brought about madness, in effect, making man into wild animal.[97] The stray became feared and reviled.

As in other turn-of-the-century cities, cities and towns across Mexico experienced the street dog as a gradually ubiquitous presence, and in most they remain a significant issue.[98] The special place in human society of the dog suggests that at times of great human changes in life conditions, we would find a similar shift for man's best friend. As Stanley Coren argues, since dogs shape human lives they therefore shape human history.[99] As with other cities, Mexico City relied on its canine scavengers as a significant element of its waste disposal system.[100] Alongside hogs, dogs swept the streets of larger carrion and offal. This was not without a price, as the dogs' own wastes also accumulated, but heavy rains and flooding, with occasional sweeping, could at least ameliorate this. In Mexico, governments commonly resorted to strychnine poisoning and bounties. Newspapers routinely informed residents of impending purges, so they could safeguard household animals.[101] Yet apparently the street dogs thrived in numbers if not quality of living. One American visitor was quite impressed in 1880 by the hundreds of stray dogs he encountered in the small city of Guaymas, Sonora.[102] At frequent intervals, municipal governments across the country would take action to purge the excessive numbers of strays with poison campaigns and roundups.[103]

This is not to suggest that only Mexican cities confronted dog control issues, and elsewhere municipalities proved somewhat chaotic in their responses. In a single year in London officials massacred between 150,000 and 250,000 abandoned dogs, which led reformers there to create orphanage-modeled refuges for the animals. The RSPCA (Royal Society for the Protection and Care of Animals) rescued the working dogs first. Governments implemented animal welfare laws by 1836 with the unintended consequence that the suddenly unemployed dogs found themselves abandoned and mistreated.[104] In the United States, activists founded the ASPCA (American Society for the Protection and Care of Animals) on April 10, 1866, again over concerns for working dogs and especially those on turnspits.[105] Animal subjectivity remained tied closely to recognizing human cruelties. In Henry Bergh's words, "Men will be just towards men, when they are charitable toward animals." Answering the hopes of those who looked to this progress, animal rights evolved over time into children's rights.[106] Mexican newspapers noted the work of societies in animal protection, and the SPCMA (see chapter 4) followed suit.

Nevertheless, in defiance of activists and humanitarians, government officials worked tirelessly to eradicate dog populations. In 1887 New York City papers recorded a culling of 700 dogs loaded into crates and dropped in the Hudson River—in a single day.[107] Concerns of cruelty met logistic challenges, and officials chose the easiest route. Beyond the level of an individual responsible for killing a single dangerous dog, at industrial scales humans become rather inventively evil.

Numbers like these seem exaggerated, even unbelievable. Could a similar body count have been seen in Mexico City?[108] It may never be possible to fully know any exact reckoning, but stingy bureaucrats proved loath to pay out contractors for animals they could not verify the dead. Attempts to defraud the officials in the early nineteenth century meant that by the later period proof in the form of animal skins was required. And so we can get an idea of what the official count came to (at least those with proof, done for the money, and not counting the dogs killed privately, accidentally, and so on). In 1879, amid complaints about people stealing his cadavers, a contractor collected 1,217.5 pesos for 9,774 dogs.[109] Five years later, Dr. Victor Revueltas verified that he had killed over 50 dogs a day for three months' time and was paid 750 pesos for 6,000 dogs. He was lauded for removing "foci of infection." At the same time, his competitors Luis Palacio and Gabriel Soto reported killing 5,000 dogs in two months and 45 a day for 3 months (about 4,000), respectively.[110] Another 6 years passed, and Rafael M. Carmona in 1900 received the contract for the Establicimiento de Utilización de Despojes Animales in Santa Cruz Acatlán. He reported to police that he killed 9,527 dogs with venom and without any "lamentable accidents."[111] At minimum, contractors executed more than 2,000 dogs a month, more than 70 each day, through legal verified channels, and at times up to double these numbers. This constitutes a necropolitics on a significant scale.

Massacres of dogs seems counter to our intuitions about "man's best friend."[112] Biopolitics, the control over life itself as governance, and its necropolitical extensions overpowered whatever sentimental attachments that people might hold. The apparent absence of empathy, I argue, represented a significant breach in the usual moral ecological view of this animal. Earlier in the century, Mexicans reacted to killing of dogs with distaste and resistance.[113] Community norms and relationships evolved and clashed with a changing vision of the street dog from a fellow subject to becoming a disposable property of the city or state, and one of potential danger. Travelers complained of the spectacle the animals presented. Some had run-ins with dangerous dogs, some simply disliked Chihuahuas, others noted that all porters had a pack of hounds as assistants, and another blamed them for fleas.[114] According to the latter, a huge number of dogs "complement[ed] the life of the average Mexican" and the poorer the peon, the more numerous the animals.[115] Rabies or health issues aside, the size and smell and noise of numerous packs of strays became a justification for eradications. A claim of "too many" always led to mass killing. The street dog became a not-really-a-dog, an Other and object, to be discarded as a casualty to attaining security despite how the community might feel about dogs on emotional levels. Necropolitics imbued society with a sense of calloused indifference toward the death of the Other as a sad necessity, an unquestioned fact, and dismissed alternatives as irrational romanticism. It built a sense of belonging in its own emotional appeals for unity and shared identity but did so in a way that denies sentiment for those it excludes. Dog-loving advocates became outlying voices.

Some hoped that perhaps the canine dangers could be mitigated in other, less final ways or, at least, not at the hands of the city officers. Laws dictated using muzzles (*bozal*) to incapacitate dogs, and the removal of the mouth incapacitated their senses, their ability to interact, and their main means of self-defense. One might consider a human equivalent in taking arms away from people. Mexicans of different classes wandered the city (despite police efforts) carrying weapons. Knives, machetes, and pistols remained commonplace sights. According to Laurence Rolfe, it seemed the least-armed member of the public might well have been the average police officer.[116] For dogs, in contrast, the law expected they appear in public wearing the canine equivalent of a straitjacket and blindfolded. It seems most owners disregarded this muzzle law, which city officials continually reissued since the late eighteenth century. Dog owners attributed their own good intentions to their animals, asserting that only other peoples' beasts needed restraints since their own animal was well behaved and orderly. Some, no doubt, kept a dog as protection and saw little point in disarming themselves. City ordinances, a form of political ecology, had in this case little capacity to change customary practices or moral ecology. By late century muzzles seem to have been little used, but public safety rose in discursive prominence.

If many dogs had a special insouciance to police rules, so, too, did rabies or hydrophobia. Newspaper reports made routine mention of rabid dogs and the occasional pig, and where they had been encountered. The usual wording noted that the beast suffered hydrophobia, thus visibly foaming at the mouth, but little more. Notably, the animal was never reported to be at large or a danger.[117]

By press time the threat had been killed in all such cases.[118] On first glance, these reports did not capture my attention. But their repetition, their blasé tone, was meaningful. A rabid dog is frightening; the rare-but-hard-to-kill rabid hog is closer

FIGURE 1.3. Shoe stalls in the *mercado volador* (thieves' market), Mexico City, Mexico. Mexico, 1908. Photograph. H. C. White Co., Publisher. www.loc.gov/item/2021635000/.

to nightmare. What is striking, then, is that these reports suggest that in any ordinary street in the city one would find individuals with guns and the willingness to take on a rabid beast, and that they did not hesitate to fire away. Technically, one could only carry a gun with government license, two people swearing a bond, and offenders faced a fine up to 500 pesos (but less for hunters).[119] Only rare reports indicated such armament being an issue, for example that a man in a bar had "let his gun fall" and set off an alarm.[120] Technically, the police were expected to take care of rabid animals, but police reports suggest they did not.[121] In other words, ordinary Mexico City folk packed enough firepower to take down a rabid boar in a high noon shootout, and did so as needed and as a matter of course. Travelers, who otherwise commented on the relative silence of the city, noted that "none in Mexico [seemed] alarmed by gunshots."[122] Others from the United States made it clear that everyone in the country walked around armed and ready to fire.[123]

And murderers lurked in the shadows.

Contract Dog killers

Strays and their dangerous bites long terrorized the people of Mexico City.[124] By 1703 officials remarked on their fear of the corruption and vapors that emanated from all the dead animals, accumulating on the streets, and they worried about how many men and women were dying from rabid bites.[125] The century of Bourbon enlightened reforms had little effect. By 1778–1779 officials reported a city "inundated with dogs," perhaps 20,000 of them, who "impeded quietude and broke rest in the silence of the night," besides spreading the dreaded rabies. One Ignacio García Bravo nonetheless had some mixed feelings on killing them en masse. He believed that it risked "the spiritual ruin that these brutalities cause" but agreed reluctantly that it must be done against, at least, the ownerless dogs on the streets.[126] The city hired men to assist the night watchmen to clear out the animals. A decade later, dog killers attempted to cheat the bounty system (ear counts) by bringing in two per animal. Officials complained also of newcomers to the city who did not understand the city customs and fed and protected the dogs.[127] In other words, they differed in their moral ecology from long-suffering urbanites in still recognizing animals as fellow beings. A couple of years later, a seven-year-old boy selling ducks in the market died from a dog bite, and officials charged a fine to a market woman they deemed the dog's apparent owner. She paid but objected that the dog did not belong to her, but rather to the entire meat market as their common property.[128] The dog clearly belonged there as part of the community, but this accepted status became unusual over the century.

As Mexico neared its independence, on August 29, 1820, one Benito José Agustin de la Peña y Santiago sent a rare letter to the *cabildo* (city council) in defense of the dogs, but only if they could be properly controlled. He pointed out their many uses: their feces can be used to tan hides, they eat dead animals and even bones, they deter thieves, they are loyal and grateful, and "ultimately, they contribute to the harmony of the Universal." He dismissed the furor over noise, saying simply that dogs all bark, and that was what they did. And he urged for controlling, but not killing them, since after all, "dogs have a powerful ascendance in the hearts of women." Nonetheless, he insisted that urban animals needed discipline. Burros and goats were putting on "espectáculos lascivos" (lascivious spectacles) in public, and dogs frequently created disorders in churches "contrary to Christian piety." He implied that this animal restraint could only come from better-off families, perhaps like his own. Dogs, he claimed, were the enemies of the poor. As an integral part of families, they took food from the mouths of poor children. Dogs ate while orphans faced cruelties, hunger, and misery.[129]

Whether he succeeded in bringing refined morals to his city's animals or not, the dogs continued as a problem. Some forty years later, numerous bites and complaints led French Intervention (1862–1867) authorities to instigate large-scale poisonings—with costly rations of poison paid for each month by the city.[130] After the Intervention, press pieces in *La Opinión Nacional* called for even further poisonings to eliminate the "raza canina" (canine race) who wandered in packs of five or six. These perros callejeros (street dogs), the author complained, had frightened women and his daughter.[131] In 1866, the city acknowledged that rabies and dogs simply went together.[132] Beyond poisoned bait, the City began to employ contract killers by the 1870s in a practice that continued well into the twentieth century.

Typically, contractors made a bid each year to the city that set out demands: the hours they would do the killing, the price they would charge per dog, the amount they would need to pay for wood for burning cadavers, and usually set a maximum weekly pay cap. Generally, the City would revise these conditions before approving the contract. An average contract then would include these terms: killing to be done between evening and early morning, each dog fetching about eleven or twelve centavos, about eight to twelve pesos provided a week for firewood, and a maximum pay set at around ninety pesos per week. The city often also added other conditions. For example, in response to Juan Torres they noted that he would earn twelve and a half centavos, he could work early mornings and after evening prayers, they specified seven areas of the city where he could go, determined that any dog without a muzzle was eligible, and that he may only use rapid-acting poisons. Interestingly, they made no note that he should wait for the legally required three-day period for owners to claim the animal. Seasonal issues made the municipality seek further contracts.

The city commented on the problem the dogs pose, especially during hot months when rabies became more prevalent, and on how the press daily spoke on the problems. Agreeing with newspapers, they said it was "not only convenient but indispensable that they destroy the multitude of dogs that roam the city, causing discomfort and presenting a disgusting spectacle that can become a danger since the strong heat has already begun to be felt."[133] The following year, Torres reduced his price to eleven centavos per animal, and proposed a plan to "open an establishment for using the offal and remains of animals that died in the city." Again, the City specified he only take animals with no muzzle or collar and that he only receive ten centavos per dog.[134] The animal corpse became a commodity. This represents a fairly standard agreement.

Most contracts followed this pattern with demands, language, and the mentions of a connection between hot weather and rabies.[135] At times the contractors tried to get extra renumeration by selling off cadavers. For example, Jesús Vasquez in June 1894 received a standard contract, but "with no right to collect the dead animals" during the contracted time "with the aim of taking advantage of their spoils in the national industry." That said, in view of the season, the heat, and the great number of animals in the city, his contract was otherwise approved. His contract again stressed taking only dogs without muzzle or collar (which suggests this was an issue) and the need for fast-acting poisons. The animal remains seem to have been a normal point of contention in this industry. Due to conflicts over corpses, Vasquez wrote to the Regidor de Policía in 1892 asking them to enforce that no one without authorization picks up dead animals because it prejudiced his interests since he had established a business where "the offal of these animals is processed."[136] Contracts and these squabbles continued with regularity into the twentieth century:[137] for example, the

City signed regular contracts with Bao Juan Francisco and Karl Cook in 1910, and the Trepiedig Company (working since 1905) renewed theirs in 1911.[138] These men and their small companies did a vital and awful chore for the City and its well-being, even if one that made them occasionally uncomfortable. At times even these contract killers had qualms of conscience that made it into the record.

Contractor Pedro Murguia showed some nuance in his stance. He began by complaining (as others did) about monopolies on the trade some had been establishing. He mentioned also the other pests of the city, the innumerable flies and mosquitoes that made spring and summer miserable, and he forecast that with summer heat the rabies would return. Here, however, his correspondence took a turn from the normal. He argued that the killers' current methods set against the dogs seemed inhumane. In his estimation, the use of poison caused innumerable evils including leaving dead dogs on streets up to two to three days putrefying, with detriment to public health and producing "a thousand sicknesses." He called out the current system of contracting as trampling the rights of citizens to dispose of remains on their own property. He also claimed it exposed children and unwary people to poison by accidental contact. He recommended, therefore, that contractors should have to wait five days for owners, and only then try to sell the dog, and only if all failed, kill the dogs. In other words, they should capture and cage the dogs. Dogs, he argued, should have to have official collars (the fees going to fund catchers) and a fee would be charged to owners to pick up their animal. He suggested twenty-five centavos within five days, thirty centavos after, and that the police should assist in this. Moreover, he suggested that all killing be done "out of sight of public." The City liked the idea. They set the price of dog licenses at three pesos or two pesos for second class, and one peso for ill owners. They also give Murguia a contract to kill for eight centavos per animal.[139]

What Murguia posed as radical ideas had already been discussed at length in city hall. Some fifteen years earlier, counselors had entertained a lengthy and scientific debate over the best way to massacre captured dogs.

In an 1880 letter to the city, Gustavo Ruiz, Fernando Finclon and Ruiz Sandoval (representing the Superior Health Council) decried the killing of the dogs by poison as "tan repugnante espectáculo" (such a repugnant spectacle). They claimed that those charged with maintaining order had become public poisoners who undermined the police. They particularly worried over the many vultures "dropped" by strychnine. This was tragic because these animals acted as positive agents for cleaning up. At times their science fell a bit short, as when they claimed that while some dogs contracted rabies by contagion, some got it spontaneously. They did make a nod to dogs having a social place, saying they were "not denying that dogs are often useful and faithful and deserve distinction—but strays [were] a problem." The letter then made some recommendations. They suggested the use of catchpoles (*laza corredizo* with wood pole) as was done in Rome or Naples, along with baiting using non-poisonous meats. The licensed owners could then pick dogs up at their own expense or, if no owner came forward, the dog would be killed by veterinarians on retainer using carbolic acid.

A follow-up letter from the Veterinary Commission addressed possible strychnine substitutes since the killing should be done "with morals and good hygiene and with attention to the degree of culture" that such warranted. The author said that other nations also massacred dogs, and that he was hesitant to give advice since science knows "so little about rabies." Nonetheless, while strychnine to him represented a practice both evil and repugnant, the catchpole also seemed too violent, and pragmatically capture programs would require too many agents because the city boasted so many hiding spots.

Beyond the capture, he identified other issues. Officials needed to keep dog pounds clean to avoid infections and "emanaciones" (foul smells). Maybe this could be funded in part by selling some of the dogs off to medical and veterinary schools. He also looked to other nations for ways to kill more efficiently. In London they used prussic acid, but this was tricky and expensive, electrocution also seemed pricy, and delivering a sharp blow to the front of the skull was uncertain and, again, "a repugnant spectacle." Drowning dogs, like they did in Milan and New York was "cheap, quick, and not too repugnant." To avoid strychnine-poisoned corpses strewn about, as appeared too often in *Prensa Ilustrado* and which created "foci of infection," he argued that they should emulate what many nations (like Italy) did and kill with asphyxiation. Specifically, he recommended carbolic acid in a closed chamber—only a cupful was needed in a semi-airtight space. He persuaded the city council. They instituted the carbolic acid-death chamber method in their facilities, and they regulated against the use of these dangerous cadavers for anything. At the same time, they retained the policy of killing rabid animals immediately (no captures) and then cleaning the site with hot water and burning any flammable materials in dens. This satisfied the laws in the Bando of 1856. They also pointed out yet again, "los dolorosas espectáculos" (painful spectacles) of poisoned bodies as a problem. This sight affected the morality and health of the public who witnessed the terrible agony of the dogs. Some did speak out on the subject.

In an odd addition to the file dated October 25, 1880, Luis C. Curiel warned against imposing onerous license requirements on dogs.[140] A former journalist, Curiel would later become governor of both Jalisco and Yucatán, a senator, a general, a judge on the Military Supreme Court, and served as a consul in Paris.[141] His letter to the government seemed to carry some weight, and his comments reached the front page of *El Diario*.[142] Enforcing licensing, in his view, would punish the law-abiding and contribute little to the national industry. It also set a tax on having noble feelings, and officials should not "penalize those who feel affection for animals," nor those too poor to pay. We "cannot deprive the heart of man from his friend," and "generally, the most helpless and miserable of poor have the most affection for their dogs, from whom they have never had injustice, ingratitude, or disloyalty." Besides, he pointed out in a libertarian aside, one could easily hide a dog, and would we really wish to have Inquisitors (powerful investigators) permitted to break into homes and violate the Constitution to find canines?[143] Despite his letter, municipal officials had already decided on the alternate solution to their problems, if slowly.

Despite what might have seemed an easy choice, the City did not hand down an actual policy for a year. On May 9, 1881, it finally opted to switch to asphyxia to avoid the "sad spectacle that the agony of animals in the streets presents." They noted that children should not witness this pain and, worse, that the city cannot sell poisoned meats and hides.[144] Less reputable scientists also weighed in, including a contractor who suggested switching to the use of KCn (potassium cyanide) in 1882. While a very deadly poison, and possibly more humane, the City dismissed the idea because of the contractor's prior bad press and his habit of leaving dead animals out on the street for up to two days.[145] In the city, the abundant dead became a public issue of aesthetics and visibility.

Cadavers as Spectacle

The resulting cadavers created a concern in their own fashion and connected to a transforming set of discourses in the city about the disposal of bodies.[146] As historian Amanda Lopezargues, cremation of the dead raised serious issues for the occasionally secular Catholic Mexican society.[147] Cremating humans troubled many who feared that in the days of resurrection their ashes would be excluded (while those who rotted to dust, presumably, would reconstitute just fine). Theological niceties aside, animal corpses raised different questions.

Since the Bible says nothing of animals having souls, the fate of their remains proved less religiously problematic, even if many of the indigenous groups of Mexico (e.g., the Tzeltal) held no such distinction.[148] Indeed, from the earliest contacts with Europeans the indigenous beliefs in more universal "en-soulment" had left Franciscan friars at a loss, since they could not easily convince their converts of man's religious domination over the animal world.[149] Tremendously complex indigenous views on animals, on non-human subjectivity, and on religious meaning nonetheless had little bearing on the pragmatic efforts to dispose of remains.[150] From the point of view of all modern scientists, the quite real need to fully burn away cadavers trumped any residual religious misgivings or debates, at least in the case of animals.

The cremating of animal corpses nevertheless proved an issue, due simply to manpower and the expense of fuel and collection. A century earlier, night watchmen simply dumped the bodies in a swamp outside town.[151] When even some human bodies could remain in a bad alley for some time, the priority on cleaning up beasts was reduced—except in the case of the rabid.[152] Considered "envenomed," the rabid dead became a high priority pickup for city officials, since their rabies could pass to another that ate the corpses. By extension, any beast of questionable health would also be taken away as a precaution of public hygiene, even though dead horses could sometimes lie rotting in the mud for considerable time.[153] Even here, modern industry had solutions. Contractors picked up the fetid cadavers to deliver to *casas de despojes* where, even if rotten, they could be rendered down for glue, hides, bone, and, at times, for the meat as well.[154] The process of turning animals into products, "rendering" in many senses of the term, related also to broader biopolitics.[155] Usually this happened relatively quickly and with the usual efficiency of capitalist incentives.

This created an interesting dynamic in that the absence of haste for the human cadaver compared unfavorably with the attention given "mere" beasts. At times, in fact, the dogs themselves took care of human corpses, as in a case in 1895. Several large dogs in Santo Domingo, noted as ones who barked too much, devoured all but the forearm and hand of a body. Officials had no luck identifying the human as a victim of crime or accident.[156] Rather, their concern seemed more focused on the noise and the apparent free comings and goings of the dogs themselves. Broader connections between society and the place of the dogs also echoed developments in other lands.

As with the inception of humane societies in Britain and in the United States, where the RSPCA and ASPCA gave rise to children's rights, the treatment of animals (dead or living) in Mexico became an entry point to questioning attitudes about humans.[157] As the societies pointed out, if inhumane circumstances for dogs or horses morally required ethical intervention and legal protections, then this equally applied to the mistreatment of workers, migrants, and children. They appeared ahead of their time in extending their opposition to necropolitics to include animal subjects as fully worthy of human intervention. This led to a shift in labor practices, as government officials reconciled the move away from working dogs and animals toward mechanization (just as the spit dogs gave way elsewhere to rotisserie devices). The unintended effect, unemployed dogs, could lead to mass purges of the now "useless." On a more positive note, the inevitable argument that perhaps children, too, deserved better care and less onerous work also took hold in Mexico, and the Porfirian regime gradually reformed laws regarding child rights.[158] Yet, in the meantime, the slaughter of animals in the streets continued.

One should note that the logic here fit entirely in keeping with capitalist society's expectations. Purging the unproductive, the parasites, and the lumpenproletariat had been concerns of social reformers of all bents, with differing solutions (some pinned unfairly on population philosopher Thomas Malthus). As animals proved less useful to production their rights to life also became dubious. Lack of living wages for the poorest Mexicans reflected another attribution of inhumanity or value. The least useful animals became used—glue factories, knackers, tanners, and others found industrial value in the animal cadaver. The "least productive" unemployed humans had fewer uses until the great wars of the twentieth century, when they would serve (along with underemployed horses) in the millions. The dogs of the lower classes, experts asserted, proved more likely to suffer from rabies than those of the well-off.[159] Of course, Mexican society embraced its animals less than its humans. Yet it is not in any way stretching beyond the elite discourses of the time to point out a connection between lower classes and the non-human animals.[160] Policy and literature and pseudoscience and press equated these (if at times as mere metaphors of anthropomorphism), and they rhetorically bestialized the less well-off. The moral ecology that applied to labeling city beasts thus rendered meanings to other communities. Poor and indigenous connections to the natural world takes us back to street dogs, perros callejeros, in other ways.

The Other Street Dogs of the Modern Cityscape

Some of the elite referred to lower-class and indigenous Mexicans as *léperos*, a term invoking images of scruffiness, mange, and street diseases. Tellingly, higher classes and novelists also referred to them as perros callejeros.[161] This denigration held racial overtones in addition to the hygienic.[162] The long held elite concerns over racial mixture, in place as early in Mexico as Cortés's fling with Malintzin (Doña Marina), or earlier in Spain's Limpieza de sangre (Purity of Blood) laws, comes to the fore when the common poor were labeled as curs, mongrels, and thrown-out strays.[163] This accords with an argument by Donna Harraway that "race like nature is at the heart of stories about the origins and the purposes of the nation."[164] Similarly, the elite framed the poor as inheriting criminality and disorder as a breed unto themselves.[165] This denigration held racial overtones in addition to the hygienic.[166]

Racists attached proper place, or lack thereof, to status and breed, and thus to nation.[167] The overlapping discourse of the street dog and the poor reinforced hierarchy and extended into visual performances. For the poorest Mexicans, those rural folks living in servitude as the "proletariat of the fields," writers noted that the poor live in "rooms that do not differ from the dens of beasts."[168] The overlapping discourse of the street dog and the poor consumed great attention in the corridors of Porfirian power.

Dogs, quite like poor people, faced increasing restrictions to their presence and mobility in the city over the years. They lost their subjectivity to the same forces of disenchantment and bureaucratization.[169] By the early years of the nineteenth

FIGURE 1.4. J. M. Villasana, "Pauperismo y Plutocracia, la limosna de Año Nuevo," sketch, *El Mundo*, Jan. 3, 1897 no. 1, 1.

century, their welcome in churches seems to have worn out. By the midcentury, they could no longer attend bullfights or horse races.[170] By the Porfiriato, legally, dogs needed to stay within the bounds of the house at most times and muzzled when outside.[171] In language, the stray dog became synonymous with poverty and often lumped in alongside urban criminality, as they lived among the various "pickpokts" [sic] of the city.[172]

Many travelers imported their own racist discourses toward the poor, often set within tropes about the "land of mañana" and conflating poverty with the indigenous. According to their often-contradictory claims, climate made the peons lazy and drunk, and they smelled of pulque.[173] Moreover, when "mountain Indians drift to city, they degenerated" becoming even less ambitious and more drunken.[174] Some literally Orientalized them, others pointed out with disgust that the peons made love in public.[175] Another made a half-hearted defense for them, blaming religious influences for flaws. Carlos Weiner claimed, "The Indian, always the same, seems as immutable as fate," never changing in their "food, costume, and customs" for ten centuries or more. "They keep the same cabana, the same games, the same foods, the same drunkenness, and the same vices. Christianity 'has brutalized them.'"[176] At the same time, peons and indigenous peoples impressed racist viewers in other ways. As workers, they proved nimble as monkeys or squirrels, had the endurance of horses, and despite being short and long-limbed showed great endurance.[177] The porters carried huge loads of up to 150 lbs. and still managed to tread twenty miles a day. The same author nonetheless somehow still complained how these workers had proved lazy and indolent.[178] In the eyes of these foreigners, the poor of Mexico represented an animality barely concealed.

The meaning of the animal depended on the era, the place, and historical contexts. Notably, "street dogs" as a term often changed since cultural constructions of the meaning of dog has local (moral ecological) influences. It could also apply differently in other lands. For example, in the former slave-based colonies in the Caribbean, dogs have a predominantly negative association as a tool for foreign colonizers and a terroristic one at that. Historical memory and artwork in Mexico also tied ferocious Spanish war dogs to the Conquest, but there seems less permanence to the distaste for the animal in general. The scientifically bred dog provided a counterpoint to the street animal. Animal husbandry of the nineteenth century reinvented or created whole new breeds and embraced whole-heartedly an idea of

FIGURE 1.5. José Guadalupe Posada, "Décimas: La perra brava," hoja suelta, pub. por A. Vanegas Arroyo., 1910.

eugenics (if in this case, animal-based).[179] The street dog, the mutt, and the mongrel represented an affront to these scientific efforts. In either of these two cases, consider how the forces of colonial pasts and (pseudo)scientific futurism embraced the animal as loaded with human meanings. The reverse, the human as animal, also pertained.

The regime attempted to remedy the cityscape before the arrival of influential foreigners for larger state theater, and in their discourse revealed more similarities. Ridding the street of unsightly breeds meant, in the case of the lower orders, that the Porfirian regime imposed on the poor clothing regulations like banning the common white cotton pants and sandals that the poor and indigenous wore. They even rented out pants for such events as the 1910 Centennial festivities.[180] If foreigners did not see the indigenous, or the poor, the elite reasoned that Mexico could be restored in the esteem and credit of the world.[181]

At the same time, some vagabond dogs found their social equals in another urban venue, as they took nighttime refuge in the army barracks. There, they denned with forcibly recruited and marginalized men, with their partner *soldaderas* (women of the troops), their children, and found a degree of safety.[182] According to one paper, a soldier needed tobacco, a dog, and a *vieja* (old lady, slang for soldadera), to be happy.[183] The dogs liked it, too, apparently getting at least some scraps to eat, if little space to sleep, and soon learned the military routine. In the morning, along with the women and children, they exited from the barracks. According to one observer, these *canes militares* (military canines) spent their free time chasing the new-fangled bicyclists down the streets all day. Much like the soldiers who caused evening disorder in nearby communities, the dogs created problems during their daytime sojourns and scared the populace.[184] Also similarly, officially the soldiers should not freely leave the barracks for the first few years of their service, while these unmuzzled unlicensed hounds should not (legally) wander at all. The police provided a common enemy for both. And like many others of the perros callejeros, an appreciation of military music affected the dogs.

During the end of the US-Mexico war, a paper reported that a dozen canines of the 11th Battalion in Chihuahua moved in tandem with the musical direction, left, right, or up, and even barked along with the signal to "fire." The writer sardonically remarked that the army needs to learn from them how to best follow orders.[185] The association of strays, even ones so well-adapted to semi-wild living, with some of

FIGURE 1.6. J. M. Villasana, "Los desheredados," sketch, *El Mundo Ilustrado*, Jan. 10, 1897 no. 2, 1.

the most miserable of the proletariat only reinforces the rhetorical inseparability of poverty and animal nature.

Callejero as a description seems also suggestive of some powerful ideas. To be "of the street" has few positive connotations. It entailed a disconnection from home, work, and family connections or identities. Who are those considered "street"? The term means severance from the things most humans consider important and comforting. It relegated the callejero to a status without place, but with position as *los de abajo*, those at the bottom. It provoked images of violence and despair. Callejero implied the loss of hope. And it did so naturally as a social statement against the embodied Other, upon whom these meanings were inscribed. The out-of-place body became the enemy to ideal society. These street bodies now found themselves left in a world where they lacked a voice, a place of anomie and distant tragedy, by a population that found reasons to believe those of the street exist there by choice or by flaw.

Aesthetically, the callejero somehow stands opposite to the monumental, the palatial, and the natural at the same time. Rather, the street speaks to something tough but ugly, something made less worthy for its association with grime and garbage. Those of the callejero become an unthinkable element, something unknowable and inconsequential.[186] The poor and strays alike, by this dint, became the dismal remnants of potential that the better-off could dismiss. They lost, as Mbembe notes, the status of "fellow creature."[187] To necropolitical agents, society would better thrive in these beings' absence.

Conclusions

The better sorts in society preferred that their urban animals remain largely invisible. An absence of the mangy, the wild, the unleashed, the noisy, and the smelly might just sell the claims made by officials regarding the nation and its modern advances. The silence from animal noise, or from disorderly humans, some assert as a particular privilege of the wealthy and powerful. Not much to be done about smell, of course. The city itself was an animal replete with sensory experiences and disorienting changes, affecting most classes, though the best-off humans had some protections to avoid this. And for either poor or animal, the ways the social elite, the critical press, and the middle classes devalued them mattered.

Attempts to "disappear" societal problems had many facets. Ideally, the lower classes would cooperate. If the poor stopped so adamantly wearing their traditional clothes outside or eating foods associated with indigenous peoples, they might cease being an obstacle to progress and become patriotic citizens. Of course, having all the lower orders standing about in new pants could not furnish the modern image in its own right—the regime spent great sums in paving, electric lights, modern architecture, groomed parks, and massive drainage projects.[188] And, of course, they also rounded up or poisoned vast numbers of stray animals across the city. In fitting coincidence, the poison of choice was strychnine, which they also prescribed medically to the many poor people suffering from tubercular coughs.[189] Ultimately, the image of the modern capital had no room for perros callejeros of any kind. High society had set science and the law on the "problem" of who owned the ecological capital of Mexico.

Clearly this was not a shoot-on-sight type order for humans, but consider how legal strictures worked to reproduce order in society. Police could arrest poorly dressed men in Mexico for "suspicion of desertion" and return them to army officials who might illegally conscript them on the spot. Vagrancy laws made poverty criminal. Wrongdoers sent to cells received little to no food, poor sanitation, and the possibility of further sanction on repeated arrests. For some sent to military service, this might include active duty in places with persistent violent fighting and dangerous disease exposures. Recourse to social scientific, pseudoscientific, and eugenic excuses allowed the regime great latitude in how it treated the lower classes and animals alike. For the necropolitical improvement of the breed, much would be forgiven.

Control over animals, loosely construed by elites, extended the lethal taming of the city frontiers across the entire terrain of the imagined nation. Resisted at times by perros callejeros of all stripes, the move toward a modern Mexico without unsightly beasts inexorably pushed forward.

CHAPTER TWO

Lurking in the Outskirts

Great Separations and Visible Death

> Loving and quarreling—like roosters—is the characteristic of the legitimate national[1]

> The whole mystery of commodities, all the magic and necromancy that surrounds the products of labor as long as they take the form of commodities, vanishes therefore, so soon as we come to other forms of production.[2]

> Indifference to death is a cultural construction.[3]

In wooded and marshy areas surrounding the cities, common folk pursued game large and small, while in the suburban alleyways and leafy boulevards, swine smugglers herded animals to clandestine market fates. Harried officials worked tenaciously to oppose these practices and to hide all traces of animal death from public view. They fought to eradicate animals' presence as well as the slaughter of undocumented meats. Locals went about their business, largely unconcerned. Animals moved freely with a mobility many humans might have envied. And for all the officials' efforts to displace death, the suburbs resounded to the sound of Sunday blood sports that brought it back to a violent forefront. Practices in the outskirts of the city highlighted contrasts between the visibility of dead and dying animals as they became objects of social relations.

In the mixed city of semi-rural suburbs and metropolis, animal lives and deaths reveal a moral ecology resistant to outside interference. Contrasts thrived.

Meat, wild or raised, made it to the tables of inhabitants. Valuable pink pork went to the gray markets of the city. Customary practices like the pelea de gallos (cockfight) provided lucrative popular entertainments. Animals wandered throughout.

This chapter reflects two facets of a regulatory creation process that stripped animals of subjective selfhood. Animal worth and reason to exist revolved entirely around markets and human cultural values that made them into useful objects and limited their lives. Seeming contrast appeared in the ways that death was hidden or celebrated, but in both cases the animal emerged as fetish. The creature invisibly went from living to meat product in the markets or became a symbol-laden gladiator that existed as representation of masculinity, identity, and fortune.

In contrast to the necropolitics of dog control, official limits on visibly killing food animals directly opposed the traditions, norms, and expectations of the population. People shaped their foodways and choices despite a political ecology that made killing subject to official invisibility.[4] In this Great Separation of people from seeing food slaughter (as spectacle, and as described by Nigel Thrift), animal death represented an element of class struggles.[5] Becoming modern meant hiding practices like meat preparation. Thrift argues that this rose when "the emotional redefinition of what constitutes the animal has combined with the sequestration of the business of killing away from the public gaze."[6] Humans were to see only the product in the market, to think (or better, not think at all) that meat came not from animals but from packages.[7] They removed slaughter away from everyday urban experience, mitigating the intimacy of killing, and removed victims from view.[8] Yet always it was the privilege of the wealthy to have clean separation in this manner, since the lower classes had blood on their aprons and an honest relation to their meat. The Great Separation then represented a bourgeois ideal or as some have referred to it, a "technological veil."[9] Animals have their own classes and status hierarchies in other ways, but for this discussion, the focus stays on human relations to the means of meat production. Who got to kill and to eat what, and where, became determined by limits on markets. The poor, like the rich, now had to buy their food in approved sites and official markets.

In the absence of a strong scientific justification, market officials proved less able to enforce norms that merely envisioned human discomforts with visible death as a non-modern, chaotic, or tacky subject. This motivation did not rely on scientific biopolitics, since in this case officials' cultural choices dominated. Government ideology normally justified its policies with clearly scientific rationales featuring strongly utilitarian objectives, as with the killing of street dogs for rabies control. Displacing animal slaughter for meat from public view, regardless of weak hygiene claims, had little to do with the science. Rather, ideological concerns portrayed meat harvests as a vile spectacle that simply should not be seen by the general public for reasons of aesthetics and morality. It seemed wrong, or backward, and so all legitimate slaughter would legally take place behind abattoir walls. Yet government controls failed to fully hide animal death from public vision.

Beginning from a discussion of the environs and its diverse creatures, the wider mixed city emerges as site of commodification. This chapter turns next to the informal game and meat foodways of the outskirts *poblaciónes* (populations) and ends with the spectacle of the cockfight. The smuggling of meat to markets shows how hogs presented a danger and opportunity outside of legal strictures. Meat, divorced from the process of its production, became a commodity fetish as the animal disappeared from public spaces. While city officials tried to curb home production and worked to clear streets of vagrant critters, animals died for cheers nearby. The next section shows the cockfight as an overt and legal display of animal demise, where again, the symbolic animal became a commodity. From its historical roots to the reasons for its persistence, the practice of cockfighting demonstrates the complexity of ideas attached to moral ecology of the crowd.

The residents had their own notions of the acceptable. One facet of necropolitical power is that it disappears from normal life the spectacle of any deaths or collateral damages, and the official and clandestine meat markets certainly reflected this impulse. Through policies and simple normalization practices, "decent" society selected which animal deaths fit with their vision of proper living and commodification. At the same time and in plain sight, the cockfight presented the death of the Other as a ritualized and community supported practice.

Green Boulevards and Busy Outskirts

Wildness intruded into greater Mexico City's spaces and suburban surrounds. Green spaces, gardens, canals, woods, and undeveloped lots encircled and dotted the map. Between 1900 and 1910 formally inaugurated park space had increased eight times over in response to new modern ideas about rejuvenating the lower orders.[10] In these new areas some of the elite hoped to see a lower class recreating itself away from the bars and pulquerías that ruined families and morality.[11] But calling it a park did not create a new space; it simply set standards and limits on how green spaces were used or maintained.[12] That is, places without homes or shops did not dramatically increase; only rules and ideas did.

Greenery had an implied set of values provided it did not go too far. Undeveloped lots could be reframed as opportunities for commerce, or denigrated as nests for vermin and, not exclusively, as a dumping ground for trash. Clean manicured park spaces showed off human prowess in scientific and aesthetic management of nature. The aesthetics in fact had profound roots in the evolutionary human psyche. We prefer grass too short for predators, trees with easily reached lower branches for safe escapes, good lines of sight to spot prey and danger—ancient impulses continue even now to shape our aesthetic landscape preferences. In a changing and modernizing nation, this drive to visibly order a society otherwise recalcitrant to change proved inconsistent. This extended from the heart to the outskirts of the great metropolis.

Much of this chapter focuses on the outer municipalities. What to call these outlying neighborhoods adjoining urban centers or sometimes with considerable remove? Historical sources call these places *alrededores* (surrounds), *poblaciónes* (populations), or *afueras* (outsides), and these include what we might term *suburbs* or *satellites* (defined by their geographic proximity and legal subordination to the larger municipality) and slightly farther out the exurbs (distant suburbs).[13] Their vague status makes them more, not less, appropriate here to a chapter focused on ambiguity and contradictions. These places shared a separate sense of identity from Mexico City, a different historical relationship, and often a population more indigenous than that of the urban proper. More broadly, and as it had been since precolonial times, these communities represented political extensions to the city itself for farming and housing only a short distance away. This fluid migration between these afueras and the city created what some termed a "mixed city" both rural and urban in nature. The greater turn-of-the-century city presented a sort of liminal space where the animal experience also varied wildly. At the outskirts of legal power, the limits to a new sort of society were bound to appear as well.

For many beasts and critters, the larger city remained relatively hospitable even as it modernized and became a more efficient killer. This modernizing ecology was not, per se, natural.[14] But the animals of the modern city adapted to these changes more readily than many of their human-animal counterparts. Rats, squirrels, bats, ducks, songbirds, pigeons, coyotes, and others, even the odd deer or ocelot, ignored

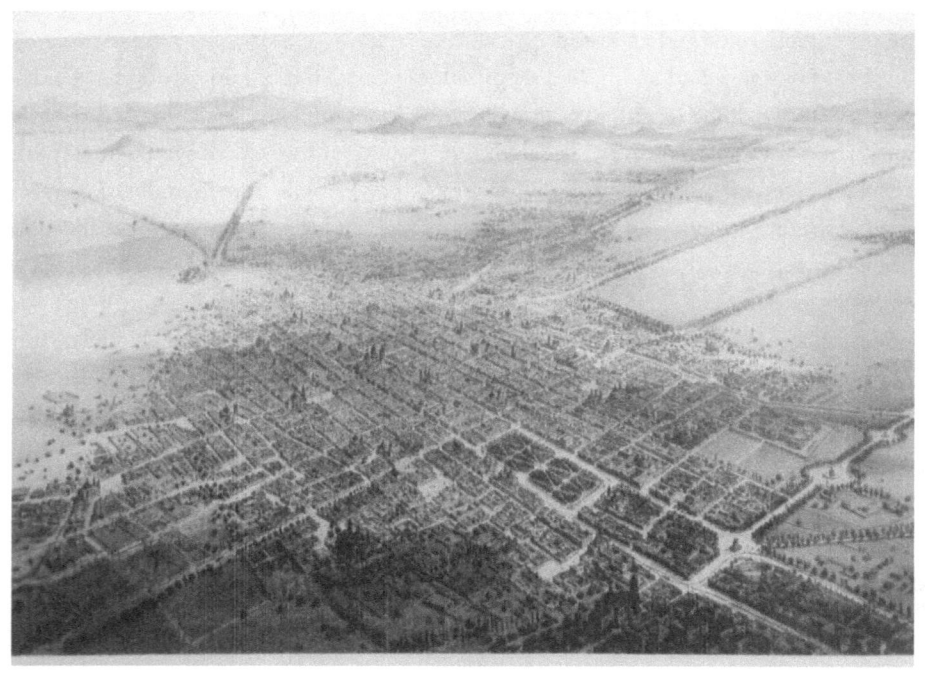

FIGURE 2.1. Casimiro Castro, "La Ciudad de México desde un Globo," painting, 1869.

the wishes of city legislators.[15] Some spoke of the urban as a garden, as the female counter to the masculine challenge of the wilderness, or the wilderness as properly regulated urban playground. These conceptions all fall short since urban ecology of animals indicates a more complex hybrid of space use.[16] Overall, many officials sought to make green the cityscape.

The increase of parks nonetheless pointed to the drive to improve and control conditions of life in the swelling Mexico City. The garden model sought to remedy the apparent ailments created by urban environs—in particular, the disorder and chaos of industrialized half-modernized streetscapes. The disordered life (*vida desordenada*) preoccupied *científicos*, like José Yves Limantour, who attributed messiness with amorality and disease.[17] Under the general auspices of hygiene, they worked to make the city fit ideals of order largely borrowed from European models. They built on to broad leafy boulevards begun by Emperor Maximilian during the French Intervention (the five-year invasion and occupation of Mexico by a French-supported Hapsburg monarchy, 1862–1867) and finished work on shining new architecture like the Palace of Fine Arts. They added statues and monuments. They emptied the city's troublesome lake bed with a Great Drain (Gran Desagüe) and inaugurated it, along with new rail stations, hospitals, and cemeteries, with delegations of ambassadors, cannonades, and marching bands.[18] They initiated or reformed police forces and firefighting units. They sent the health police into slums and brothels and barracks, seeking orderly living and hygiene via speculum.[19] The increased parks represented simply one more element of the government's fight against local wildness.[20]

The Junto Central de Bosques sought to give all the country a model of "well-preserved mountains" in places where the vegetation had been stripped and thus, instill a "recognizable patriotism."[21] The importance of maintaining greenery for the environment appeared as early as 1914 too. Writers claimed that the forest should be reserved for *salubridad publico* (public healthiness), because it regulated temperature, humidity, and flooding.[22] Increasing parks added one more element in the fight against local wildness by the scientifically minded.

The modernizers, driven by the engine of public health institutions, drew on the finest European colonial examples and the best sciences of the day.[23] Their vision had prescribed places for animal lives. Most beasts could stay, if only in traces and harnesses, in muzzles and laps, in pens and stables, in parks and menageries, and for some, in cages and laboratories. Not all that differently, scientists framed the least fortunate of non-human and human animals alike as social problems and the cause of disorder, violence, and illnesses. Leaves and grass would cure animal inclinations.

The elite intention to tame the baser instincts of the working class by sending them to the parks had considerable support from "ordinary" families. They sought safe and clean places to gather. While the poor were not always respectful of the various rules (and the upper classes were not either), parks provided them a social space they sorely needed. This love of the green and natural came despite customary aversions to the wilderness. Fear of the wilds, of the untamed forest and a "place of beasts," had a long legacy among indigenous and mestizo populations in Mexico since before Conquest.[24]

The woods in premodern eyes represented a fearful dangerous place—consider for Europeans the tales of the Brothers Grimm.[25] In Mexico, too, the forest hosted the abodes of devils, the ill-omened owl, or Tecolote, as well as witches and brujas, and other unseen dangers of supernatural origins. This deep anxiety did not apply to smaller safer city parks, but the Chapultepec Forest certainly drew unhappy suicides and other rumors. Only with the beginnings of the twentieth century did a rapidly urbanizing society reimagine the mostly tamed "wilds" as reframing the wilderness as a place of meditation in the heart of natural beauty.[26] Even in this, the possibility of being eaten adds a certain adrenaline to the affair. In cities, more generally, the perils and the communing both paled. Yet exposure to nature in this carefully orchestrated way had a laudable impact on the population as it enjoyed vegetation. The domestication of urban green spaces, some of them quite large, also countered the prejudices against outdoor leisure that marked the "non-savage" (i.e., non-traditional) poor and indigenous.[27] Scientist Pedro Escobedo directly connected the issue of poor people's lodgings to the idea that the forests, a part of the riqueza pública (public wealth), could remedy any shortcomings.[28] City folks could enjoy it, too, if only in proper settings.

Occasionally deer did make their way in. An 1892 letter to the city government requested permission to disperse some, claiming "the need to remove from the Alameda a growing number of deer that exist in the center of the meadows at the entrance that leads to the city center." He reasoned that this was not an appropriate place for these animals who will get sick there (not having hooves for this terrain), and so they should be relocated to the park at Chapultepec away from the public, and from women and children.[29] The urban-rural boundaries blur again.

Suburban *Afueras*

Around the great city orbited the older villages and towns and suburbs not yet absorbed into the metropolis.[30] Here, migrants and indigenous people brought rural lifeways to urban living and constituted a part of the expanding urban frontier as *colonias* grew and the "indigenous wards" at edges of city became something new.[31]

Nonetheless, from the point of view of many in the city proper, the moat of working class and indigenous peoples whose homes surrounded the official urban center seemed to represent a backward element. Their neighborhoods fell short of modern. Whether termed *pueblos*, colonias, exurbs, suburbs, or poblaciónes, they occupied an intriguing space between the city and countryside, with elements of both incorporated. According to Tenorio-Trillo, these crucial spaces "were the city, and the city constituted them."[32] The inhabitants' moral ecology and treatment of animals likewise falls somewhere in between the killer city and the great wilderness. The boundary between these three zones was far more permeable than one might assume, and its fluidity significant. Critters wandered.

On the streets of the wider cityscape animals ranged relatively openly. Residents actively executed some categories of vermin, for example, rats and mice, or at times found themselves faced with animals dangerous and diseased. Other animals scavenged and bred, to be killed only when their numbers seemed problematic. Vultures flocked, acting as "general garbage commissioners."[33] Livestock and pets escaped into the mix, some becoming feral while others sought out human contact or care. Domestic working beasts occupied street space alongside workers. The relations that people had with these various types of beasts shaped urban life in ways rarely considered.

These urban critters fell into multiple categories depending on their relationship to humans' expectations. The domestics included creatures deliberately brought into city and used, kept, and managed by human beings. Among these would be pets, work animals (like horses, mules, guard dogs, and messenger pigeons), and livestock (including hogs, chickens, turkeys, and rabbits). Some of these creatures fall into a more malleable category, as they escaped, or as humans abandoned them. In a state not quite feral, not quite domestic, they adapt as best they can and often come into conflicts of various sorts with human life. Those fully feral, or those who have migrated into the towns, adapted, and never domesticated, fall into the category of synanthropes. The final category, atanthropes, comprised wild animals that might incidentally find themselves in town. They all have some degree of agency, as animals' choices to obey, to depart, to go wild, to escape, or to adapt to the city represented (within boundaries) a type of subjectivity. Adding to the complexity, many animal categories here also overlapped. Consider the "outdoor" cat that receives some of its food and shelter from its domesticated human but continuing huge killing sprees against the local bird populations, and breeding where it wants.[34] Some of these even got a degree of legal immunity by simply being a pet-type of animal, if perhaps not safety from the many other perils of the city.

The urban and suburban wildlife also interacted with domesticated beasts like dogs and cats, and of course with feral or stray animals of all sorts. This meant sharing microbes and parasites, including fleas, lice, and rabies, and this also entailed sharing with humans, their main predator. Coyotes mixed on edges of the city and moved into the center on occasion. Ironically, the presence of large numbers of stray dogs in packs limited these ventures more then than now, as competitive pressure worked better than any human-animal controls. Dogs fought one another too.[35] Possums, skunks, and cats shared habitats and pathways and hiding spots. Bats roosted with birds in human attic spaces. Ocelots prowled in bigger parks, competing with wild, feral, and domesticated predators for food.[36] Officials knew the risks of rabies infection and sought to prevent animal cross-contaminations but could do relatively little. City planning, and often the lack thereof, did not usually help these efforts, and animals flowed from place to place with few checks on their freedom.

Displacing Death in City— Moving Meat and Visible Mortality

As the hazy-edged city often fed from the suburbs, foodways long connected poblaciónes and suburbs to "true" urbanites. People, animals, livestock, and ecologies flowed between, and inhabitants marked only the truly far off as the rural hinterland.[37] The suburbs remained zones of production that did not fit with Mexico City, which thus continued to represent a mixed city.[38] Inhabitants of the city continued in their normal way of life much as they always had, but emphasized differences from suburban moral ecologies.[39] In what James Serpell refers to as concealment, and

Nigel Thrift as "the Great Separation," officials attempted to obscure the visible slaughter of animals and remove it from the end product of meat.[40] The invisibility of death (commodity fetishism) connoted modernity and hygiene—it offered a type of comfort.[41] It notably also exists as a feature of necropolitics that the death of the lesser ideally takes place away from bourgeois eyes. In the "proper" system, society sets the conditions of acceptability for seeing death and creates the terms for dying.

Historically, consumption of meat in the wider metropolitan area represented balances between producers, religion, nature, and social norms.[42] Meat appeared seasonally, with beef in low supply from January to March, and hogs available all year but cheapest from January to May.[43] Religious prohibitions limited meat eating to about 30 percent of days.[44] In late colonial eras, the supply could be generous—in 1791 Mexicans ate 189 pounds of meat per year compared with Revolutionary Parisians at 163 pounds or France in general at 48.5 pounds.[45] Of course, even these figures ignore the likelihood of informally obtained meats.

Class identities formed around meat choices. Even in the colonial era, some restrictions on suppliers meant growers sometimes smuggled food into city.[46] This supplemented the pork already raised on patios and in backyards in the city, of course, and made meat an element of egalitarian practices.[47] In the country side, due to theft, campesinos often kept livestock in their homes.[48] Clever entrepreneurs moved meat from better supplied outskirts where indigenous producers had plenty, to the city where the money waited.[49] Over time, the exact meat eaten also had a role in class formation. Indigenous consumers apparently did not favor bacon or *asadero* (barbeque), while mestizos took pride in the cuts they served.[50] In part this pressure would be sustained by economics, and by 1896 observers noted that indigenous peoples near Guadalajara mainly ate corn, beans, and *atole* (gruel) with little meat at all.[51] If you are what you eat, this implied also that class erasures constituted a part of the changing moral ecologies. A cuisine suited to the rural, semi-rural, and indigenous became difficult or illegal to obtain, and that of the impoverished urban classes became the only legitimate option. Again, this accorded with a biopolitical agenda that sorted classes neatly in how they lived, and where the managing of slaughter and meat remained the prerogative of the government officials. Access to specific foods and animals changed class identities.

The lower-class neighborhoods of the city did not lay isolated from those of the wealthy, nor were any areas somehow forbidden to rural folk. The human parts of Mexico City thus had a diverse population and no clear separation from the "rougher" practices of the subsistence hunter or the livestock farmer. Found or slaughtered animals supplemented the dinner table of poor families, despite the many issues that the wealthier classes had with the idea.[52] Certainly, too, many continued to eat *bichos* (creatures) including insects like grasshoppers or ants, and other small animals.[53] Some also ate *huitlacoche* (a corn smut fungus). One traveler claimed that the food of the poor included "nasty messes of which offal and rotten meat often form part."[54] He went on to describe that the man carrying offal from slaughterhouse for sale to the poor presented a disgusting object smeared with blood from head to feet (and loaded with a heavy basket).[55] Consistent game meat remained more common to the countryside.

To the degree it was possible, lower-class urbanites did obtain some extra food from non-domestic animal sources. For the semi-urban poor, significant obstacles limited hunting for meat since few deer ventured near the city and ammunition and guns were expensive.[56] Still, residents did seem quite comfortable with harvesting their own turkeys, ducks, chickens, and so on. The problems of various wandering critters and market animals had always confronted municipal officials.[57] A February 7, 1825, law forbade city folk from throwing out dead animals, from allowing their pigs to forage widely, and dictated that all birds, rabbits, and hares must be sold with feet and skin. Presumably, this would prevent fraud (*dar gato por liebre*, or "giving cat for hare," was a venerable euphemism for a swindle). Equally clearly, repeated laws of this kind suggest they did not have great success enforcing this. In 1844 pigs, game hens, turkeys, hens, and other creatures were once again forbidden from wandering.[58] Some thirty years later, 1871 saw new laws against the wanderers and a regulation that their meat not be sent to hospitals or asylums (suggesting some sort of issues there with bad meat).[59] They also set a limit of six months for hogs to be penned within city pigpens.[60] For another example, in 1888 people still ate significant numbers of "birds and animals of the hunt," enough to warrant a discussion by the director of the meat market (*rastro*) to impose a tax on them.[61]

This meant that throughout a very mixed city death often presented itself to viewers. Inhabitants routinely discovered cadavers of animals and sometimes humans in the city streets and spoke of the buzzards and scavengers that they fed.[62] Class based notions of animal rights, of appropriate hunting, or of sensitivity to killing, would have meant something quite different in such a context.[63] Separating residents from the process of slaughter rose largely as an aesthetic ideal rather than an effective strategy.

Estimates of home-slaughtered meat, a commodity often shared through extensive kin and neighborhood networking, suggests a thriving hidden meat industry primarily in pork, chicken, fish, and turkey. One foreigner wrongly believed that all beef and chicken in Mexico City came from slaughterhouses.[64] Meat had become a relative luxury in some poor areas and, nonetheless, sources suggest that it continued to get to people in less than official ways.

Apparently, plentiful game could be found in and around Mexico City, including duck, snipe, plover, and these especially in the fall.[65] Fish from canals like the Viga or from Xochimilco continued to make it to market and to table.

Boys sold six-pound carp from the canal for fifty centavos each.[66] Not only did some fish the canal, but careless hunters fired guns from boats (likely at ducks) and ended up scaring the locals, leading to a new law in 1878.[67] To some observers, trade on the Viga also had unpleasant facets, with one describing the filthy canal with pigskins full of pulque loaded high on barges. She noted, amusingly, that Edinburgh was "infinitely worse."[68] Pheasants and partridges remained a common enough food source to create a conservation issue. By law these became restricted to wealthy plates by 1900. Turkeys and chickens featured in many city homes until well into the 1960s. Rabbits bred well and certainly ended up on the menu of the poor (especially those in exurbs) long into the century. Less savory perhaps, meat also came sometimes from horses, roadkill, stray livestock, squirrels, and less identifiable bits ended up (reputedly) in the *guisanos* (stews) of certain ill-favored vendors.[69] An early account exposed how some of the poor had sold the meat of stray dogs to unsuspecting consumers.[70] More acceptable family-level slaughtering had simply moved from openly visible to the back of houses over the course of the nineteenth century. Killing animals legally became the purview, at least officially, for those sanctioned by the state.

With a mobile fluid population moving between the urban and rural, for whom hunting and fishing of abundant game had long been a way of life, extra-market meats certainly graced tables more often than inspectors guessed.[71] In times of scarcity, they also made use of other resources to provide protein. For instance, thieves from the poorer quarters plagued the rastro (meat markets).[72] Others obtained their meat from unofficial markets that deeply concerned the authorized dealers.[73] Local entrepreneurs also brought game into the city for sale, as for instance Otomí women with ducks who arrived by canoe.[74] The hungry found a way.

This created potential conflicts between customary moral ecologies and political ecologies or legal precepts. The law limited duck hunts with quotas and

FIGURE 2.2. Viga Canal and "Floating Gardens" Santa Anita, Mexico City, Mexico. 1908. Photograph. H. C. White Co., Publisher. www.loc.gov/item/2021637134/.

enforced this occasionally.[75] Officers charged Benito Acevedo in Ixtapalapa in 1905 with duck hunting by *armada* (using a battery of connected guns firing a volley all at once) in the swamp "la Calzadilla." He inquired if he could "exploit the ducks" on his own lands, but officials denied this because the ducks are "property of the nation." He followed up with the Department of Hacienda, asking verification for how armadas might be authorized. He also produced a copy of his lease arrangement that permitted him and his sons to take 1,500 ducks per year, with a three-year term. A Victoriano Acevedo (likely a relative) bonded the document.[76] Some official notice did apparently reach the bogs and unhappy duck hunters. Nevertheless, fourteen years later, a 1919 police report takes for granted that hunters still prowled the canyon edges of the city of Tacubaya. Hunters there had followed a trail of vultures to the body of an unknown male human body.[77] That they discovered this while hunting did not occasion any concern or note, but police noted it simply as context for a murder mystery. Stipulated, perhaps, was that some opportunistic hunting remained a normal feature of afuera living.

One could not argue that game frequently accounted for a great deal of the diet, but certainly it provided a special treat for those who normally could only purchase less than 200 grams of meat per family each month.[78] Beyond small game, hogs presented themselves more consistently, sometimes for sale, and sometimes opportunistically since locals reported pigs escaping every day.[79]

Ninja Pigs—Clandestine Pork and the Displacing of Slaughter

On a sunny day in June 1902, a rabid hog threatened the lives of city strollers with deadly tusks. This powerful and aggressive animal now sported a lethal bite, and even normal swine can be difficult to stop and hard to kill. Yet seemingly nonchalant bystanders simply drew a powerful gun and shot the animal down before it did any harm. Newspapers reported this without any great uproar, taking for granted that people packed that kind of weapon, that rabid hogs raised little concern, and that readers needed no further details. Historians, on the other hand, have a lot of questions.[80]

Some wandering pigs shot in self-defense likely proved to be less rabid than merely delicious-looking and on the loose. Also, one might have seen fewer pigeons in some areas, rabbits remained shy, and rural cousins may well have been prized for what they brought for dinner from just outside town. In any case, animals died in the wider city for all sorts of reasons and did not simply disappear from view.

The killing of the infected swine in the street raised a whole other set of questions as it might not always be clear that a rabid beast's shooting was truly "justified." It is impossible to estimate the degree to which the poor might have taken advantage of chance-found meat in their diets, for example, of things like roadkill in a city where the new trolleys were taking a toll on anything that walked. Moreover, pork had long been a staple for rich and poor alike in the city.[81] The unsettling association between cadaver removal and the burgeoning sausage industry raised some questions in general about hygiene and the provenance of meat products. Jeffrey Pilcher argues that unlike the political outcome of Upton Sinclair's exposé for the United States, in Mexico the sausage makers held tightly to their autonomy.[82] I suggest that rather than accepting that the market and the government colluded to force all residents to a table of their choosing, the lower classes did (and still do) find alternatives that accord with taste and opportunity.

A clearly well-organized *plaza* (furtive set of routes) existed in Mexico City to move clandestine meat past the inspectors and law enforcement into the popular quarters.[83] Hogs came in, by night, but only as quiet as pigs can be. Not at all secret, in that case, but common enough to suggest police look the other way. Smugglers brought these animals not to the official licensed abattoirs (filthy but regulated) but, rather, to community yards and places of clandestine meat packing. Whether police truly saw this or not, they did not squeal. This pork remained an important part of the non-indigenous Mexican cuisine and table, despite the complaints of local sausage moguls.

City inhabitants and officials tried to manage the clandestine and official flow of hooved bacon into the center of Mexico. They set careful restrictions on licensed hogs' movements, ruling, for example, that when bringing pigs into city they should do so at night, since it was a "disgusting spectacle that made streets into toilets." They should also limit their routes and just move between the train station and the pig sties, and only between 1 to 5 a.m.[84] The racket and confusion this would entail in the middle of the night hardly seems like an improvement in any case. But the meat had to move.

The enormous rise of the industrial abattoir, so well described by Pilcher, meant a boom in slaughterhouses and meat markets.[85] These increased in both size and quantities.[86] Certainly, one solid improvement did come with this as the price of beef (at least in some markets) dropped significantly, and by 1899 some markets sold 100 kg (220 lb.) of beef for 50 pesos.[87] Of course for animals in the city, this merely reflected yet another place and venue of urban death, if one a bit outside the scope of this study.

Killing itself went undercover. In counterpose to the sad repugnant spectacle of stray dog control, or the loud carnivalesque spectacle of the blood sports, the modern age made a point of removing death from food. Animals from the outskirts of the city or held as livestock within still died but did so more secretly than before. They often did so illegally. They existed as commodities, never seen as animals by those who would eat them later. The authorities did their best to halt or at least to conceal clandestine trade, citing public health, and by imposing their political ecology on city foodways and public commons.

Frequently reissued laws dictated how people slaughtered animals in the city. They ruled that butchers only could only kill within the bounds of the market, or later, in specifically regulated abattoirs.[88] They inspected and shut down clandestine *tocinerías* (bacon shops) in 1900.[89] The sanitary police chased down reports of clandestine meat reaching the market even in times of relative scarcity like during the later armed revolution in 1919.[90] Even before the Código Sanitario came into effect, veterinary meat market inspectors reported on February 12, 1885, that some occasional clandestine meat (usually just lacking an official seal of approval) could be found, and that some had already turned bad.[91] Despite their inconsistent efforts, animals still flowed into the city.

Whole herds made their way inside at times. In 1881 a man fought the municipal law on behalf of his unlicensed pigs. The Ayuntamiento had charged him a fine that might reach as much as 500 pesos, much more than the fine for illegal guns and more than an average working man might make in two years' time. The City relented a little and charged him a 200-peso fine, citing as justification the negative impact his undocumented hogs had for others' property and human rights, and problems they caused to public health. He tried to argue that Article 27 of the Constitution was on his side, but the Ayuntamiento upheld their fine in court.[92] Other critters also found themselves in city custody over lack of official identification.

Lost and Found

The city government also found itself responsible for a huge variety of vagrant creatures found wandering the city without clear ownership. The *corral de mostrenco*, or a missing animals lost and found, collected the animals and kept them fed and cared for while waiting for the owners to claim them. They published missing animals' descriptions in seven daily newspapers. The wayward creatures included hogs, horses, mules, dogs, and cattle, some kept for over a year. Usually, they took in about thirty-five animals a year, or three per month, which does not seem too high, but the costs added up.

The gendarmes collected them and then attempted to ransom them back to owners to cover their costs, for example, charging ten centavos each for three little piglets. Depending on the expense of the creature, the owner might need to pay a bond (*fiador*) of up to one hundred pesos to cover the liability created when the real owner might show up to make a claim. This unreasonable expense, of course, meant that poorer animal owners might be out of luck when trying to retrieve their animals. The accounts also indicate that gendarmes found many of the creatures in bad shape, and possibly abandoned for that reason. Still, even for a skinny horse with a suspected case of *muermo* (glanders, a communicative bacterial infection in horses, possibly dangerous to humans too) could fetch a sixty-peso retrieval fee despite the need to destroy the animal immediately thereafter. The city faced a cost for keeping these animals that came to about twenty-five to fifty centavos per day, and on average they kept lost creatures for between four months up to a year. The public corral seems to have often sat on the edge of bankruptcy as a result. Some fortunate animals might be sent to a new occupation, handed over to the Department of Public Works, as were nine mules in 1919.[93] But for the horses, mules, and burros they cared for, and occasionally for the collared dogs as well, after a half year they faced execution. Vagrancy led to loss of status, value, and eventually to disposal. If the government carefully managed the pure fetishization of animals in markets, streets, and abattoirs, in other venues the fetish provided raw entertainment.

The afueras also featured animal deaths more deliberate, more staged, and more raucous in the palenques (arenas) where cockfighting drew crowds. The contrast, the Great Separation, between the smuggled hog and the festive gallo highlights the cultural artifice surrounding animal deaths.

FIGURE 2.3. Hendrik Hondius and Antonio Tempesta, "Two Roosters Fighting," 1610. Etching. Courtesy of LACMA.

Peleas de gallos

The pelea de gallos, or cockfight, represented an incredibly common part of life in the towns and suburbs of turn-of-the-century Mexico. Travelers, for instance, noted seeing frequent fights done in light pyramidal structures of wood or thatch (called *palenques*). They saw numerous *galleros* (cockfighters) in the streets, most commonly during lent, and noted how the fights allowed towns to work out rivalries with one another. Fights occurred with one weeks' notice, across the countryside (including New Mexico).[94] The pelea had a central place in the lives of many Mexicans of all classes and in our analysis.

Despite numerous prohibitions, the sport in Mexico endured. The cockfight has fascinated modern scholars since the influential "thick description" of Clifford Geertz revealed the way to use these as a window into social historical and cultural meanings.[95] The pelea seemingly offers a view of the highly ritualized leisure life that has changed little for centuries. The fights brought together upper echelons of society with working-class participants and in peasant venues. Gambling conflicts and injustices they dealt with together, and often with little recourse to formal legal structures. In some ways, the palenque provided a vision of the natural world largely outside of state regulation or, at least, one with only minimal controls. Due to relatively low audience numbers, reasonably cheap costs, and the lack of ethical oppositions, state officials imposed only enough to mitigate conflicts and to ensure that local governments received a small cut of the profits. Although often banned in Mexico City itself, palenques abounded in the poblaciónes and afueras. And city dwellers seem also to have held frequent illegal fights in any case. Since police, soldiers, and politicians made up a sizable portion of the audiences, cockfights have rarely faced legal consequences.

A counterpoint to this might have been the dogfight—as old, as frowned upon, as cheap, and like the peleas de gallos, only effectively criminalized in the 2010s. With no cash cut given to government, no rules officially published, and no legitimate arenas, the history of the dogfight can only be found in literary sources or the odd mention of travelers. The latter, quite accustomed to dogfights in their home countries, tended not to comment at length. As such, I am happy to leave the dogfight to others' future scholarship.

The sport of the Porfirian cockfight ran in relatively simple and standard ways.⁹⁶ Breeders provided birds selected for strength and ferocity. They prepared them in advance by cutting off crests, removing some feathers (*tusado*), and "training" them for thirty or so days using expendable, weaker, opponents. These presumably went into the stew pot after. *Amarradores* (handlers, rather like cutmen in boxing) attached knives and spikes to the birds' feet and treated their wounds. The knives, or *navajas*, could be made of various materials and had lengths between an inch and three inches.⁹⁷ Two *soltadores* (releasers) presented the two birds beak-to-beak a set number of times to get them riled and angry, in what they called *pruebas* (proofs). At a signal, the soltadores then tossed the birds into the ring, attempting to mimic exactly one another's movements to keep things perfectly fair.⁹⁸ A *juez* (judge) watched closely to determine winners, losers, and breaches of the rules. The fight itself ran about twenty to thirty minutes, with only a few breaks as needed to treat wounds or revive courage. Security often looked on, too, especially for fights where alcohol was served. The audience tended to be largely male.⁹⁹ Some men held bets, some took bets, and others still functioned as doormen, announcers (*gritón*), wranglers, and so on. During the actual fight, the audience was supposed to stay quiet, on pain of a 150-peso fine (despite the unlikelihood of this since there was money on the line).¹⁰⁰ On a normal day, an event would go for three to four hours (at least five fights) on a Sunday afternoon (which presented a conflict with the bullfighting schedule). At least in the licensed fights of Porfirian Mexico City "suburbs," a normal crowd brought around 150 spectators.¹⁰¹

The venue at Tlalpan suggests the normal operations of a palenque. In what the report termed "verified" data for May 3, 1908, the city received 437 pesos as its cut for June. This came from 18 fight days, with an average three- to four-hour length of event. These were attended by 114–248 people, with an average of 158. The empresario's income ranged from 102–321 pesos with an average take of 182 pesos.¹⁰² Not a bad profit at all, and no doubt, part of the longevity for the sport.

Mexicans held cockfights since the earliest days of the colony until today, and not always with state sanction.¹⁰³ The first recorded fight in the Americas came with the first European invaders in 1492. The fights faced occasional opposition.¹⁰⁴ By 1687, the church sought to ban the sport, as the Archbishop of Mexico City called for a Real Cédula. His concern centered on the "spiritual and temporal ruin" that cockfighting brought to men who gambled.¹⁰⁵ For colonial officials, gambling, it

FIGURE 2.4. Unknown, "Mexico. Cock fight," ca. 1919–1920. Photograph. www.loc.gov/item/2016821918/.

should be noted, represented an existential threat. Since they had colonized by divine providence, and since gambling suggested chance or variability in God's plan, then permitting things like the cockfight represented a blasphemy that could undermine the colonial enterprise.[106] The ban, nonetheless, did not hold. One last royal Hapsburg order to prohibit the fights came in 1701.[107] As the Bourbon regime came to power in the eighteenth century, the fights seem, in fact, to have grown to enormous audiences, with one boasting some 1,350 spectators.[108] Popularity vied with the need for order.

By 1730, governors set down new regulations. No children, slaves, *jornaleros* (day laborers), or officers could attend. Fights could not take place on workdays and required an official license.[109] To Enlightened officials the cockfight exposed children and slaves to bad language and gambling. They never invoked discourses against bloodshed or animal cruelty. For the workers, they also feared corruption, and worse, a distraction from their labors and the possibility of facing further impoverishment. The rule they set against officers' attendance suggests that perhaps this spectacle reflected poorly on the men whom they expected to act as examples for civilians. Alternately, it might have been acknowledging that officers may have been prone to using their influence to abuse their powers, and that the pelea had a corrupting influence. Some of the late Bourbon rationale appears in the 1805 regulations. These entitled the increasingly influential cabildos to take larger cuts of profits and to ban fights as they wished, citing concerns, again, about blasphemy and betting.[110] Independence Wars did not end the sport.

Cockfights continued as the colony became national with all its heroes and villains. The clerical bad boy and father of modern Mexico, priest Miguel Hidalgo, who already fell under Inquisitorial attention for his radical politics, book clubs, and bastard children, seems also to have been a fan. Purportedly, he took his gallos with him everywhere, even into the confessional booth.[111] Decades later, Antonio López de Santa Ana became almost as famous for his cockfights (at least among contemporaries) as for his eleven terms as president and dictator. Rumors suggested that when hard-pressed for money he even wagered his many military decorations at the palenque.[112] As the Second Empire came, the French Intervention witnessed yet another temporary, and largely ignored, ban of the fights in 1865. France itself had held fights until 1853, and even until 1876 in some northern departments.[113] Perhaps influenced by the Intervention, in 1884 Mexico City officials again banned the palenque stating that "cockfights, besides being an improper spectacle of a civilized people" remained illegal along with other games of chance and betting.[114] This did not last long.

The late nineteenth century saw important changes as the practice became bureaucratic, commercial, legalized, and formalized. Famed author Luis Inclán published a set of rules that became the standard, and these continue to be the basis of rules today.[115] According to the founder of the veterinary school at UNAM (National Autonomous University of Mexico), also the president of the national fighting-cock growers association, these rules had not changed as late as 2018.[116] By the early twentieth century, state after state had legalized the sport. Each published similar laws and rules, though gambling regulations varied somewhat. Eventually, only Mexico City stood apart as the government sent the fights to the suburbs, but they continued to take their share, of course.[117] The formalized rules now called for specifics from what had been customs, and rules made fights more standardized. The palenque had a specific size and marked lines on the ground at exact intervals that set the bounds for soltadores. Judges could declare a fight invalid for violations including excessive crowd noise, crowing by the roosters (as a sign of cowardice), or other issues that might unfairly prejudice the match. Navajas needed careful measurement. The palenques no longer welcomed children, cursing, drunks, and guns.[118] If promoters served drinks, they needed security on hand.[119] Government vetted the judges for honesty and wisdom. Birds needed to match each other fairly in terms of weight. Although largely muted, some reformers did see the sport as problematic.

The early twentieth century witnessed an opportunity, perhaps, for those who might have driven the sport underground or out of existence. Petitions still regularly reached the government to permit fights, even though most they denied.[120] Nonetheless, high-level officials from the countryside continued to love the sport and supported it right through into the Revolutionary period, keeping it viable. Even when banned, loud matches continued and clearly police chose not to enforce laws.[121] There are no quiet cockfights or *galleros*. For example, one evening in 1911, at 5 p.m., ten rowdy men left a Mexico City pool hall with six gallos (that they just happened to have along). A corporal and three gendarmes attempted to arrest them. The cock-toting men claimed they had *comisario* permission, and besides, argued that the drunken corporal had no right to bother them. Pressed later, the accused changed their claim, saying they simply carried the birds around with them, which was not a crime. The authorities in this circumstance seemed more concerned with the possibly drunk non-commissioned officer—and so the men went free.[122] It may be that they had a narrow escape.

According to one old veteran, Porfirio Díaz's Mexico City ban did not stop the fights, but officials sent any galleros captured directly to the barracks as conscripts. The vet himself had been taken by this anti-cockfight *leva* (impressment). He spent years in the army, rising from conscript to second captain in a highly unusual career trajectory.[123] During that time he saw many cockfights, and at them, witnessed all the highest officers of the Revolutionary era including Porfirio Díaz himself, but also figures like Tomás Urbina, Rodolfo Fierro, and Emiliano Zapata.[124] The best known aficionado of the era seems to have been Francisco "Pancho" Villa, who brought the fights along with him on the lengthy campaign trail.[125] New revolutionary regulations, despite temporary bans by some of President Venustiano Carranza's governors, included assigning palenque inspectors by 1920, even as the same regime had banned bullfights.[126] Other elements of the fights also changed with the years.

The science of the gallos did evolve alongside the discourse of progress. Husbandry bred, as with bulls for the corrida, better and more fierce competitors. Some breeds picked up new tricks and maneuvers, like those called *ratoneros* for their sneaky motions.[127] Medical care improved—if slowly—with professional attention and germ theory. Early wound care simply called for the washing of injuries with water.[128] Later, handlers administered cooking oil potions and creosote tinctures to wounds.[129] Actual astringents came later. Navajas improved somewhat, too, with some of forged steel and others made from claws taken from larger roosters or even turkeys. Amarradores attached them with glue and sometimes tied them with cords as well. Veterinary schools trained students to raise the roosters, and in how to train them, and continue to offer this training. Although fights might be banned, after all, owning the gallos themselves remains legal. The unspoken part, of course, was that no one would raise and care for these nasty-tempered and otherwise useless birds if not for the fights. Only heartfelt attachments could preserve the breed, as well as deep connections to social meaning.

Culturally, the cockfight in Mexico had an integral part in the cultivations of leisure and sociability and taste among multiple classes. It entered language. To "run the cock," *correr el gallo*, became slang for going wild in a night of drinking, or cutting loose.[130] The fights also had an odd relation to religion, taking place on holy days and ultimately facing attempts to ban it from Revolutionary-era anticlerical reformers. They also became a significant marker for cultural elements of national and local identity.

Broadly, the fights built on a sense of nationalism, with locally grown roosters and a sense of broad community. In the words of one observer, the cock represented a "work of nature and a symbol of love."[131] Others clearly stated, the Mexican cock *was* Mexico, and those that attended fights had a deep bond: "in the gallos, all are a brotherhood."[132] The bird served as a synecdoche and metaphor for the nation. According to Octavio S. Gomez, "The bloodied navaja, the small brave feathered gladiators, whose victory resounds in song and death as well, they are, after all, México and México resounds with their fairs and revelries."[133] Beyond this, the sport resounded, too, with superstitions and folklore. Fans interpreted crowing, amarradores administered strange cures, and the breeders widely knew that rooster crests should be cut under the quarter moon to reduce bleeding.[134] Beyond esoteric lore, the sport also contributed to senses of pride in place, of local farm, town, and region. Fights often served to "settle" conflicts between these rivals, though in many cases this could simply lead to further and persistent vendettas. Beyond region, the sport also played up national pride and nationalism (particularly through cock breeding and particularities in their version of the sport). The nation became seen primarily in this case as a male concern and area of knowledge. Community pride and identity played a secondary role to masculine constructions.

The sport publicly featured at its heart gambling, and betting on the fights appealed to men as risktakers—spurred on by pride and greed, as well as, often, by addiction.[135] The gambling was also a part of the performance of public manliness, proffering signs of confidence, of wealth, of devil-may-care insouciance. When one won, victory signaled confidence, competence, and good luck, and when one lost, defeat prompted an opportunity to posture or show stoicism. Complementing and complicating this, drinking together bonded men and loosened inhibitions regarding gambling and cheering. If one was unlucky with their cocks, perhaps they could regain face through appropriately manly binge drinking. Then, as now, the cock ring remained a predominantly homosocial male space where performed masculinity had a near completely male audience. Behavior at the palenque need not necessarily translate back to the home or to workplaces, though certainly the impact of gambling would and machismo did tend to persist as men identified in their home communities as proud galleros. This type of cross-class male bonding provided them an antidote to the seemingly sterile mundane modern life and its manliness, built upon a shared killing.

In the Marxist sense of the term, Mexico had a cock fetish. The rooster became separated from its subjectivity, from its place as an animal with sensations and behaviors and personality, to become a shaved trimmed object. It became, instead of a fellow creature, a disposable stand-in for regional or even national pride, and the arbitrary vehicle driving one's financial fortunes. If the bird suffered, and they surely did, proponents dismissed this in myriad ways. The animal, they said, simply mattered less than the sport and their entertainment, and, besides, it was the animal's inherent nature to do this, since they wanted to fight. The bird was, some others argued, too stupid to feel real distress, and, finally, some argued that the pampered if short life of the cock was better than it would have on a farm. Regardless of specific excuses, proponents systemically maintained that the bird had no individual right to exist outside the ring. Its reason for being became essentially as commercial and cultural fetish.

With the mixing of classes and gendered performances that were built around this practice, this might fit as a metaphor for political culture. Some have argued that the bullfight represents such a model for class structures, hierarchy, and so on, but I would argue that this has been more flawed than useful.[136] Perhaps the cockfight better represents some of the Revolutionary underpinnings of male society in this era. These events, messy, loud, drunken, local, patriarchal, and brutal, brought together broad cross-class groups performing masculine norms and bonding, with little regard for the official approvals of church or state. They persisted, and persist, despite changes from colonial to independence to revolutionary and so on.

As importantly, the behaviors of the crowd suggested a degree of class dissolution and democratic expectations. Their collective ideas about the sport represented a robust moral ecology. The judge needed to build trust and rapport with the crowd, they needed to cooperate to follow rules, and the fight and its result was held to be something of a group effort.[137] Variations on the fight reflected local tastes but, also, local approval. For instance, different blows by the birds like *golpes de pico*, *cuerdo*, and *cañazo* were dealt with in distinct ways depending on the crowds.[138] This community building notwithstanding, a French primary school text compared the peleas to corridas as markers of *mexicanidad* (Mexicanness), perhaps, but in the author's view, also as backward.[139] But many loved it dearly.

According to outside observers, for these rural aficionados and cock-raisers the sport took a preeminent place in life. Owners grew greatly attached to their favorites, naming them in accord with their personalities, calling them Sparrow, Tyrant, and Cat. A decent fighting bird cost about fifty pesos and represented a considerable investment for the average villager.[140] One traveler noted how an indigenous family in the countryside kept hobbled cocks inside their house for fighting on Sundays after church, where the man of the house wagered his week's wages.[141] Betting could be expensive and addictive. Bets ranged from 5 to 10 pesos on average, but some risked up to 1,000 pesos on wagers.[142] For those seeking a good cock, the price could vary, but in some cases, money was no object because "the motive was revenge" (presumably against village rivals).[143] Given this deep attachment, abolition of the sport had little chance of success.

Two factors proved crucial to dodging outright bans, as occurred elsewhere with various sports. Fighting birds lack charisma for the non-fan. Compared with horses, dogs, or other creatures, short-lived, bad-tempered roosters were less prone to considerations of animal cruelty. Some claimed that the birds did not have the brains to feel pain.[144] Handlers removed the roosters even further from any semblance of their natural appearance through decresting and defeathering. They armed the birds with nasty little weapons and fed them a sometimes unusual diet that might include things like liver, beer, and sardines.[145] Notably, this latter remained the case in the 1970s United States.[146] This weird little fighter became a living tool for a local and closed industry and did not occasion the sympathy that other animals facing cruelty might receive.

Beyond this, cockfighting faced little conflict between opposing local (or moral) ecologies and political actors. Spectators came from all stations of society.[147] A cross-class alliance of the poor and rich as well as law enforcement all enjoyed the sport together.[148] As late as 1983, a cockfighting book noted in the acknowledgments Mexico's chief of police Colonel P. López as a "great aficionado."[149] When the SPCMA had arrived on the scene in the early years of the twentieth century, the honorary society president and first lady of the nation, Carmen Romero Rubio, could not even prevent her husband from attending fights (nor bullfights). The Revolution, as Roderic Ai Camp shows, brought in generations of likeminded politicians.[150] Many of these, from rural roots and military backgrounds, had the rough persuasion of those who enjoyed the practice.

The sport has only recently, in 2018, faced effective federal and state legislative bans. Those arguing against the ban in Veracruz did so in the language of a largely shared moral ecology. They cited their rights to property, rights to culture, rights to work, and called for courts to recognize their "usos y costumbres" (uses and customs).[151] They also pointed to the legal hypocrisy, since other sports, especially the bullfight, had not faced the same banning. The court denied their argument and perhaps set a precedent that might extend animal rights beyond being mere property to some recognition of them as living beings. Regardless, cockfights likely will continue for decades to come.

Conclusions

In the leafy outskirts of the mixed city, society managed slaughters at two scales: one at the commodity levels that graced household dinner tables, and the other in the narrow and specific indifferences contained within the practice of cockfighting.

In this way, stealthy swine and crazed cocks bring us to the same point, a place where local practices remained outside of ideal controls by the liberal state. The city proved not so isolated from its surrounding communities as one might assume. Adjoining communities bled creatures, practices, and contraband into the metropolis. The killer city reached out into the boundary zones of the mixed city. What constituted the mixed city was not always clear to people who lived there either but was generally portrayed as a fluid identity in a site considered rough, dirty, and largely indigenous. Yet it also created a broader city with mixes of new culture and practices. The outskirts were bucolic and green, wild and tamed, liminal and dynamic. As a site, they represent a great place to sort out practices with an extra degree of clarity and to see limitations of governability. Urban and rural blends persisted without great difference.

Practices of the "suburbs" tied to *modas de vida* (ways of living) and competing foodways. Meat centered the diet for some, and long-time sources began to wane. Game scarcity, new regulations, and increased poverty changed diets. Food and subsistence formed class identities and represented a moral ecology. Death was displaced from the city to the suburbs, and at times trotted back into town on its own cloven hooves. Clandestine and smuggled meat gave agency to pigs and their noise.

Residents gathered game, fished canals, and smuggled country food in exchange for city money. Gray markets proved immune to "sausage" rebellions, so long as killing remained discrete.

As a first point, the Great Separation made animal slaughter an issue of putative hygiene but actual propriety, as it displaced death from markets and everyday foodways. In the second point, blood sports prioritizing entertainment continued despite lingering religious unease and limited prohibitions by the regulatory government. In this, the assumed "nature" of the animal meant any possible suffering could be largely set aside by proponents of the sport.[152] Both processes turned the animal as subject, as creature, into an object commodity fetish and a symbolic representation. The question then: why ban the sight of animal killing for the table and yet allow it when attached to the fights?

This disparity has roots in how people perceived the meaningful existence of the animal, a meaning described and managed and focused on the ending of life. The creature's body, where it existed and how it thrived, carried the imprint of power, as structures informed by a necropolitics that inscribed it with new meanings. In other words, this chapter examines two phases of necropolitics, one at the level of social controls (security) in edible commodities and their use by the poor, and another in a set of relations where broad class alliances insulated sport animal deaths from critics.

In the former, medically worded moral hygiene pushed a market agenda and exercised controls over the use of animal bodies. In the latter, watching cocks fight became a participation in a community stressing honor, hypermasculinity, and competition, via ritual, with rival groups, ranches, or individuals. Classes blended and mixed, not unlike how the afueras and city proper mixed freely. Cultural trappings like music, drinks, gambling, and hostesses set the cockfight into a milieu where the fate of the individual birds held little weight.

Moving out from centers of power, if not far, a different set of relations to animal death held sway. The mixed city represents a complex site, filled with ambiguities and contradictions. It should not surprise that practices and cultures also mixed.

In a way, this chapter speaks to limits and to class differences. Not all people or animals appeared equal in the eyes of the population. Here the contradiction in practices sets the invisible against the glaring to prove the point. The varied types of power inscribed on bodies in different ways, and with vastly different rationales about suitability and acceptability. The result rendered some deaths invisible, while others stayed both blatant and bloody.

A deliberate and gleeful blindness to animals killed in sport enjoyed wide popular and elite support. An adherence to custom, not at all scientific or rational but purely cultural, held sway. The contradiction, the relief, between public meat slaughter and the pelea de gallos shows how in practice, necropolitical assumptions and the absences or omissions of official power worked. This had to do with proximity to governments but also revealed the limits of power in certain spheres of behavior.

Officials and ordinary people made deliberate decisions on how to live, on how to see death and animals, and on which cocks were worth fighting. Power in fandom and cultural resources enabled ways to justify practices that took precedence over mere food politics. Selective visions led to the hiding of the abattoir, to caring for lost animals, and to displacing home slaughter, all contrasted to showcased killing at the palenque.

Clearly, too, cock fans did not care much about the questionable legality of their fun. Governments came on board, making the sport legal and regulated, and profited from it. Moralists and activists did little to stop it, perhaps realizing that the clientele at fights included the same officials that they might normally hope to lobby. Or, perhaps, they did not see poultry as worthy of protections.

Suburban death became less visible outside of the deliberate pageantry of the cockfight. But if the palenque made animal cruelties a fetish and an entertainment on display, the sporting giant that truly brought this impulse to new heights rose in the sandy arena where the bullfights reigned.

PART II

In the Arena

CHAPTER THREE

Birth of the *Fanático*

Cultural Takes on the Bullfight Audience

"Jump in the ring with your hidden cape
The bull can't decide what it is that he really hates."[1]

Horns answered the roar of the crowd and in front of thousands of eager fans the picadors and their nervous horses trotted out on to the blood-stained sands of the ring. High walls draped with banners advertising all manners of goods separated arena from row after row of seating. The rich cheered from cushioned seats in the shade while the ragged hollered under the blazing sun. Ignoring the jabs of lances, the confused young bull tossed a horse and rider to the ground and gored the animal with his horns. The lightly armored horses bore the brunt of this. The bull, not yet villain or hero, bled next from the darts of the banderilleros and lashed his tail in frustration and anger. The enemies were too many, the animal already bled and blown, and as exhaustion set in a new figure emerged from the wings. The surviving horses and crews disappeared. The matador in his garish silks and red cape flourished his thin sword and caught the bull's weary enraged eye. A dozen charges, a dozen clever dodges—acrobatic veronicas, mosquitoes, and a myriad of cape-swirled maneuvers—and the toro, panting, drooped weary. The crowd's cheers went quiet. The matador tempted his target into one last charge and struck. He made a precise thrust atop the neck, deep between the shoulders, and the crowd roared again. The great beast and its thousands of voices screamed their approval, and the fight ended. Horses dragged the bull's carcass, minus a severed ear, out across the sand while the matador caught up thrown flowers, hats, and cigars, and waved to his admirers.

CHAPTER THREE

The bullfight in all its sordid glory demonstrated a vision of the mass spectacle where hardcore *corrida* (bullfight) fans created cultural meanings. This offers a perspective on life in an early consumer economy and of class expression during the Porfiriato. By the peculiar logics of consumer capitalism, the fans became, in their own minds, entitled to a great show and to the death of the Object. They built a subjectivity around this and, in the case of the bronca (riot), fought for it, and if denied they even burned venues down. They deserved the show. The animal, too, as they saw it, deserved its fate.

The crowd re-created the event's significance as a collective. They emphasized nostalgic ideas and traditional norms, and related to the animal victims of this vicious sport in complex ways. They cheered their own society as they saw it. The fight, its promotion and lead-up, and its aftermath, represented a transforming set of practices that brought a new modernity into connection with an older moral ecology and its economic elements. They built community around the whole of the event.[2] Community influences also constructed the wider world of the corrida, insisting for example, that the sanguinary display provided a truly social "good." As a new take on an old, ritualized sport or way of life, the emerging capitalist market interceded. The event became a broadly produced pageant of merchandising, advertising, and product branding. The audiences swelled. To one viewer, "repugnant mercantilism" had defiled the sport itself by 1910.[3] The spectator became a modern consumer.

Beyond conspicuous consumption with merchandise, the new bullfight also included subtle forms of inclusionary fandom and tribalist masculinity. Fans proved affiliations with their wallets. They did not watch alone—they absorbed, opined, yelled, and participated as group members. They did so as a tribe, one gendered masculine or feminine in complex ways, but as a group with its own identity. Us against other towns, regions, or nations. Us against this or that *cuartilla* (team), or against that bull breeder. Us against the bull. Us, the non-animal, against beasts. This took on new aspects as the old sport became the new spectacular. Mexico, and fans, became modern through an ancient rite.

This chapter describes how an altered form of mass entertainment, married to the media and marketplace, provided insights into shared leisure experience. It explores a shifting point in the behavioral landscape of a modern urban space and its new classes.[4] The moral ecology, the set of relations a community makes with nature, lay at the heart of these. Overcoming the violently bloody scene and the deep discomfort with witnessing death required a constructed cultural mediation.

The tortuous death of the bulls, often of horses, occasionally of humans, passed from horrible to permissible to heroic through a filter of ritual and shared understandings.

An indifference to death, indeed an enthusiasm to see it, represents here another form of necropolitics where in cultural practices certain subjects formed new identities at the expense of animals that became objects. Death incarnated both progress (modern spectacle) and community solidarity at the same time in the world of mass fandom.

The fan became a subject through experience, absorbing papers and expert opinions, throwing riots, dwelling on nostalgia and memory, and enjoying music. The experience and reflections created the modern sports fan as a new type of subject made through cultural influences. This chapter begins with the idea of this subjectivity and the ways that fans encountered mass spectacle. This identity then shines through and was refined with the introduction of specialized mass media, newspapers, and professed expert opinions. Fans integrated these and made them part of who they were. Softer sides of the culture developed around nostalgia and folk music. At other times they expressed themselves violently through the *bronca* or riot in the stands.

These modern times constructed new consumers who maintained traditional roots and for whom animal deaths (of horses and bulls) became cultural freight. They constructed sociability around norms of hypermasculine posturing and the personal identities performed at the sports venue and without. The cultural values of the inured or callous spectators devoted to the art of *tauromachia* (i.e., the bullfighting arts) became essential facets of their identity.

Creating the Fan

Self-understanding came through selected leisure. You are what you buy into. It required personal investments, of time and attention, and even financial sacrifices—the pawnshops boomed every day before a fight as consumers borrowed to feed their fandom.[5] As a very general guide (depended on venue, year, and promoters), the best box seats in sections of ten went for twenty pesos each, the good seats in the shade cost about two and half pesos, and the rougher seats in the direct sun went for about thirty centavos. To set this in perspective, a skilled laborer earned a peso a day, but peons and soldiers about twenty-five centavos. Mexicans of new growing social classes had agency and made choices about their time and limited income as thousands filled the bullrings around the country and cities. Some also bet on the fights, though this seems less common than gambling at cockfights.[6] Expertise was culturally prized.

Fans followed the corrida (bullfight) news, bought or borrowed playbills for home and business decor, and they talked and gossiped and emulated and played bullfighting. Moral ecologies were not separate from economic considerations, but rather, came prior and superior to mere finances. At times the crowd acted in ways consistent with moral economic aspects (à la James Scott) when family subsistence took second place to purchasing tickets or placing bets.[7] Those lined up at the city pawnshops before fights knew this. Some of the poorest, as in orphanages, connected to subsistence moral economies, too, as they received a donation of tough gamey bull meat once the fight finished. Of course, if the modern consumer made rational choices for entertainment, few industries would survive.

Whatever circumstances found the fan (whether employed or not, decently housed or enduring slums, campesino or urbanite), taking on the identity of fan (or *porra*) allowed for them some brief moments of transcendental escape. They found in this experience a holiday from mundane concerns. It would be too much to insist that this created lasting interclass solidarities, and certainly the Revolution would give this the lie.[8] But some degree of at least temporary camaraderie did emerge and, even at times, elements of a shared nationalism. The crowd allowed themselves the release of the spectacle and became a part of something shared and grander. This escape built meaning beyond the sport itself.[9] The broader literature on sports and fans supports the idea of turn-of-the-century transformations and the importance of sport in identity formation.[10] For the new fans, this came with a displaced sense of attachment and community—not necessarily place-based identity—but an individually chosen affiliation to an activity that was its own sphere.

Consider the options the individual subject had previously used to self-define. Social roles marked one as part of a family (for good or ill), as from this town or that region, as a member of guilds at work, or as a member of one's parish. Even politically, people often had few choices in adherence to a *patrón* or at least to a party. By contrast, the modern fan dissociated from these identities, however briefly, to become their "own" invention in "the eminently modern experience."[11] This had deep and significant effects as a piece of the psychological shifts that made them modern subjects. Perhaps, ironically, it also cemented an urban identity through fandom over what was originally a rural practice. Becoming a fan thus channeled energy and attention away from family, from work, from church. This happened to the chagrin of families and employers, of course, where the church officials proved most vocal, and the fights at times even earned papal disapproval. They diverted churchgoers from attending Mass.[12]

In fight season, priests saw fewer souls and received less in collections, and depending on the church hierarchy, this might represent something of a crisis. Moral questions also came up, rarely about the problematic killings, but instead about diverting good Christians from pious activities and exposing them to raucous mobs. The social good that proponents tried to claim seemed not at all obvious to those who had to deal with an overly rabid fight aficionado or, as one writer called the audiences, the monster with a hundred thousand heads.[13]

A great change came late in the nineteenth century when the scale and scope of the *corrida de toros* meant it became truly massive in numbers and frequency of events.[14] This context changed experiences. Most of all, I see the bullring as a space of sociability that quickly became something greater. Different genders, ages and classes mixed in the stands while promoters did what they could to manage and cater to each. Sociability represented a secular sphere, charged with politics, that emerged in certain spaces during the Enlightenment.[15] People mixed for reasons other than religion, war, or work. The bullfighting crowd created a separated social community, shaped by marketing, and sharing an experience or phenomenon like Pierre Bourdieu's habitus.[16] The meanings of animals mingled freely with how people envisioned themselves in a new world. In this context, the "new" sociability included class mixture, leisure purpose, serious fun, and shared intensity (or facing consequences). This created a set of normative habits in formation (albeit one roughly governed by the regulations of the *diversiones públicos* section of the municipality). The city tried to manage.

Despite attempts at urban planning, Mexico City featured few areas where disparate classes met, even at hygienic distances. The so-called Porfirian Persuasion discouraged mingling.[17] Nevertheless, and the politics of seating aside, much as today, attending a large public event brings people together.[18] The idea within the new sociability where purposeful leisure creates social mixing applies differently to this sort of experience in contrast to visiting a bar or walking in a park. The destination-event changed the cultural meaning. Fights drained money and required some degree of planning ahead. Afficionados put in their time. The corridas were serious fun but requiring knowledge, attention, and investment, and one's fellow fans enforced a sense of shared intensity.

And certainly not all attendees in audience came as true *fanáticos*—many arrived there incidentally, or for lack of other options, and so on, but the true fans drowned them out and brought them, at least a bit, into their world.[19] Superfans educated and constrained the casual attendees. One learned quickly what to cheer, how, and when, as well as the limits to rowdy behavior. Simple rules that modern audiences might take for granted had to be taught: queuing, seat assignments (if only in general), washroom etiquette, concessions, and the thin line between dangerous rioting and enthusiastic expression. At times the world of the corrida also poured out into the streets.[20]

This sort of attention and focus went beyond the few hours of the show, and the event spilled into streets, bars, homes and so forth. This contagion (fostered by promoters, ads, etc.) created a part of what makes this new experience different from centuries before. In other words, fandom wafted out into society as young women hung posters of bullfighters in their bedrooms, and advertising papered the public spaces and streets.[21] María Louisa Noecker (her sad story is in chapter 5) was one of numerous ladies adorning their rooms with torero posters. The advertising world of modern consumption worked well with this newly constructed fandom and its demands in an emerging global and capitalist market. Advertisements reified the unreal divinity of the product and displayed ideals, and they sold the bullfight fantasy as a package entire. Enshrined in images of never-aging beauty on poster boards, the torero embodied an ideal type and interacted with fans and promoters. This consumer perspective came about not dishonestly, but as result of a sort of mutual fantasy.

The modern consumer experience, at the heart of consumer capitalism, required the "rendering of all things" into fetish, with even gender represented as a commodity with market value.[22] The subject with choices and agency becomes a mere object of capital worth. This did not occur accidentally, as Michael Taussig points out, but as a feature of the system that enables it to work.[23] In this case, both celebrity bullfighters and their victims alike can be stripped of humanity. To the point that not only the bulls but also the toreros and even hapless bystanders became figments of the fetishizing imagination purchased by fans embedded in the world of the bullfight.[24]

The Bullfight as Experience

The bullfight as modern event had become something not far removed from big shows of the twenty-first century. In contrast to the colonial-era or rural bullrings, by 1900 the experience had vastly increased in scale, in size, and in becoming increasingly uniform in its form and regulation. Through practice, it became normal to act as modern consumers, and spectators learned appropriate behaviors associated with taking part in mass public events. Orderly queuing for a public non-church event clearly posed something of a challenge. Security where police were scant and not well respected was an issue, and deploying soldiers proved only a minimal fix.[25] Generally this meant pushing, line cutting, fights, and discomforts. But on the other hand, the existence of a line-up also helped sell the idea that the destination was worthwhile.[26] The event had its own life.

A foreign visitor provided an exceptional description of the fan's prefight experience. In 1906, William Edwards wrote at the height of the corrida's popularity. He claimed that the fights mainly took place a couple of miles to the northwest of the city, Sundays at 3 p.m., but that tickets could be purchased in advance on the street out front or at cigar stores.[27] The day of the fight brought surge pricing; with street cars, carriages, and cabs all full, drivers doubled their prices.[28] Upon arrival, fans threaded between hundreds of eating stands, past firefighters and mounted police, and at gates surrendered half of their ticket (keeping the stub).[29] Ominously, they also passed two companies of infantry with fixed bayonets since "often the mob becomes so mad with bloodlust, that bayonets were needed to keep order, sometimes also bullets."[30] At the *entrada* (entry way), they could also pay for a ticket, still at 5 pesos if available. There, the traveler recounted a small gang of five loitering boys who "cheered every pretty well-dressed woman, they howled for the band, and they burst for the matador."[31] They had been well taught.

Another feature of the modern show came in the form of ubiquitous advertising and aggressive marketing. Walls of the ring and available flat spaces feature posters, broadsheets, and all manner of sales. Huge banners adorned the interior heights of the bullring.[32] Overhead, dirigible advertising sailed by (long before the Goodyear blimp) as the El Buen Tono cigarettes blimp overflew bullfighting rings.[33] The awe-inspiring sight in an age when flight was still young built a modern experience (if one dependent on winds and weather). Collectors' cards, intended for children, also appeared later in Buen Tono brand cigarette packages, encouraging habits among young markets.[34] As an extension of ads that Steve Bunker mentions, this furthered decades-old attempts to build young consumers.[35] Smoking in the wooden stands, of course, was normal, and given the flammable construction of seats and cushions, seemed not always as a great idea. The event certainly encouraged some bad habits.

The interplay of cigarette consumption and media worked to build consumers and community customs. Children could purchase these cigarettes legally, but not easily, from stores. More problematic to eyes of authorities, some children obtained their smokes from vending machines that had popped up everywhere from *cines* (cinemas) to cantinas.[36] Police did take issue with this, and occasionally destroyed the machines with hammers.[37] Other options included winning cigarettes at shooting galleries with air rifles and darts, for a mere two centavos a shot.[38] The cigarette companies added extra incentives to children and to customers more generally, as they printed *historietas* (short cartoon stories) in newspapers. These lithographed images highlighted stereotyped versions of social types (the soldier, the businessman, et al.), showed events from the news including bullfights, and featured racist depictions of the Chinese. These added to creating a shared culture among the lower classes and smokers in Mexico.[39] That the company itself had a strong penchant for the corrida also seems clear from the huge advertisements for bullfighters like Luis Mazzantini that they posted on their offices, not far from Bucareli Plaza.[40] The experience created consumers.

Going to the bullfight involved learning acceptable, appropriate public behaviors and some participation in monetized recreation. For the fan with ready cash, merchandise abounded.[41] Some purchases made the event and its memory permanent as the souvenir allowed tangible connection to a treasured experience. Many, of course, remained as tacky as any other modern souvenir. Fans could purchase ties, *zarzuelas* (operas) in pamphlets, novels, collars, canes, pictures, hankies, endorsed sherry, and even relics from fights (like pieces of horn and bits of capes).[42] Merchandise reinforced and signaled devotion. Fans' enthusiasms echoed through the streets.

Most marketing for the shows came in less spectacular ways than blimps. In the times leading up to a corrida, pedestrians in the city faced inundations of leaflets and shouting vendors with programs, who attended corridas as well. Newspapers publicized the corridas and even at times sponsored them themselves.[43] Programs, some merchandise, and other items could be purchased at the hands of street hawkers called *pajuelas*. Some items sold lacked legitimacy.

Another scourge of the modern event appeared in the form of the scalper. Taking advantage of sold-out shows, with tickets fake or resold with markups, they sought out procrastinators with money. The scalper had already been noted as a problem by 1815. Nearly one hundred years later, officials still tried to combat this. They banned scalpers, arrested them, and drove them away from gates, but rarely and briefly. Unfortunately for stadium owners seeking maximum profits, torero promoters simply wanted full seats, and some fans simply bought their tickets late. It did eventually lead to some increased ticket prices. More problematic for everyone, forged tickets also appeared in scalpers' hands. If unchecked, this could lead at least to overcrowding, conflicts, and diminished revenues. Officials attempted to combat this by making it harder to copy tickets, largely unsuccessfully, and by issuing all tickets with shorter notice (thus taking away the time to make fakes). This last measure had its own drawback since limiting the sales window reduced ticket sales, too, and created unmanageable lines on fight day. Few scalpers seem to ever have been prosecuted.[44]

At times God herself intervened in ruining a decent event by throwing more rain at the ring than was decently manageable. Mexico City, especially in summer months but occasionally in fight season, enjoys a solid burst of rain almost every afternoon whether inhabitants had made plans or not. Angry and near riotous fans responded poorly to cancellations and rightly demanded refunds. The City government ran a set of much debated laws on the matter in 1887, in the interest of public safety and as a relatively neutral party. They determined how much rain or weather warranted a canceled or postponed event. They issued vouchers to fans as "rain checks" to see postponed shows later. They occasionally mandated refunds for tickets when the show could not be repeated.

Promoters in numerous media worked to counter passage of official regulations on this. For example, they addressed City attempts to ban fights during rainy season citing the complications in offering refunds and rainchecks. They questioned the specificity in rules, the amount of rain that dictated closing, the fate of travelers who could not attend later corridas, and most importantly, municipal liability in the case of rioting in reaction to a cancellation (which fans deemed *estafa* or fraud).[45] Promoters themselves could also be fined for any issues with the "entrada" and the matter of refunds became more complicated since fans typically failed to keep their ticket stubs (*talón de boleta*).⁴⁶ Within all these possibilities, clever scalpers found yet more ways to forge ticketing (like rain checks) and otherwise find scams to take advantage.

Even if the fight went on, if the ticket held value, and if the queues remained in motion, the big show posed other issues. Crowd control in the case of panics, riots, or disaster began with architecture. As in ancient Rome, a stadium needed clearly marked entrances and (vomitorium) exits to move large mobs in incidentally coherent ways. Little had changed save a few nods to science and surveillance. A further problem was that the fights do last some time and viewers consumed refreshments, and so washroom facilities had to be built, cleaned, and maintained. To modernize these sanitary installations, the Porfirians hired a military engineer named Samuel de Cuellar in 1899.⁴⁷ After lengthy foreign travels as a military attaché, surveyor, and observer, he made substantial changes as bullfighting rings renovated or as new ones were built.⁴⁸ The regulations on facilities needed in relation to flow of foot traffic, and even the urinals themselves, all changed. Not surprisingly, the ex-military de Cuellar also called for increased security personnel. Often the authorities provided too little assistance due to penury.

Promoters got what they had paid for. Security did not do much, patrons frequently brought in banned drinks and food, and only serious issues might warrant interventions. The size of the crowd and its passionate emotions likely discouraged an overly proactive policing. The city made ordinances to bring back peace, while the promoters built separate gates to insulate the wealthy patrons from the chaos.

The lowly sun-sitting crowds could best be dealt with by keeping them at least somewhat separate from their social betters. This started with arrival as the high-class fans had their own entryway without the loud large lines. Greeted on arrival and ushered to their assigned seating area, they had a somewhat smoother experience. Music by military bands and speeches by announcers or politicians preceded the fights and helped to build an overall sense of the spectacle as "muy pecho" (heartfelt).⁴⁹ They even offered valet service for carriages to ensure safe parking spaces and easy post-show pickups. Promoters made a point of noting that this all especially benefited wealthy ladies who could not be expected to rub elbows with *los de abajo* (the underclass).⁵⁰ Sadly for the organizers' pocketbooks, one could not fill stadiums with only the well-to-do.

Special events intended to bring in more of certain crowds who normally could not attend. For instance, on certain festival days (as religion again popped in), events catered specifically to the workers and their families, or to students in the city. Any given show had to be special in some way, memorable, in a way that helped to form the fan community. This group had learned expectations on how to participate in the huge new venues.

Again, none of this would be especially strange to our eyes, all things quite normal to attending a large concert, football match, or even political rally. But for late nineteenth-century crowds the amazing novelty would truly be part of the experience. Fees, rules, and regulations irritated but also set a modern stamp on the corrida. The sheer size of the new stadiums and "the crowd" gave it power well beyond what had been seen in the colonial era.

This new mass market and its implications took advantage of a fully participatory fandom. If any of the attendees had misgivings over the brutality of what they would watch, this sentiment was overcome by cultural reframing. Most of this came from the fans themselves, but promoters and industry organizers had a clear stake in making sure the corrida continued. So how to build this cultural consensus? How to convince the audience and fans that obvious animal pain did not matter? How to reframe the event as suitably modern in the face of elite oppositions?

Changes to the fight and its organization distanced it from the corridas of the past. The church had no place in this industry. The brutality seen, they argued, was relatively mild in consideration with other parts of sport or life. Promoters emphasized that the event provided a social good. They argued that business was something too valuable to eschew over tender feelings. And, above all, promoters promised a good show. Market demands shaped the sport itself—the corrida needed to appear novel and modern from consumers' viewpoint and "not your grandpa's" bullfight. The matador stole the stage, the entourage becoming a lesser set of actors. Ranches bred bigger, better bulls. International stars appeared on circuit. The new merchandise and more concessions suggested changes had come. Did this succeed? One effect of popular demands saw riskier moves and deadlier bulls combine to increase deaths by the 1910s.[51] Audiences witnessed the ultimate in dramas. And they bought more tickets.

Other human factors potentially shaped the experience in negative ways. Petty thieves and rateros or pickpockets took advantage of the crowded venues despite the presence of numerous police and soldiers. Some overly rambunctious, offensive, and profane hecklers exceeded the considerable leeway afforded the crowd. This seems to have been something relatively new for corridas as a problem not mentioned in earlier sources. The loud and obnoxious humans likely did not bother many bulls or toreros, and few enough among most of the crowd, but promoters sought the approval of their "classy" clients and so new rules made their way through city council. Profanity itself might also have been an issue for a family sporting event. Rowdiness also kept security busy with overcrowding and profanities in the gate areas.

For instance, in 1898, the City of Mexico prohibited drunks and alcohol and guns, and ruled that fans could no longer "mistreat in word or deed" the workers and bullfighters. Further, they said "we ask all to be ladies and gentlemen at the gates"[52] implying that this was not the usual case. They also specifically worried about behaviors that the children in the audience were exposed to by the mob. They did allow that police and soldiers could bring their guns, so at least some there would be armed. This did not bring order.

Security staff seem to have often been at a disadvantage. One solution to this saw the city bringing in soldiers from nearby garrisons. Sometimes, these received compensation in the form of tickets for future events (subject to gaining permission from officers to leave barracks, of course). Likely, many of these "comped" tickets were then scalped by officers. More often, the soldiers worked without pay on orders. Venues supplying appropriate security often drew on soldiers for the task, but this did have complications. In 1895, Luis G. Tornal wrote a six-page letter to the City on the topic, where he urged that while the army was accustomed to doing security, they should just assist the police who he saw as "essentially the protectors of the public order, of people, and of property." He also drew a line, stating that the military must remain within its own chain of command, not following orders given by police or the empresario.[53] As in foreign arenas, this represented how the crowd's pretense of sovereignty (and democracy) tended to be reined in with armed force and exemplary punishments.[54] The unruly fans presented a new breed.

The modern audience had changed. Promoters attempted to sell spectators on their own status as experts—they were the ones who really understand the art and the animals, not the teams down below. Since the fans read all the periodicals and closely followed their favorites, they enjoyed an implied status as the diestros of the stands. The "could-have-gone-pro" armchair quarterbacks of the bullfighting world built on a sense of personal knowledge base as identity, like knowing baseball stats as a matter of pride.

In other words, they made consumer participation into personal identity. Fans argued their opinions on fights, bulls, moves, and outcomes. They identified with and shared the experiences of matadors and bulls in pain vicariously.[55] They communicated these with one another and with all other attendees in shouting range. Some posed themselves as master analysts of all things tauromachia. Perhaps some of their neighbors even believed them, but it matters little. In the construction of the general moral ecology of the bullring, these loud and insistent fans acted as a sort of sketchy "organic intellectual" giving voice and reason to the events witnessed. As with the concept of identity in fandom, the broader literature has explored the authority of the self-declared expert in this sporting context.[56] These few, of course, spoke to a greater collective, if not necessarily for them.

This went beyond the individual, too, as the crowd evolved into its own beast with its own sense of a group identity. The crowd that had projected so much on to the torero in terms of gender also considered itself as hypervirile and took this as proof of social Darwinism in action.[57] They, as a group, negotiated ideas of "taste," fandom, understandings, and status as they negotiated "a social terrain" of mass and class.[58] They also, perhaps, envisioned themselves as holding power as a democratic voice.[59]

This coincided with the growing presence of specialized media such as newspapers and penny presses like *El Toreo* in 1898, and *Ratas y Mamarrachos* from 1903, dedicated entirely to the sport. They offered images, poems, songs, news, and raw data to satiate the cultural desires of their most dedicated fans.

Specialty Papers

Specialist newspapers had a crucial place in the world of the bullfight. They sought, among other things, to give voices to the fanbase and they defined the sport going into the modern age. Commentary and opinion created context for the spectacles. A handful of papers appear over the years, including *Arte de Lidia Imparcial* and *La Careta* and *Heraldo Taurino*, but two of particular importance were *El Toreo* and *Ratas y Mamarrachas*.[60] These papers did an especially good job of coverage during the years between 1895 and 1905, when the bullfight transitioned most toward its modern form. Comparatively cheap, the newspapers went for between two to five centavos for an issue and generally offered about eight pages with some illustrations (or later, photos), and about a page of advertising. Both papers feature a somewhat obvious Spanish bias, which no doubt, the editors embraced as a boost to their credibility. The select audience would need to be literate (not enough images to appeal otherwise), though certainly one copy could be shared between less well-off fans and with a reader.[61] They also demanded currency of coverage.

While *El Toreo* began with a Monday publication they seem to have felt some pressure to provide swifter coverage, and by January 1897 they began to publish one hour after the last fight on Sunday. They received news from bullfights across the country by telegraph. By the time *Ratas* began publication, the need to publish immediately after the fights seems accepted as they did nothing else.

In terms of content, the papers often published portrait sketches or photos of the bullfighters, of big events, and rarely, featured a ganadero (cattleman) or empresario. *El Toreo* paired its cover portraits with biographical pieces within and featured mainly the big-name Spanish matadors. They included details like date and place of birth, debut fight ("baptism of blood"), and career highlights. This was not mere hero worship though, since the writers also critiqued the torero's style as a fighter with some honesty. For example, in discussing "el Boto," Antonio Escobar, they noted his "baptism" date, admitted that he was good at *pasos* and *veronicas*, but chastised him for choosing to use cheap moves and thus boring bulls and public.[62] In later issues they also called him out as terrible and full of self-love,[63] and "un maleta, jindamón, fatuo é ignorante" (a piece of broken luggage, a coward, fatuous, and ignorant).[64] With such outspoken critiques many of the authors actually used a pen name (a common practice in the era), including Fierabrás or Don Justa or el Criticón. Periodicals followed standard formulas.

The usual issue started with a graphic image if available, such as dramatic gorings, and especially ones to the groin or rear. They followed this with a page of opinions and commentary on the bullfight generally. Writers used a colorful mix of colloquial terms (like *mamarracha* or muleta) and formal Castilian Spanish. The following sections detailed and analyzed the fights at a favorite local plaza, with critique of bulls, fighters, *ganaderías* (breeding farms), and officials, and usually a brief description of attendance. This could vary from *flojo* (minimal) to regular and was always divided into sun and shadow. *El Toreo* offered news from Spanish plazas for a couple of years, and then switched to solely discussing fights across Mexico. This may have reflected the availability of telegram in the country, and certainly the later papers, like *Ratas*, always covered Mexican fights exclusively. When bulls gored toreros, a rarity in this period, the press covered the story and interviewed the attending physicians. Following sections tended to be lighter fare, including poetry at times (occasionally about the corridas), and advertising.

Advertisements reflect the consumer audience that advertisers sought to reach, and hence, the possible audience for these papers. These ads did not seem to market to the "public of the sun" who in any case, might have had less interest in reading. They did reflect a modern consumer whose interests might be overlapping as leisure reading created shopping opportunities. So who was this ideal consumer and fan? They do not seem a pretty picture. They had asthma, digestion issues, and were drunkenly smoking amid their collection of books, antiques, and crystal ware. The advertisements included medicine for asthma, crystal wares, doctor service, tailors, shoes, jewelers, Spaulding sports store, digestives, antiques, books, wines, tobacco, theaters, insurance, tequila, stationary, typewriters, cognac, dentists, and cold cream. They catered to a middle- or upper-class clientele, and at times in surprisingly modern ways.

In 1903 a famous matador named "El Faico" bought a pair of shoes, and his trip to the store, along with its address, the paper carefully reproduced. This seems an early example of celebrity sports endorsement.[65] One hopes the torero at least received a discount. The bullfighter Bombito, likewise, endorsed goods, and Gaona had a cigarette brand named after him.[66] By early 1904, matadors and banderillas also had their own section of the paper that listed their names, occupations, and addresses. The toreros paid for this, fifty centavos for ten issues, not including any added mentions in fight coverage. Deadbeat toreros who had not paid their bill earned extra press coverage and none of it positive.[67] The matadors had an awareness that the papers reached their fans and empresarios, and that coverage could influence their careers. One self-aware example came when Salieri visited the *Ratas* offices to get publicity. He may be the source of a rumor they published that week, claiming that Antonio Montes, Ramón López, and the owner of the Torreón Plaza were having disagreements.[68] Salieri, in contrast, received positive attention and "ink." He knew how to play the celebrity game and appeal to the fandom.

Ratas and a New Fandom in Papers

The creation of the *afición taurino*, the bullfighting fandom, came in no small part through the efforts of these specialized newspapers and their editorial choices. Carefully expert and selectively Spanish, the editors and writers turned the singular event of a corrida into a narrative line that passed back into times immemorial. They built heroes, they excoriated villains, and they fought one another, the city officials, the various ganaderos, certain toreros, their profit margins, and most notably, the "greedy" empresarios.[69] The editors clearly claimed to do so on behalf of the true fans. *El Toreo* claimed they would keep honest the empresarios who offered "hare and gave cat," and who presented matadors of low quality ("suitcases"). They would uphold the faith of the fans, against fight presidents who allowed abuses, and who brought decadence instead of improving the spectacle "most enthusiastic in all the universe." They would also defend the great sport against "the protests of the 'sensitivists' that should remain in the classroom."[70] Instead, they preached to the select.

The *Ratas* editors planned to create a group of fans for the "virile Spanish spectacle" of the "fiesta so beautiful and engrained in our customs." They would do so, not just for profits, unlike some empresarios, but for Mexican fans, Spanish fans, toreros, Mexican ganaderos, and empresarios. They would create, therefore, a community of afición (supporters). They continued with a qualified boast that they employed only well-known and expert authors, but not presumptuous ones. As in other newspapers, they mourn nostalgically that the corrida had turned "repugnant."[71] The bullfight itself came across as perpetually waning. In elegiac tones, the press proclaimed erroneously: "Our poor art! No wonder that in Mexico the supporters diminish rapidly."[72]

The pessimistic papers also harshly and constantly critiqued many of the contemporary fighters and the bulls, at least until publishing their obituary. They employed a wide range of derogatory slang terms, including Villamelón, *camelos*, *mojigangas*, *monos sabios*, and *maletas*.[73] The paper's name, *Ratas y Mamarrachas*, came from editors' negative opinion on the current situation in Mexican bullfighting. As they explained, bulls in Mexico, with rare and honorable exceptions, were *ratas* (rats, skinny and unimpressive). Toreros in Mexico, "with or without bells," were mamarrachas.[74] The term *mamarracha* referred to a buffoon, but in typical *alburre* style, may also have obliquely combined this with *marimacho* (a manly woman), *maricón* (homosexual), *cucaracha* (cockroach), and may have been the root for the colloquial phrase "no mames" in later decades.[75] Name calling aside, the toreo became bigger than any single fight.

By creating a running storyline, they set the fan experience as part of a greater and longer narrative. They highlighted the expectations of the fans, reinforcing or inventing them, and pointed blame for any failings in the show at select antagonists. Opponents, whether real or cultivated, provided a touchstone for a fan community to rally around and gave justifications for crowd behaviors, usually after the fact. In this sense the editors became a somewhat regulating and standardizing influence on what the bullfight meant across the city and the country. Fans did not always act as the press hoped.

If the editors defined the aficionados in predictably glowing terms, they also at times called them out on their behaviors. The real fan, they claimed, lived for the sport. After the corrida, they go tranquilly to the streets and think about the event as "a fan of the intelligent class." They judged judges, calves, and horses. They rejected any false fans as cowards who would need to change their underwear if they ever faced a bull.[76] With a new season approaching, fans and diestros (expert bullfighters) prepared, and children played at bullfighting. Others consulted the work of Sánchez de Neira (a technique manual) and discussed "toros bizcos" (crossed bulls), pondering whether these were "suspicious looking or sweet as a damsel in love?" These various people, the paper claimed, represented "the rabid fans, they have a girlfriend called Lidia (the Fight) and live in Bull Alley."[77] In other words, they lived for the corrida.

That said, fans could act notably fickle and expected continued entertainments. The editors dismissed the baseball game as taking away fans but admitted that Mexicans did like novelties and the new-fangled game itself. Nonetheless, they asserted that the bullfight remained better as a "virile spectacle." The critics then blamed Ayuntamiento, plazas, and empresarios (who are "immoderately greedy for profit") for any fans lost to a new pastime.[78] What the fans needed, above all, was education from print sources like their own, at only two to three centavos an issue. That this required literacy they do not comment on. The fans should also learn to receive bad news, like temporary bans, with stoicism and patience, and hope for better outcomes.

For example, when the government canceled fights in DF in late 1895 (temporarily) the news was received with "great astonishment by the fans." In contrast, the editors thought a short suspension (due to fines imposed on Bucareli

Plaza) would be corrective and prevent owners from fraudulent practices. They also pointed out that, once again, the public did not keep ticket stubs so that the fault for not receiving refunds fell on them. Ultimately, the blame for the disappointment they cast on empresario Ponciano Díaz, "the public's idol, who has deprived them of their favorite diversion."[79] So, sometimes, they urged patience.

In one dismal era of poor-quality entertainment, they held out hopes for the future. In "Recuerdos y suplicas a Don Ponciano" the writers connect the fans of the empresario (former torero) to civilized patriotism (in a facetious tone). They added that to Díaz, the wealthy fans were "agachupines" (a negative slur, implying overly Spanish pretension). Nonetheless, all could be saved, if only Díaz managed to bring the famed Mazzantini and his *cuadrilla* (team) to Bucareli in January, to fight good bulls from Tepeyahualco.[80] Indeed, "the bullfights had fallen like a destructive avalanche, and now most Sunday afternoons had become cold, monotonous, and desperate." But they promised everything will get better with Mazzantini's arrival.[81]

In preparation for this big tour, promoters published new prices for seating. During the famous Spaniard's set of three corridas, prices went up with seats for *lumbreras* (luminaries) running 200 pesos for an 8-seat box, seats at the *barrera* (barrier) in shade at 15 pesos, in the sun at 6 pesos, and general seating for 5 pesos in shade or 1 1/2 in the sun.[82] Nonetheless, organizers struggled to guarantee Mazzantini would come, having raised only 17,500 pesos out of the 50,000 required.[83] Travelers also thronged to see the great torero fight, remarking on his nonchalant smoking in the ring, how the crowd threw him canes, hats, and cigars, and claimed he had been paid 15,000 pesos for two shows.[84] Perhaps less of an informed fan, an American named Bates excitedly reported spoke of the arrival of the famous "Manzanillo."[85] Whether the renowned matador changed the sport or not, the fandom as a whole still needed education.

In a telling article clipped from Madrid's *Sol y Sombra*, written by the fandom's favorite Spanish expert José Sanchez de Neira, the project of shaping audiences appeared explicitly in "How to Make a Good Fan." This defined, from the Iberian view, an ideal. The article called for objectivity, saying that fans should not pick any favorite toreros to become an authority. The good fan should be intelligent, well read on the subject, and objective with their own personal views on toreros, aptitudes, and so on. They preferred to call matadors "serene" rather than cold-blooded. The great secret of expert fandom was knowing how to judge the ganaderías. They also should never attribute cowardice to the animal, since all bulls acted differently.

Fans ought to know that the fight is art, not science. A good bullfighter can modify any bad instincts that a bull might have."[86] The fans, he implied, should live up to Spanish standards.

Did this set of admonitions lose potency, coming from a Spanish source? The papers did have a Hispanophilic bias, to be sure. They asserted that the fans should change their ways and that the editors were not giving a lecture or sermon but just observing. They went on to say that the Mexican fans needed to behave better and not throw things in ring and they should also applaud only when deserved. They warned that the Spanish were watching and judging them.[87] Whether that proved true, the reverse did appear. An article in Mexico from their Madrid correspondent noted that women, young and old, powdered themselves up to the point of being "glacial," to attend corridas.[88]

Of course, in ways not always so splendidly overt, the fans also learned their world's expectations in more subtle ways. Art and poetry, for instance, could convey a fan culture as in this poem by Luis el Tumbón:

Y el toro murío diciendo	And the dying bull said
vaya un matador valiente	what a brave matador
y aplaudío toa la gente	and all the people applauded
y toos nos juimos diendo	and everyone joined together
Resumen: una corría	Summary: a corrida
alegre y ehtretenía	cheerful and entertaining
trabadora la gente	the working people
y animada y complaciente	lively and complacent
y hasta er domingo señores	and until Sunday gentlemen
que hay que dir a la corría	say they will go to the corrida
pues son los toros mayores	for they are the old bulls
y va á ser la despedia.[89]	And they go for the farewell.

The poet called for a solidarity among fans and suggested the bull's gratitude for taking part. He presented an image of happy complacent worker-fans content to look forward to the following Sunday. The somewhat broken Spanish lent the poem Castilian credibility and a hint of culture while presenting something almost colloquial in tone. Sometimes the cheery and complacent audience felt let down.

CHAPTER THREE

The Nostalgic Fandom

The fan—intelligent and deliberate, fiery and impulsive, and thoroughly immersed—had nonetheless arrived at the bullfight in a sad time. The old fighters, the old ways, claimed the papers, had been better. Nostalgia reigned over this genre. *Modernistas* and any novelties the expert press largely dismissed and disdained; the toreras they accepted in part because they came as a part of a long tradition in Spain. Modern new moves they impugned as buffoonery: preferring instead the *salto de la garrocha* (pole-vaulting bull using spear), the *paso en redondo* (round step), the *cerrado punta de capote* (closed cape), the *frente por detrás* (front from back), the *quite galleado* (cape behind back), and the *farol* (cape at side, one hand high one low). Modern moves like those done seated in a chair or on one knee like the *cambio de rodillas* (veronica on one knee), or the *paso en rodillas* (turn from the knees), the *Ratas* purists absolutely hated. The traditionalist fighters always received better press, at least until they retired to became empresarios, and then again when they finally died.

  Even including the occasional arena riots, fan expectations and moral ecology changed the meaning for otherwise carefully managed affairs. Crowds at times turned to the side of the bull when toreros failed to perform as expected. Opinions on what they witnessed also influenced the decision by the juez (judge) or president on whether the matador could take an ear, two, or a tail. His repute and prestige hung in part on the loudly voiced opinion of the crowd. The adrenaline-fed moral ecology could be a harsh master. Coded transcripts of masculine public behavior and tribalism fed into fairly wild behaviors but also created something of its own reality in the ring. This represented a form of performative involvement for the fan who got to be a part of events and a piece of history in the making.

  Despite the presence of women and children, and they were included in this collective new group, the overall focus reflected primarily a masculine veneer. Women proved their worth, in the words of the fan magazines, in their unflinching indifference to the blood and gore. They set aside their "natural" animal sympathies in place of national and regional pride, adherence to specific stars, and their love of the sport. In a collective sense, women transcended their gender and animality in becoming fans. Children gained role models as they, too, learned how to handle the spectacle.[90] They would learn manly behaviors.

To be sure, the entirety of the bullfight involved a sort of acting out of masculinity often termed pejoratively as *machismo*.[91] The torero of course was supposed to be the exemplar of manly behaviors. The following chapters delve more into the matador and gender, but from the fan's perspective there was always a gendered nostalgia (bullfighters always used to be more manly). In a general sense, corrido folksongs also modeled of a specific kind of manliness where risk-taking earned feminine approvals.

Singing to the Fans

For fans, including those unable to read the specialty papers, the world of the bullfights came in musical forms and on illustrated broadsheets or the big screen. Filmmakers created footage of 51 bullfights between 1896 and 1906, and a further 148 between 1907 and 1914. About half of these films featured Mexican rings, but some went abroad to Spain and even Nimes, France. All but 35 appeared on screens in Mexico, the others mostly in Spain.[92] By contrast to this new-fangled media, the *corrido*, or folksong (not to be confused with corrida), had a venerable history in Mexico.[93] This analysis examines a few dozen of the most widely published, and thus best known, from between the 1880s and 1930s. These reveal which topics interested the fans, how they spoke to nationalism, and how the songs helped to build the overall sphere of the greater fandom.

Many corridos naturally focused their attentions on the diestros as potentially doomed and tragic hero figures. Although other corridos may well have existed, surviving copies give a sense of the popularity of various matadors in the best known fifty-one songs.[94] These tunes told the tales of sixteen toreros, six with Spanish origins: Ponciano Díaz proved most popular with some fourteen, Rodolfo Gaona next with nine, and others like Juan Silveti or Bernardo Gaviño with a handful each. For any diestro, death gave the best chance of immortality in song.

One of the early greats fits the narrative well. Bernardo Gaviño's Spanish background seemed largely forgiven due to his achievements in Mexican rings, and his role as teacher to the popular Díaz. He first arrived in Mexico in 1835, fought there for over fifty-one years, and was finally gored to death by a bull at age seventy-three (though at least one corrido got this wrong and claimed he was eighty-three). Corridos of his death questioned why he had to go, asking "Why did you mercilessly leave Bernardo Gaviño dead?"[95] They formulaically asserted that he would be missed, spoke of his greatness, told details of how he died (painfully, and over ten awful days), and dropped the names of all the famous people he knew. With Gaviño, the songs proclaimed, "the king of the bullfighters died," having fought always with great arrogance and no fear.[96] Lyrics lauded him for serenity and nobility, as they would for other diestros honored in songs, and they lamented that his death came simply as fate. As the song "Verdaderos y últimos versos de Bernardo Gaviño" noted, "From the piercing sight—of the bull, nothing escaped."[97]

His most famous student, Ponciano Díaz, famed for his moustache, was born in Atenco hacienda where his teachers' deadly bull had been raised. He rose to *alternativa* (promotion to matador) in 1879 and earned fame for his skills on horse or on foot, and his skilled application of two banderillas at the same time. By the end of his career, Díaz had toured widely in Spain, played in New Orleans, and of course, dominated the Mexican circuit. In 1888 he turned businessman, and opened the Plaza Bucareli, which seems to have diminished his popularity somewhat. He fought his last corrida in 1895 and died in 1899.[98]

The songs to Díaz spoke often of his manliness and his charro authenticity.[99] One claimed: "He is too manly for the bulls—and for the females too."[100] Even attending his fights made one more virile: "It's nice to go to the bulls—with your pretty girl."[101] When he killed, he set the animal's soul to peace; when he fought, it was a dance. The fans loved him, at least early on, and the songs speak of them as "feverish and full of joy—all the Mexican people."[102] The corridos followed his tour closely and related all the news as he earned *alternativa* (promotion) in Spain, who he fought alongside, and especially, when he would return (which received multiple songs alone). The music emphasized his lack of ostentation and clean style of bullfighting. When he died of complications during liver surgery, the songs eulogized him. They recalled, for instance, how the fans had taken him from his coach in Puebla to carry him on their shoulders to the plaza.[103] They remembered him as treating his mother well. And they said little of the various debacles that plagued his business at Bucareli, a plaza which only survived him a few months.

The sad songs of Antonio Montes (1876–1907) strayed from usual formulas and from bullring. The half-deaf torero had acquired an uncanny reputation due to how his disability limited his conversations, and some even considered him mystical.

After a mortal goring in Plaza Mexico, and four agonizing days, he died. Corridos detailed this, singing of his high fever, weakness, and inability to move, as well as details about the wound breaking his tailbone and penetrating to spine.[104] Upon his death, the songs also related his last will and how some 3,000 pesos of his fortune would go to his lover Grace, from Chicago, and the rest to a finca estate. As odd as all this specificity may have been, Montes's odd tale got more macabre thereafter.

The mortuary where they took the poor dead diestro had careless and incompetent *veladores* (watchmen). These failed to notice fallen candles that caused a fire which burned the cadaver to charcoal. The songs went on to detail how he now lost both eyes (leaving only deep wells), his left leg detached, and that the fire left him "buen barniz" or varnished black all over.[105] Adding insult to injury, on the way to Spain his coffined remains fell off the ship and suffered water damage before being retrieved. Nothing natural could be responsible for all of this; the corridos suggested a superstitious curse fell upon Montes. The day of his death, it claimed, had been filled with unlucky "thirteens," from counting the letters of his name, to the lances used in the fight, to the number of toreros, and even in the date. Curses sealed his mystic fate.

Less magically, Rodolfo Gaono (1888–1975) received a great deal of attention from the corridos because of his preeminence as a torero, his Mexican roots, his serious injuries in the ring, and of course, due to the scandal of the Noecker case (see chapter 5).[106] He universalized the sport and made it global due to his popularity abroad as an authentic diestro first, and as a Mexican second. Songs labeled him with nicknames including the usual Califa de Léon, but also with the less complimentary Petronio of the Rings (Petronius was famous in Rome for his love of luxuries) and Indio Grande (Big Indian).[107] He nonetheless had a great following.

Corridos to Gaona largely followed the usual formula and spoke to his skills, and when he was gored in 1908, a corrido detailed the 20-cm-deep injury from the "criminal ox."[108] In an odd linguistic slip, the author used the term "van dos" perhaps from the French (Catalan?) pronunciation of twenty. Other gorings also featured in songs, but apparently did not have enough impact to warrant inclusion in Gaona's memoirs. The Noecker affair figured prominently in corridos, and broadsheets included further details of the case as it unfolded each week to keep fans up to date.[109]

Other corridos presented news beyond the doings of matadors for those interested in bullfighting world, more broadly. They sang, for example, of the feud between two rival toreros who planned to settle a 2,000-peso bet with a competitive corrida. Ultimately, their performance at the fight failed to entertain a crowd so bored that they walked out, in the words of the song, "soaked" by the poor show.[110] In another corrido, the singers gave voice to the great Spanish star Mazzantini in 1888. They complained on his behalf about the terrible quality of bulls he had faced in Mexico that fought "scared" as dogs or chickens. If Mazzantini had actual complaints about the animals, he did not mention it in the official press accounts at the time.[111] Yet another corrido told the tale of fourteen fighting bulls that got loose in the Mexico City center. The briefly liberated animals tore up the Alameda Park, charged trains and cars, gored a boy with a basket on his head, and injured twelve others. When passing toreros saw them, according to the song, they turned tail and "ran like children." The bulls, the lyrics joked, had now survived one fight, and thus earned the title "rebravo" as veterans.[112] Indeed, a few bulls even earned their own corridos. Gorrión, Platimo, and others, usually posthumously, the songs proclaimed as beautiful, brave, noble, and fated to die.[113] They enjoyed a place in the greater community. Their dooms still came, as inevitable as any humans, but the songs lent at least a sense of immortality in story form.

Corridos provided an easy, quick, and formulaic media to bring the bullfight out to broader publics. They helped to create fans. Community feelings like mourning or guilt became shared, as when songs claimed of the geriatric Gaviño's death, "We killed our good captain."[114] Fans could picture the narrative in musical narrative or, at times, in print.

José Guadalupe Posada's images that accompanied songs about the fights remained largely respectful and further established social norms about the practice. Nevertheless, in other venues, his images showed more nuance. His character of Don Chepito mocked society and presented a social critique of the rabid fans (whether of horses, boxing, dance, bulls, or marijuana).[115] Posado showed ideas and people that he disapproved of by having them tossed on the bull's horns. The bull represented a form of justice, or divine consequence, and a powerful imagery with which Mexicans identified. The toro became the counterpart to Don Chepito and the ills of society, much as Posado's Caterina brought humility to pretentious mortals.[116] The bullfighter's arrogance, treasured in the corridos, stood rebuked in the art of one their chief illustrators.

Beyond novel fan identities and specialist cultural forms, the devotion of the crowd burned brightest when they rioted.

FIGURE 3.1. José Guadalupe Posada, "Corrido don chepito mariguano," hoja suelta, pub. por A. Vanegas Arroyo. 1902.

Riots, Disorders, and *Broncas*

Songs, media, and press releases could aspire to social progress but could not guarantee order. Despite clear instructions, the fans did not always behave well. Papers regularly reported on violent disturbances at corridas in Mexico (and beyond) as *broncas* (fights) rather than as riots or using any other stronger terminology. The fault for a bronca rarely fell on the fans, according to journalists, but rather on the City, the veterinarians, the empresarios, the bullfighters, and occasionally, the bulls. The inflammatory press itself never took any blame despite working ceaselessly to rile up the fan base and their expectations. Just as they claimed for the matador Reverte, they, too, wished to "electrify the public." The blame fell elsewhere. The crowd acted up in response to outrages in a fully natural and just way.

When fights turned out disappointing, when bulls or toreros acted cowardly, or when empresarios switched out advertised fighters with lesser substitutes, the fans reacted. They tore out seats, planks, cushions, and threw these, along with any other items at hand, like bottles, hats, or food. At times, they lit these aflame first, to make certain their points had been made. In 1895, they did sufficient structural damage to Bucareli Plaza such that it had to close for business for months.[117] The most common claim from the papers asserted that broncas resulted from poor-quality bulls and bad "teams of buffoons (mamarrachas)."[118] Seeing this motivated "the public, that great witness . . . to rise up evening by evening with noisy protests arose and tumultuous activity . . . [and] with wild fury" including throwing planks into the bullring.[119] At a bronca in San Luis Potosí, a "totality of the public" without distinctions of age or class, began throwing chairs and apples and oranges at cowardly bullfighters, and calling on them to be jailed. This terrible showing, with great cowardice, so offended the crowd that they called on formal justice to avenge them. The owner of the plaza was in fact briefly jailed (perhaps for his own safety).[120] The audience had found its voice.

Crowds demonstrated their in-group inclusionary status loudly, and things sometimes got out of hand. Fans chanted and heckled, shouting over the noise of the vendors.[121] Some even threw odd items into the ring to demonstrate their earned and expert opinion. For instance, in Spain spectators hurled dead dogs and cats, in as horrifying a barrage as one could imagine.[122] One must wonder, how did fans manage to bring these? Did they carry these around all day? And how disappointed

FIGURE 3.2. Unknown, "Bronca al 'Sanluqueño," *El Toreo*, Nov. 30, 1896, 1. Sketch.

was a fan when they had to take this stinking ammunition home unthrown after an unexpectedly good fight? Fan bonding and participations sometimes went far too far.

Usually, fandom meant simply throwing seat cushions as a part of inclusion and participation in the shared experience, but when heckling went bad, some actors made it worse. The song "Corrido relative a la ¡La Gran destrucción y terrible incendiado de la plaza de toros de Puebla el 12 de enero del presente año! ¡Un muerto, muchos heridos y contusos!" told the tale of a bronca gone wrong.[123] The song tells of a disgusted crowd of thousands who whistled about a bad bull in third round, calmed a little with the next, but grew enraged during the fifth and sixth rounds. The crowd turned ugly when a Spaniard "threw his cushion with all force." With shouts of Gachupin, the crowd began to whistle and throw rocks, and the gendarmes could not contain them. As the corrido described it, "The audience became a beast—shouted madly and frantic, more than people, they seemed—the demons of hell." Even the children of the better classes, the song said with some amazement, joined in and became savage. Fire broke out. In the end, they destroyed everything, one person died, and the Spanish instigator paid a mere 200 pesos bond and fled justice. Other venues learned from this, and started to install at least some firefighting equipment, with, for example, the Plaza de Toros adding four hand pumps in 1897.[124] In the eyes of fans, the fault for the disaster seemed clear.

In "Las autoridades y el Reglamento: Los empresarios y el Público," the press discussed a typical bad fight and questions of blame. They declared that the Ayuntamiento should have rigidly followed regulations and cancelled the fight earlier, that the ganaderos should not sell cart oxen, and blamed the empresario (Ponciano Díaz) as he should have known better. They admit that while normally some bulls have no confidence, when all fail to fight there can be no explanation. They ultimately found that the empresarios, the officials, and the cattlemen all shared fault and that "their abuses and idiocy exasperate the fans."[125] The various authorities had plainly failed to meet the expectations of the entitled audience.

Foreign plazas did not prove immune to this phenomenon either. In a ring in Cartagena Spain in 1885, fans tore apart all the seating in rage.[126] At a bronco in Saint Louis, Missouri in June 1904, a riot and fire broke out.[127] Some 7,000 World's Fair goers had just enjoyed a Wild West–style show and impatiently awaited the bullfight main event to follow. Unfortunately, due to pressure from religious and humanitarian groups, Missouri state Governor Dockery gave in and dispatched the sheriff to shut

FIGURE 3.3. José Guadalupe Posada, "Terrible incendiado de la plaza de toros de Puebla," hoja suelta, pub. por A. Vanegas Arroyo, 1902.

the show down and to arrest the manager. Irate spectators became impassioned. The crowd "gathered for the barbaric spectacle, was howling 'toro toro.'" Adding insult to injury, police officers then came out carrying a placard announcing that the authorities had cancelled the corrida, because it was a "inhumane fiesta." Even worse, there would be no refunds and with tickets at $1 USD each, the crowd had had enough. Everyone in the audience became furious, and a mob sought to lynch the hapless manager (Richard Norris), his uninvolved wife, and the obedient sheriff. Deputies, backed by a dozen humanitarians, enflamed the situation and could not restrain the audience as they began to throw objects and howl with anger. According to the Mexican source, "They tore the square to pieces, set it on fire, and then the horde of savages threw themselves at fruit and refreshments kiosks, stole merchandise and money, and crushed the stands to powder. There were uncountable victims."[128] The *New York Times* reported one serious injury and several minor, and that the rioters prevented firefighters from saving the arena that burned to the ground. Clearly, the audience had made its point.

Unusually, the Mexican papers partially blamed the crowd in one case. The editors did not blame the empresario, authorities, or others for riotous bottle throwing, but called out the public for this "porqueria" (bullshit). The paper then backtracked; the crowd had acted correctly enough, since they were protesting energetically against bullfighters' *cabriolas* (prancing). They went on: "Every audience has the show they deserve."[129] In other words, fans got the quality of fight that they were willing to fight for.

The people believed themselves entitled to what they considered a good show, upholding a certain level of expectation and entertainment. The bronca reveals interesting facets of how the public audibly reacted to a breaking point in its moral ecology. Fans expressed themselves to protest poor fights or to celebrate better ones. The stands echoed with the noise. Terrible shows led to the roar of a riotous bronca or riot, slightly better ones brought on a piercing chorus of whistles, an acceptable fight got the ovation or *palmas*. Fans punctuated this with projectiles, throwing cigars, cigarillos, and sometimes hats to the torero, with cheers like "a dragon's roar."[130] Shouts and wild adulation, at times, could persuade the *presidente* to award an ear, or two, and sometimes a tail, to a particularly skilled matador.

Applause suggested more approval than one might assume and went beyond mere politeness as it might now. When the audience received bullfighter el Reverte

FIGURE 3.4. Unknown, "Por tantiar salir tantiado," *El Toreo*, Dec. 9, 1895, 1. Sketch.

"el Azteca" with loud applause, the *Ratas* editors proclaimed it as a great show of patriotism.[131] The whistling seems tightly tied to proper fandom, where writers spoke of "la silba más justa" (most fair whistle) or whistling at "poco valor" (little valor) that came as part of a fan's expected duty. One fan spoke to the paper about a fight that had led to cancellations due to excessive whistling, saying "'This is not living,' a young amateur said to me with tears in his eyes; 'If they suspend bullfighting, what will become of me?'"[132] The tumults themselves involved a devolution along the expression spectrum, as whistles failed to vent enough anger and active destruction began. Yet, again and again, the specialist presses not only forgave the crowd but attempted to justify their violent outbursts.

So, who, if not the rioters, held blame for broncas? Sometimes the toreros, particularly those not favored by the papers, caused the trouble by prancing or showing outright cowardice. Some misled the public, as with matador Machaquito who they claimed as the "rey de embustería" (king of lies).[133] Not only did he lie, but some fans had fallen for Machaquito (*caído bien*) and thus, had no mind of their own. On this claim, public outrage forced the editor to defend his critiques as not coming from his Spanish bias but based rather on the matador's technique.[134] Other actors failed to meet their critical standards. For example, they called out some diestros as "modernists" and "niños zangolotinos" who were all talk and only faced the smallest bulls.[135]

Beyond the toreros, blame for bad fights and resulting disorder often fell on the City, especially the section of Public Diversions and its appointed officials. These men had a duty to protect the fans from greedy businessmen, and to mitigate the fans' reactions to bad fights (even if justified). According to the papers, the public tired of taking all this abuse and mockery from empresarios, and the city needed to step up enforcement of regulations.[136] They demanded authorities find better men and appoint them to the important roles of director of the change of *suertes* (who determines the stages of the fight), the *regidor* (who oversaw the fights more generally), and the inspectors or sometimes veterinarians (who approved quality of bulls and horses for the fight). The fine points of these professions became public debate.

The papers could, at times, become quite heated on the subject. The editors sent an open letter in 1903 to the head of Diversiones Públicas, Augustin Alfredo Nuñez, saying that the fans entrust him to care for their interests. The editors said that they know Nuñez was smart and not malicious but that the many disorders at bullfights could be easily fixed. Specifically, they called for him to fire Inspector Julio Periá and the Director de cambio de suertes, Fernando Gutiérrez "el Niño." They said that the inspector knew "nothing about bullfighting" and should be made the inspector of theaters with his "shenanigans and bullshit." They added that the director was not much better. The two, sarcastically referred to as experts, should not be acting as the employees of the plaza but of the City instead.[137] This conflict of interest, a basic injustice, drove tumult in the stands.

That the rioting, whatever caused it, might be an overreaction could not be admitted by the specialist press. If the crowd behaved too well, in too sterile a manner, it denied itself the justified passion that the sport had tried so hard to promote as part of the "virile spectacle." Beyond all, the fandom insisted that promotors owed them the high-quality fights to which they knew they were entitled. Since the fight embodied the fandom as a body, since it spoke directly to their own collective worth and value, they demanded the best. This, as in other sports, built senses of both euphoria (at the great fights) and more often, disappointment, unrest, and dysphoria when expectations fell short.[138] Carefully cultivated fans fully embraced their right to enjoy the highest quality fights, the corrida to which they felt entitled, and for this they would fiercely revolt.

Conclusions

Modern corridas sold an experience responsible for the phenomenological formation of a new, modern, and nationalist fan. The idea of a new Mexican identity drew from traditions of the colonial and Catholic pasts while embracing novel and enticing entertainment industries and new spectacles. The *culto*, the fanático, the porra—who constructed a new off-work and out-of-church identity, maybe even a "self" separate or outside of family, found in bullfighting a powerful draw that even superseded normal financial concerns. Fans forsook the church, their studies, attendance at work, and hit the pawnshop to attend the "big event." Regardless of the course of the fight, they made it important by talking about for weeks, making songs, and reading and discussing specialized newspapers. They rioted. And they waited eagerly for the next match.

The greater industry and fandom also made this an indubitably a Mexican sport! Even if it had persistent Spanish touches with toreros emulating and comparing their corridas with Peninsular counterparts, by the late nineteenth century it had become a truly Mexican thing. Much as with the Mexicanization of boxing—there was a need to convince the public that it is not betrayal or foreign to be a fan.[139] As with other sports, promoters found that the key was the consumer and in making the fan invest in it personally. Through merchandise and specialized newspapers, fans became overtly affiliated with the sport and sharers of lore. Readers continued to develop a learned expertise, find a place among fellow fans who will listen to them, and they become vicarious professionals, if never men with capes themselves. Ultimately, and with multiple levels of media polish, a shiny new fandom on an old sport emerged. This raucous mass fellowship, centered on the death of the Other as packaged by capitalist entrepreneurs, became a shared entitlement and collective identity.

At its base the practice they revered depended on a shared set of traditions and expectations for the acceptable death (and degree of indifference to it) of the animal. This, monetized, wed a consumer moral ecology to a necropolitical assumption. Relations between the living fans and the dying animals helped to form modern sport, economy, and society. The porra chose their "natural" position in the overall order of things with the contents of their wallet.

The bullring echoed with the roar of a modern age of superfans and consumption.

CHAPTER FOUR

Owners and Haters

Capitalism and Activism in the Bullring Business

"The curses of the humanitarians will be silenced by the proofs of the economists."[1]

Huge iron skeletons clad in stone facades rose along the edges of the great city. From modest starts in 1886, a sudden boom in building and promoting had transformed the cityscape. Enormous stadiums seating tens of thousands competed for audiences only short distances apart. They took advantage of modern transit and architecture to provide unique experiences to the largest number of possible paying fans. A modern age of entertainment consumption had arrived.

Sporadic bans did little to interrupt the rise of a massive leisure industry. The fervent fans, and their moral ecological beliefs, acted as gleeful accomplice to profit motivations. The industry of modern leisure tapped into shifting capacities for spectacle, into broader multimedia means of creating and sustaining fan bases, and into the opportunities of the age. The corrida expressed the best in Mexican and Spanish traditions and showcased the potentials of local capitalists and promoters. These groups revived the stadiums and built numerous plazas. They built investment, they created merchandise, they advertised, and they lobbied the city at every turn. They created stars of men and bulls. They promoted a rabid fandom. If some rings rose on foundations of shoddy materials and low bids, others represented truly innovative changes in architecture and modernized facilities. While some heralded the possibility of a new golden age of bullfighting that would rival nostalgically remembered pasts, others, Mexican and foreign, spoke against what they saw as terrible cruelty.

Protection societies raised fierce, if often rhetorical, resistance against the bullfights. Largely, they failed. Drowned out by the cacophony of the crowds, drowned out by the money and influence of the investors, the bans fell short. Temporary successes (1880–1886, 1890, 1916–1920) only briefly displaced the fights to rural venues. Indeed, by 2025, repeated calls to abolish the fights have continued and sputtered.

The power of the show and industry at higher levels helped to constitute a powerful political lobby. The owners drew on adherence to capitalism and to nationalist character and relied on popular support from the mass audiences as a base. The haters opposed them, with foreign support and sentiments, calling for empathy and presenting a humane, animal-friendly, and ethical modern image of Mexico. In this clash, money won out. The owners, much as a successful matador carving an ear off a fallen bull, took their own trophy.

The underpinning impetus of capitalism made out art, memory, and the animal a mere commodity. The corrida, embedded in nostalgia and in fan narratives, spoke to the underlying fantasy of the necropolitical where the Other and its extermination legitimized the security and stability of the social order. It distanced the bull from a living breathing creature to become a symbolic antagonist to be ritually dispatched in the name of commerce, tradition, and leisure. Death, once purchased, became a fetish commodity for personal enjoyment.

This chapter begins with the history of the venerable art in Mexico, turning next to modern changes made to the sport and to the spectacle. As the bullfight matured, so too did the business investor. The owners and infrastructure, along with the ganaderías that supplied bulls, come next. After these, the chapter turns to the activists, in particular the SPCMA (protection society) and the numerous foreigners whose shocked accounts appealed to Mexicans' better natures. The empresarios and fans gave little heed. At the highest levels, two ideological struggles set out different terms for framing the killing of animals in the bullring.

The emergent capitalist culture facilitated the mingling of "authenticities" and of traditional practices with modern trappings. It constructed an experience centered around the shared enthusiasm for a sport that saw animals as Other and expendable. The abolitionists, in contrast to public hygienists, sought not to manage animals but to erase certain practices on aesthetic or ethical grounds. Bullfights represented a social experience re-created by modern venues and moneymen to construct a story about Mexican values absent any humanitarian ideals. As an organizing form for death, the entertainment industry of the bullring shrouded brutal logics in capitalist and modern trappings. Some elements of humanity did indeed intrude and struggled for the abolition of the sport. Those involved in the halls of power proved quite capable of dismissing animal deaths in the name of progress and capitalism. Business superseded any moralist, humanist attempts to call attention to the rights of animals to be seen as subjects or, even, to stay alive.

In Porfirian Mexico, as before and for a good time after, the experience of the bullfight arena stands out as the truly big show. It offered a unique mass entertainment that drew thousands of spectators together in a shared event unlike any other. By situating the sacrifice of animals as constituent to new capitalist enterprises, it established a bloody logic at the heart of modern Mexican consumer of sports culture. The fight itself had greatly changed over time.

A Brief History of the Bullfight

In its earliest form in Spain, participants closely tied bullfights to slaughterhouses, to religion, to marriages, and over the centuries to social welfare by raising funds for church charities.[2] Later fights persisted despite official clerical distaste and periodic opposition from among the powerful. Yet if it diverted some from attending Mass, if some critics found the sport too barbaric, nonetheless the church had been tied to the corrida since its earliest days. The bullfight as ritual had been a cultural industry that supported pilgrimages and religious causes with the full-throated unofficial approval of the clergy.[3] They also raised funds for natural disaster relief.[4] The sacred stamp in many ways remained, and remains, in the moral ecology that sees the spilled blood as sacrifice and the event as a social good.

Mexicans had a long and contentious history with the bullfight. The fights had a marked political and sacred place—on August 13, 1529, only ten years after Cortés's landing at Veracruz, a commemorative celebration saw one of the earliest matches celebrated on San Hipólito's Day in Mexico City.[5] The bulls that fought there arrived as new and alien to Mexico as their human Spanish opponents. Conquistadors celebrated their "God-given" victory via this bloody ritual while they politically claimed their legitimate place in Tenochtitlán.[6] Spectating Mexica would not, presumably, have noted a great deal of difference between the Spanish use of blood rituals in political theater and their own religious sacrifices and ceremonials. Despite a different deity, the meaning nonetheless would have made perfect symbolic sense.

Afterward in the colony bullfights frequently accompanied major political events. The important 1535 entrada to install the first viceroy, Mendoza, featured a three-day corrida, while the Galvéz entrada in 1789 had two weeks of bullfights at a new plaza (built in 1784). As Linda Curcio-Nagy points out, bullfights represented both an opportunity for private entrepreneurship and a Bourbon ceremonial cornerstone. During the late eighteenth century, these provided much of the revenue the government depended on to fund its other lavish political events.[7] Into the national period, Agustín Iturbide inaugurated his rule with a bullfight in 1821, as did Benito Juárez half a century later.[8] New plazas appeared in the 1850s at Paseo Nuevo and a bit later, at the Plaza de Colón.[9] The ritual nature of this had a political theater aspect.

Juan Pedro Viqueira Albán likewise shows that the bullfight had long been used in New Spain as a model ceremony that represented social order and hierarchy. It reflected tensions between viceroy and church, and even reflected, in the Bourbon era, a breakdown of old orders instigated by the Enlightenment reproach of elitism. He also showed how the sport changed in the eighteenth century to favor the torero on foot over the mounted version, even as horses had become increasingly available.[10] Further, he detailed how additional diversions like dogfights, greased pole climbs, and female matadors at times appeared.[11] The "innovative" shows that took place in the late nineteenth century, therefore, appear not so novel, but as a recurring attempt by organizers to meet the demand for varied entertainment. Stated reasons for colonial bans emphasized the overspending on events by the poor and the unruly behaviors of the crowd, and never spoke of brutality.

The move to ban the fight had started much earlier, with precedents during the colonial era, but the law and precedents had begun to support some sort of ban by the middle of the nineteenth century. One clever work-around by A. José Soledad in February 1868 proposed to show animals other than man fighting "since the principal motive of the law versus the corrida is the grave risk to human life." In that case, animals killing one another was just fine. The City agreed, and permitted a show pitting a bull against a bear, and displaying other *fieros* (wild beasts) in the plaza de Paseo.[12] But the law reiterated a few year later that this did not pass muster. The mistreatment of, or cruelty against, animals had long been illegal, even in combat sports. The Criminal Code in 1871, Chapter XI, prohibits the mistreatment of any animal with excessive loads, illness, or act of cruelty, including condemning "those who in combats, games, or public amusements torments animals."[13] Perhaps this law made some impact since three years later, when Olivera Cardos requested to exhibit wild beasts and other animals in the plaza, 1874, and they denied him permission.[14] The fighting between a bull and tiger, on the other hand, could at times be allowed. Usually, as in a fight in the Plaza de Madrid, the bulls won.[15] In Mexico, ordinary bullfights remained the norm.

The Great Spectacle

No other mass spectacles drew in audiences in Mexico on the scale of the corrida. Horse racing drew fewer fans, cockfights only dozens, circuses and theaters slightly more than these but with similar issues of bad behavior and, worse, of political murmuring.[16] The corrida won out over other types of spectacles like animal shows and dramatic theater. Officials, convinced in part by the overly political nature of stage theater presentations and audience participations, believed those venues to be chaotic and harmful for the moral well-being of the public.[17] The audiences rarely behaved, and officials closed shows to conserve "the good order at public spectacles."[18] Owners learned to adapt.

Entrepreneurs who offered other choices had difficulties when their venues failed to meet community standards. Prominent circus proprietors like the J. J. Orrin Brothers operated a show in Santa Domingo neighborhood in the mid-1880s, when bullfights faced a ban, but could not persuade the City to allow them to add a zoological museum, let alone to continue their operations. They assured the city that they kept the circus area "perfectly clean and odorless," which might have been a suggestion of the contrary. City officials noted that the show obstructed people's passage, caused floods, threatened fires, and disturbed families in the neighborhood with its "unbearable music." The Orrin Brothers proposed as a solution that they would add greenery to screen the site.[19] The City report then noted that the circus's neighbors also reported that they could not use their balconies without seeing acts against decency and morality. Moving slowly to respond to these citizen complaints, the city made the circus transfer to a new site . . . nine years later.[20] Among other entertainments, hundreds listened to military bands in city parks or found smaller shows. But the sheer numbers in a bullfight crowd dwarfed all these options. The bullring itself represented an architectural transformation as the late nineteenth century would see huge modern facilities and the first truly giant stadiums of the modern era.[21] Even the public had transformed.

A subtle change by the late nineteenth-century corrida came as organizers explicitly took out religion and minimized civic duty as reasons to attend. The show instead shifted toward a capitalist mass spectacle of leisure. The display of agency and preferences made by the consuming public now connected to a secular identity, and one with a collective moral ecological discourse. Among the many changes as the corrida became modern came through the influences of the emerging capitalist market. The spectacle became more purely a commercial moneymaker than ever before. While entrepreneurs had always been involved in grabbing profit, the new architectures, regulations, and promotions built something bigger—an industry. Safety measures, city ordinances, veterinary attendance, and many other features now became requisite. The church faded away. The international market beckoned and marketing specialized.

Promoters like Ponciano Díaz at Bucareli, Ramón López, Ecijano, Cuatrodedos, and others, ushered in a new experience for the fan and reached out into society to build a base. They catered to the female fans, and they sexualized marketing. They provided collectibles for children. They printed posters for the hardcore fans. Newspapers with access to the toreadors catered to a broad middle-class audience base. Luxury boxes and other expensive services catered to the wealthy. Stars were made, managed, and marketed. Even the management acquired a celebrity burnish. For example, when Spanish matador Fernando Gutiérrez el Niño grew too old to fight, he became the Director of Fights at El Toreo bullring in 1896.[22] Even the animals had been redesigned.

The industry constructed a new antagonist by making the bulls modern celebrities in their own rights. Careful breeding made the new generation noteworthy for their "bravery, nobility, and appearance."[23] They brought them in from abroad, too, to breed in increasingly skilled ganaderías on the Mexico side.[24] One consequence, the tougher bulls and new closer-to-the-bull maneuvers led inevitably to a marked increase in dead bullfighters. This hardly proved bad for ticket sales.

Most importantly in many ways, they created the modern celebrity matador (see chapter 5). Promoters deliberately tapped into a need for hero figures as they built their market, and they stoked the extravagant and fantastical hero "rock star" figures of the sport, including figures like Antonio Montes, Rodolfo Gaona, and Bernardo Gaviño. These men sold bravado and flash, and the machismo, the finesse, and the discipline that ideally marked the great matador. They did not engage (much) in politics, appeared not overtly religious, and had no connections to the military or other industry. The promoters constructed secular fandoms for a modern age.

The Industry of the Corrida

As governments overturned the first set of federal bans in 1886, entrepreneurs initiated a building spree to bring the sport back to full profitability. Most of these new plazas, somewhat hastily constructed, lasted only a short time as in the case of San Rafael, Colón, Paseo, and Coliseo, which ran from 1887 to 1889. In 1889–1890 a new ban closed their doors; most did not reopen.[25] For a time, the most important plaza belonged to a former matador, Ponciano Díaz, who ran the Plaza Bucareli since 1888 until his death in April 1899, and the plaza's demolition a month later. This ring, located near the Garita de Belén and conveniently close to the offices of their biggest advertiser, El Buen Tono cigars, had a reputation for inconsistent quality.[26] Díaz excelled at public relations and used his fame and press coverage to convey an image of "mexicanismo" in charro outfits and events.[27] Nonetheless, *El Toreo* relentlessly hounded him as providing bad fights for too much cost, and indeed, for forcing fans to tear up Bucareli in protest. The plaza does seem to have been somewhat lower in scale than some, with a reasonable 8,000 seat capacity and decent 38-meter diameter ring size. Unfortunately, it also had inadequate elements like a mere steel cable to protect first row seating from a leaping bull.[28] Cheaper construction did allow for further expansions.

Fans won out as the sport boomed again in the first years of the twentieth century. Promoters opening new venues regularly with bullrings at San Rafael, Plaza Mexico (Condesa) in 1899–1913, Plaza de Toros in 1899, Chapultepec from 1902 to 1907, México's Old Plaza opened in 1903 (and still running), and the huge El Toreo in the Condesa opening in 1907, among others. Former diestros often fronted groups of investors in these enterprises, for example, with Cuatrodedos at Chapultepec and Ecijano at Plaza de Toros. Investor groups, often with engineers credited, too, sunk

FIGURE 4.1. José Guadalupe Posada, "Desde la barrera," hoja suelta, pub. por A. Vanegas Arroyo and Gil Blas. 1909.

significant money into these ventures. These included many of the notable family names in Mexico, such as Mondragón, Alamán, Robles Gil, and so forth.[29] New expertise also changed the architecture of the rondel.

The complexity of the construction grew as the scale of plazas did. When Jesús de Yeaza proposed his new ring (the Romita) in the Condesa in 1899, he initially built for a 14,000 capacity, and he brought in the military engineer Samuel de Cuellar to manage the details.[30] With a unique structure of stone facing and steel skeleton it finally opened July 27, 1903, guaranteed to the City with a 10,000-peso bond.[31] Blocks away, September 22, 1907, saw the opening of El Toreo under Ignacio del Torre (son-in-law to President Díaz), which at time was the largest in the world with over 20,000-seat capacity, and some claimed it held over 25,000.[32] Featuring a slightly larger ring, multiple entries for both sun and shadow spectators, and Belgian steel, the outsides of the stadium also featured huge advertisements for beer, hats, and other goods. More practically, it also boasted a series of *carrederas* (walkways) for emergency exiting.[33] December 1905 saw Ramón López obtain approval for his Plaza de Toros with capacity for 16–18,000 spectators.[34] In November 1908, the plaza at Tacuba opened.[35] Enthusiasm for the enterprise seemed high, and the municipal governments proved eager to join along. It certainly did not hurt that the city got a cut on the tickets sold, usually, 5–15 percent depending on venues, with smaller suburbs also getting a cut of tickets. For the City of Mexico, laws often slated these funds to pay for public works, like the Gran Desagüe (Great Drain water project).[36] Money flowed.

All this activity represented a huge commercial investment. Each of the stadiums took up to a year to build and cost between 200,000 to 300,000 pesos depending on size.[37] As an example, an iron-framed structure for 6,500 seats cost 218,000 pesos, with price going up to 397,000 pesos for a 12,000-seat structure. Seats themselves cost about 20,000 pesos, carpentry about 50,000 pesos, and another 20,000 pesos for general labor. Land, often at edges of city and relatively inexpensive, still ran at 5–7 centavos per square yard, or about 145,000 pesos for an average stadium.[38] Owners often looked for savings.

Land prices and local politics tended to drive bullfights to the edges of the city. Bidding on labor at times created conflicts. Adding on extra seats also meant adding on bad seating and counting on courting larger crowds of the poorer customers. Starting from scratch after the 1880s and 1890 bans, this huge boom in building new stadiums with modern architecture nevertheless seems amazing. The average stadium cost 14,500 pounds sterling, or $70,470 USD, in today's prices, running about $2,159,000 USD. The promoters who could afford this represented a select group within high society.[39] Most often this included foreign (Spanish) investors, groups of Mexicans, a celebrity front man, and well-known engineers. It should come as no surprise that many in the public considered the general reputation of opportunistic bullfight promoters as notably seedy.[40] Outsiders alleged dishonest business practices including wage theft, false advertising, and outright fraud. But the industry thrived.

Clearly a bullring came as a good investment since even with sunny seats selling at a mere thirty centavos each, multiplied by tens of thousands this represents a tidy income. Three full audience fights could pay for the construction of a ring. In the first years of the century (1904–1907), Mexico City hosted over 131 *festejos taurinos* (bullfight events). This meant profit, even after the official cut to the City (15 percent) and undoubtedly paying out for other political arrangements and further kickbacks to government officials. Numerous investors stepped forward.

One, a former bullfighting star himself, was Ponciano Díaz. He proposed a new plaza in 1894 in a letter rife with spelling errors. He wrote that he "knows from criminal statistics that the day of a corrida drunkenness decreases since those types are waiting at the entrance of the ring rather than at cantinas. The virile show gives the masses not a barbarous amusement but shows them that the courage and intelligence of man are superior to the simple force of a beast." He added: Besides, Spain has corridas too, and the practice makes a great deal of money. The initial counterbid from the government suggested that maybe this plaza could be permitted, but with an extortionate 60 percent of the entrada donated to the city.[41] Profit drew further investors.

Other famed matador businessmen offered to run their own plazas. Cuatrodedos (who had lost a finger as a child) was born in Spain 1856 and had a successful career in Mexico from age thirty-one to almost fifty. Beyond fame in the ring, he became better known for his business dealings as he got caught up in a deal with two other Spaniards, the former banderilla Ramón López and one Ángel Caso. Rather than following through with building the Plaza de Toros México with the unliked López, he broke from the deal and built the Plaza Chapultepec in Condesa, in 1902. This ring lasted until 1907, but with financial difficulties. Bulls never got Cuatrodedos, but he died, impoverished, in 1918. Some had more savvy.

Another proprietor, Yñigo Noriego Laso, disingenuously wrote to the Ayuntamiento in 1894 that he could not build his new bullring at La Viga.[42] He argued that it would fail because the "aristocracy of our society, especially the ladies, would resist going there." In contrast to the norm, he wanted to provide an arena with the beauty and luxury of Paris, and with beautiful access points for vehicles. He went on, nevertheless, conceding that the corrida de toros was not the favorite of the aristocracy, much less of ladies who scarcely and rarely went, since the spectacle was too overwhelming for their exquisite sensibilities. Rather he would cater to the great mass of the people, who would prefer pulquerías and *viñas* (wineshops), as the statistics of criminality had shown. With his contradictory arguments and willingness to altruistically save the workers from drinking, he seems to have convinced the council of his legitimacy. They approved his proposal to build a 300,000-peso stadium.[43] Arenas sprang up everywhere, as did new regulations.

Reacting to various scandals and disasters, the city and other governments began to rein in the burgeoning stadium complex with added requirements. The appearance of sick and contagious animals, in shamefully bad shape, led officials to require that promoters hire a veterinarian. Officials noted that proper stabling should be installed, that any questionable meat should not be sold to markets, and denounced the recurring problems of muermo (glander) that plagued the horses used in the ring.[44] The City determined that while veterinarians certainly met a critical requirement, the stables, water supply, meat storage, and overall hygiene all still needed critical improvements.[45] Related to horse health, bullrings often spent as little as possible for their horses knowing full well that most would die on the horns of the bulls.[46] Health problems in the stands, but more often down in the ring, led to requirements for an on-staff doctor.[47] After the 1896 disaster in the ring at Puebla, cities required the rings to provide firefighting capacity (see chapter 3). They also mandated where rings could be built and weighed in on everything from urinals to security arrangements.[48]

In addition to setting hygiene regulations, government officials also began to regulate general policies and other details for operations. In a sample contract for the Mixcoac arena in August of 1894, they explicitly set out: (1) time limits for fights, (2) ticket cuts paid to the city (5 percent to Mixcoac and 15 percent to DF), (3) three horses made available per bull, (4) the number of reserve bulls on hand, obtained only from known *ganaderías de lidia*, (5) the exclusive use of diestros with known aptitude and license, (6) a doctor and veterinarian on site for all fights in city, and finally (7) the City's reserving of the right to cancel the contract.[49] While governments took a hand in some matters, critics in the press paid careful attention to the operational side of the corrida. Special venom from the taurino press fell on the business and industry of the bullfight.[50]

El Toreo had many contentions with former torero Ponciano Díaz, who they called the unique and tenacious enemy of the fandom in Mexico. According to the opening of the first issue, he broke all the regulations and made changes to the fights with "his stale ideas." They set up that by contrast the Plaza Bucareli generally should have worked for fans' current interests rather than turning backward to 1860 as Díaz would have it.[51] Among his many ascribed crimes, they held him responsible in 1895 for switching out advertised fighters and allowing the president to choose bad bulls from a low-quality ganadería for fight. The editor, going by the penname "el Criticón," also claimed that Díaz had failed to provide enough horses for each bull, which breached regulations and led to a poor fight.[52]

Another issue that provoked the newspaper seems to have been the empresario's buying and selling of new bullrings. They accused Díaz of "monopolizar económica-ambiciosa" (economically ambitious monopolies) because he tried to buy yet another plaza at Tepeyahualco (the site of a famed ganadería). He was selling Tacubaya to Juan Jiménez "Ecijano" (a fellow matador), who offered cheaper fights and yet the paper seemed to see this as a negative step. They also pointed to Díaz's persistent problems with tickets and refunds, and what they termed problems at the entrance.[53] Indeed, outrages over his actions and the riot that followed cost Bucareli the opportunity to offer any public amends through hosting a charity benefit fight. When the empresario petitioned to do a benefit for the Colón Asylum, the City denied it due to extensive damage in the stands, and the benefit moved to a smaller out of town plaza in San Bartolo.[54] This struck some as an appropriately just punishment for greed.

This was not an arbitrarily anti-business stance by the press. Regarding the bullfights at Pachuca, they had only glowing reports, including wonderment at the cheap prices; promoters there offered seats for fifty centavos in shade, ten in sun, gave an under-thirty-years-old discount, and provided a free train rides to the city with the purchase of a corrida ticket.[55] But Díaz could do nothing to win them over nearer to home. The paper even reported somewhat gleefully of a rumor that a new play about Díaz called *Lo barato cuesta caro* (Cheap Is Expensive) that would be performed in city theaters.⁵⁶ Press vitriol did extend well past poor Díaz.

For their part, *Ratas y Mamarrachas* spewed some hatred toward the matador Machaquito, but their real editorial anger they directed toward the empresario Ramón López. The former banderillero and Spanish empresario made the cover of *El Toreo* (the only empresario ever thus featured) and ran the Plaza de Toros México.⁵⁷ The *Ratas* did not share *El Toreo*'s enthusiasm.

They accused him of many flaws. The powerful López did not lower his prices despite his elevated income, he used the worst bulls, and now he planned to open another plaza at Chapultepec. He should not "prostitute the seriousness of the fiestas" with his despotism. In his last fight, fines were levied against the wrong people, since the director did his job, the veterinarian did his, and so the plaza (and hence López) earned the blame.⁵⁸ Injustice bothered the editors, but shoddy business practices drew the worst press.

They pilloried López for not keeping up with the new plazas being built in city. They commented on a stadium proposed with stone facades and 20,000-person seating, that would lower prices from five to three pesos in shade and from two pesos to fifty centavos in sun. In this case, Luis Aguilar and Domingo Carrodegiias sold their stakes to Dr. Carlos Bringas and Gonzalo Alfaro (leaving Ramón López out of the deal) and had already put a 10,000-peso deposit down with bank to get started construction.⁵⁹ Meanwhile, the paper noted the lamentable state of the López's Plaza de México, which, though only four years old, had poor construction showing through, especially with a year of bad rains and flooding across southern part of city. The paper urged the city to help with engineering to get his rival's Covadonga Plaza ready to take 16,000 spectators.⁶⁰ In a follow-up article, they claimed also that the Plaza de México's stairs needed reinforcement and new planks, and that the plaza had flood damage.⁶¹

Ratas also repeatedly called out Ramón López for his parsimony, perhaps because he was a native of Madrid (foreigner) and the son of a shoe salesman (working class). His excessive ticket sales had led to conflict and overcrowding in oversold stands. The editors also called for him to compensate his toreros more fairly, pointing out that matadors at Covadonga earned only 150 pesos and banderillas only 60 pesos.

Since the gate took in over 14,000 pesos, this struck them as inadequate.[62] If true, this does seem like low payment. An article compared Spanish pay at 800 pesos with normal Mexican pay that usually hit between 200 to 300 pesos.[63]

Ratas continued their attacks with even more complaints versus López, claiming that he did not permit benefit fights, his prices were too high, he did not give away meat where it was needed, and so on. He also employed a whole collection of "maletas."[64] These complaints, as well as his use of inadequate bulls and toreros, continued almost weekly.[65] The editors also claimed that López purchased biased favorable press in other periodicals.[66]

Although the various papers at times criticized the government and its agents this did occasion somewhat more caution. They had high expectations for the City and pointed out that the municipality should consider their recommendations since the bullfight provided so much income for their budgets.[67] The large percentage of entrada that the government took (15 percent for DF, and often another 5 percent for the municipality of the plaza) struck the journalists as fundamentally unfair. They pointed out that the City only took 3 percent of theaters' ticket sales. The bullfight, by contrast, represented "the only true diversion for the people," since they did not attend city-subsidized operas, casinos, or horse racing. Therefore, taxing the bullfight unjustly penalized the common people.[68] Not only did the City take extra from the bullrings (and its poor fans), but at the same time they handed out tax money to the well-off with the prizes they awarded at the Jockey Club.[69] The issues with the city, beyond their excessive taxation, generally revolved around personnel. The Ayuntamiento's role included properly regulating operations through appointed staff positions, especially the Director de cambio de suertes, inspectors, and medical or veterinary staffing.

From specialist press coverage, it would seem that the city made its appointments based on patronage or favoritism rather than meritocracy. Editors pointed to the fights and to fans' reactions as proof of incompetence. For instance, they facetiously claimed that the honorable Ayuntamiento in its "reformative mania" made a parody of regulating and was "metamorphosizing" the bullfight to an extreme. Instead, the Director Taurino should be selected from among the intelligent fans, rather than picking an ex-torero like León Cortés. The proof was in the last fight, where bulls received forty-five *varas* (lances) and killed eighteen horses which indicated negligence.⁷⁰ They called repeatedly for better, more professional veterinary staff to disallow bad bulls before they entered the ring and ruined the show.⁷¹ They even asked that these men have actual degrees.⁷² To be fair, the editors did note that the Director Taurino position and the job of president proved almost impossible since the ganaderías, diestros, city, and fans all had different opinions and agendas. You cannot please everyone. They did add, though, that the Director de cambio de suertes position should be a City employee (to be objective) and at least competent.⁷³

They reported each new appointment and scrutinized the officials closely.⁷⁴ Many writers held little back, as in an article in *La Careta* that called out the government as embodying a country of the deaf (unresponsive) where the officials helped defraud the public.⁷⁵ That said, at times the government pushed back with a chilling effect. In 1904, police jailed an editor of a weekly events magazine named Vega because he criticized Inspector Julio Pería (an ex-comic turned official).⁷⁶ This case also appeared in *Diario del Hogar*, a large mainstream paper that opposed the corrida both as spectacle and as a business but took exception with the jailing of a journalist. Vega had strongly suggested that the inspector needed to prevent sick and overly young bulls with bad horns from being used. The use of these inadequate animals, they pointed out, caused the crowd to protest in violent ways. The *Diario* also suggested that the inspector might have corruptly been working with the empresarios Feliciano Rodríguez (of Spain) and Francisco Peréz Vizcaino, who owned the "industrial" company of the Plaza México.⁷⁷

Not to be left out, the editors of *Ratas* sent an open letter to the District Government. They wrote on behalf of "the citizens and fans in our *patria* who wanted magnificent fights instead of *raquitíco* (spineless) and repugnant ones." They wanted a spectacle that enflamed the spirit and exalted the passions. Somewhat abruptly they then concluded that the government should therefore not prosecute Vega, nor give in to pressures from empresarios like Ramón López, who was getting unfairly good reviews for his new plaza at Chapultepec.⁷⁸ Although they had to add in a bit of their own pet rivalry into letter at the end, they at least spoke in favor of Vega, which, given some of their own critiques of officials, had an element of journalistic self-defense. Ultimately, a great deal of the papers' many complaints fell on those who supplied the bulls.

Ganaderos

While bulls could no doubt be encountered in any corner of Mexico, the true fans only entrusted a certain select few breeders to provide their *toros bravos* (fighting bulls). The number of these varied over the years, but the important ones at this time included San Diego de los Padres (owned by Barabosa), Tepeyahualco (of José María González Pavón), Parangueo, Piedras Negras, Santín, and Atenco (which papers gave a bad repute for its *ratas feas* or ugly skinny livestock). Atenco was known, too, as the oldest of all ganaderías, having belonged to either the cousin or cousin-in-law of Hernan Cortés.[79] Bullfights ran from the first Sunday of October to last Sunday of April, which sometimes led to debates over whether organizers had sufficient animals for so lengthy a season.[80] The papers pointed out that a handful of farms could not properly provide for the over thirty corridas in the capital alone during 1896.[81] The fights killed six bulls per afternoon, and by early century often seven. And the demand for more, and better bulls, always pressured breeders.

Other ganaderías popped up from time to time, including, according to *Ratas*, one of the best in 1904 at San Nicolás Peralta. This one belonged to the wealthy and influential son-in-law of Porfirio Díaz, Ignacio de la Torre. Since he was going to supply bulls to the Colonia Españoles ring at Covadonga (the clear favorite of the Spanish-biased editors of the paper), one might take that particular recommendation with a grain of sand.[82] De la Torre owned a highly traditional hacienda, and required his peons to line up and kiss his or his wife's (Amada Díaz) hands while they sat atop what one visitor called a type of throne. There, it was said, the brothers Zapata became angry and revolutionary working as horse wranglers for the pretentious hacendado.[83] Of any bulls, the visitor made no mention.

The actual beasts garnered careful judgment by experts, not least because of their expense. For the most part, these specialist bulls sold for at least 200 pesos at the cheapest, depending on their lineage and qualities.[84] In the ring the experts often characterized the bulls either as *la casta* (with good breeding), *el trapío* (with shiny coat, good horns, small ears), or *novedad* (those who have not fought yet). In the last years of the nineteenth century, the bulls began to improve through careful breeding, and little resembled the animals of the past. Breeders judged the ferocity of the bulls by the number of varas (spears) that the animal withstood, and the number of horses

FIGURE 4.2. Unknown, "Tepeyahualco bull," *El Toreo*, Mon., Nov. 2, 1896, 4–5. Sketch.

that it killed. More and more breeding stock from Spain arrived to add danger to the ring. In 1896, Alberto Zayas brought thirty bulls to Mexico in three shipments by October.[85] Likewise, the ganadero González Pavón earned fame for his modern approach to breeding and had brought Spanish bulls in since 1888 (these fought in 1893). He brought still more from the Duque de Veragua in 1890, and six more in the summer of 1896. His Tepeyahualco ganadería received consistently positive coverage from the press, even featuring on *El Toreo*'s cover, and they proclaimed further his bulls very well cared for.[86]

The new Spanish bulls brought attitude to the ring. One newcomer to Mexico promptly killed four horses, wounded a picador, and then gored the matador.[87] The up-and-coming ganadería at Santín received good press when two of their bulls leaped into the stands during a fight, with one being barely held back by a matador pulling on its tail.[88] The press also pointed out nationalist differences between the animals, claiming that the Spanish bulls, while fierce, tended to be somewhat predictable in terms of acting with the right aggression at the right times. In contrast, the Mexican stock tended to need more attention to fight them properly, they acted oddly at times and needed more prodding. For those gambling on the bulls, this added uncertainty. Writers said that the bulls in Spain work with you, but in Mexico they needed more work. They referred here to a *toro codicioso* (greedy) that gored Antonio Montes in the leg. It had succeeded in landing its blow because it had "pocas facultades de bicho" (little capacity as a creature) and not because it was gifted.[89] Overall, the beasts had become more dangerous.

Despite this, and perhaps as a result of cheap empresarios, papers continued to point out the poor quality of stock. The beleaguered Bucareli swapped out advertised fighters, they used bad fighters, but worse of all, they used oxen rather than bulls. This also held the veterinarian to blame, since the Regulations Article 13 said bulls must be four and a half to six years old, and Article 15 said that bulls cannot be "defective." The editors urged a boycott against the empresarios.[90] Even with new blood, by 1904 the papers continued to be pessimistic about the state of the bull. In what the writer called a sad confession, he asserted that Mexico would never have good bulls because they had no real ganaderos, and they needed better breeders and high-quality land and water. The best they had, he admitted, came from Tepeyahualco and Piedras Negras.[91]

A final note on why having the best bulls possible really mattered ties back to broncas, construction, and the aficionados. The writers argued for rapidly improving the animals used at a new plaza to avoid difficulties. They warned of the implications of further bad bulls as Chapultepec Plaza opened, putting stress on the supply of good toros. To illustrate the risk, they called on the government to imagine a fire gutting the Plaza de México, and in the tragic aftermath, all the wailing orphans it would leave behind. Therefore, the city should, for public interest, clamp down on inspection of bulls and ensure the use of good ganaderías. For the sake of the children.[92]

Sometimes even the best toros and canniest industrialists had to find new ways to spur the interest of the crowds, and novelties, many seen in the colonial era, reappeared.

The Weird

To overcome lingering opposition and fill seats, promoters again brought in the exotic and the sale of excess and the weird. Ponciano Díaz and his acolytes brought the Buffalo Bill Show to Madrid, along with Mexican charros in 1894.[93] Now with a precedent in Spain, American Will Pickett visited Mexico where he wrestled bulls to their knees with "only the ring in their nose." His Wild West–style show (May 5, 1900) featured a *jaripeo* (rodeo show) with cash prizes for the best "amarrar un novilo" (calf-roping) and *baqueros* [sic] Tejanos demonstrating steer wrestling.[94] Going full-on Roman-style, another fight had set a bull versus a lion, with implied symbolic ideas about empires and nations. These animal-on-animal fights, nothing new, had been featured in Plaza Nuevo in the 1850s where Mexicans had pit bulldogs in a series of fights, against a bear, young mules, hares, deer, and once, a lion.[95] Again, this style had also took place in Spain, where they had pitted tigers and lions versus bulls in a show in 1894 (the bulls won).[96] In any case, unusual spectacles sold tickets.

Novelty acts, of course, did not play only to Mexican audiences. This era also saw the success of the Wild West Show in the United States with its enormous popularity at the Chicago World's Fair, as well as innumerable smaller shows and traveling exhibits.[97] Raúl de Anda, professional charro, rode the rodeo and charro circuit for years, and for a time with the Wild West Show. Later he would become a minor movie star with roles in, among other films, *Vámanos con Pancho Villa* (1936).[98] Novelties also provided proponents of the corrida ammunition against bans by making it harder to define exactly the type of activity could be shown. Was the ban specifically against bulls versus men? What of other animal shows, or what if the matador was not a man but a woman? Perhaps of limited use in taking the focus off animal cruelty, but female matadoras like Lolita Guerrera y Angelita and others faced temporary bans in DF, despite having great success in venues across Spain earlier.[99] The promoters argued that the old prohibitions against female fighters came from French moralists legislating against prostitution, and so clearly had become irrelevant (for more on toreras, see chapter 5).

Far beyond the promoters and performers, the creation of the bullfight as a modern spectacle depended enormously on changing infrastructure in the nation. In an odd irony, the greatest cultural show that the nation put on did not make it to the big screen until much later. The earliest film companies could not film bullfights in the early century due to lack of rights, though the goring of Gaona in 1908 does have a short footage.[100] Ganaderías flourished, *gremios* (guilds) of toreros appeared, and caudrillos had no difficulties filling spots.[101] Fights increased and gained better quality, new novelty acts appeared, the industry made increased connections to Spain for animals and people, and physical buildings transformed enormously. The fights became entirely different as rings rose from a mere single 10,000-seat plaza to multiple rings with double the capacity, and now with electric trams to shuttle in spectators.[102] Nonetheless, despite modern trappings and broad cultural acceptance, some raised their voices against the blood on the sand.

Bans and Reformers

Far from the maddened crowd, some Mexicans questioned the entire industry of bullfighting and called for new bans. They questioned assumptions of the moral ecology, for instance, claiming that the violence against the animals represented an unnecessary cruelty.

Among the proponents, many felt the bull to be an appropriately "distant" target—a mere animal—and therefore fights were not truly cruel. As an Othered object, the beast fell prey to popular indifference. The bull as a creature was different enough to ignore, and, after all, the meat was sent on to good purposes.[103] Through the whole of the bull's life, up to the last hour or so, it had a far better time of things than most cattle could hope for. The Bible said man had lordship over animals and could use them as they would. Some also made claims of bringing natural world to the city: at times in Spain fierce dogs would be brought into the ring to goad cowardly bulls into fighting back.[104] This could not be cruel, they argued, since dogs were simply a part of the natural world, and nature could not be cruel or kind—it simply was. The fight was not orchestrated torture because it harmonized with nature. This consensus of moral ecology nonetheless faced detractors among the elite who had a rival perspective.

The sport clashed with a small group of the wealthy elite acting as animal rights proponents, including the president's wife, Carmen Rubio Romero, by the 1890s. In this, it also highlighted a culture war between conflicting views on animals, entertainment, sports, and national image. The Society for the Protection and Care of Mexican Animals (SPCMA) took a lead role in this fight. They held monthly public meetings with the goal of working with authorities and the law to reduce animal suffering. Members, upon paying dues ranging from one to one hundred pesos per year depending on one's "station," received a special badge to wear in public to be seen by all.[105] They certainly saw themselves as working on the side of heaven, with the society seal showing a man with a stick threatening a horse, with an angel interceding. Education reforms would allow them to challenge animal cruelty in the longer term, and Article 3 of their rules required them to propagate and spread ideas in schools, books, pictures, and printed matter, and to encourage teachers to join the society. The following articles mainly laid out roles for their appointed agents and inspectors, their lobbyists, and offered some salaried roles like veterinarians and lawyers to join a board of nine officers. They also proposed to have a Special Committee of Ladies, with its own board and officers. Presumably, they would address feminine issues of animal welfare? In any case, the society would meet on the first Monday of each month, having posted a notice in English and Spanish papers three days in advance.

For the society, some of their efforts bore fruit. In one small victory, they managed to install a water fountain, proposed on June 22, 1904, with help from the Ayuntamiento. This fountain was to be artistic, granite, six feet high, with a low trough for small animals and a middle trough for horses or mules, and with an iron-capped section for people. Luis Espinosa of Public Works okayed the request and offered possible locations, subject to traffic and water pressure available and ultimately approved two such fountains.[106] Broader changes proved more elusive.

The SPCMA argued that being modern and civilized and good meant banning the cruel sport of bullfights. Notably, dogfights and cockfights and small-scale shows, as well as hunting, continued without specific attention from these organizations. Their concerns focused on the great visible prominence of the corrida in major cities where someone might actually see the bloodshed. Animal rights efforts did not prove terribly successful despite bans in Mexico City from 1880 to 1886, in part of 1890, and from 1916 to 1920. Romero Rubio and her friends never got their way with the whole country, or for long.

Given its limited successes in improving the actual lot of animals, it seems likely that the SPCMA played a role both performative and incremental. Merely having constituted such a society reflected well on elite claims to the country's place among modern Western counterparts. That its voice went unheard mattered less than that it existed at all, even if as something of a symbol. Perhaps less cynically, the society also permitted incremental and gradual changes to animal treatment that did improve in the long run. This "war of position" allowed for the potential shifts of opinion and culture in a space where the society could voice alternative perspectives.[107] Equally likely, of course, many would-be reformers found themselves frustrated and discouraged by the small gains that they could enact.

Society rhetoric occasionally appeared in bullfighting periodicals. "A los impugnadores de las corridas de Toros," responded to these moral reformers. Not only "the ladies of the Mexican society" (SPCMA) but also the international Society for the Protection of Animals had written a complaint about the fights. The letter, according to the *Ratas* editors, contained a list of barbarities that would even leave (nefarious promoter) Ramón López open-mouthed. Rather than respond directly, they simply cited a Spanish article ("Avenzado") that discussed issues of animals and beauty that the activists should read. They did decry a Mr. Berjoin, an active member of the society and known *zoófilo* (animal lover) who they said was leading a deplorable French invasion into the corrida de toros. As a result, Berjoin intended to pose an "affront to human beings provided with sensibility and an immortal soul" who, at the same time, "had no qualms with animal suffering and death." The nationalist editors met his diatribes with "crazed laughter" and dismissed him as French and, perhaps worse, as an artist.[108] They also found a witness who claimed Berjoin had given a standing ovation to a bullfighter, therefore pointing out hypocrisy between his actions and philosophy. The larger fight, according to the press, rising between *taurófilos* and *taurófobos*, set intelligence against dullness, art against vulgarity, and virility against aestheticism. They defensively concluded that the corrida demonstrated the greatest art in the world and "not a nauseating pantomime that turns the stomach and makes everyone, from farmers to the general public, vile."[109]

Clearly, the letter had hit a nerve. Editors penned a follow-up article the next week calling the SPMCA the "Society de marras" (the deficient) and rejecting the idea that toros and gallos could be compared at all. The society's rejection of all forms of cruelty toward rational creatures would eventually lead to absurdities. The editors called the activists idiots who would do better cleaning up problems back in their own countries since they did not understand the beauty and grandiosity of the corrida. Comparing sports like boxing or pelea de gallos only created "more idiocy and a thousand stupidities." They also argued that the fighting bull gets to end its life with nobility and meaning but did agree that the bulls should be well treated and healthy—at least until they got to the ring.[110] In following weeks editors printed a copy of the society's letter to the press, and they carefully left in (or added) a great number of errors and typos. The editors again dismissed criticisms since the corrida always became the target for "progressives of delicate feelings." They rejected entirely any notion of creating an office of Ayudador (protection) to monitor the sport or impose an outside philosophy by the so-called "paladins of humanity."[111] The conflict given voice in these letters and rebuttals represented a political ecological clash, and one that crossed nationalities.

Foreign writers also called out the inability of the SPCMA to oppose the bullfights. One spoke of how the humane society published in the *Mexican Herald* and boasted only a half dozen members, mostly sympathetic to burros. He asked, how can Mexicans hope to treat animals kindly with crowds flocking to the bullrings?[112] Another blamed the SPCMA's lack of success on the inherent cruelty of "half-breeds" and "Indians." He argued, "What chance of existence could such an institution have in a country where bullfighting is sanctioned by law and society?" He went on: "The native seems to be cruel from birth," Mexican children amuse themselves by torturing animals, and even the adults (and the thieves) had a propensity to torment their victims. In such a society, he claimed, the SPCA's hair would stand on end.[113]

The international roots of the society also had a chilling effect in Mexico. The elite generally seemed foreign themselves as they consumed French cuisine and fashion, for example. But French and foreign ideals played against, rather than with, the efforts to ban the bull. France's last big bullfight came in 1889, by 1890 revolutionaries formed bans and a League of Protection for animals.[114] This may have been spurred by bullfighting that appeared at the Paris Exposition in 1889, and the last Spanish toreros left France in 1894.[115] For the French, the question of animal rights had been connected to popular politics and rights discourses. Yet in contrast, the pressures to keep the Mexican bullfight came from all levels of society, none of whom cared to be French, and the only rights they saw trammeled were their own. By association, perhaps those calling for bans were themselves too French, or as many said, *afrancesado*? Emperor Maximilian's court had left some influences. He had mandated certain rules intended for animal welfare, for instance, mandating water dishes for public storefronts for dogs by 1863 (partially for rabies detection). Even these were not seemingly installed until 1904.[116] Water bowls and fountains set up in public spaces also seemed to suggest animals' labor rights (but with limits).[117] Despite the desperate war against the French Intervention some decades earlier, a conflict that had made President Díaz a hero, some critics suggested that perhaps the Porfirian elite had gone French too.

Using this xenophobic claim, nationalists had further ammunition to keep bullfighting as a social and cultural practice. The enormous profits did not hurt either. Mexican government attempts to sell the nation and create a new image for themselves, some argued, had failed because of foreign opinions about things like bullfights. Better treatment of animals, the absences of animals in streets, and the disappearance of blood sports could only help the image sold to investors. Yet it seemed that this argument did not persuade lawmakers, and the government failed to bring in restrictions.

Other ban attempts took different approaches. For instance, as part of a broader urban shift some sided with the "positivists" (the científico or scientist faction within the government), who sought to reform recreations. This would draw common folk out of bars and cantinas and allow a "better and more clear delineation between nature and man."[118] They also suggested that young fans should be otherwise diverted. Opponents to the fights stressed that even attending corridas took youngsters away from classrooms and workshops, and so should be avoided in the name of a civilized people.[119] Some reformers sought "good leisure" in place of blood sports.[120] As always, the bullring had an answer for them.

The fight promoters in 1894 for their part pointed out that going to corridas actually reduced crime in the streets considerably and should be considered a positive. They added that since they limited or restricted completely the sale of alcohol during the events, the fights also encouraged moderation.[121] Promoters also had to overcome public worries over workers and students skipping their duties due to "their immoderate passion for bullfighting." This they countered citing support from secular científicos like José Yves Limantour, who argued that everyone agreed that society should "have a day dedicated to rest."[122] Perhaps they deserved even more than one day. A group of owners, including Lorenzo R. Ferrar, Enrique Martínez, and A. Cerdan and Company, urged that more corrida days be permitted to compensate for rain delays at the least. They argued that "we believe it is already in the public's consciousness" to rest and re-create on their days off. They added that there already were theaters, circuses, and parks to divert them and yet workers seemed to get along just fine and without disrespecting their work. Therefore, the corrida should be allowed on all Sundays, fiestas, and non-workdays.[123] Moving somewhat slowly, the City finally approved in 1894 (seven years later) the holding of fights on non-festival days.[124]

Boxing fans also opposed the special status of the bullfights.[125] In August 1910, the Club Atlético Internacional in Mexico City demanded that the municipal government permit boxing as a sport. In a petition with 300 signatures, they pointed out that since 1907 there had been a Japanese school of jujitsu, and various martial arts including kenjitsu, judo, and esgrima trained in city. The other sports they permitted, like billiards, racing, target shooting, and even, bullfighting, made no more sense to them. Boxing, they claimed, was not "brutality," but a means to make more robust individuals and get rid of effeminate men and "raquiticos" (the spineless). Boxing created the ideal race, and also propagated anti-smoking, anti-alcohol, and family-oriented values. They particularly used the corrida as a foil to argue for their sport. "The public that attends sporting events is not at the same low level intellectually and socially [as those] that drunkenly attend the corrida de toros" that "Sunday to Sunday create scandals." They said that the bullfight caused so many incidents that the practice "negatively regenerated the race." They continued, saying that bullfighting "being our national custom—a regrettable backwardness and it is a pity we do not hide it—yet we do not abolish the fights FOREVER despite them openly clashing with civilization and culture." They asserted that Mexicans cannot deny "the harms caused in taking the lives of men and animals in the sand inked with blood." The government did not apparently read the document or respond until one year later in July 1911, perhaps due to the ongoing Revolution.[126] In similar fashion, opponents to the bullfight in Spain also pointed to boxing, horse racing, and car racing as dangerous but morally superior activities.[127] Defenders of the bullfight responded with traditional claims and customary rights.

Proponents of the sport used a common vocabulary in their claims that bullfights represented a social good worth keeping, whether one agreed there was cruelty or not. Promoters also gave special fights for charity, for example raising relief funds in October 1891 for a flood in Spain or for children's welfare.[128] The petition for the flood relief was denied, due to the decrepit state of the wooden stands and stairs at Bucareli. The children's assistance did however take place in years later. Luz Cosío de López and others asked in April 1895 to hold a corrida to benefit the Asilo Colón, without tax, to help the "unhappy class" of a respectable number of "asylum children." They ultimately raised 4,620 pesos, gave the city their 15 percent (693 pesos), and raised an additional 1,424 pesos on the side. For some reason, the asylum was only to receive 243.20 pesos, but organizers reluctantly raised this to 449.87 pesos.[129] Regular benefits could be held, and empresarios who did not, received negative press. For just two examples, *El Imparcial* announced one for Guanajuato,[130] while another article wrote of a benefit that responded to a flood in Sinaloa, covered with amazingly over the top graphics and praise.[131]

In terms of the social good, some also argued abstractly for the bullfight as creating better citizens. Much earlier, in support of building the 1866 hippodrome during the empire, proponents argued that "arts and sports have the capacity to introduce into social relations notions esteemed and noble" as "instituted by most civilized people."[132] Proponents insisted on the artistic merits and tragic narrative that created something far more intense and important than prolonging a bull's life a few years. They spoke to the ritual and historical value of the corrida and how it spoke to essential human nature and pride in the traditions of the past. They claimed that national pride insisted on holding corridas. Some pointed out that bulls lived comfortably and usually longer while awaiting their fight than they would if sent to pasture. They claimed that the bull's life had true meaning as a fighter, and that its death likewise could now truly matter. They claimed that the beastly character of the matador demanded this sacred battle to save his very soul, and so the fight offered a sacrifice to an unknown god. Spiritual blessings aside, the debate continued.

Even today, the argument over animal rights is complex and perhaps selective. Opponents of bans appealed to cultural rights, property rights, and the right to work.[133] Proponents of cockfighting rightly pointed out the hypocrisy in the law where dogfighting could be banned early on, and cocks next, while the bullfights continued to be perfectly legal. One commentator pointed out the possible hypocrisy of preferring that fighting bulls not be bred in first place: it was "not enough to say that maltreatment of animals is immoral, because what is maltreatment? Should fighting bulls die in pens and disappear as species? Avoiding suffering is only one norm of ethics among many."[134] The question of bans did not go away.

Attempted wars of morality against bullfighting did not fully bring back the 1880–1886 bans. The brief 1890 ban had little purchase, and the later 1916–1920 ban under Carranza reflected anti-Porfirian politics rather than ethical concerns.[135] Despite their efforts, Mexico continued, and continues (by 2025), to have legal bullfighting. One problem for these reformers might have been the affected class attitude as many saw an out-of-touch elite attempting to rob the masses of their main entertainment for purely sentimental reasons. Mexican promoters had largely succeeded in framing their events as intended for the lower classes, as their rightful culture, and as inherently nationalist. They had significant high-level backing. When men like Tino Hidalgo petitioned the City for a change to the rules, he did so with considerable written support from Congress in 1885.[136] The president ignored his own wife and calls for abolition in newspapers by the likes of the anti-bullfighting club.[137] For bans to gain traction the opponents would need to prove that bullfighting was not Mexican, that the lower classes should not see them, and that they represented cultural vacuum.

Entrepreneurs, veterinarians, farmers, nationalists, fans, artists, and others came together in creating a cultural message to argue against bans. Building a shared understanding as to how community members related to animals, to one another, and to nature, and how this tied sport to tradition and custom, this powerful and purely moral ecological web broke the efforts to get a ban. Not incidentally, the broad consensus intersected with new levels of large capitalist industry. The fights drew wide audiences.

Whether from antipathy, curiosity for a cruel display, or to witness an industrial wonder, foreign visitors made special efforts to attend the bullfight.

Ineffable Memories of the Foreigner

One group not so culturally entangled with the Mexican moral ecology made extensive, almost required, commentary on the corrida. In survey of some twenty-five foreign travel accounts, none failed to describe their experience at a bullfight. Of course, travelers' biases meant that only the unusual, the dangerous, the awesome, and the disgusting made it to print. Their colorful tales offered ammunition to would-be reformers.

Those Mexicans who would ban the fights did so in realization that its brutality did not neatly fit with foreign modernity. The modern world was something neat, European, clean, and absent of evident cruelties. They pointed to France, the United States, and England where government had relegated blood sports out of public view, and bullfights, hard to disguise, they outlawed entirely. Foreign travel accounts without fail spoke of attending the fights in horrified tones. Yet tellingly, tourists always did go to see one. None followed with their line of reasoning on animal cruelty to even mention the "lesser" blood sports of dog- and cockfighting. Perhaps this reflected that these "sports" certainly continued to take place in their own home nations, back in the so-called modern world. Those in the Mexican elite who wanted to ban the fights mostly discounted the cultural value of the practice, and they exaggerated the damage done to the national image. This aside, the travelers' reports had a lot in common. They explained the course of the entire fights in lurid detail.

Foreigners nearly always made commentary on the bullfights, which as one put it, had been "stamped so ineffably among [his] memories."[138] They spoke of the impressive size of the ring.[139] Those arriving between the 1880s and 1910 spoke of the great building boom for Plazas.[140] Wherever they went, they found bullrings and cockpits in every Mexican city, with cheap admission, and saw a growing fandom for even the amateur bullfights.[141] Some suburban fights had, in their eyes, a somewhat different character, for example, one at Tlanepantla (famed for bullfights) where the viewer found it as "festivals of merriment, rather than festivals of murder."[142] Others, as in Huisachal, proved more the norm.[143] Most writers detailed the course of the fights for their audience.[144] They spoke of the layout of the ring, the use of military bands for musical interludes, the role of different toreros, and even the types of seating (straw-filled). Some described the colorful costumes and mentioned other entertainments like lariat duels and *colear* or bull-tail pulling.[145] An early visitor saw a somewhat different version of the fights. He reported that at the corridas, the *cachetero* used a dagger to finish the bull, and that, unlike in Spain, the horses had good leather protections, and that bullhorn tips were sometimes sawed short for safety.[146] Clearly, these measures had changed by the time later outsiders visited.

Despite their obvious fascination and impressions of the facilities, these witnesses strongly criticized the fights as barbarous and as one of the "objectionable legacies of the Spaniards."[147] The experience usually started off well enough with ceremonies and military bands and excitement, until the bulls began to kill the picadors' horses. One detailed how the bull immediately disemboweled one picador's horse, then another, and then maimed the picador. Nonchalantly, the diestro Caballero stepped up while the famous Mazzantini casually had a smoke. The traveler seemed impressed by their sangfroid, but noted that his female companion began crying in horror over the hurt horses.[148] Another writer claimed (not incorrectly) that the picadors' horses had been purchased simply to die.[149] Even the bulls seemed surprised by this violence, with one, having gored two horses, standing "amazed."[150] Another author noted that despite brutality, cruelty, and horror of it all, where six bulls and thirteen horses had died, a small boy near his seat declared it as "magnifico."[151]

The foreign perspectives nearly universally expressed deep disgust with the cruelty of the spectacle. A rare exception to all the travelers who attended a corrida, Emil Blichfeldt, called it the exhibition of a tortured animal impaling a poor old horse, in a sight both sickening and revolting, and blamed tourists for perpetuating what he called the "glee of killing."[152] A less convinced viewer hedged, saying "Cruel, you say? Well, yes! And therefore, intensely wrong! Y-y-yes; even I can make no defense."[153] A less conflicted observer asserted: "To me, who love most animals, who recognize in them in a lesser degree the emotions and many of the mental traits, and certainly a great share of the susceptibility to perish of the human race, the spectacle I have just witnessed was inexpressibly shocking."[154] Others referred to the taking of ears as a "trophy of the wicked sport," or of the low animal instincts of fans, and of the "pernicious evils" that the fights comprised.[155]

The greatest shock to outsiders seemed to rise from observing the audience itself. One remarked on the vast crowd, its wild cries, the stamping, and "that indescribable bass hum which easily deepens in a roar and strikes one with a sense of awe."[156] The same traveler who had noted the fights as cruel and wrong also called it a "gorgeous feast of bravery" and particularly seemed taken by the "excited admiration which betrays itself in the usually pensive eyes of the dark-skinned tropical beauties."[157] For most the violence and noise of the spectators came across as frightening and unpleasant. One commented on how the ring featured two companies of soldiers, with fixed bayonets ready, to contain the crowd gone "mad with bloodlust."[158] The mobs had "the savage aroused in their hearts."[159] Despite this, the plaza did not exclude the better classes or women or children. As one man noted, "Gentlemen take their wives and children and make it an enjoyable pastime, varying the everyday occurrences of life."[160] Another noted that at the event he saw Mexicans of all classes, and that despite representing "cruel disgusting spectacle," the corrida could not be banned since "the vox populi must be respected."[161] The entitled fan and the duty of the promoters to provide them the show they deserved seemed clear even to the outsiders' perspective.

Again, despite these often-vociferous criticisms, almost every traveler went to the fights, and almost all claimed to stay to the end.[162] Only the abstinent Blichfeldt avoided fights altogether, and he asserted that Americans went with an air of bravado but in truth "proved unable to sit through one killing."[163] How he knew this was unclear, and perhaps it rose from his hopes that his countrymen secretly shared his distaste for the sport.

All the writers became somewhat somber or grim as the matador made the final strike. With the bull's dragged-off exodus, they became elegiac in their tone. All commented, too, on what they believed the corrida revealed about Mexican character, usually in negative ways.

From the point of view of elite Mexicans seeking to improve their national image this witnessing had mixed blessings. Clearly, this was a practice persistently and closely linked in foreign minds to Mexico's questionable place as a civilized or modern country. The national image had become attached to not only the old institution but also to the rabid crowds and their excitement. The colonial connections to Spanish tradition, however cruel, at least had some ties to a European identity. The occasional and temporary bans of the sport highlighted an ambivalence in how Mexicans saw their own character. And yet, unwittingly, the travelers also framed a snapshot or moment in a broader way of how traditional cultures forged a relationship with the natural world in the context of a modernizing society. They reveal the disconnection between the moral ecological narrative and the ways that Mexico hoped to present itself to the outside world. Foreign sentiments, much like that of the SPCMA rhetoric, nonetheless fell mostly on deaf ears.

Conclusions

The torturous and slow death of the bull fit poorly with notions of civility and the "Christian" duties of the human animal to show care for animals. A moral ecology of the crowd permitted a cultural reframing of the obvious bloodiness to take on new, and acceptable, meanings. The sport became at once artistic expression, sacred ritual, and nostalgic tragedy. Art and memory intervened against feelings of horror or disgust. Nature became a backdrop for understanding, and cheering, the death of the animals. The crowd, and the promoters, had their way. Moral ecological expectations, capitalist marketing, and necropolitical underpinnings reinforced cultural acceptance and resilience. Technological advances in mass spectator events played into creating a grand spectacle of death and fantasy. Cultural modes that underpinned capitalism, and vice versa, thus revolved around the emergent modern sport.

Owners tapped into fans as a base for building a great industrial-entertainment complex. Their own agendas did not always align, of course, as seen in the riotous broncas when fans found the show lacking. Nevertheless, promoters rode on a wave of enthusiasm and spurred it forward as best they could. These high-profile entrepreneurs insulated themselves from anti-Spanish sentiments behind the facade of figurehead bullfighting celebrity-owners. They catered to the crowds with unusual events and walked a fine line between cost and quality as they organized corridas. Savvy owners found ways to profit, and to counter the complaints of anti-corrida newspapers, activists, and foreigners.

Protection societies applied political pressure with uneven results. They harnessed foreign outrage to back their assertions. They proclaimed the shows as self-evidently barbaric and *atrasado* (backward). They suggested that the bullfight subjected the nation to international mockery and hindered foreign investment and recognition. They argued that the fights damaged the soul of humanity. And they largely preached to a Mexican society dismissive of their cause.

Attempts to ban the sport fell flat, and the new industrial plazas thrived. The raucous shouts of the massed fans, marshaled by marketers and promoters, drowned out legislators, moral reformers, and even poor Carmen and her society friends.

CHAPTER FIVE

Dancing with Bulls

Gender and the Porfirian Bullfighter

"Again he bowed to the vast multitude and no human being ever received a more overwhelming ovation than did he. Flowers were thrown him in heaps. Sometimes women even take off their jewels and throw them and kiss the hero when they meet him in the streets."[1]

In mid-December 1909, master bullfighter Rodolfo Gaona stared at the walls of a Mexico City's Belem prison and pondered his fate for the twenty-second day. A woman from a good family, María Luisa Noecker, lay dead. Folksongs and newspapers broadcast her tragic suicide and speculated wildly about the torero's presumed responsibility. His actual crime, seemingly, lay in failure to attend a bullfighters' party. The senorita Noecker had snuck out of her uncle's home to attend the gathering in full expectation of meeting with Gaona. Her suicide followed a presumed dishonoring, with much left for readers to assume between the lines. Sexual ideals interwove with the world of the bullfight.

The case as it developed revealed much about social and gender norms, expectations for toreros, and the price of fame paid by the professional killers of bulls. His brother initially took the blame, until investigators proved medically that he could not have dishonored the girl. Her autopsy proved "scientifically" that she had not been drunk, and had had sex, but asserted that she did so consensually.[2] Gaona's guilt, many felt sure, had been proved by the fact that the girl had his portrait in her locket (a *prueba del amor*), a romantic artifact that indicated a relationship between the fifteen-year-old and the twenty-year-old bullfighter, even though he claimed to have never met her in person.[3] He denied wrongdoing despite some witnesses who testified he had indeed met the girl at either a hotel or his own home, late at night, and after more drinking. Some of his public supporters went so far as to put his thoughts in verse, with a fervent denial of guilt calling melodramatically for him to die at the horns of a bull if he were actually at fault.[4] Celebrity thrived on this drama.

The bullfighter, stereotypically the rock star bad boy of his time, officials briefly sent to a prison. Many of his fans would come to believe this event had cursed his luck, as bulls turned treacherously against him and his good fortunes failed for a time. In his own words, he had, despite "many enemies," managed to be a good man, citizen, and father, and he took pride in his artistry with solid cause.[5] Ultimately, he became a renowned torero in both Spain and Mexico. In the words of one commentator, "The greats were Ponciano Díaz, Rodolfo Gaona, and Fermín Espinosa—and of these Gaona was the most elegant and complete torero that ever existed."[6] By 1915, he had already fought more than 400 corridas, and he continued until 1920. He achieved fame as an innovator of new moves like the *gaonera* where the cape is held behind one's body, adding to the danger of the paso.[7] He died in 1975 at age eighty-seven.

The world of the matador celebrity illustrates a changing conception of fame and masculinities. This chapter argues that the diestro (the master matador) and his experience represented a narrative of gender constructions that intersected between elite and common norms of sexual behaviors. The expected and traditional behaviors in this world, shaped by cultural norms, set the death of the beast into an acceptable context. Social relations of the moral ecology permeated society. Popular and upper classes alike constructed the world of the corrida with stereotyped ideas for toreros, animals, and the spectators or bystanders. Gaona, as a premier celebrity, embodied fantasy. And when he broke with unwritten expectations, it fell to fate and the horns of a bull to bring him back in line. By analyzing his place in turn-of-the-century Mexico, a gendered world fraught with notions of animality comes into view, especially that of its heart, the diestro or matador del toros.

Celebrity matadors became embodiments of cultural conflicts, caught between the horns of the bull. The celebrity figure as a category of modern life, with its rewards and prices, reveals a whole suite of cultural aspirations. The torero sexualized capitalism, with his body as commodity, and with collateral damage merely the predictable cost for mass spectacles of agony and ecstasy. The fantasies of death extended, too, to the exoticized killer. As models of elegant, graceful hypermasculinity, the matadors embodied in this era an archetype of mixed virtues and the dawn for troubled celebrity.

Necropolitics ties in as well to the world of the famous matador, if less directly. Society sets up relationships that determine the acceptability of life and death within the boundaries of practice. The diestro, or matador, embodied the ritual nature of the bullfight and adds celebrity trappings to the ritualist role.[8] Around the bullfighter, society works out fantasies, imaginations, and cultures of death and its meaning. Social expectations for this role interfaced with law, customs, families, and gendered ideals.

This chapter intrudes into the world of the matador, using Gaona's life and troubles as a case study into the nature of celebrity in this odd corner of the human-animal relationship. His life and trials illustrated connections between gender and modern sport, and how cultural work shaped social and political experiences. After his story, this chapter section turns to matadors more broadly, and to their construction as idols in song and image. As agents to a very specific cultural sphere, they represent the keen point of connection between modern liberal society and the killing urge.

Gaona, The Califa de León

The Gaona story demonstrates the cross-contamination between class, gender, and animality in the context of the bullfight as mass spectacle. Kathryn Sloan has already examined the death of Maria Luisa Noecker in *Runaway Daughters* and *Death in the City*, but my attention is drawn here more toward the context of the bullfighter and his own masculine identity that adds further insights to the tragedy. The meanings of the animal in a modernized mass arena complicated elements of gender relations that went beyond the show itself and into daily experiences.[9]

Rodolfo Gaona, twenty at the time of the incident, represented the epitome of the Mexican bullfighter. Noted for his looks and elegance, he also represented the small-town boy made good, an indigenous heritage (at least in looks), and of course, his raw machismo. The bullfighter torero as a public figure nonetheless holds a particular ambiguity in the eyes of the masses. The macho figure carried the weight of childhood memories and constructed ideals, including profound nostalgia, where the bullfighters had always used to be manly (not like "today").[10] As Sloan points out, he and his entourage (the *gente de coleta*), had a repute as immoral, sexual, and vile. They drank heavily together.[11] They encouraged fans' adulation and prided

FIGURE 5.1. José Guadalupe Posada, "Cogida de Rodolfo Gaona en la plaza de toros de Puebla, el 13 de Diciembre de 1908," hoja suelta, pub. por A. Vanegas Arroyo. 1908.

themselves on sexual escapades, often without much discretion.[12] They reflected the complex inversion of the ring. It set man versus the beast—yet . . . the bullfighter himself embodied the wild side, barely controlled passions, more animal than not. Nonetheless, he came from normal society.

The so-called "pontífice de la torería" (pontiff of bullfighting), also called El Califa (the Caliph), Gaona rose from humble stock. He was born January 22, 1888, in León de las Aldamas. As an apprentice shoemaker, he frequented the corridas and saw the great Pimiento and Reverte Mexicano early on, and in 1897 witnessed the goring of Santiago Gil. The bad boy Braulio Díaz became his mentor early on (this Díaz later famously shot a rival named Lino Zamora in the back). Gaona later began his serious training with the Cuban exile Saturnino Frutos, called "Ojitos" (Squinty), which lasted one and a half years.[13] During this time, he went by the nickname "el Relampaguito" (Tiny Lightning).[14] In his successful career as torero and banderillo, he quickly rose to the top of his dangerous trade.[15] After a debut fight at Covadonga, he accompanied Frutos on a brief Spanish tour in 1908.[16] According to his memoirs, he learned from Ojitos that "toreros could be gente decente and well-looked-at in society." More, he took from him that a good torero had to learn to play guitar, sing flamenco, dance, and entertain.[17] His eventual fights would take him from village to international circles.

The matador also sometimes called "el doctor sapientísimo" (wisest doctor), toured extensively. He played at Madrid and six other Spanish plazas with sixteen toros, at Mexico in 1908 he faced fourteen corridas and thirty-nine bulls, in 1909 five more fights in Mexico, and then moved back to Spain for a time. He rarely rested from working unless recovering from terrible injuries, which happened, to be honest, fairly often. Even his bulls became temporarily famous, with their names published in programs and corrido broadsheets.[18] Leaving Spain came with complications.

Flush with victories on the big tour circuit, he returned to Mexico to find a mixed reaction. In his fight in 1909 at El Toreo, he first encountered what he called "anti-gaonismo" from *niños bienes* (snooty rich youth) and foreigners who denigrated him as *indio bolero* (Indian bootblack). His response years later was to clarify, "No, I was a *zapatero* (shoemaker)."[19] It was at this point that, in his words, he first "mixed with politics," though it seems notable that he made relatively little mention in his autobiography of all the presidents he met.[20]

The Political Figure

In higher circles cynics found use for the celebrity matador to suit political ends. Press opportunities saw toreros thrown in with presidents and politicians at highly staged luncheons or public events. They generally avoided overtly political topics, but took photos, exchanged small talk and niceties, and visited. The matador presented himself as polished, civilized, and grateful. The politician basked in the reflected glory of the fighter. Being near to the presumed hypermasculine reinforced an image of virility and courage that the politicians wished to own—if only by association. Canny toreros played along.

Gaona provided good examples for this political phenomenon, in his numerous meetings with Mexican presidents over the years. He did not discriminate much between them, and only occasionally waxed political in his comments. He impressively met four different presidents in this era.

In 1908 he met briefly with President Porfirio Díaz, who was a fan of corridas. Díaz (purportedly worth 800,000 pesos) advised him, and presciently it turned out, to be careful with his money and "not to let himself be exploited by those clever opportunists who swarm" the bullfights. The president attended Gaona's fight of November 1 in Plaza de México. There, Gaona offered in homage "the death of his first bull to the president." For this he received a wallet with Díaz's initials and a 1000-peso bonus.[21] Unfortunately, the bull named "el Gorgojito" had other ideas.

The luck of "el indio diestro de León" did not hold.[22] Seriously injured by a bull on December 13, 1908, in Puebla, he was rushed by car to Mexico City and given into the care of Dr. Aureliano Urrutia Sandoval (the foremost physician in the nation and one of the heads of the Department of Salubridad). The surgery made the physician's reputation, and he went on to befriend Victoriano Huerta and briefly reached the heights of government power during the early Revolution.[23] Despite a coma and serious surgery, Gaona went back to action in time for Mexico's great Centenario celebrations in 1910. At a February 20, 1910, afternoon show at El Toreo, with Díaz and his vice president Ramón Corral in attendance, he fought again. Drumming home the patriotic politics of the corrida as ritual, the matadors were played in with national anthem. Gaona's luck had not changed much, this time also proved unlucky, and the bull tossed (*embistió*) him on its horns. But by the next year, he healed and went back on tour in Spain.[24] One observer credited his recovery to his indigenous background and "the spiritual reserves of the virtues of his race."[25]

More politics followed. Two years passed, and Gaona fought on January 28, 1912, at El Toreo once more. President Francisco Madero attended and received personal updates on Gaona's condition as, once again, he had been injured. For his part, Gaona treated Madero as a fan and warmly hugged him.[26] Notably, he made no mention of this in his own autobiography. It would not be long before the matador would embrace Madero's assassin. Only a year later, on November 23, 1913, President Victoriano Huerta attended the El Toreo. Once again, organizers played the national anthem, and announced him to much "hat waving, chaos, and cheering from the people." After the fight, Gaona received gifts and rode with the president in his car to sip champagne at a downtown restaurant. The torero toasted Huerta as having "pacified the country and dealt with the authors of its disorder" thanks to the support of the people.[27] The press also attended, and *El Independiente* newspaper claimed that Gaona had given a speech noble, patriotic, and in favor of peace. It seemed that the bullfighter had acquired a taste for the political limelight.

Rather than passively accepting the courtship of politicians, on January 11, 1914, he hosted a banquet at Huipilco for invitees including Huerta, Dr. Urrutia, the Secretary of War, and other notables. There he toasted Huerta as an "exceptional man who rose at the country's most difficult time . . . and with an iron fist averted catastrophe." Gaona also suggested that Pancho Villa "was like a fighting bull due for punishment.'" Huerta replied that he would solve his problems with Villa exactly "as the remarkable torero said." They then listened to more national anthems.[28] Perhaps Gaona had cultivated the wrong politician.

A few weeks later, Huerta was gone, and soon after President Venustiano Carranza took power and promptly banned the bullfight. Someone informed Gaona that he would be executed as a traitor if he returned to Mexico (according to the Law of 1862), but he seems never to have been added to the blacklist. Showing rare discretion, he nonetheless prolonged his tour in Spain from 1915 to 1917 doing thirty-five corridas, with a brief tour in Lima, Peru for which he earned a cool 6,000 pesos, tax-free, and with all covered expenses.[29] During this time, at twenty-nine years old, he met a nineteen-year-old blond actress, Carmen Ruiz de Maragas, and they wed in 1917.[30] Three whirlwind months later, they divorced, and she then pursued King Alfonso XIII of Spain (who was ten years married by this time). She became the royal's lover for sixteen years and bore him two children.[31] Her ex-husband struggled on.

Gaona fell on difficult times. Although he fought sixty more corridas, he had serious money issues and lost some 40,000 pesos as well as having his house destroyed.[32] Back in Mexico, in late 1919 the Carranza bullfighting ban lifted. The would-be President Adolfo de la Huerta sent Gaona a guarantee of safety, and with his new wife, Enriqueta Gómez, and his son returned home. On November 21, 1920, El Toreo reopened, and the matador returned to work.

On September 20, 1921, the nation celebrated the centenary of the consummation of independence with a bullfight, of course. President Alvaro Obregón and his cabinet attended a show with 25,000 fans, again featuring the national anthem and standing ovations. This fight, more expensive than those before the Revolution, charged five pesos in the shade and two in the sun. As part of the ritual, matadors offered more toasts, more musical *marchas* played bullfighters in, and then to cap it off, the anthem played a second time. Meeting the chief executive one final time, on November 16, 1924, President Obregón and future President Calles unofficially attended one of Gaona's corridas. A year later, December 14, 1925, Gaona finally retired from the sport and from politics.[33]

Beyond ordinary political narratives the torero's peculiar status as both modern and traditional premised a unity or healing during the throes of Revolutionary upheaval. Posing with presidents like Huerta, for instance, suggested some return to normality for a city rocked by the death of Madero and the ten tragic days (Decena Tragíca). The sadness of that time turned instead to considerations about the upcoming season and making up for lost corridas. Formal politics had no place in the ring. Yet in the old sense of bread and circuses, the bullfight most definitely made the matador a potent political icon.

Celebrity politics put the matador on his best behavior, but a wilder side seemingly waited just beneath the veneer and had the potential to spread to fans. For Gaona, his greatest notoriety rose from the suicide of Maria Luisa Noecker.

The Gaona Trial

In contrast to the simpler narratives put forward in the public press and folk songs, the trial record reveals some important nuances. Noecker, the daughter of a German businessman, had shot herself twice in her bedroom on December 3, 1909. Officials promptly arrested Gaona, but also his brother Enrique and an associate named Cirilo Pérez (noted as a seller of eggs and small items, and brother to the diestro nicknamed the Refulgente, or Brilliant). On the evening of December 2, the *huevero* Pérez had escorted the teenaged girl to a party.[34] Public opinion on the incident split.

A brawl between supporters, bullfight abolitionists, and different presses ensued. As Gaona later wrote, it was the press that made a torero's success, not the bulls. In this case, papers debated his guilt.[35] The *Imparcial* fought *El Toreo*, in some of the bitterest infighting among the various presses, and others like *El Heraldo* and *El País* added their voices against papers like *Ratas*.[36] Anti-torero press like *El Sol* frequently reported "Indio bolero" calls in the bullring. Some papers like *El País* called for Gaona to be lynched, and most papers ignored all the evidence.[37] Among those finding the bullfighter guilty on mere suspicion, *Abogado Cristiano* put the overall blame on a seedy industry making idols of bad men.[38] Eventually, after a lengthy published defense of the matador in *Ratas* that called out the *Heraldo* and *Imparcial*, Gaona claimed that the public began to leave him alone, with papers having used him simply as a scapegoat (*chiva expiatorio*) to sell print.[39] Newspapers generally proved more interested in Rodolfo than in the young naive girl, but officials looked deeply into everything.

An incredibly detailed investigation into the case proved inconclusive.[40] An inquest (355-pages long) examined the girl's home and her body.[41] Doctors found a newly torn hymen and two gunshots, one to her stomach and one to her head. They insisted without further evidence that she had been penetrated by a penis, even though they found no semen. Investigators searched Rodolfo's room but found no blood. They searched Frutos's room, too, but determined that the blood found there belonged to his wife. Gaona's brother Enrique freely admitted having sex with Luisa, but doctors argued that he physically could not, as he suffered from erectile issues due to the chancres of early-stage syphilis. Enrique insisted this was a mistake, perhaps

FIGURE 5.2. Mexico City, Inspección de policía, E1718, Juzgado Quinto de Instrucción, Dec. 5, 1909. Rodolfo Gaona, photo.

to save his brother, or perhaps for his own sexual reputation. The inquest ruled the same about Cirilio Pérez's inability for the same reasons, syphilis. For his own part, Gaona insisted on his innocence, claiming that he never met her at all, that some acquaintance had given her an image to put in her locket, and that he was at Teatro Colón that night with friends.[42] Nonetheless, doctors determined that he possessed a perfectly functional penis and set suspicion toward him.

When the investigators failed to find physical evidence, they made do with innuendo. They painted a picture of an innocent girl obsessed with a celebrity, with multiple prints of his playbills in her room, and with his image in a locket. This they suggested was a *prueba del amor* (token of love) that meant a legally binding promise had been made to its recipient. Even more damning, many emphasized the ill repute of the "mafia de coleta" and assumed the worst of any torero.[43]

Nonetheless, the courts did not agree. Rodolfo Gaona paid a 5,000-pesos bond and they released him on December 30 after twenty-two days in Belén prison. He fought that next Sunday at the plaza.[44] By March, the court dropped all charges against him and against Noecker's maid, who prosecutors had not proved negligent in her duties of care. The judge further found that since the father could not prove he was truly the girl's father, he had no right to press any charges of *estupro* (deflowering). The court found that prosecutors could not prove Gaona attended the party, and since Pérez had taken her from her home, that Gaona could not be charged with *rapto* (kidnapping, basically). Further, since the girl apparently went to a hotel willingly, this could not be considered rapto in any case. Others echoed the call for his innocence.

The popular bullfighting press expected nothing less of a hot-blooded torero and proclaimed his innocence in the matter. As Schubert writes of Spanish toreros, the fans wanted a "bullfighter in the streets," with the implied sexualized seediness.[45] Neither account gave credence to Maria Luisa as a real agent capable of choices and honest mistakes. Neither press conceded her to be a woman with the capacity for desire, even that of an overheated teenaged sort. The only aspect of her own embodied and animal wishes they might ascribe to her was a beast-like confusion, and any sexual agency they attributed to the guiles of Satan. Many agreed that her innocence had been destroyed by the uncivilized Gaona. He proved himself a matador to more than just non-human animals. Songs spoke to the people who did not all read the news.

Several corridos related to the Noecker affair quickly bloomed during the twenty-two days while Gaona languished in jail. In contrast to sections of detailed information published on the back of the broadsheets, the lyrics took certain liberties. "Reflexiones dolorosos de Rodolfo Gaona en su bartolina de Belem" presented how the diestro grappled with his horrible crime, how he hoped to be an example for others to do better, and how he now had to mourn his loss of reputation. "I appear to be a delinquent, as the author of her dishonor, and here I will be suffering—having lost my honor also," said the song, on behalf of a man who continuously claimed to have never met the girl. Said lady also earned a corrido to speak for her perspective.[46] She told her story in "Sufrimientos, reflexiones y consejos de la suicida Maria Luisa Noecker: en la otra vida."[47] According to this song, the girl, now in hell, offered to parents her words of wisdom in controlling their children and preventing them from following in her passionate but foolish path.

Triumphant corridos greeted Gaona upon his return to the ring only a week after his brief imprisonment. The songs featured none of the "anti-gaonismos" that the diestro spoke of in his memoirs, nor any of the slurs that major papers eagerly reported to have been shouted from the fans. Instead, the corridos spoke of the "delirious public" and celebrated his race as "el Indio Mexicano," and his lavish style by labeling him the "king of the elegancies."[48] Throughout his career, songs occasionally did make further mention of his race, for example, with the backhanded compliment that he fought "good, for his blood."[49] One final voice also spoke on Gaona, as "Corrido de la Muerte" dismissed his courage and skill as ultimately pointless. Death asks, "What good is it for Gaona—to be brave with the bulls—and the same for Count Koma—to show off his strength in the forums?"[50] The torero's world passed beyond the mundane.

Religion could not be separated from the world of the corrida. The Gaona case harked back to this too, the young lady was hell-bound as *suicida*, and if it were Gaona's fault: "If I don't tell the truth, let a bull kill me!"[51] His animal counterparts would act as arbiter of God's will, standing in as justice to judge the torero's honor, his manhood. Given Rodolfo's longevity (he made it to 1975) and his likely guilt, we can rule out direct divine intervention on this.

In a world where bulls could be "muy hombre" (very manly) and honorable, while men acted as crazed beasts—what of poor María Luisa? In the absence of her

FIGURE 5.3. José Guadalupe Posada, "Sufrimientos, Reflexiones y Consejos de la Suicida María Luisa Noeker: en la Otra Vida," hoja suelta, pub. por A. Vanegas Arroyo. 1908.

father, away in his native Germany on rail business, and her mother, ill in hospital, she lived with her uncle and had developed her affection for the torero, according to the sources, without ever meeting Gaona.[52] With her death the press stripped her of any agency in life, denying her choices validity. Nothing she had done came of her own will—they reframed her as a victim-object in a tragic morality tale.[53] Where could this golden-haired girl have learned to make the right choices in the absence of the "angel del hogar" mother figure, or attentive father-patriarch?[54] Everyone knew the sad disintegration of Santa in the contemporary novel, a girl much the same: innocent, seduced, and destroyed by the modern city and its hypersexual predators.

The popular novel *Santa*, later made into plays and movies, posed an image of the countryside as perfectly idyllic and natural.[55] The city as counterpoint represented degradations and the inevitable fall from grace for rural innocents who urbanized.[56] The animal nature of man was made into its worst in the city, and a central figure in the novel was a matador, who ironically, fails to save the girl from her own depravity. This heroic torero, though referred to as an *espadachín* or swordsman in a sexual innuendo, attempted to rescue the girl. He could not save Santa from her fate, as she betrayed him and ultimately lost all that was good and innocent inside her. The figure of the matador resonated with readers of the novel and with eventual filmgoers. The broader trope of the fall from paradise became Mexicanized with the details from society and the inclusion of a good old-fashioned corrida reference point. Hardly a stretch of imagination, the figure of the matador echoed the fears and fantasies within the common and popular cultures.

The novel's juxtaposition of pristine nature with the degrading urban landscape prescribed ideal gender behavior. Humans should overcome and live in nature while resisting the corruptions of the questionably civilized. It was for Santa quite the same as for Gaona, each time succeeding in the ring yet failing to control himself in nighttime debauchery. For her, her human nature proved both failure and ideal at the same time, both remedy and poison (or what some call *pharmakon*). The elite press proposed her tale as others' failure, too: of the parents, of the maid, of the caretakers, even perhaps of the huevero Cirilio Pérez, but especially the failure of Gaona from whom they hypocritically expected sexual self-control. Yet what could one expect of the debauched class of men that became matadors?

Diestros and Matadors

Sensationalist cases aside, other larger than life figures defined the corrida in Mexico and brought international fame and innovative adaptations to the sport. Their work created a "Mexican" style. The "father of modern bullfighting," Bernardo Gaviño (born 1812) first signed on in 1835 and fought on well into his seventies—a bull gored him in his forty-second year of fighting at age seventy-four (on February 11, 1886).[57] Among his contributions was the maneuver called the Mexican Mosquito. Arcadio Ramírez, the Reverte Mexicano, thrilled audiences who seem largely to have glamorized his mestizo appearance. Spanish transplants also thrived. The tour of famed diestro Luis Mazzantini y Esguia drew huge audiences and fervent press.[58] The infamous Ponciano Díaz changed the public face of the sport with his renowned moustache, which earned him the nickname Bigotes.[59] Perhaps something was needed to compensate for otherwise feminine looking apparel, but a beard would have been too wild and going too far (and difficult for some with indigenous lineage). Certainly, some without moustaches were denigrated by crowds as girlish or priestly.[60] Bullfighters also had great vanity for their *coleta* (ponytail) for which their cliques took the name *gente de coleta*, or less generously, *mafia de coleta*.[61] When they retired, the matador ceremonially cut this off. Scars and wounds would also add to manly repute, and even identified some, like Diego Prieto Barrera Cuatrodedos and his maimed hand. A sense of Mexican ownership grew with the burgeoning industry.

Over time, the sport became a nationalist point of pride. Some celebrities brought an exotic touch from abroad, like the Spanish Antonio Montes, who fought from 1876 to 1907, with the last four years in Mexico. But fans also claimed that this proved Mexico's premier place in international bullfighting and used apparent Spanish approval to argue for the sport as appropriately Mexican. Homegrown Mexican toreros increasingly became stars. One later fighter, Juan Silveti, became known as "the pride of the race" and a "purely Mexican being," with nicknames including El Meco, el Tigre de Guanajuato, and bizarrely, El hombre de la regadera (The Man of the Watering Can).[62] His other nickname, Juan sin Miedo (Juan without Fear), became the slogan on the official stamp for the Department of Health inspectors in the 1910s.[63] This latter presents an accidental conjunction between necropolitical public health and the practice of the matador. Celebrity did not guarantee public acceptance.

Among the diestros, few were seen as heroes on their own hearth, and few heroes survived life between the horns. According to some press, there existed no such thing as a good bullfighter. Even the generally pro-corrida papers like *Ratas* occasionally picked on the entire profession, claiming that bullfighters were entirely ruffians, dirty, and cowards in one diatribe.[64] Many bullfighters became known as *galleros* (cockfight fans) suggesting an unsavory and gambling nature.[65] Anti-bullfighting mainstream press like *Imparcial* or *El País* would likely have agreed.

Much more commonly, the specialty press saved its venom for specific toreros who meddled in business, or who acted as mamarrachas (buffoons) in other critical ways. *El Toreo* had little love for the business-savvy Ponciano Díaz, and none for the diestro el Boto, Antonio Escobar. He, they claimed, fought well with pasos and veronicas but then always chose "to be tricky and bore bull and public."[66] They called him out as terrible and full of self-love.[67] Similarly, the editors of *Ratas* hated Machaco Machaquito, Rafael González, who proved the decadence of the art, and the *rebajimiento de afición* (lowering of the fans). They mourned that he was a product of his times, shameless, and effeminate—and also—short. His style offended, too, as it proved typical of the *niños modernistas* of whom they did not approve.[68] Perhaps worst of all, he earned 300 pesos a fight, which they considered overpaid up "to the clouds."[69]

For the most part, the specialty papers treated diestros more gently, and the eulogies when they died (especially in the ring) ascended to heroic proportions. *El Toreo* mourned the death of Juan Romero Salieri gored in Puebla in 1896 at age twenty-five. They wrote of his grand funeral and spoke no ill of the bull. Rather, they set the blame on Death or fate itself, claiming that "Death had hovered vengefully on his laurels of triumph."[70] In October 1903, when Spanish bullfighter Reverte died, they proclaimed him the last of his kind. His tragic death during liver surgery had deprived them of a man who was "all heart" unlike all the mamarrachas with their "chanchullos y chapucerías" (shenanigans and sloppiness) that plagued the profession.[71]

Some of the greats of Mexico also returned this favor, as Gaona and others did tours in the Peninsula, bringing indigenous Mexico to Spanish corridas on the big circuit. This made logistic sense since the Spanish corrida season differed from that in Mexico. In all cases though, it does seem that the matadors brought a certain edgy character to their performed celebrity. As one of their defenders tepidly noted, toreros embodied not "the most despicable of society" but perhaps nearly so.[72]

FIGURE 5.4. José Guadalupe Posada, "Cogida y muerte de Timoteo Rodríguez," hoja suelta, pub. por A. Vanegas Arroyo. 1895.

Matador Reputations

The diestros, matadors, and cuadrilla members alike had an often-troubled image to overcome as public figures. Even aficionados made frequent comment about wild drinking stories.[73] A former Spanish matador made tongue-in-cheek commentary about himself that reveals public impressions. According to Dalmacio Higueras, "el Enaguitos," he agreed that diestros should bathe monthly, but complained how there was "now no end to hygiene!" He went on to disparage manicures, pedicures, and clean clothes as crazy lengths to expect of them.[74] He played to the stereotypes, admitting to his own superstitious nature, using crude innuendos like equating a fifteen-centimeter wound from a bull horn to a sexual penetration, and suggesting that matadors would happily sacrifice their picadors for safety. His preferred that a bull "should be noble, small, with horns like snails, that as soon as they touch [the fighter] they hide, very brave with the picadores but considerate and kind with the matador."[75] He nonetheless would not give up the lifestyle of a *tió de coleta*, admitting that the applause made him drunk as if in love.[76] Other matadors capitalized on their reputations to build a brand. According to "Corrido a la despedida de Rodolfo Gaona," marketers used his image for selling cigarettes, perhaps taking advantage of a reputation for luxurious living and style: "There are already cigars whose brand—his proud name shows. . . ."[77] Personal aesthetics, branding, and innuendo created one facet, but could interfere with the perfect show that the fans felt completely entitled to see.

One thing much of the specialty press would agree on: the toreros of the day could not live up to the great figures of the past. The idea that the sport fell into in a decline featured in works on both sides of the Atlantic. Joaquín Vargas Coto wrote a scathing review of the art and its many contemporary signs of decay.[78] For him the worst problem was the diestro who tried for perfect science but achieved sterile lifeless performances. This, he claimed, happened because toreros all wanted to be stars, and they used to fight for glory and reputation, but "today the torero is an industry like any other." They sought only to grow capital and have a life of luxury and comfort and making a parody of the art.[79] As a result, the cuadrillos had been eclipsed, the best picadors posed atop the most agile horses (thus taking less risk), and the matador had become a "figurina parisién" (Parisian figurine) concerned primarily with fashion.[80] Bad veterinarians made things worse, and bad bull breeders who get greedy, but the desire of empresarios and toreros and their agents (*apoderados*) to become millionaires had the worst effect. Not finished he went on to critique the press, the *monos sabios* (staff, president, and veterinarians), and even the public itself for the decline of his beloved fiesta.

Nostalgic reframing and fluid historical memories aside, the art of the toreros did follow certain core criteria that spectators expected. A proper number of picadors and banderillos, with appropriate equipment and horses, had to plant their lances bravely and to good effect. The correct level of risk could be judged by the number of injured, maimed, and killed horses. The bull, large and healthy, needed to be fierce but not too unconventional in its movements and tactics, and should be well-bloodied but still quite dangerous before the matador came into play. The crowd expected the matador to have a certain style, elegance, and arrogance, as he strutted into the ring with total apparent calm. His maneuvers should always bring him perilously close to horns and trampling but also reveal his complete control and management of the bull in every moment. He should use a variety of pasos, all graceful, and in keeping with classical styles. Daring innovations, like fighting while sitting in a chair, needed to be balanced with more conventional and accepted techniques. The bull, fully in his control, should almost appear to be acting in concert with its executioner, as if in a dance between cooperating partners. The final strike should be sudden, clean, precise, and occur only at the perfect moment. The higher the apparent risk of the fight and the colder the blood of the matador, the better the performance. Beyond this, the all-time greats of the sport built a sort of contextual narrative in each event where the death of the bull came as the climax, almost tragic, of a storied struggle. By the 1920s the sport in Mexico began to value the domination of the bull over specific details of the kill.[81] Adapting to the many elements of the fight that remained outside of human control with perfect grace made it artistry.

Travel accounts readily identified the diestros' celebrity status and offered observations on the fighters. Some remarked, perhaps surprised, on the "mixed race" of the toreros.[82] They noted the high level approval of the sport, suggested in the role of José Yves Limantour, who was both the national Secretary of State and president of the "Bullfighting Club."[83] Matadors apparently received ovations as if they were a famous actor.[84] Women threw them jewels and kissed them on the streets.[85] The diestros even turned the heads of young gringas and sold souvenirs to the masses.[86]

And one traveler even claimed that Mexicans see the toreador as a "demi-god."[87] If so, he represented a deity with a dark aspect.

It was the wild side, the natural, that he enacted outside the arena, yet inside had to overcome this if he would live. Overcoming his base natures became all the more laudable in the contrast, and a great deal of the torero's appeal rested on the perception of him as the untamed man. The industry nonetheless had an interest in managing this image. In an era of rapid social upheaval, the sport spoke to the self-civilizing essence of discipline. Those who enacted and embodied community standards of acceptable killing gained fame. The ritual performance intersected with the rise of commercial celebrity.

Making Stars, the *Cuadrilla* shift, and Managing Matadors

In marketing their stars, promoters followed suit from Spanish industry. The corrida was not all about the matadors, originally, the attention was focused on the whole team—the cuadrilla of five men—from whom the gente de coleta later also emerged. It was a relatively recent change in the late nineteenth century that the corrida became all about front man or star; this man they termed the espadachín, the diestro, or the matador. Indeed, one matador described forming a cuadrilla much like one would put together a rock band today.[88] The typical cast of the cuadrillas, as brought by Ibañez and Company to Bucareli in November and December 1898, included two swordsmen, four picadors, six banderillas, a puntcillero, and at least six bulls per show.[89] The posters specifically named the matadors and ganaderías, but other participants only showed up in lesser press or on programs. Rarely did the common fighter make it to the big time.

The progression of careers from rags to riches in trajectory followed a set course. The novices began in small towns and ranches, working on technique, encountering less deadly bulls or even steers, and learning from the more talented or experienced diestros. Most cut their teeth for years working in cuadrillas and as picadors or banderillas to prepare the bulls for the "real" stars. The long apprenticeship allowed promoters to discover the budding superstars early on.

Promoters watched for and groomed those with the skills and the charisma to make the transition from small markets to the larger city arenas. Matadors like Gaona they cynically celebrated also for their indigenous roots and their rural authenticity, even as they disdained this in all other venues. The would-be torero worked their way up and endured the process in ways that apprentices to any other tradesman would recognize: grunt work, longer hours, and less pay with few guarantees for advancement. In many venues youngsters in Mexico fought as opening acts against steers, providing the next generation of toreros. Officials banned this in 1887 due to frequent serious injuries. In response, promoters suggested the possibility of opening a proper bullfighting school to teach the next crop of matadors.[90] Over time and with increased commercial influences, the prospect of real fame held more reward but less likelihood as the gente de coleta team fell into shadow of the matadors. Only the rarest made it to that highest level, and all the others could at best hope for was being a part of the rare teams that toured together in the big-league circuits in places like Spain.

Toreros dreamed of one day performing well enough, consistently, to rise from banderilla to matador in the *ritual alternativa* whereby a known matador (the *padrino*, godfather) passed on the role. The promotion came with a cape and sword, and the right to the first kill. The best became diestros at the hands of the most renowned old professionals and in the biggest and most prestigious plazas.[91] Over the course of a successful career, the superstar matador received the alternativa in each country where they fought.

The successful matador left behind humble roots and took on the new role as a celebrity with expected behaviors both fair and foul. Aware that the diestro's womanizing might cross a fine line between manly and debauched, among other tawdry behaviors, professional agents (called *apoderas*) worked to manage the star's image (though these seem less common than in Spain). Matadors earned a degree of respectability by 1904, but this remained somewhat defensive. As one author remarked, the audiences understood "he smelled like a bullfighter" without explanation. Moreover, a matador could not act humbly and maintain his repute that way because to audiences any show of modesty became equated with timidity.[92] Those from "better" backgrounds stood out, too; for example, part of Reverte's lauded reputation came because he liked to read and had an educated view on affairs.[93] With celebrity came wealth and fame, and some new expectations and responsibilities. Surprisingly, given their ill repute, toreros became sought after as godfather compadres.[94]

Compadrazgo in Mexico represented a venerable tradition of extended kinship networking. The godparents acknowledged in a public ritual with witnesses agreed to certain duties. On one hand, they provide a simple safety net to care for orphaned children and assist in emergency circumstances. Beyond this function they also attached to the reputation of both sets of parents. The rite demonstrated the worthiness, honor, and prestige of the selected godparent, and, simultaneously, the respect and trust the parents feel for them. It specifically required that the godparents see to the proper Christian upbringing of any children, whether orphaned or not, and to their general spiritual well-being. Certainly, a wealthy torero made sense in terms of providing financially, but a man with a debauched reputation who behaved like an animal seems problematic.[95] This was certainly the reason why this public relations spin worked. In becoming an apparently respectable Christian gentleman some of the matador's drunken shenanigans and bad attitudes fell off into the distance. If nothing else, it might create some degree of reasonable doubt in the public.

Matadors, or perhaps just their managers, also attempted to repair their image through works of obvious social good. In an extension of their public personas, some became the figurehead spokesmen for disaster relief efforts. Floods, hurricanes, quakes, or fires could allow the torero as valuable opportunity to show his true colors as a leader and raise funds to assist those imperiled by acts of God. And really, who better to do so than the man accustomed to such deadly whims of fate like the temperament of an enraged bull? Ultimately, profits ran alongside branding and public relations in the creation of the matador fantasy.

Since all of this occurred alongside the commercialization of the sport, and the building of competing rings, the promoters certainly had a hand in encouraging this. Each company claimed in their ads to have the best most *bravo* bulls, the wildest yet most skilled diestros, and the softest, most shaded seating. Pricing always proved a complicated issue, too, as they sought to milk the wealthy and poor alike, and even catered with group rates for school children and military barracks outings. Historically, this had meant that the day before the fights saw increased business at the pawnshops.[96] It stands to reason that with such pressures to make the sport both respectable and reach the broadest possible audience, the need to at least make some pretense of managing the bullfighter would also come into play. The behaviors as *muy hombre* (very manly) of course also were part of the popular charm of the figure, but modern sales sensibility also had its power.

If it made some stars into animals, it also made animals into brief star celebrities.

Bulls as Stars

The crowd had a brief relief from their normal animal life when they sat in the arena. In the expected suspension of the rules, the idea of a "moral vacation," nonetheless, does not quite fit with what was clearly a regular practice for the fandom of fights. The unusually vocal and even rowdy nature of these crowds suggests a site of transgression, a steam release, where an internal logic kept things (mostly) from reaching levels of real danger. In a word, the bullfight encouraged a set of gendered and public-facing behaviors that witnesses deemed "animal." Rules set by promoters and city officials could scarcely be enforced in the face of such a crowd. The moral ecology of the bullfighting mob had its own ideas of public propriety, of animal expectations, and of torero performance, that rose from ideas of what was natural. When bulls did their own thing, the crowd reacted.

If the animal nature of the torero and the audience blurred lines, and if ideas of masculinity itself assumed wild beastly behaviors, then what of the character of the bull itself? The spectators and press anthropomorphized and attributed to the bull a human character. Indeed, some rioters in the stands set the blame for their mayhem on the bull's moral qualities in the ring. Bulls represented regional pride of *patria chica*, bolstered by owners' and ganadería promotions.[97] Their ferocity or timidity stood in for the men of their home regions. The viewers recognized agency in the bull—his choices within the literal and figurative structures of the ring determined his fate and fame. This was agency far beyond the interactive notion of *agencement* proposed by Vinciane Despret, as a means to understand animals in historical thought.[98]

In the sense of it here, I privilege animal consequences over animal intentions that humans can never fully understand or define. The crowd understood the bull not as a thinking but limited animal, but more often as the carrier of cultural cargoes. When bulls fought back in unpredictable ways, the fans (and the torero entourage, the ranchers, and the promoters) explained it in ways that emphasized cleverness of an unnatural sort. Flashes of genius came from spiritual places, perhaps from the devil, and met only incidentally with careful breeding to create a deadlier bull.

Once bled and dead, the bull became a mere pile of meat in the dirt, a sad beast, but before this it could transcend its animal nature. In the fight, of course, there could be no drama without risk, and no risk if the animal stayed true and predictable in its bovine habits. The transformation from near-human to stringy beef could not happen without the matador's intervention. At least some bulls showed signs of real thinking as an antagonist. In this the accounts of bullfights show similarity to tales of the sport hunter where a beast's inherent clever nature, its stealth, its violence, all gave proof to the bravery of the human and the justice or fairness that underlay the fight. Animals with this genius became worthy of manly killing and lauded for their cooperation.

In addition to a simple agency, the bull also revealed something of how society envisioned particular traits, including those typically coded in masculinities (such as courage and vengefulness) and in ways more religiously framed. A chief one of these was the implication that actions deemed treacherous labeled the bull as a *moro*. The bull that acted unpredictably, wild (in fact, not all that differently from a late-night torero party), pointed to an evil alien nature, without proper manners, rather than the clever ruse of a desperate animal. The bull that gored Gaona in 1908, for instance, songsters declared in a corrido as a "rancorous, treacherous, and hypocritical Moor" and, furthermore, a "criminal ox."[99] An Orientalist perspective of the bullfighter also played on this "alienness" at times, emerging for instance with Gaona's nickname (made more popular in Spain) of El Califa de León—a reference to his swarthy looks, his style, and to his mastery of Spain's old enemy, the Moor.

Yet if the bull could be coded Muslim, he also had a direct connection to the Christian god. Since the earliest known fights, the corrida had an association with religious rituals, it celebrated marriages and festivals, and it eventually became the chief means to fundraise for church charities. Only later did it commercialize, yet even then some deep meanings of blood sacrifice, holy destiny, and risky ritual remained. Moreover, fights held on Sundays (to the unhappiness of many clerics) interfered with the piety of the most fanatic of bullfighting fans. Bullfights acted as a substitute religion and deliberately ritualized the sport in every way. According to one astute writer, due to their frequent blood sacrifices, the toreros performed as a priesthood.[100] The ritual made sense of what could otherwise be a disturbing scene by implying deeper holy meanings to the event. Rituals give cultural frameworks to practices otherwise mundane or distasteful. In terms of moral ecology, the deep ritual of the show mediated the unusual sight of slaughter. When the ritual fell apart, participants rioted. Elevated by the ritual, the sacrificial bull, if not devil-touched or genius-gifted, became sacred and its death both sensible and tragic and perversely, beautiful. Holy days became bullfight holidays. This even included the fiesta of Saint Francis, the patron of animals. Bulls, sacred since our earliest cave paintings, now served in a mass commercial industry as sacrifices on an altar of nostalgia and nationalism. Death became a matter of consumer tastes, with a religious undertone.

If the worst behaviors of the hypermasculine matador and fickle bulls could not always be reined in, promoters had other tricks up their sleeves to distract and attract fans.

Toreras and Women in the Stands

Finding or creating a popular market at times required experimentation or innovation in the types of shows that they put on. Gender became in these cases quite explicitly part of the sales pitch. Foreign animal shows, like a man who wrestled bulls by the nose, and novelty acts like female toreras, added to the sense of the "proper" fights' claim to representing proper traditions and "normal" Mexican masculinities. For instance, the press highlighted how female matadors still had housework to do between fights, or at times, illustrated the ones who fought from horseback complete in long dresses. Others jokingly claimed that the crowds threw household goods like a sewing machine and cooking pans into the ring.[101] It points though to some uneasiness with the hypermasculine matador roles played out by women and to an uncertainty that extended possible sexual dangers to the stands as a social place.

Images exclusively depicted the toreras as well dressed in middle-class clothes and sometimes dresses, and in contrast to the males, they obscured or blurred any markers of race. Expectations for the ladies afforded them few masculine signs. The women did a man's job as an exception proving a rule, and as a show of the unusual. Yet in no ways should these women show signs of things like independence, intellect, or sexual agency. Custom could only be bent so far. Moreover, the "unnatural" display shaped a sense of expectations, a moral ecology, wherein women had highly limited roles in the killing of animals. Women inhabiting the exceptional role of torera proved by contrast the notion of "masculine by nature."[102]

To fight a bull, in however feminine a fashion, offended the crowd's sensibility unless promoters carefully framed the event as freakishly strange and weird. And no commentators made any suggestion that the ladies shared in the matadors' usual appetites for nightlife and vices. Yet two Spanish women arrived in 1898 to challenge social expectations.

Promoters repeatedly tried to bring in toreras, often by downplaying the dangers faced when they spoke to city officials. With bullfights barely back in operation after bans, toreras began to reappear.[103] Petitions made the argument that the practice had already been made normal in other countries, suggesting that Mexico would be backward if they did not follow suit. In December of 1897 promoters first asked for the corrida with *señoritas toreras* and then assured the City that the women "command the art," that there was no risk, and that it was only steers used. They also informed the council that the ladies planned to live in the reputable Hotel Humboldt, suggesting that their whereabouts and behavior could be managed and remain proper.

The matadoras Lolita and Angelita wanted to do two or three corridas but legally this remained prohibited in DF where law forbade women in bullfighting shows. The promoters pointed out that toreras had performed there in the past, even if in one case an empresario had "tricked the public with prostitutes." Nonetheless, women had shown in Madrid, Sevilla, Barcelona, Valencia, Cadiz, and Malaga, so the Ayuntamiento should reconsider.[104] Another team called the La Dulzaras had played in Madrid in 1898 and petitioned to come as well.[105] On February 6, 1898, Antonio Medina finally received permission to bring in a cuadrilla de señoritas toreras to Bucareli. Given that this bullring had experienced many difficulties (and was one year from demolition), this perhaps also showed some desperation on the part of the owner, Ponciano Díaz.[106] Certainly the women's arrival stirred up the fandom.

Lolita Pretel, lauded as the cute one, caught the specialty press's attention first, which earned her both a cover picture and a page-three biography. They reported that as part of the señoritas toreras cuadrilla, the sixteen-year-old girl was neither pretty or ugly, but still nice and modest. They assured the readers that the Barcelona-born girl would only be fighting steers. The paper also covered its bases, suggesting that perhaps the girl instead should apply herself to labors appropriate to her sex, like attending college or playing piano, and then no one would ever need shed tears over her. After all, "Was there not shame in watching an angel bullfight?" They slated her to fight at Bucareli on February 20, directed by Don Mariano Armengel, against four two-year-old bulls along with Angelita. Lolita took ill, and stepped out, leaving her compatriot to do the honors and affirming the editor's preconception of her fragile nature. The cuadrilla nonetheless fought well, and the audience applauded loudly for their bravery and ability.[107]

Not so "sensitive" or photogenic, Angelita, Angela Pagés, featured on the cover of the next issue. She was a daughter of a Barcelona brewer and less elegant in appearance than Lolita, but strong and tough, and "only lacking experience to fully excel." She had already suffered three gorings but succeeded as a torero despite her "violent temperament." What this description might have entailed was unclear, but they claim she, too, was modest, and so apparently forgave her other flaws. Again, they claim all the fights as well attended and well received.[108] As the toreras moved on through the Mexican circuit after, they played Puebla next, where both made kills and Angelita put on such a good show that she was awarded an ear.[109]

The criticisms of these women and others like them nevertheless still appeared in press. When Ignacia Fernández, bellicosely nicknamed "La guerrita," did a lengthy Latin American tour running from 1898 to 1910, many commented on her origins as a domestic servant. Some no doubt meant to emphasize her rise in status, others, her feminine essence. Others still critiqued her as a marimacho (unnaturally manly woman).[110] A travel account spoke of the *toreadoras* [sic] as presenting horrifying spectacle and a "good joke." He told how the crowd threw "darning cotton and spools of thread at the fair señoritas instead of the usual offering of cigarettes."[111] The audience offered its own sense of humor to the affair, although they clearly seemed titillated.

Beyond the ring, some commentators reflected on how the corridas themselves brought about a degree of sexual arousal among audiences. The architecture itself added to the perils—the promoters eventually added "foot covers" to prevent *los de abajo* (the lower class and also those seated lower) from looking up ladies' skirts.[112] Not incidentally, this risky new sexual space shared many anxieties with Michael Matthews's railway cars.[113] In both places, a degree of chaos and the mixing of various classes caused uneasiness, but also a sort of opportunity or possibility for taboo relations. States of passion or arousal caused by the exciting spectacle or the novelty of experience, built up by expectations, represented a modern sense of sociability. Perhaps inevitably this tied to sexual desires and the susceptibility of some folks simply caught up in the excitement.[114] Anonymity within the crowd, an excuse for vocal excesses, a time-marking event with its own import, and the convivial expectation of the mob allowed women a space to express themselves regardless of who did the fighting below. The enthusiastic participation of women as active spectators caught the eye of foreign attendees and represented yet again the popular sense of the "acceptable" that ruled the bullfight.

Society and Its Tastes

In other words, the arena played out not simply the sun-side versus shaded seats and they were not so orderly as William Beezley's caudillo metaphor. In fact, if the ring were political metaphor, it seems much more like the post-Revolution in many cases, or at least, democratic chaos.[115] Others have proposed that the fight's political message reflected messages about monarchy, social prestige, nation, and so on (including the last Royal Spanish bullfight in 1906) and created a model of proper power.[116] Some have even argued for a Freudian reading where the bullfights represent resentments against family authority figures.[117] Perhaps.

The bullfights of the Porfiriato greatly expanded in prominence, featured acrobatic interactions between bull and matador, and the official bans proved brief and due more to mismanaged venues than any other consideration.[118] In contrast to the influential model proposed by Beezley, the presidents, whether visiting dignitaries or those appointed to each fight, regularly faced the opprobrium of the fans who loudly derided them and showed no signs of meekly bowing to the theoretical authority of the caudillo.[119] Rowdy behaviors and near-riots did not generally reflect "basking in the patriarch's presence," nor did the stoic endurance of the common man reflect clearly in the adulation of the celebrity matador.[120] The latter may have represented some elements of shared solidarity with the people, but more than that, the matador also showcased hypermasculinity and ambition in ways that set them apart, and even above, the audiences. The corrida as a political metaphor brought together a messy, cross-class, cross-gender, and potentially violent crowd—democratic and even revolutionary in its fervor. But the crowd had its own moral ecology, one based in part on the human character of the bulls, the taurine character of the matador, and the aesthetic expectations of the viewers. Society adapted to the sport.

Matadors as the face of the bullfight took on increasingly celebrity places in a society embracing modern mass spectacles.[121] Boys (and some girls) aspired to be them—playing at the roles of bull and matador in streets, towns, and farms.[122] The specialty press and promoters created the matador as stars.[123] Rags to riches and the lure of wealth certainly motivated some. Matadors at the top levels earned fortunes and moved in prestigious circles.[124]

In leisure, Mexicans' deeper cultural understandings of concepts such as sacrifice, honor, courage, and gender played out as contests of nature and man. They defined through laws an idea of the civilized boundaries for the new nation, as they controlled or banned casual cruelties. They made assertions about social classes, and they enacted traditions in paradoxically modern fashions. The corridas and the exalted matadors fit cultural categories within a particular gendered moral ecology.

And if the corrida could be chaotic, sexy, and wild, it was also paradoxically managed, ordered, and orchestrated. The moral ecology of those sitting in the sun at times coaligned with the political ecology of those in the shade. They watched the same spectacle.

The sight, it should not be forgotten, entailed gore, pain, and cruelty. In a textbook for French primary school children, later translated in Mexico, an extremely graphic description of the bullfight ended with the author calling it an "orgy of blood."[125] Spectator and fans do not, to this day, deny the torment and confusion of the bull (and the horses). Nonetheless, in the love of the corrida something stands in the way of spectators acknowledging the unnecessary violence and for then considering it to be inherently wrong and avoidable. It is here again that the moral ecology tipped the cultural scales toward meanings that might not exist, and erased any discomforts felt.

The entire ritual in its new commercial setting imposed narratives on the bulls, fighters, and even on types within the audiences—especially on gender. Finding elegance in cruelty, a habit engrained in the bullfight aficionado, perhaps replayed in the numerous press narratives when it came to the case of María Luisa and Rodolfo Gaona. Between the lurid rumors and the defensive rebuttals, a sort of middle-class narrative did emerge as a somewhat stereotyping and melodramatic storyline. Partisans made the two protagonists into the villain and victim according to taste and class positions. The suffering of both, most spectators assumed. Where they differed was in interpreting the differences of station between the wealthy slightly older man and the youthful but socially respectable girl. Her place as a dangerous prize, a fair and foreign-seeming girl from a good family, stood in contrast to his rags-to-riches status and indigenous appearance. As such, the tale presented one dramatic warning to well-off parents of daughters and a different warning to the parents of ambitious boys.

The elite had their own aspersions and expectations from those of the lower classes, with influences sometimes shadowed by European ideas. An idea of elegance permeated events, and in the case of the corrida and expectation (demand) for accommodations to their class. Being "classy" or exhibiting "taste," according to Pierre Bourdieu, represents socially constructed class markers originating in the eighteenth century.[126] The difficulty for promoters came in finding ways to upgrade the experience to match these desires for their Mexican elite audiences. Improved facilities, smaller perquisites like private entrances, valet parking, and in-seat drink service, as well as generally improved bulls, shows, and organization, brought the wealthy back to the sport. More rules, too, to bring some degree of order to the unruly crowds, helped to assure the shade-sitters that they participated in a thoroughly modern, and classy, event. They could even argue that the fights served a greater social good by asserting a non-indigenous character among the popular classes. In an era that associated whiteness with progress, the Hispanic roots of the corrida had a traditionalist appeal. The Mexican innovations in the ring, and the authenticity of the bulls and matadors as national, they deemed proof of entering a modern age and leaving indigenous pasts behind. And if the matadors' occasional depravities might hint at an unsightly backwardness, then at least the actual attendance of the masses at the bullfight might itself be a civilizing influence—eventually.

Conclusions

The bullfighter fit oddly into both the highest circles and the lowest cultures, a civil-minded killer, and as a little bit of country in the big city. He thus helped people make sense of some elements of urban life. Killing animals in the city now supposed to be the place of regulated abattoirs under city officials, also included the ritualistic role of the celebrity torero. Necropolitics took on a celebrity face. The relationship to animals moved in strange ways.

The broader ideals of the bullfight crowd shaped around a moral ecology rooted in traditions, interrelated needs of community, and internal logics. The political ecology imposed an outside vision set down by "those in charge," even if rarely clarifying who exactly this meant. Some behaviors the elite wrote into regulations. Others stemmed unobtrusively from economic differences, such as seating in sun or shadow. Equally stark delineations came from differing services offered the better classes—valet services, private entries, and refreshment services. The choices made by promoters on show contents also related more to a capitalist logic and less to the expectations or hopes among the popular classes. Rules about behavior infringed on community norms. City governors' attempts to manage the crowd, at an extreme, could also lead to the corrida moving out to the countryside in search of authenticity. Different relations to this animal practice, the moral and political ecologies, therefore permeated the world of the corrida and the event transmitted gendered norms into society more broadly. Gaona's hypermasculine attribution, real or imagined, fit the moral ecological culture of the crowd. His time in jail, on the other hand, reflected a political influence. Corridos and popular pressures saw him released; culture had mediated the gap between two different visions of appropriate behavior.

Animals intersected into many areas of society including religiosity, leisure, labor, science, and even into family dynamics—as such they represented a host of challenges that played out in conflicts of the modern age and helped shape the stories told about gender. Bullfights intercede in this. Masculinity in tight pink pants met with horned human character.

Animals defined much of what it meant to be human: they incarnated notions of sexuality and fed the hungry; they participated in rituals of state and church, and they labored in the street; they provided company to the lonely and died for entertainment. In the world of the bullfighters and fans, an arena for María Luisa's unfortunate demise, the animal side always lurked nearby.

Moving beyond this, in a swirl of the veronica, and to the death of other animals, we make expedition to the wilds.

PART III

In the Wilds

CHAPTER SIX

Stalking the Modern

Sportsmen, Wild Beasts, and Conservation in Mexico

"Hunting has changed man's relations to other animals in his view of what is natural."[1]

A cold, wet, half-starved hunter stepped carefully past the rattling viper, took aim, and shot the massive bear at a hundred yards. Carefully having it hauled back to camp through packs of ravenous wolves and treacherous bandit gangs, he was greeted by his joyfully drunken companions. Back in his city home, experts mounted the creature in an angry snarling pose as the hunter composed his well-embellished tale. He omitted mention of indigenous guides or porters and promptly began to once again mourn his sterile urban life.

Well-embellished stories of the hunt represent an ancient human tradition almost as venerable as the hunt itself. In the final decades of the nineteenth century, Mexicans and foreign adventurers continued these practices. They hunted any and all creatures, from the tiny axolotl to the rapidly disappearing grizzly bear. In accounts loaded with masculine posturing, they recounted the many hardships they endured and the dangers they confronted. But if their experiences remained much the same, the practice and institutions and meaning of hunting had begun to deform under the pressures of modern life. This had profound implications.

Powerful broad-based conceptions about conservation and nature developed from the hunters' tales. In the hunt, some individuals engaging in death dealing as identity become a part of state policy constructing the statistical relegation of deaths, the art of the necropolitical. Hunters used their tales to share didactic anecdotes about civilizing and self-civilizing.[2] A norm of conservation among sports hunters created a tension between subsistence groups and the luxuries of the wealthy. This legalist scientific political ecology ran contrary to common moral ecologies and played out when state power (laws and agents) got involved on behalf of a new vision of "nature."

Most importantly, the government set a new set of biopolitical claims over the *riqueza pública*, or nature as national wealth, as the domain of the "nature state." The building of culturally consistent political ecologies, infused with necropolitical logics, made hunting into a site of class injustices and modern sensibilities. Moving from critter to criminal, from an animal perspective, many animalities became illegal in the countryside as they had in the city for errant dogs.

Wildlife constituted a facet of this new sphere of property. State agents categorized, studied, and regulated the fates of rural creatures. These displaced the foodways of indigenous and other subsistence hunters into farming and meat markets. The gap between the subsistence-based moral ecology and the ideology of the sportsman also created pejorative and criminal labels like "butcher" and "poacher." In this venue of power-clashes, a history of hunting reveals the dialectic clash between cultural frameworks. Generations of hunters contributed to the creation of an accepted version the wilds for national legislation. These also helped to consign certain creatures into categories that made their deaths both inevitable and unmourned.

Idealized versions of the abstract idea of nature suited huntsmen reformers as they brought to bear legal and rhetorical devices. Drawn from this, conservation became an assumed or self-evident truth of social good, with a few limited means to achieve it. The way Mexican society chose to deal with wild animals therefore offered another lens by which to see changes in social relations. Conservationism as a political ecology had been fed ammunition by limited numbers of non-indigenous Mexican hunter-writers who had offered them commentary.

Competing visions of what it meant to be civilized, and of the appropriate role of death within this, dictated the development of a regime of hunting laws. Rugged, wealthy, and non-indigenous individuals told their tales of the hunt and shaped the discourses within which animal lives in the wilderness would exist. A genealogy of sorts shows the correlation between the boastful didactic tales of these men and the formal policies that followed.

Conservationists, like the public health officials, acted in good faith to apply scientific and professional approaches to the issues of animal populations and welfare.[3] Yet they nonetheless worked within necropolitical systems that had unintended consequences for prey creatures and dispossessed peoples. The conservationists sought to do good in the name of public wealth and a political ecology where animals represented a property to be hoarded. That the benefits would be unevenly distributed and poorly enforced could neither be surprising nor avoided. The central ideas of who should be permitted to kill, and which animals should die and how, did not rise from science alone. Rather, a cultural niche occupied by the hunter-naturalist defined "proper" and modern ways. Their writings spread to a wider audience as their ideas migrated from backwoods campfires to the halls of legislation. The government literally categorized creatures into lists that declared their life or death as acceptable.

Philosophies about the meaning of the hunt underpinned the discourses that shaped the new political ecology. This chapter begins with a discussion of thinkers whose views highlight this philosophical vision. On the ground, of course, hunters had their own ideas. Three generations of prominent hunters lay out their perspectives of the good hunter, the good hunt, and the good society. Their ideas changed into legal assumptions. The final section examines how conservation laws echoed the sportsmen's cultural practices but exposed many animals to danger. Legal attempts to regulate animal-man relationships divided society into gentleman and beast, game and vermin, urban and rural.

A Philosophy of the Intimate Kill

Philosophical couching made the killing of wild animals, just as with other blood sports, permissible and laudable. In other words, cultural constructs intervened between the practice and any inherent hesitancy to kill.[4] The hunt transformed as animals became game. In contrast to fighting bulls or cocks, opponents tended to criticize hunting poorly rather than the idea of hunting in and of itself. José Ortega y Gasset provides one of the clearest arguments in favor of hunting.[5] As the prominent philosopher said, hunting represents the "privilege and torment of our species."[6] It was a part of us and could not be avoided. To some, this suggested an inherent human nature as a killer ape rooted in evolutionary developments.[7]

For proponents, hunting seemed necessary as a requirement for the modern man where only wildness could act as antidote for sterile and meaningless modern ways of life, even if at its heart, the practice meant killing. In a world where most of mundane life was filled with forced occupations, the hunt offered a suspension from the daily grind and a "true life."[8] Chasing game offered the illusion of getting away from civilization, from other men, civitas, ordinance, and the state, and saved the "man condemned to progress."[9] Man went from killing to eat to fulfilling a "spiritual necessity" and acting on his "sacred right, his passion" in a search for solitude. This allowed them to forget work, money, and all that was forced on him, where he labored for wages merely to live.[10] At the same time, the search for this meaning could only be done deliberately as one worked to return to nature and descended to the bestial. This represented the key to "este rito sutil es la caza" (the subtle ritual that is hunting).[11] By getting in touch with this side of their being, the hunters could enjoy "vacations from humanity."[12] Hunters' many motives went far beyond the fable of the killer ape.[13]

Non-subsistence hunters generally state other motives, of course, and go beyond broad abstracts with overlapping reasoning. Some certainly stress the taking of meat as economic necessity, despite the various added expenses from licensing, butchering, and the expedition itself. Some emphasize ecological rationales of controlling animal populations subject to minimal natural predation to save the survivors from the cruel death of starvation. Other hunters focus more on social and ritualistic elements such as male bonding and family traditions. These all, sometimes in combination, suffice for many hunters, but others claim more esoteric motives.[14]

Hunters may appeal to cultural understandings as rationales. For some the sense of becoming an "animal" as a predator allows them to approach and appreciate nature in profound aesthetic and quasi-religious ways. Their love of nature is reinforced by their experience and overcomes any misgivings they may feel or any buck fever for that matter. For a few the stark reality, the "harsh truth," of the hunt becomes the intrinsic reality that justifies their sense of indifference or triumph as well as a dismissal of any sense of tragedy. Yet if a commonality does tie these hunters together, it lay in the reality that the experience has a dramatic energy and emotional effect. It spurs excitement, guilt, longings, and makes man confront some primal aspects. Beyond all, it defines a boundary between human and the animal Other in the starkest way.[15] This chasm nonetheless could be bridged in idyllic reimagining.

This Romantic view connected the hunter to the animal. Through the hunt, man could live in the orbit of animal existence.[16] To many hunters, the creatures of the wild had a type of purity that made them "Other" from normal animals. Domestic animals lived in an intermediary reality between pure animals and man.[17] Nevertheless, the pure animals needed killing, even if the hunter might have emotional ties to them.

The moral ecology of the hunting community was not, of course, fixed but equally as dynamic as the broader competing notions in the meanings of civilization. The discourses on hunting thus balanced between different ideas of man and nature, and between love of the subjective animal and the civilized necessity to hunt it.[18] As Ortega y Gasset puts it, "A good hunter has restless depths in his conscience faced with the death he will deal to the charming animal."[19] To quiet these qualms, the hunter differed from other sportsmen by seeking out danger (either in animal or circumstances), but walked a fine line. If the killing transformed into a pure massacre and destruction, this was not hunting, but something else. Equally, if the animal can fight back, "where the aggression was mutual, then this was not hunting (it was bullfighting)." The sweet spot for him was where the hunter, with skill, overpowered an inferior species.[20] Moreover, the hunter cannot need the meat, since there existed a huge difference between hunt and sport, or between survival versus diversion.[21] Many hunters would disagree.

In any case, whatever philosophical bent the hunter carried, the death of the animal remained the necessary element. To Ortega y Gasset, man can only try to understand his own death through killing, and must grasp that the animal experience multiplied the enigma of death.[22] Where some might think this sense of wonder should excuse the prey animal, he instead insists that death was essential because without it there is no authentic hunt: "One does not hunt to kill, but, on the contrary, one kills to have hunted."[23] Only in killing then, can one live.

Generations of the Sportsman's Creed: Blazquez, Lopez, and Imaz

From early in the national era, spokesmen for the "new age" of hunting proclaimed the boundaries of their own relations to the natural world and wider society. Their ideas changed slowly over the better part of a century, at least. Comparing this elite moral ecology over three generations of hunter-authors, Pedro Blazquez, Carlos López and Carlos M. López, and Arturo Imaz Baume, between the 1840s and 1940s, illuminate continuity. How they viewed the hunt, their conception of the good hunter, their ideas of dangers and rewards, and broadly, how they saw the hunt in relations to wider society, all informed developing conservationist discourses.

The earliest of them, Pedro Blazquez, wrote his 1868 work as a helpful guide from the perspective of a twenty-five-year hunter eager to share his passions. Blazquez owned a hacienda in Puebla, where his brother taught natural history at the state college.[24] For him, the hunt represented an artistry that developed the soul and the self. He insisted on his love for natural history in his descriptions of animals and his relating of adventures and lessons from the field.[25] He began with a nostalgic sonnet claiming that "when the deer falls, all is forgotten."[26] The hunt, to him, entailed a sacred and all-consuming practice. It dominated the hunter's spirit until he found other diversions tedious and indifferent.[27] He asked, "What diversion can compete with the beauty, hygiene, morality, and philosophy of the hunt?" To him, theater, dance, lectures, gambling, and meetings had all become corrupt, mere "bacchanals of drunkenness and gluttony." Above all, hunting was not disorder.[28] Philosophically, exposure to the wilds provided an "immense school into the Omnipotent" in which one could seek sublimity.[29]

His view of society stood in stark contrast to the realms of nature. Already by the 1850s we find a fierce opponent to urbanization. The hunter, by virtue of his surrounds, had better health than city dwellers.[30] Cities, he claimed, had been fouled by pollution, their air foul, with feces strewn everywhere, and he pointed to hospitals and cemeteries as especially nasty places.[31] Urban society degraded man. The lone hunter remained superior, since "group recreation reproduced the perversities of the majority" and diminished individual morality. Meanwhile, "the rich went to theaters, dance, gambling, or orgies, the poor to the tavern and houses of prostitution."[32] In contrast, hunting charted the way to "true civilization," as a meditation that brought knowledge of the self, and so represented a noble entertainment.[33] It taught good customs and the arranging of life.[34] Far from taking up the mantle of pure environmental crusader, Blazquez made clear that his meditations required violence against animals; his next chapter carefully detailed his recommended weaponry.

Blazquez's "good hunter" stands mostly in contrast to those he disparaged. He hated what he called *idiot hunters*, or *Sunday hunters*, as really just interested in shooting and wasting ammunition.[35] Real hunters had to be naturalists, though he proved vague at what this might mean.[36] In typical fall-from-grace writing common to conservationist tracts, he noted the dangerous decline of France that had already been hunted bare by 1862. He proclaimed the need for Mexico to sound the alarm against the ruin of their own woods and waters.[37] Closer to home, he acknowledged the Mexican indigenous peoples as natural hunters. He then undermined the compliment by noting that those that truly excelled at the hunt were "revered by the 'savage hordes' as equals to European princes."[38] Making accusation by implication, to Blazquez the good hunter regulated what he takes on his own volition with healthy moral moderation rather than killing too many or blindly following laws.[39] He also needed skills. To be a "real man, honorable in society, he must know how to handle firearms."[40] Notably, indigenous Mexicans often had no or fewer guns, and therefore, to him, could not attain approval.

Blazquez differed significantly from those who followed later in his experience in using diverse hunting methods. For him, much of the technology was still new and the game too abundant for worries about overkill. One exception here was that he acknowledged stalking as the superior way of hunting, particularly for deer, just as later authors would. Yet when he spoke of unorthodox methods, he often sounded impressed. He lauded a hunter in 1844 United States for bringing in modern means by using lanterns to dazzle his prey.[41] In discussing the use of indigenous hunting guides, he cited cases from the United States, Egypt, Canada, and other places that used armadas, ran herds off cliffs, and used other means of mass slaughter. In one instance in Ontario, Canada, hunters had killed over 282,000 animals in eight days.[42] He warmly described a farm owner in northern United States who faced a "horde of turkeys" and made use of an "infernal device" that could shoot forty-three at a time.[43] Even in his own advice, he readily turned to the use of bait and pit traps for hunting big cats, wolves, and coyotes.[44] Of course, these more dangerous creatures deserved the caution.

Dangers in the mid-nineteenth-century countryside abounded. Blazquez made little specific recommendations for hunting rifles but clearly swore by carrying a Colt-brand pistol in case of bandits or being surprised by jabalí (boars), wolves, tigers, lions, or cougars.[45] Of all the hunting tales, his alone made mention of keeping night watch in camp for the safety of people and pack animals.[46] He expressed some real worry and actual fear of the nighttime forests. He discussed how "at dawn the hunted becomes the hunter" and spoke of the fear of death among the immensity of the mountains.[47] He drove this home in his story of finding the skeleton of a lost hunter propped against a tree, in what they then called the Woods of Death.[48] Of course some of the scariest parts of life at that time would have been illness, and so he dabbled a little in medical advice (tailored to hunters), even if some of his curative advice could kill.[49] Specific tales aside, his tales also evoke powerful connections between sportsmen across time.

Commonalities between hunters over the century appeared throughout. The bane of the first-time hunter, "buck fever" (*fiebre del ciervo*) he called a natural emotion.⁵⁰ These bouts of sudden nerves, shaking hands, and reluctance to kill speak to my premise that the killing of animals has a psychosocial weight, usually and eventually overcome with cultural training.⁵¹ As one philosopher puts it, "He who takes hold of himself only at the moment he has to fire at his prey will have little luck," thus emphasizing the need for self-disciplining.⁵² Blazquez also puts great emphasis on properly treating one's dogs. Dogs in Mexico proved crucial to the hunt, he argued, and in the great hunting stories the dog was always the hero, and, of course, the animal was an instinctive hunter.⁵³ He claimed, there could be "no good hunter without good dog" and then gave instructions on the use of hunting dogs.⁵⁴ Going further, he asserted that the man who did not care for his dog was no hunter, was hard-hearted, and was not a good citizen or *padre de familia*.⁵⁵

Blazquez also stood out within the hunters' literature in his culinary focus. His ideal philosopher-poet huntsman needed a broad education (knowing for instance that a xoloitzcuintli was not a coyote).⁵⁶ But above all, he needed the ability to slap together a gourmet feast in the middle of the wilderness. His "simple" recipes ranged from difficult to insane. A basic ham stew for camp, for example, called for "clavo," pepper, cinnamon, water, vinegar, spices, and wine.⁵⁷ He provided multiple recipes for hare and rabbits, but his most ambitious recipe, "pastel frances de liebre" or French hare cake, he called a great hunting lunch. This dish, similar to a cordon bleu perhaps, seems an ordeal to prepare. It called for layered rabbit, veal, pork, ham, liver, potato, and spices to be mixed and fried in oil and wine, simmered for six hours, then baked in a tortera (wrap), then fried in two pounds of butter, basted yet again, and finally soaked in a wine sauce for two hours. Slathered in a "cloak of butter," this should then be eaten with a good wine. Not an easy camp dish.⁵⁸ If bandits or grizzlies failed to take the hunter down, heart failure just might.

Decades later, new spokesmen explicitly addressed many of the same topics as Baume, but with attention to the changed times. Their work accorded with ideals of what a hunter should be in a modern nation, what has elsewhere been called the "sportsman's creed," and it also fit with efforts to limit and erase indigenous hunting practices and cultures from the nation. These new hunters gathered in Mexico City in places like the Jockey Club, where they discussed their plan.⁵⁹

FIGURE 6.1. Unknown, "El de la Presa," *El Mundo Ilustrado*, Mar. 2, 1902, 1. Painting.

In 1911, Carlos López and Carlos M. López compiled the best articulation of the sportsman's creed.[60] The work they described as the creation of a collaboration of various "hunters of the country with stories and photos of taken animals, and also of the country" and dedicated to those who love the sierras, the mountains, the woods, and so on and to those who enjoy these with weapons, dogs, and shooting.[61] Their audience, other elite hunters and legislators, they worked to convince of the justifications for a regulated and civilized hunt. The authors detailed the four forms of hunt: the stalk (or "true hunt") where hunters tracked and shot prey on the ground, the use of beaters (*batida*) to scare prey toward the hunter, the stationary ambush from behind camouflaged blinds (*acecho*), and the use of traps (*trampas*) to disable or kill the animals.[62] Riding to the hounds they disdained, as too European and not Mexican. They significantly staked a claim here to a national identity that did not emulate foreigners, and one that carried a local freight of unique practices. The hunter embodied and exploited a national treasury. The authors stressed how the hunter experienced (and enjoyed) hardships and developed his perception of the wilds as a mysterious place where true men uncovered the secrets of life.[63] For these rugged adventurers, the hunt tapped into "lo más rico" of the nation, its deep wealth of resources, which still at this point had seen no diminution of species. Other authors concurred, noting that "Mexico abounds in game," and that animals flourished including the deer "hunted by all classes," or the wide variety of game birds and fish.[64]

Despite this abundance, the sportsmen also proclaimed the risk that civilians and technology might destroy native stocks. They proposed a "new" hunting law in 1908 that would properly preserve and conserve the national patrimony. Ironically their solutions seem to have been near-identical to the apparently unenforced 1894 legal codes, which they certainly should have been responsibly informed about. They nonetheless called for a new guild of hunters to usher in the new age.[65] Their law (very much as the existing one) specifically called for the following: land for state parks, bans for commercial game meat, seasons for each animal, permits for hunting, protection for farmer's friend animals, limits for numbers taken, bans for using venoms, and a bounty for dangerous animals.[66] Perhaps more telling, they also called for the removal of hunting from "poblaciones," that is no taking of game actually near places where humans lived and needed to eat (see chapter 2). Their proposal established the harvesting of categorized game as the sole prerogative of the sportsman class. Their ideal modern world required discipline in consumption and the careful stewardship

FIGURE 6.2. El Buen Tono, advertisement for cigarettes, *El Mundo Ilustrado*, June 5, 1904, 7. Sketch.

of ecological capital. Proper hunters (non-indigenous) became the means to reshape and safeguard modern foodways based on markets, sciences, and laws.

The idealized sportsman stood as the modern incarnation of appropriate, manly, and civilized behaviors. Hunting, according to the López brothers, would cultivate the man; it was hunting, in their eyes, that gave history both Hannibal and Napoleon.[67] Their hunter was the naturalist who, at cost to his own health, opened the national terrain on behalf of those who lacked their essential qualities. These characteristics they specified: older than twenty-five for nerve, younger than fifty for vigor, patient, intelligent, serene, stylish, and lucky.[68] He (and they never suggested women) must excel at calculations for aim and trajectory. Above all, he must not kill just to kill, or in excess, as that would not just be "stupid but criminal." This noble paragon would personally eat his permitted kills (unlike the trappers), and he would follow closely the rules and regulations of hunting clubs. These, with names like "Los Intrépidos" (the Intrepid Ones) or Club Zimatlan, would maintain his honor and educate future generations.[69] Featuring anywhere from a handful to a few dozen men, club memberships ensured consistent practices.

This sportsman embodied the epitomized mestizo citizen of the nation, a considerably romanticized masculine ideal. This new man understood that the patrimonial wealth belonged to him contingent on his honor. He would kill no female animals, he would not shoot sleeping prey, he would use neither blinds nor beaters, and he would eschew explosives or poisons. The true huntsmen looked down on non-sporting gimmicks, especially night lanterns, and used traps only for nutria and grizzlies.[70] His selective use of meat would add the exotic to the table; the authors even give numerous recipes that would civilize venison for the modern palate.[71] Clearly, cooking game was still masculine, and given the times, they felt side dishes a feminine concern and left them out of the book. Other concerns took precedence.

The true sportsman also dealt with his own medical emergencies in the vast and dangerous wilderness. In case of snake bites, they contended, a simply mix of alcohol and ammonia should do the trick.[72] Other more professional sources at the time offered opinions too. Dr. Pedro Peréz Grovas spoke of common "cures" for snakebites that included in his words "bullshit and herbs" and sometimes human feces. When asked, "Sometimes, did the patients heal?" he chuckled, "No, of course not."[73]

Alcohol figured into much of huntsmen's planning it seems, and then, as now, provided a crucial element of recreational hunting trips. American journalist Frederick Remington bemoaned the chore of quail hunting in Mexico, save that at least he found sufficient alcohol to buoy his spirits.[74] Taking the hypermasculinized mythology further, the López duo also point out that the good sportsman carries with him a pistol at all times, not as backup since he punctiliously cared for his main weapon, but in case he encountered bandits.[75] In all things then, the sportsman prepared to be the gentlemanly adventurer.

The most compelling part of the López's manual comes from their discussions of how the indigenous played counterpart to the real sportsman. They readily admitted that the best true hunter was the "indio salvaje" or savage Indian, but then they denigrated the same indigenous huntsmen for their thoughtless nature.[76] This impulse did not restrict itself simply to the *cazadores* (hunters). Rather, this discourse of ancient reverence combined with contemporary revulsion also connected the Porfirian statues of native heroes in the streets to an "unspoiled" indigenous past.[77] The sportsmen claimed that the market hunters with batteries of guns and traps were bad, but that the subsistence meat hunter had far worse effects. The indigenous, they depicted as a *carnicero* or butcher: "He is simply a bloody barbarian, without common sense, conscience, or nothing. He is a devastator, a missionary of death; the greatest enemy of the animals and the true hunters."[78]

Their vision of the indigenous pervaded the text as they patronizingly referred to how "our Indians" use nets to get birds, or how the indigenous saw a good hunt as God's favor rather than a skilled activity. When the authors did give voice to race, they did so in terms of dogs and complained of the need for a good pure-blooded Mexican breed that had no roots in coyotes.[79] This did not imply lack of nationalist awareness—they also believed that US trappers were wiping out their black bears, and that German-style hunting clubs would be a great solution for regulating their sport.[80] At the same time, they had nonetheless brought back a descriptive analogy where the racial ideas of a mongrel Mexico connected to animal lives.

Because indigenous and the rural poor (often conflated) depended on hunting for subsistence, the imposition of new laws and antagonistic discourses cannot be separated from broader efforts to disentail them from their ways of life.[81] Freedom of mobility, the carrying of arms, the taking of game, and the maintaining of cultures and traditions were all at stake. Legislators made use of the hunters' disdain to justify measures against traditional hunting not to simply press control over reluctant populations, but also to further the development of public lands.[82] Beyond this, as peasants lost the commons, they contributed to the labor available for hacendados and the other powerful rich in the countryside.[83] As a part of how the liberal state created security (in the sense of fixing in place), this worked in tandem with acculturating measures, and of course, with pushing the poor into normalized market relations.[84] While none of this represents entirely new ground, perhaps, the ways that conservationist discourses constrained subsistence hunters and facilitated this system of dispossession has been little considered.[85]

The imagined wilderness wandered by this exemplar of the sportsman's creed had little basis in reality. Yet the code informed a general shift away from accessibility of game animals for the poorer quarters and indigenous hunters. Modernizing the nation and elite practices called for the assimilation and integration of the indigenous into so-called civilized economies and into mandatory consumption. It would thus reorganize socio-spatial relations and regularize "cognitive geographies"—in other words, it reshaped ecological understandings.[86] The rules made hunted food into exotic meats suitable for a sophisticate and turned indigenous foodways into backward and primitive desperations.[87] The sportsman, as model, fashioned himself in law and literature as the "Other" to Mexico's less fortunate majority of subsistence-level indigenous. Huntsmen changed little in the years following the Mexican Revolution of 1910–1920.

Arturo Imaz Baume's 1948 work alternated his discussions of conservation and animals with decades of stories (both his and from others). He featured tales from many military men featuring dramatic snake and bear encounters. In other ways it followed many of the formulas of our other hunter-authors. He describes the ideal of the good hunter, the hardships and rewards of the expedition, and his vision of the hunter in society.

He began similarly to the others with an invocation sent out to true hunters, and discussion of how the hunt makes man civilized.[88] The good hunter loved his dogs, and knew to use them, especially for *jabalí*.[89] His idea of the good hunter and moral ecology derived from certain "unwritten laws" of hunting, customs of law, respect for old hunters, giving right of way, camping politely, and gunfire safety.[90] For example, among these ideas, he believed that wounded animals belonged to the first hunter who shot it. He calls this the *moral law* or *hunter's law*, and he connected the hunter's overall respect for laws to the cause of conservation.[91] Coming later in the century, he also set hunting into a discourse about animal cruelty using the bullfight as a foil to justify his practice.[92] Cruelty to animals played on hunters' emotions, setting the cruel against the sensitive among those who witnessed what he called the "painful spectacle." Nonetheless, he argued, prey animals had many natural predators and bullets killed more humanely than tooth and claw.[93] He also discussed hunting as necessary at times, as with destructive rabbits.[94] Still, at times hints of conscience or buck fever seemed briefly to trouble him. At one point he mused, "What right do I have to kill so beautiful a creature?" But then he did so, shooting a deer with a dumdum expansive bullet.[95]

One difference from the earliest tales reflected the increasing prevalence of hunting laws. Imaz clearly states that the good hunter must follow all the laws, where Blazquez still favored the use of a moral compass. To Imaz, poachers were pirates, and all hunters hated the use of the armada against ducks.[96] While he acknowledged that different regions had their own preferences for hunting methods (whether blinds, calling, running to hounds, etc.), he also adhered to the idea that stalking remained the only proper way to do things.[97] He nevertheless confessed that he had broken laws by using lantern (*linterna y con reclamas*) in a hunt.[98]

He differed in other small ways as well. Imaz and his storytellers made few mentions of indigenous or campesino hunters, and only in one tale does a native appear and he was a modern border-crossing Kikapoo most notable for his love of American Chesterfield cigarettes.[99] In contrast to the rather pretentious class claims in other accounts, Imaz and his fellow hunters had a rough edge. He equated the fans of corridas, boxing, football, and hunting with one trait—they all used a lot of bad language.[100] He specifically also argued that hunters should generally stay sober, or at least, somewhat so.[101] That said, he also believed that a ration of four beers a day in camp meant the party had fallen on low rations, and that pulque was acceptable if shots of hard liquor topped the drinks up.[102]

Indeed, camp provisions had simplified somewhat over the years. His lists included evaporated milk, coffee, eggs, rice, potatoes, onions, fruits, sweets, flour, spices, and of course, beer.[103] He also favored eating game in the field, whether hares or the delicious (in his words) armadillo.[104] He believed that the key to a good hunting camp came in finding compatible companions who shared in the overall experience, even if the hunter actually stalked alone.[105]

In the tales of Imaz and his contributors, danger added drama as usual. Added to the perils of beasts and weather, some of their hunts took place in areas actively at war. For example, they relate how "savage" Yaquis shot at them, though they do not bother to mention this took place during the ongoing Revolution.[106] Imaz seemed to fear other hunters most of all and made numerous calls for better gun discipline and awareness. There appeared to be little risk in big game hunts, perhaps because

FIGURE 6.3. Unknown, "Arturo Imaz con un jabalí," Arturo Imaz Baume, *Cacería*, 2nd ed. (Mexico City: Secretaría de Educación Pública, 1949), 121. Photo.

these had become staged with spotlights for jaguars or pumas, and traps for bears.[107] Some threat appeared in the form of coyotes or wolves, but only due to rabies.[108]

In contrast, and possibly due to a small phobia of the author, a significant part of the book covers dangerous snakes. Imaz devoted a whole chapter to vipers, their bites, effects, and remedies. He had no faith in ranch remedies (which included an alcoholic concoction and a hot bath) and gave some good advice; the bitten hunter should relax, elevate the wound, and see a doctor. He then ruined this advice, by recommending that the victim find someone to suck out the poison.[109] Of course, danger and hardships represented an indispensable part of the experience. Having complaints made it fun, even if it did not seem so at the time. As he once declared at the end of tough trip, "!Quién demonios inventó la cacería!" (Who the hell invented the hunt!).[110]

For nearly a century, the stolidly conservative world of the modern hunter scarcely changed. The spokesmen demanded that hunters take care of their guns and dogs and beware of bandits and biting creatures, and that they drink and dine at nights while spinning yarns. Over time their language changed somewhat, with more attention to law, conservation, and cruelty, and moving slowly away from overt negative comments about the indigenous. Dangers had shifted a little, but as always, the three real challenges (as Imaz stated) remained: getting lost in the wilds, finding the prey, and hauling dead deer back to campsite.[111] Most importantly, the moral ecology of the elite mestizo huntsmen came over time to blend with ideas from state and scientists to become the new political ecology of conservation.

Hunting Laws Abroad

Conservation laws in Mexico's northern neighbors had already long worked to enforce power over nature and the rural populace. They facilitated, perhaps unintentionally, the forces of colonization and imperialism, and they shaped the cultural practices of hunting.[112] In contrast to some ideal of a generally unpeopled wilderness, scholars turned their attention to the ways that killing animals in those places mattered to the young nation-state. Tina Loo argues that the difference in terminology used to describe and categorize animals represented an ideology inherent to state interventions in attitudes.[113] *Wild, tame, domestic, vermin,* and *game* thus help in formation of a normative agenda with implications for inclusive citizenship and local knowledge. Paternalistic states set restrictions on taking prey that related to racial understandings of animal use and to national claims of ownership over land and beasts held in a common patrimony. Looking at the rise of game wardens in Canada since 1909, she points to how loss of game animal access pushed indigenous populations into a state of dependency or, at best, a limited living as guides for outside hunters.[114] In this scenario, local (racialized) knowledge became a commodity for the wider market, and, indeed, animals themselves became yet another simple product.[115] Game laws become class injustice.[116]

As part of the new economy and biopower, wild animals became property. Both Louis Warren and Karl Jacoby persuasively argue that this drive toward market capitalism drove hunting laws in the United States with deeper racial motivations justified on the nation-state's claim to ownership over all lands and animals.[117] Animals represented the focal point of colonial conflicts and the key to establishment of the idea of frontier.[118] The discourse of "progress" depended on a movement toward enclosure, where hunting led to livestock and farms, and eventually to an industry associated with frontier mythologies. In this, "the freedom to hunt will bring ruin to all" and so the regime would attempt to regulate commons against the will of local communities by dividing them on basis of class, race, gender, and generation.[119] The nation-state staked its claim to animals as a national good or commodity for sportsman against local subsistence or market hunters. To accomplish this, the government applied permits and laws against poaching, grazing, and logging. But it did so on terms that privileged racial hegemony. Scholars pointed to anti-immigrant hunting permit requirements in the eastern United States and the selective enforcement of laws in the West against the "unnaturally" skilled indigenous hunters.[120] Part and parcel of this, legislature created the national parks as off-limits, areas of national patrimony to be held in a state of stasis and denied local exploitation.[121]

At least in theory, Mexican laws sought quite similar outcomes in terms of limiting who could use lands, exploit resources, or make wilderness livings. One area of contrast came in enforcing these restrictions effectively as the Mexican government had less capacity to enact laws in the countryside. A second contrast rose from the populations targeted, as Mexican policies targeted a majority indigenous community that had not been relegated to reservations. The end result of this conflict saw interactions with nature heavily controlled and redefined as national issues of power and citizenship.

The use of the commons, especially the game animals, represented one element of this clash along with forest and water uses. Even some elite hunting clubs in Mexico felt that more game meat for the poor would help the country into progress and civilization. They compared their people with Europeans and claimed (somewhat outrageously) that game made up 25 percent of the average diet in Europe in 1910.[122] They mistakenly went on to say that this was not true of Mexico simply because although deer were abundant, they were not allowed for sale in markets, and people had forgotten how to cook it. That hunting and wild meat remained essential to a racial and ethnic identity for the indigenous, they left quite aside—the sportsmen had their own ideas of who should hunt and where. And now with police as a part of the situation, the state had added to their involvement and worked to rid the poor of yet another use of what might be considered local commons. This reformed the terms of capitalism in the countryside.[123]

Society shaped a new political ecology through measures of law. Mexicans proved well aware of the richness of their wildlife, and a book made for natural historians in 1895 detailed the dozens of larger mammals typical to the nation. Coyotes, bison, and grizzlies and their ranges painted a picture of the wild in the imaginations of urban readers. Pumas the authors noted especially as a problem pest due to their aggression and large numbers.[124] In just a few decades, nonetheless, only the coyote would still range in any kind of real numbers. But a consensus appeared that animals represented sources of national wealth and "the common patrimony of Mexicans."[125] For wild animals, nonetheless, problems of overhunting and habitat loss created the conditions for species extinction. Legal solutions proposed to solve this depreciation of nature's assets. Well-intentioned lawmakers and lobbyists worked toward a nomological political ecology burnished with scientific claims and intuitive conservatism. They would be informed by the prominent Mexican huntsmen and the volumes they wrote about their experiences.

The Historical Trajectory of Conservation

Far from some modern imposition, hunting entailed a quintessentially Mexican practice.[126] Wild meat made up a substantial part of the food supply before European contact.[127] In 1540, Spaniards reported with amazement how 15,000 *ojeadores* (scouts) killed 600 deer between dawn to dusk in what the Europeans termed the "traditional exploitation."[128] They noted in the same year how the Spanish already valued the hunting of the desert bighorn sheep, not for meat, but for the prestige of the horns. This continued to be the case through the centuries.[129]

The idea of conservation had long roots. Hunters claimed that conservation gave society a moral virtue and asserted that old indigenous practices stood out in contrast. The true hunter "harvested" his kills without endangering the species.[130] He was not a carnicero (butcher) or *catrin banquetero* (city dandy), and respected laws rather than leaving kills in a pile to show their ferocity.[131] Like other modern hunters, this author started his justification of anti-indigenous conservation measures with an invocation of the perceived abuses rampant since time immemorial. In Mexico, the crown issued the oldest wildlife law in the 1567 Novísima recopilación de las leyes de España.[132] For centuries this law governed, at least theoretically, the colonial hunt.

Conservation laws in the independent nation largely followed suit. The Código Civil in 1870 instituted the first modern hunting laws, and a near identical law followed in 1884. A decree made hunts on public lands subject to policing in 1894 (*Decreto en terrenos baldías*, Chap. IV). The Ministry of Development added to this in 1909, and the Constitution of 1917 (Art. 27) continued in much the same light. In Revolutionary years following, the Directorate of Forestry, Hunting, and Fishing was established in 1918, Presidential Accords added on in 1924, and in 1928 and 1932, and legislators made some alterations to the Civil Code of the Federation. Nonetheless, most new laws changed little in practice, and by the mid-twentieth-century officials still reported that the continuing problem was simply that the Mexicans did not follow the laws.[133] Despite the passage of time, the Porfirian regime's hunting laws from 1894, in fact, continued as the legal basis well into the twentieth century.[134]

At the heart of the new conservation and wildlife laws lay good intentions. Populations of animals could be self-sustaining, protected from overhunting but hunted sufficiently to maintain balances. Some animals, vermin and nuisance, should be hunted without limits. With law enforcement and scientific knowledge, the political ecology could manage the riqueza pública for the good of the nation. Yet some actors needed official constraints.

Illegal hunting and poaching threatened to ruin the wilderness for all. Animals belonged as property to the nation, and so it was a public utility to conserve them and to prohibit commercial hunts.[135] Those people, like the indigenous, who hunted in ways deemed excessive needed to be reined in, according to the new political ecology. This notion applied as well to overly hungry or greedy campesinos and to invading foreigners. Furthermore, new laws echoed the marginalizing of minority hunting groups in other lands (for example, the Italians or rural poor in northeastern United States).[136] The old ideas of conservation had to change with the times.

Official policies on conservation had in fact been the rule since the earliest years of New Spain in the fifteenth century, but by the Porfiriato took on new urgency and intensity. Wildlife laws from the old Novísima recopilación de las Leyes de España combined with scientific prospects, for example, with a medical thesis that stressed the need for forests as a source of public health.[137] The laws continued to make exceptions for animals thought to be dangerous like big cats or bears, being rather pragmatic on these issues. The great course change came with the new Wildlife Law of 1894.

These new regulations marked the evolution of thought toward shifting animals into categories as a basis for control of national resources.[138] Animals became objects of property. The law redefined each animal in accordance with perceived usefulness to the country's requirements for agriculture, security, and commons. Some animals became off limits as farmer's friends due to their role in pollination or insect control. Others termed vermin were subject to no restrictions on their demise. Included among them were all types of cats, crows, possums, raptors, wild pigs, and some farmers wanted to add deer.[139] This could have political ramifications as ranchers viewed predators like wolves as mere vermin and set bounties that defied the word of the law. Perhaps the most consequential new idea was that some animals now became "game." The English term evokes their place in a sport, in play, and changes essential food to mere frivolity. Laws along this nature often became the instruments of class injustice; *game* for one might mean starvation for another.[140] Animal control and wildlife management sought to instill order upon the frontier spaces of Mexico, whether those dwelled a block from the downtown Zócalo or in the middle of the Sierra Madres.[141] The 1894 Code set limits and defined acceptable practices for hunting, and upon the meaning of hunting in a modern nation. It redefined animals themselves and their relationship to man.

Though not well enforced for decades to come, these laws again should be seen as another necropolitical effort to tame humans, and especially to regulate the lower-class men and men of indigenous descent. What did this mean in practice? It prohibited the hunting of certain night birds, songbirds, and those deemed bug-eaters. It specified that the hunters could not take the young, the females, or the very rare breeds. It specified certain animals as highly valued and rare, deserving of preservation as national wealth. Regulators elsewhere made cultural choices as part of an ethic of exploitation that some "wildlife is too important for eating," because it added value to modern life and an antidote to "over-civilizing sterility."[142] It relegated some species to the status of born to die.

Some of this had little to do with scientific conservation since the few who took part in that discourse admitted that most of Mexico teemed with every sort of creature. One visitor pointed to the hundreds of thousands of ducks on Lake Chapala and stated that for hunting all parts of Mexico were comparable to Asia and Africa.[143] Further, the law had no real concern for the subsistence hunter—the category of food animal or different rules for large-scale food hunting were not addressed. Articles banning the use of traps, nets, night lanterns, gun batteries (armadas), dynamite, and poison further sought to eliminate commercial and subsistence hunting in favor of the leisurely sporting of the gentleman.[144] Non-shooting hunting forms became legally prohibited, not for moral or scientific reasons, but because they were the practice of indigenous subsistence gatherers.[145] Easy and high-yield methods now carried stigma and legal bans.

Legislators reimagined hunting itself as unconnected to dietary needs or class customs. The code also demanded that all hunters pay for permits and hunt in appropriate seasons—again privileging the leisured class with money as the poor could not wait seasons for their food, nor purchase permits.[146] As a result, feeding one's family in a traditional way had become an act of poaching, of piracy against nationally owned resource animals. The poor, the lawmakers implied, needed to find sustenance in new ways, modern ways, like working in factories and buying in markets.[147] In this way, the Wildlife Code could be seen as the attempt of state agents to push recalcitrant lower classes, especially the elusive urban "Indian," into a capitalist system that emulated Europe and the United States.

In fact, the entire 1894 Wildlife Code spoke primarily to the construction of a new sportsman and to marginalizing those whose hunting legislators deemed traditional and backward. It dealt with the perception of certain populations of animals as out of control where man could assert himself as the chief predator and regulate problem animals whether bears or deer.[148] The prohibition on taking does and fawns, as an example, appealed to a gendered argument about chivalrous manly hunting far more than it looked to biological rationality.[149] Many in the countryside took game with little concern for "city" rules.

The issue of the rural population recklessly hunting gravely concerned the conservationists. Officials considered these hunters as ignorant at best, and butchers and pirates at worst. In the late 1950s some argued that the predators ate all the good game, but for more, blame fell on furtive campesino hunters without education.[150] These poachers needed government education, to learn not to destroy all the birds and to limit themselves to shooting varmints.[151] According to the prominent Puebla politician Gonzalo Bautista O'Farril, officials needed to educate the rural masses since while the sportsmen can be trained by club peers to "elevate ethical values and cultural superiority" more generally over 80 percent of hunters still had not even a gun license.[152] Said one writer as late as 1995, the campesino hunter posed the principal problem for fauna in general since "they kill for hunger, for necessity, and for love of profits" with a .22, lose two (wounded) for every one killed, and then sell exotic skins in every town.[153] Years later, nothing had changed. A report in 1963 divided hunters into sportsmen, hungry campesinos, campesinos defending their interests (against crop eaters), and commercial hunters.[154] They argued that education ought to come from peers and especially that hunting clubs needed to instill civic consciousness, conservation, and true citizen spirit.[155]

The idea that proper hunters represented Mexicans of better quality and more virtue appeared with some regularity in the conservation reports and legislation. As one example, in the rules for grizzly hunting they specify that Mexican hunters should be older than eighteen, that foreigners needed extra licenses, and that hunters were to be "disqualified by the commission of certain crimes and certain misdemeanors." They specified that this meant no hunter should be "deprived of intelligence by madness, idiotism, or imbecility," nor a drunk or drug addict, on pain of fines from 1,000–15,000 pesos and three years in prison.[156] Genuinely desperate hunting only occasionally earned formal recognition.

A few conservationists in the mid-twentieth century realized that painfully real hunger could drive the rural hunter in ways that no education or extra regulation could stop. In so doing, they opened a small space room to alternative moral ecologies. The rural poor had needs: "In our country there is still poverty, and our country men are obliged to satisfy by any means the urgent needs of the family, and they use even the most primitive systems to bring into their homes the meat, the skin, and, if possible, other offal that will serve to produce their well-being."[157] According to the same report in 1958, the national territory was 15 percent agricultural, 44 percent livestock use, 34 percent forest, and 7 percent useless.[158] Considering this dearth of farmland, what were the hungry to do? Added to this, the weakness of law enforcement made choices clear. The author admitted the impossibility to enforce protections (*coto*) against ranches where groups enjoyed total "privilege," nor against the ignorant, uneducated, and hungry. He pointed out that deer cost nothing, while a calf costs 500–600 pesos. He added that draconian conservation laws sounded like imperialism and needed to be run democratically (e.g., by ejidos), or they would face justifiable opposition.[159]

A different conservationist sounded more resigned noting that many hunters mistakenly kill the wrong animals, and the great mass of campesinos had serious protein deficiencies. Thus, it seemed reasonable that out-of-season or illegal hunting took place. He did go on to state that it was not fair to other (legal non-local) hunters since these rural dwellers know the land so well and were always there (not just on brief vacations), and so they could easily hunt it out.[160] An observer during the Revolution noticed that peons still had little meat in their diet, aside from what could be hunted.[161] If nothing else, meat recovered from poachers had an official use as early as 1918. Legally, all recovered poached meat went straight to prisons and hospitals or public beneficiaries.[162]

The conservationists also had some nuance to their ideas beyond blaming everything on poachers. Many had seen commercial hunters as especially pernicious since early on. Frequent laws forbade the use of armadas to take down flocks of migrating fowl. As in 1884 and 1894, a law in 1918 set fees on armada hunting and for overkill (five- to ten-pesos fines).[163] During the armed phase of the Revolution and in years immediately after, numerous laws came out to limit the impact of commerce. A decree suspended export of birds in 1923—due to them being a part of the "natural wealth"—especially quail and partridges, and extended the ban on beaver hunting from 1909.[164] In 1926, they prohibited the sale of commercial quail meat to hotels or restaurants, without proper permitting.[165] The attempts seem to have had limited effects, since over one hundred ducks a week were being taken just twenty minutes from the capital, sometimes with a thousand shot at a time and sold to restaurants despite laws.[166] The commercial hunters focused especially on ducks and feathers, but also took hides and some meat from other animals to markets (the report had no issue with the meat sales, oddly enough).[167] Hunting did have some financial positives.

Nor did the reformers want to see all hunting stop. If only because of the sport's significant economic value, conservationists recognized the limits of their influence. According to an official 1956 report, the national income from hunting, fines, taxes, products, and sales of permits reached 8 million pesos in 1956, or one-ninth Mexico's income.[168] Additionally, the nation boasted more than a million hunters: "It is a growing and necessary recreation for the modern man."[169] In terms of balance, problems of conservation could not necessarily be remedied by law enforcement. According to the experts, even though habitat destruction could be identified as the most pernicious problem in conservation, game laws needed proper administration.[170] Unfortunately, they claimed, this meant hiring as many police as there were hunters, an impossibility, and so they shifted the responsibility to clubs and associations to take an active role.[171] Many types of illegal activity came in ways beyond any club or police force's ability to curb. For example, eventual overhunting of certain ungulates resulted from the use of automobiles, which provided poachers with easy access and escapes.

Slow changes to the laws did add at least to the types and numbers of protected animals and limited the kinds of hunting methods. Laws banned traps and restricted hunters to use only guns or knives, even if they set no season on dangerous animals or vermin.[172] Antelope and wild sheep hunting they banned by 1909.[173] Deer hunting became limited in Baja California, Coahuila, and Chihuahua in 1924.[174] Specific seasons and regulations for everything from swans to howler monkeys to whitetail deer to squirrels to coyote, and the numbers of kills permitted, covered all the wildlife in Mexico by the 1960s.[175] In tandem with these rules, and to quell civil conflicts, efforts led to increased gun controls.

Legislators in the aftermath of the years of Revolution and ongoing Cristero War, also used conservation regulations to adjust some limits on firearms in 1929. Hunters could claim an exemption from normal arms laws but had to carry weapons openly.[176] By midcentury, Mexicans had limited rights to have guns for self-defense (unless serving in army), but they needed a police permit to carry arms, unless they had a hunting license from government.[177] This, of course, cost money, as did the other requirements for hunting, and licensing remained a practical obstacle to actually getting campesino or indigenous obedience to the laws. Joining a club or association for hunting and association could get one licenses and arms permits, but meant a fee paid directly to government.[178] These and other costs reached prohibitive levels (as proposed by conservationists): for a hunting license, they suggested 120 pesos a year if in club, 150 if not, and for foreigners 1,500 pesos for a six-month permit. Beyond this they suggested special permits including 30 pesos for whitetail deer, 10 pesos for jabalí, and guide licenses would cost 10 pesos.[179] Only officially approved hunting would remain legal.

The efforts had limited impact on poachers and continued overhunting continued to appear in reports. One issue, beyond the diminishing numbers of some animals (and extinctions of others, like the grizzly) was that modern hunting brought hunters more easily to remote areas. By early century this meant rail, in later years automobiles provided access.[180] For the most threatened game, like the *borrega desierto* (desert sheep), their numbers diminished quickly—in 1922 there were 25,000, in 1936 15,000, in 1947–1949 between 2,000 to 8,000. The building and use of new roads exacerbated this, since, according to reports "a big issue was car hunting."[181] Remote areas had their own lawless experiences, for example, hungry cowboys in the Sierra de Mamulique trapped or poisoned and eventually shot (with .22 and .30-30 rifles) fourteen black bears.[182] Likewise, private lands also saw little enforcement, according to one report, and on rented ejido lands it became common to see outside hunters taking six deer each.[183]

Mexico's great wealth in wild animal populations proved the one positive upside for the conservation movement, even if perhaps a temporary one. According to one estimate, twenty-one million ducks migrated through each year.[184] According to deer distribution mapping in 1950, whitetail were still widespread and numerous.[185] The experts nonetheless pointed out the overhunting of the deer as something "uncontrolled and irrational."[186] Yet according to constitutional lawyer Carlos Sánchez Mejarada in 1966, Pachuca abounded with deer, hare, and rabbits, and these used to be shot right in the street.[187] He added, "And I do not think you can punish a poor Indian, a poor *ejiditario* dying of hunger, because he kills a pregnant female."[188] Other smaller game animals have likewise done fine, but the big cats grow scarce and some animals like the Mexican wolf or grizzly were effectively extinct in the nation early in the century. The government did eventually set some effort to problems of hunting and conservation, particularly by 1955, but claimed that it still was not on US levels at that point.[189] Despite all their laws, and a certain degree of scarcity, poached meat reportedly remained common in the rural diet in 1988.[190]

How well, or if at all, the laws affected conservation seems quite questionable. The significance of these attempts reflected changes in managing human-animal relations, and in both the moral and political ecology. It became—de jure, if not de facto—the province of the public officials to maintain new laws and to intervene in animal executions.

Conclusions

Mexican game hunters played a crucial role in the forming of ideas about wildlife and conservation laws. Limited numbers of vocal professed hunters, who worked out ideas within their own community, spun tales that pre-echoed conservationist aspirations. This created a basis for the state to lay claim over the public riches of the wilds. Sportsmen exercised tremendous influence over how emerging conservationists viewed the hunt. Their tales of masculine heroism and hardship created common ideals, and their associations or clubs defined for wider society who should count as a good hunter.

Those appointed to government positions in conservation drew on the sportsmen's worldviews and naturalism as they set up laws to preserve or cull animal populations. Those creatures who did not increase the national wealth and those who hunted the wrong way, like many indigenous peoples, became Others, pirates, and prey. Efforts to legally control and preserve populations failed to save Mexican grizzlies or bison, and many other creatures faced near extinction. This may have been inevitable, but more crucial to this discussion, the choices made by officials did carry weight. Despite disparate views relating to race or class, hunting laws in general exacerbated the dispossession of the poor and indigenous. They became the assumed enemy of rational practices. The resources allotted, the spaces conserved, and hunting policies all rose from cultural constructions tied back to the sportsman. Some animal death died not from rifles but as prey to the pens of bureaucrats.

The sportsman ideal set out a figure rife with fantasies and artificial memories. As the self-professed and appointed steward of nature he set the rhetorical limits and definitions for proper hunting practices. The hunter, his coteries, and his associations, set an internationally recognized image of the hunt that built into legal efforts almost word for word. Few lobbyists could have dreamed of this level of influence or efficacy.

The organizing of death in the wild places of the land fell clearly into necropolitical systems and their logics. A sportsmen culture played a crucial role in shaping the language and assumptions and images that laid the foundation for the legal efforts that made the death of wild animals a bureaucratic matter. The political ecology of the "nature state," infused with logics that sorted out and justified killing the Other, became synonymous with the scientifically worded and humanitarian conservationist movement. If it seemed beyond reproach and of the highest ideals and used objective language, conservation practices nonetheless remained cold to animals as subjects. Utilitarian and necropolitical logics not only permitted, but actively encouraged, a seemingly necessary culling of herds.

Conservationist efforts that followed represented a political ecology with few teeth. Well-intentioned, and not inherently inferior to the moral ecologies of other communities, the drive to limit the hunt nonetheless had negative aspects. The legal and scientific discourse formed another facet of colonization and normalized necropolitics, even if the government found game laws difficult to implement.[191] Ideals came easy, rural law enforcement not so much. Reports lamented the continued diminishing of species each year. Lack of resources in this, as with so many Mexican laws, meant that little accomplishment occurred in timely fashion. Skilled mestizo huntsman and conservationists, of course, did not constitute all those who took game in the wilds or fought to preserve it.

Indigenous peoples, foreign expeditions, and elite politicians brought their own ideas toward nature and the hunt in cultures alien to that of the sportsman.

CHAPTER SEVEN

Imperial Huntsmen and Missionaries of Death

Colonizing Practices, Indigenous Ways, and Symbolic Big Game

> Humanity in nature has never constituted one empire within the other; not being the image of nature, or above it, humanity is integrated into the intimate heart of nature.[1]

Bottles of fine red burgundy and a clean white tablecloth covered the heavy wooden table set out in the middle of the forest. The prey of the day, not yet prepared for eating, hung nearby. Intrepid hunters awaited a multiple course meal of French cuisine as they recovered from the day's exertions. Servitors, tired from a long day of beating the bush to flush game, hurried to bring the meal to politicians busy gossiping and networking. Photographers attended. The native guides, once free of duties, had returned to their local villages with small fees, perhaps some meat. When opportunity presented, they took their own small game as they wandered home. Meanwhile, the heroic hunter at the table's head regaled all with tales of daring pursuits and masculine achievements. Sharp differences marked the ravine between the ceremonial and the practical kill.

The "subtle ritual" of hunting carried significant cargo as a practice and a pageant. For indigenous and rural communities, the hunt tied into historical identities and ways of life. Hunting put meat on tables, protected crops, and affirmed masculine norms. It built on subjectivities while meeting subsistence needs. For the upper crust of hunters, the wealthy and the foreign, the hunt became a performance of tales and taxidermies. Big-game hunting's importance proved more symbolic than economic.[2] In contrast to the moral ecologies (and economies) of other classes, travelers and local elite hunted purposefully without need. Indeed, the need to hunt obviated its meaning for them. The wealthy made use of new roads and rails, they hired and denigrated locals as guides, and when the hunts ended, they refashioned them into legend. Trophies created significance and fostered remembrance. The appraisal of naturalists and hunters from abroad spoke to a vision of Mexican nature and the nature of Mexico.

At these levels, the biopolitics of the nation turned from law to art. The power of performing in the self-colonization of the nation allowed elites to repurpose an indigenous practice and its products as the exclusive rightful property of powerful non-indigenous men. The "kill" as a pure cultural artifact became limited to certain groups as a privilege of their social standing, and one enforced not just by laws but by norms and established power.[3]

The fetish performs a central role in this wilderness arena, setting the distance between the living animal and the commodity that it became in death. Subsistence hunters, increasingly bound by laws, remained closely linked to the animal and the meat it became. On the other end of the spectrum, game and trophy hunters reconstructed the animal as a fetish fantastically removed from its environs and origin. Taxidermized mounts and embellished tales reflected the enormous disconnect between the simulacrum of life and the death that had been wrought. In the Marxist sense, the distance between production and commodity echoed in the creation of the symbolic trophy. Symbolism and moral ecology interweaved, because the meanings of the kill became imbricated with the power of the necropolitical to erase the subject.[4] The animal as living, breathing, and conscious creature became a representation of imperial male power. Its new existence, as story, as carpet, as decor, proved the legitimacy of its execution, and by extension, that of its killers.

The efforts at limiting hunters through legislative dispossession and the necropolitical logics of conservation laws presumed a great deal about those who would do the hunting. This chapter moves beyond the "normal" sportsman class to address the indigenous, the foreign, and the imperial as exceptional cases. I argue that the clash between different views of the hunt manifested in areas of colonizing and self-colonizing where necropolitics inscribed power on bodies and, at times, with bodies. In the animals' case, the colonial fantasies did not dream of extermination but of sustainable, indeed, continuous, potential for killing. The imperial hunts also turned the impulses that hid the death of animals in the market on their head. In this realm, killing became authentic and legitimate representations of power. This became made most visible and made permanent in taking trophies or in photographic memory.

This chapter outlines some general aspects of indigenous and rural hunts before turning to the perspectives of travelers and the highest circles of Mexican elites. It culminates with how President Porfirio Díaz performed an imperial hunt as an orchestrated political argument. This became, perhaps, a metaphor for his doomed thirty-seven-year dictatorship. The dismissive political ecologies of the rich stood in stark contrast to the sometimes destructive moral ecologies of the poor. Wild animals died either way.

Indigenous Hunts–Perspectives from the "Missionaries of Death"

Taking game provided the poor both identity and livelihood everywhere in the country. So long as old ways and visible poverty continued, the government could make little claim that they had succeeded in their positivist mantra of "order and progress." In the countryside, life remained closer to the natural sources. Outsiders noted campesinos in Michoacan (and elsewhere) as being "always with their dogs." Clearly, the dog had a privileged place in rural lives. Similarly, guns had a big place, and one charro mentioned how, when the Revolution came, he went to war "with the arms that all the ranchers had."[5] Animals in rural places became at times the pawn of politics and war. In Porfirian times (and earlier), hacendados seized animals to cover debts and maintain peonage. During times of warfare the various armies seized *zarate* (fodder) and animals including cattle as they foraged for supplies.[6]

In rural farm areas the poor rarely got meat, according to one observer, and yet deer hunting remained an essential form of life for many living outside the farm and industrial systems.[7] Even more so, hunting represented a spiritual activity to many with ties to an indigenous past that they valued.[8] An example of this from the Yucatán was the continued inheritances of the *tunich keh* hunting charms among Maya, a group whose livelihood officials increasingly saw as poaching against the national preserve.[9] Across the nation, native peoples continued to seek game.

The dangers of generalizing and creating categories for indigenous hunters abound, and finding some overarching moral ecology seems destined for failure.[10] What might apply, generally, boiled down simply to the notion of local knowledge and the use of commons. More to the point perhaps, similarities appeared in the great suspicion and disdain that many in society held for indigenous peoples. The Guadalajara press, for instance, made it clear that to readers that civilization was urban society while "the rest was barbaric."[11] This particularly applied to warlike natives, and the government constructed the Yaqui as a criminal Other.[12] Such a mentality led to military leaders to call for a war of extermination to eradicate certain groups including the Yaqui.[13] Dispossession from the commons articulated with a necropolitical regime and a liberal rhetoric that restricted indigenous foodways or cultures.

Those outside indigenous communities also at times mistook poverty for differences in taste, claiming without basis that the native population had no desire for meat to eat. Taking their observations further, the press in Guadalajara asserted that vegetarian diets was a symptom of indigenous backwardness, and one that often paired with alcoholism. In one step more, they adopted a Lamarckian view that indigenous diets of vegetables meant they were fated to a life as beasts of burden.[14] Likely not limited to this city, the idea that indigenous diets reflected who they were essentially seemed widespread.[15] Hunting and eating game meat surely follows.

From the perspective of city dwellers and visitors to the countryside, the indigenous hunters occupied two contradictory positions. On the one hand, many critics deemed natives as ignorant barbarians that slaughtered animals indiscriminately and wastefully. This demonstrated to their eyes a people unfit to hunt since they proved unable to follow the basic rules and in their wanton ways they depleted the stock of game. At the same time as these commentators derided indigenous people as "bad" hunters, they nonetheless also called for tougher laws to limit indigenous hunting because of their unfair advantages in skill and knowledge. They pointed to how these hunters succeeded all too well because of their intimate knowledge of the terrain and creatures, their near-supernatural skills of stalking and tracking inherited from cultural upbringings, and their living year-round near to the hunting sites. They rarely mentioned that indigenous hunger also proved a great motivator for successful and patient hunting. As such, they portrayed the native hunter as both a terrible and terrific hunter, and in either case sought to have them stopped.

The paradox for indigenous hunters rose from the double standards of racism. Expected to be exceptionally skilled at taking game, the idea that native hunters lived particularly close to nature led some to overvalorize their abilities and helped to make indigeneity a category in recovery narratives.[16] As an exception to hunting laws, that the Tarahumara (Rarámuri) depended still on hunted pheasants as an important food source was acknowledged by officials.[17] Yet the image presented still could have shades of the past or simplicity, as when foreign travelers noted what they termed "true Indian hunting," or commented on a Rarámuri hunting with a bow and arrow and his wolflike dog.[18] According to another visitor, natives hunted ducks at Patzcuaro with a only canoe and a club.[19] In another example, one man remembered how important game meat remained in everyday survival, enough so that hunting overlapped with ongoing struggles of the Yaqui against the government.[20]

An understanding of indigenous hunting sets a counterpoint to the legalist and idealized conservation movements.[21] It represented a moral ecology against the political ecology. Again, this is not to assert a value of good or bad to either notion, but rather a way to examine conflicts between traditional and community-based ways of seeing nature against the opposition from modernist and external sets of relations. This did not exclude possibilities of discriminatory and exclusive practices within a community, or the adherence to parochial values.[22] The imposition of conservation or other legal limitation from the outside highlights the degree to which culture mediates different understandings of a natural world and the animals within it.

This is also not an argument for some unchanging or closed corporate community model of the indigenous world. Certainly, there existed intermediary groups, mestizo or not, between the local and national. And, certainly, local actors knew and accepted some of the conservationist ideas, and some national actors valued indigenous ways of life.[23] The issues of ecological destruction did not belong to outsiders alone. For example, the Mayo pointed to habitat loss leading as a cause of their hunger in the 1950s, despite conservationist efforts, which they supported.[24] And while I will indulge here in some "upstreaming," it is meant to highlight continuity and persistence, rather than suggesting that indigenous peoples did not change and adapt. In fact, some have argued that indigenous moral ecology can be precisely defined as ways of adaptation and marking change.[25] That all said, I agree with author José E. Martínez-Reyes that the moral ecology of the indigenous hunter may stand as an alternative to the imposed restrictions from the outside interventionist. Taking game provided the indigene both identity and livelihood.[26]

Some generalities set indigenous hunting as different from those evinced by the sportsman. The hunt frequently featured religious elements and supernatural rationalities. Nature and the environment tended not to be seen by the indigenous as separate from the human experience, and so the view of hunting tended to have a holistic quality. Killing for meat occasioned gratitude toward nature and the animal.[27] Customs, rather than science or laws, dictated the appropriateness of hunting. These included notions of sustainability but were often framed in a different language.[28] The hunt itself could not be simply limited to one form of activity, but instead needed to be set in contexts of place, space, season, and community purpose. For example, hunting on the way to work a field played a different role and set of internal logics than did organized expedition hunting that took one away from home for days or weeks. Hunting specific neighboring animals or learning to hunt by trapping smaller prey also had different roles, and they provided different stories.[29] Local groups often built identity around game.

In some regards indigenous hunting had much in common with that of any other groups. The "property" notion of meat (and animals) in indigenous communities often dissolved into common resource use since the food remained a necessary supplement for subsistence areas. This notion holds true in wider rural areas to this day, and so can scarcely be essentially indigenous, but represents yet another piece. One implication of this common property sees the riqueza pública as not the account of the greater nation-state, but held by the local community or even by a particular extended kin network. The indigenous hunt differed little from that of mestizos or foreigners in other ways. The hunt provided a rite of manhood and rights to belong in community. The tale of the chase and its hardships and lessons was as important to natives as to any other hunters. The drama of the hunt mattered for all.

Notably though, the indigenous (and many campesino) hunters differed entirely from the sportsman class in one crucial way. They became the focused subject of laws that made their practices into poaching, and they faced enforcement that criminalized eating game. Archaic means of hunting like bows and arrows became criminal. Modern but pragmatic tools like hunting from cars or using electric lights became criminal. Seasons for hunting legally matched supposedly scientific rules, rather than times of need. Hunger does not scruple to avoid poison unless luxury rules the land. The clear superiority of the indigenous hunter became illegal too. Lawmakers specifically declared it injustice since these locals knew the land and could hunt every day. That they grew up there and had no means to leave became the reason why their hunting should not be permitted.[30] That most foreign expeditions apparently faced even fewer limitations added insults to injuries and imposed a different political ecology yet again.

Hunted by Aliens

Travelers found Mexico full of exotic dangers and tantalizing opportunities to adventure. Even visiting a common village held perils. One recounted witnessing a fierce wild boar charging out of nearby jungle brush. As the town panicked, local dogs rallied to rescue a young girl certain to be killed by the animal. In the same normal town, the next day the visitor watched as townsfolk shot an intruding deer shot and immediately sold its meat in the market.[31] To outside eyes, Mexico held a wealth of nature that tempted those seeking new hunting grounds.

The starkest contrast to indigenous ways can be seen in how foreign adventurers came to kill Mexican animals. In addition to toxic racial ideas, imperialist expectations, and far too much cash, these hunters imported their own brand of political ecology. They came to the sport imbued with ideologies about social hierarchies and necropolitical fantasies about how the death of animals (or even some people) mattered or not. This, not surprisingly, eventually proposed strong elements of local conservation and sustainability that would allow them to continue hunting abroad in perpetuity. They also told tall tales like any other hunter.

Although many stories brought in different experiences, these tales also had some common facets. The hunters commented on how locals did their hunting and how they acted in nature, and so gives us some sense of moral ecologies. They tied these to racial ideas quite often, and in a shift from the sportsmen, they frequently lauded the indigenous hunter even as they racially dismissed them.[32] Mestizos they commented on in almost purely negative ways, denigrating even their hunting guides.[33] They did, nonetheless, show rhetorical respect for Mexican animals, even as they hunted them into extinction.

Foreigners often remarked on the abundance and variety of Mexican wildlife. One said that in terms of zoology, the large mammals were very rare, but they had many black bears, deer, coyote, otters, skunks, and so on. They also had centipedes up to eighteen inches long.[34] Travelers in Yucatán spotted "many large panthers, tigers, and lions."[35] Likewise, another was told of "woods teeming with deer, boar, pheasant ... game of every description."[36] Still in the southeast, one told how people there hunted alligators and caimans, ate a lot of these, and as a result were the healthiest people in the state.[37] The explorer described how a "dark-skinned mozo" hunted a fourteen-foot alligator with only a dagger, as a sort of casual demonstration![38] One claimed as well that Mexico had a four-nosed snake featuring sixteen fangs.[39] In the north, William Thomas claimed that the area between Sonora and Chihuahua had abundant game, but also "bad Indians."[40] One visitor, perhaps blessed with great luck, proclaimed the docility of all Mexican beasts claiming that even the rattlers at Chapala did not bite.[41] While this latter claim seems dubious, travelers believed in the great natural wealth of wild creatures in Mexico.

All the stories featured their hardships and the extreme difficulties that they faced due to poor help, dangerous creatures, and most often, insufficient comforts. In this they accorded with hunters everywhere: hunting was a thing with dangers, sacrifices, and discipline—the furtive hunter was not one.[42] They all created a clear sense of Otherness. They found that the more unusual of animals the better, they highlighted the enormous cultural differences they found (or implied), and above all, they all proclaimed that Mexicans could not be entrusted with their own conservation or hunting. The usual condescension applied to encounters with Mexican officials.

Despite relatively casual gun laws within Mexico, foreign expeditions did encounter stiffer controls at the borders. This came in part due to persistent rebellions in the northwest of the country, particularly the Yaqui and Mayo of the sierras, and in part due to the opportunism of guards seeking quick money.[43] The law permitted visitors to enter country duty-free with two pistols, a rifle, and four hundred rounds, but officials often required fees or bonds from the hunters and even held guns at border (requiring foreigners to acquire new weapons in Mexico).[44] Some hunters seem to have eased their way by appealing to higher authorities, and in the acknowledgments of their books explicitly thanked (and name-dropped) Mexican presidents, Ulysses S. Grant, and powerful landholders like Enrique Creel.[45] One party in 1906 had difficulty bringing guns across border, where guards feared the weapons would end up in hands of the Yaqui uprising.[46] Watchers at the border also seem to have required or encouraged foreigners to hire guides, some of whom proved inadequate.

In Donald Carpenter's *Hunting Big Game in the Sierras of Chihuahua*, his discussions of their hunting guide Valentine illuminated the gulf between foreigner and Mexican. In what he termed "mañana land," he and two friends did a ten-day expedition during which they shot six deer (over 700 lbs. of weight), and unsuccessfully sought cougars and turkeys.[47] To assist them they had hired a guide, who also dressed the kills and did some of the cooking. In Carpenter's words, Valentine "a

Peon, owns no home and few personal effects," and lived a life of continuous poverty and drudgery to eke out an existence. Previously a cowboy and a frontiersman, he now guided occasional hunting parties for fair pay.[48] His appreciation of the guide, without whom the trip would have failed, did not take away from the pitying tone he chose. On its own this might have been fine, but when Valentine made them tortillas in place of plain flapjacks, they proclaimed him the "king of bread-makers" in what comes across as condescension.[49] In this marvel Carpenter's party proved fortunate. In a different case, hunters hired a self-professed game warden, "a Yankee charlatan," who asked for four dollars a day to hunt javelina, mountain lions, or deer. With no success at all, the party ended up dismissing him.[50] Truly local guides did seem to facilitate success, and wild tales proved it.

The book *Mexican Game Trails* compiled a variety of hunting tales written by travelers and published in American periodicals between the 1860s and 1930s. Rather than spoil their stories or try to fully recount their sordid adventures, the following selections reveal a political ecological sensibility and how the foreigners set up broader patterns.

An early visitor offers the first vision of this wild wild west. In 1879 an American hunter named Wallace visited one of the hacendados where he found them quite caught up in hunting deer, wolves, and "untamable Indians," especially Apache, Comanche, and Lipan.[51] Many of the landholders continued old Iberian traditions with elaborate hunting shows on their massive tracts of wild and farmed territory. The collection of hounds and horses became as much part of the charro outfit as his silvered sombrero and guns.[52] A decent sombrero, by itself, could go for thirty pesos or the equivalent of a good month's salary for a skilled servant. The hunting entourage included a minimum of three servants (mozos) who were local "Indians" at home with the "highways of the desert" and who would shelter the intrepid sportsman from bandits and "bad Indians." In Wallace's words, while at the hunt (and while protected from Indians by Indians) "the conduct of man was never more instinctive." His account in *Scribner's Magazine* also made much hilarity of stampeding a herd of bison over a hidden "thieving Apache" who had been trying to get close to the party (or likely, to hunt his own food).[53] The old guard, like the Terrazas families, continued to run their lands as a personal game reserve complete with indigenous extras, and to some degree this situation would not abate until well into the twentieth century.[54]

Other foreign hunters in years to come focused more on complaining about the hardships they faced in pursuing their sacred right to hunt. At times this could be quite mundane, as in Carpenter's trip where he complains about riding his horse (Muchacho Negro) too long for comfort, and spending a night and a day stuck in a rainy camp.[55] Frederick Schwatta on an 1890 hunting trip for peccary in Sonora complained about having to run a mongrel or cur, but at least, in his mind, his Cuban bloodhound proved capable.[56] Others agreed with this view of Mexican hunting dogs, as William Bergtold who commented that all dogs in country were worthless and called Pancho, and overall, did no good for people.[57] Artist and journalist Frederic Remington, writing for *Harper's Magazine*, complained during a quail-hunting trip at Eagle's Pass in October of 1896. His protest was quite understandable—hunting quail was boring, they mostly just drank heavily, and not unrelated, he did not care for the early mornings required.[58] The worst of all possible bourgeois hardships that might befall the otherwise prepared hunter caught up with Humphrey in 1909 as he pursued (illegally, one might note) bighorn sheep in Baja California. To his dismay, and that of his accompanying wife, they found themselves in the wilderness without a proper tablecloth. Fortunately for the man, his wife nonetheless persevered on the trip and did all the camp chores.[59] The dangers of the wilderness seem formidable.

Foreign hunters did pursue a great variety of game, and not all hunters complained over trifles or faced merely insignificant perils. For instance, Yaqui killed a gringo hunter visiting Tiburón Island in Gulf of California. Animals also presented challenges. Another hunter, Ben Burbridge, went on lion and bear hunt in 1908 in the Sierra Madre Occidental. He took along a North Mexican Mormon as guide (reportedly about 4–5,000 of them in Mexico at the time) and four dogs (two hounds and two shepherds). Despite their extinction status today, Mexicans viewed the mountain lions and bears as vermin at the time. Rather than in complaint, Burbridge claimed that their days were full of "hardships and excitement that a hunter loves."[60] He also always kept his Kodak camera ready, suggesting a somewhat different view of the hunt as an experience that might be memorialized beyond trophies. Carpenter had a frightening moment after shooting a deer, when he became lost in the forest.[61] Other American hunters went south and into tropics, especially in the twentieth century as proper medicine made such trips less suicidal. There, some hunted alligators, ocelots, and iguanas, while some like Emmet R. Blake sought rare birds in 1934. Some faced dangers quite unwittingly.

An unlikely tale by Henry Harper illustrated how enormous luck could save an idiot traveler. Alone, in unfamiliar locale, he went deer hunting at night using a "jack," or a small lamp with reflector on top of head.[62] Seeing eyes shining some 125–150 yards away, he began to become nervous. They approached, and at fifty yards, the eyes appeared to him as being three to four feet apart, suggesting a truly giant creature. He started shooting, blazing away more or less blindly at the unidentified creature. Having lost track of it, he attempted to return to his camp but became lost and wandered in the darkness for some time before reaching safety. The next day he followed vultures back to the site and found a large dead jaguar.[63] Although he acknowledged some luck, it bordered on the miraculous that he had even seen the cat and survived it, let alone killed it.

Even for foreigners, the advent of the new political ecology and conservation laws did have some impact. The hunt became more limited, and more expensive, and expectations for behavior began to matter. With no coercions, while hunting desert sheep in 1911, Kermit Roosevelt refused to be unsportsmanlike. With the animals in sight, he held his fire rather than shooting them while they used a watering hole.[64] The same animals became highly protected in the following years. In a later instance, by the time Dale Lee went after increasingly rare jaguars in Sonora in 1935, that sort of hunt had become the preserve of only the rich and famous.[65] Yet their favored status and implied power also meant that foreign hunters often chose to act as they saw fit, rather than being plainly bound by the law.

The imperious attitudes of these hunters, even in those with the most benign commentaries, implied their superiority and civilized position. The killing of Mexican wildlife, in their eyes, belonged not simply to the nation but to some broader abstract community. Not so differently, the most powerful and wealthy elite in Mexico brought their own imperialism to their own understandings of the hunt.

Old Dogs, Not-so-new Tricks

A self-proclaimed hunter held the highest post of the nation. For men like President Porfirio Díaz, the hunt provided an opportunity for show—a theater for expressing one's manly prowess, and wealth, and connections to power.[66] Elite networking had always been implicit in participating in the hunt.[67] Sending invitations for him to go on an expedition, something easily delivered by private post or even by telephone, prospective hosts instead published in the big newspapers where all the president's literate subjects could note his manliness.[68] This also offered political capital for the host, of course. Such a trip did, nonetheless, entail a degree of expense. The president did not travel outside the city without a guard of at least fifty, plus his entourage, and general staff, and often his son Porfirio Junior.[69] The affair built prestige with pomp.

The elite classes used the hunt as a theater to display power. Through an orchestrated death ritual, their social inferiors could see the justification for hierarchy echoed in the resulting trophies. Even worse, some of servant classes had to carry the spoils home for the lucky hunter.[70] The taxidermist's art became the centerpiece to the hacienda decor, with stuffed animals featuring in all the wealthiest homes of the nation. The trophy itself as an object of fetish, a piece of bourgeois masculinity made into decor, applied as much in Mexico as elsewhere.[71] The complete lack of dietary necessity for the hunt only added to its theatrical element.[72] Notably, this recreational pattern did not apply evenly across Mexico, where decimated indigenous populations still lived on hunting throughout the colonial and national periods (and in some regions continue to do so). As theater the hunt had implications.

For leaders like Díaz, the hunt and the associated opportunity for networking had compelling appeal. Having come to the presidency by coup and holding it by force, the semi-lettered venerable warrior realized that the support of this old guard in the rural areas was a sine qua non. Díaz brought a new era of progress to the nation and its army, consolidating the liberal project and harnessing it to the rapidly accelerating technologies and social changes of his time.[73] He and his advisers turned to the philosophy of positivism, seeking in science and technology to resolve the persistent problems of the nation. Backward populations, or those unready for his new modern world, at times pushed back.

Serious internal opposition repeatedly emerged, including military rebellions and conspiracies in 1877, 1878, 1879, 1886, 1890, and 1893.[74] Scattered Indigenous attacks by Apaches, and larger uprisings by Yaqui, Mayo, and Maya continued through much of the era.[75] To counter this, he cultivated his personal supporters and intimidated his reluctant allies. The elite hunt was no less a display conceived and performed than so many of the aspects of Díaz' cult of personality. As a fighter against the French, the aging president had gained prominence, but now many of those who remembered the Intervention were dying. He thus needed to appeal to the rural power classes again, and he also needed to reassure Mexicans of his own personal virility and vitality, beyond marrying a young wife.[76] Short of war, many saw hunting as the most effective restorative to one's masculinity.[77]

On occasions that the elderly Díaz did attend a country hunt, the excursion required a large group of indigenous beaters to scare the game toward the waiting hunters.[78] This presents an intriguing practice, too, both in its marked resemblances to British imperial officials in Africa or India, and in how it reimagined the indigenous man.[79] The indigenous hunting guides of Mexico represented a racial understanding of the place of man in nature. Writers and travelers assumed that the inherent ability of the native guide came from a deeper connection to the savagery of the beast, a closer link to the untamed nature all around.[80] The upper-class harnessed this skill, even in the relatively simple task of ordering their guides to beat the bushes, and thus made an imperial statement. This featured in tales throughout the colonized worlds of the European, from Canada to India to Kenya. The power to make this assumption rose from colonial relations and racial discourses, as many have shown.[81] Still, the true progenitors of the sportsman's creed in Mexico considered the use of beaters barely acceptable, something permissible primarily in the case of terribly rough terrains or elusive game animals.[82] The high society elite paid little heed to these opinions.

Imperial Hunts, Undead Witnesses

Hunting in a colonized nation always entailed a matter of power and competing moral orders.[83] The elusive, rare, dangerous game pursued by the resolute huntsman produced one facet of a sense of fairness across nature. In the colonizing and settler-colonial worlds, indigenous collaborations made the hunt possible and proved necessary to any success. Indeed, early in Mexican history the colonial hunt included indigenous people among its prey.[84]

Meanings of the hunt as ritual and the political hierarchy echoed in its practice created an imperial performance that reinforced status and power relations. These types of hunters often seemed more similar than it might appear. The natives proved not alone in attributing supernatural aspects to their hunts, just as the masculine constructions belonged not only to colonizers. The hierarchy between hunter and native guide never remained stable, and at times the native took precedence and agency. For example, some guides thoroughly controlled the possibilities for elite hunters, set up game animals, and sold fake trophies. Power shifted in context. Local cultural norms and moral economies (like subsistence bases) set hunting against broader socio-legal structures of political ecology. The imperial drive met colonial models. The 1890s saw new game laws globally, which brought new restrictions and ethics into the field. Across the globe, the colonial hunter brought his prestige home in the form of the indivisible trophy.[85]

A practice closely connected to ideologies of the hunt and taxidermy had only begun to come into its own in the nineteenth century. Practices of preservation and mounting vastly improved in the last decades and this presented hunters with new possibilities. Earlier taxidermy had basically entailed upholstering with hides based loosely on ancient practices of mummification.[86] Additions of wiring and internal sculpting added realism and captured the semblance and beauty of the animal, if it always also remained a reminder of death. In Mexico, most trophies had been displayed in the European mounts, of simply setting bare skull and antlers up on walls. Those with more money (and museum pieces aside) might now choose to put a complete severed head and rack on the wall, with hair intact and glass eyes carefully posed. Hides displayed as rugs or tapestries also provided decor. Few had space and financial resources for a full-body-mounted display that could take over an entire room, but certainly some haciendas and mansions did so.[87] The taxidermist also preserved an animal's meaning beyond its lifetime. The object took on a new meaning.

The mounted kill created an animal frozen, silent, and preserved against death that spoke to the hunter's skill or virility.[88] It represented the encompassing of human longings and the hunter's "relationship with and within the natural world."[89] It also provided a type of limited remembrance, in a way not so unlike the souvenirs that fans brought home from bullfights.[90] The display deliberately and mutely told its part of the tale, in media res of the encounter, so that the hunter (or other witnesses) might elaborate on the rest. The story of the hardships, the stalk, the kill, the return to camp, and the meaning or lessons of it all came from the story told, while the mounted animal acted as a prompt or prop. The trophy also belonged to a single hunter, despite the contributions of other sportsmen, guides, butchers, taxidermists, and so on. As an indivisible fetish it gave all the credit to the individual hunter.

The fetishization of the kill changed its discursive power and wider meaning. The true animal disappeared in place of a simulacrum. The origin, the labor of its

FIGURE 7.1. Unknown, "Interior de Federico Lamin," in Carlos M. López and Carlos López, *Caza Mexicana: Obra escrita con la colaboración de varios cazadores del país e ilustrado con retratos y con fotografías tomadas de animales, también del país* (Mexico City: Librería de la Viuda de C. Bouret, 1911), 53. Photograph.

being (reproductive and otherwise), and the animal itself now becomes its new role as an object. Its only meaning, as with the fighting cock, the brave bull, the rabid dog, now revolved entirely around its relationship with humans, and in a tale told by its killer. The sole value of the beast, in a society grown indifferent to its death, now came from market calculations and the sentiments around its execution. Much as the street dog became an object compared to the urban poor, the mounted wolf echoed the devaluation and displacement of the rural poor. At times the fetish displaced again, where the displayed animal was not the same creature that had been hunted or had been hunted by someone else entirely.

Some guides found ways to take advantage of this commodity, and sold pre-harvested animal remains to naive hunters, giving them the impression that their bullets had struck home.[91] This fraud brings home that the meaning of the trophy depends on authenticity and that the displayer must be the actual killer. Secondhand trophies become kitsch and tacky. Much like the hunt itself, the trophy represented a cultural symbol and a social practice that established the worth of the hunter and made them part of a broader type of community.[92]

As a fetish item for a particular elite moral ecology, the trophy became a "potent object."[93] It facilitated the storytelling that lay at heart of the hunt. Especially for foreigners and colonizers, but not exclusively, the exotic trophy held contradictory meanings. It kept a beauty alive forever and thereby repudiated the act of killing. At the same time, it built on colonial dreams and fantasies, and the hunter's tale of himself became complicit in the act of subjugating new lands.[94] The animal as fantasy had to be deliberately staged with predators snarling and herbivores serenely gazing. To pose them otherwise made "tragedy into farce."[95] This observation also applied to stories told by colonizers. The stuffed creature presented a tamable form of wildness to natural history museums, educational institutions, and even to Worlds' Fairs as in 1889 Paris.[96] At the latter, they also displayed colonized humans.

Unlike the colonial aspect, the taxidermic display did bring out another side to the hunter's mentality. The fully displayed animal, unlike repackaged meat or hide made into clothing, represented an act of appreciation, perhaps even of love.[97] Nevertheless, the undead provided unsettling witnesses to act of the hunt. Many hunters speak of the closeness they feel to the natural world in which they briefly observe and take prey. They catch a glimpse of a truth and rhythm that outsiders cannot fully grasp. This, cemented to ideas of responsibility and stewardship, excludes non-hunters (who often include the critics of hunting). Performative consumptions of at least part of the prey, when possible, facilitates the idea of a responsible carnivore. More to the point, the evidence of the grand and imperial hunts revealed a political edge to the practice with little show of appreciation.

In all this, the "prevailing social hierarchy could be reflected symbolically in the arrangement of hunting methods."[98] This custom spoke against slaughter and butchery and yet made of hunting a "true wild pagan sport." Hunters in India, like elsewhere, locals supplied with guides and alcohol, and their culture devalued the beaters in favor of the shooters. The hunters' ideas set up fair play in the hunt as an inherently liberal idea, focusing on work ethic, equality, individualism, and self-discipline.[99] Hunting, and the stories about the hunt, revolved around a notion of the authentic experience.

Hunting thus allowed the building of status among peers, as well as in the eyes of outside (even foreign) observers. For colonials, it also erased indigenous presence. It presumed the "romantic sensibilities associated with the hunting experience."[100] The idea of moral ecology in this sense depends on ideas of reciprocity, renewal, and regeneration as being purely local.[101] The idea of fairness itself shifted, and becomes for some competing between two equals, for others, it assumed two unequal players and reifies power.[102] Hunting above all, is about the story told and the deprivations the hunt entailed.[103] And this artificial story, largely targeted to and told by men, reprised the colonial experience.[104] In Mexico, the self-colonizing and self-civilizing drive continued under Díaz.

The theater of the hunt represented a colonial (or self-colonizing) rather than a self-civilizing process, though certain elements do overlap.[105] Certainly, both impetuses sought a break from traditions and what elites called backwardness to become something more internationally recognizable, and in both processes, practices performed and embodied the new normal. Both colonizing and civilizing entailed emulation alongside the destruction of customary practices. They differ, nonetheless, in the importance of direct displays or exercise of power to exert control over a population and land. The civilizing may more subtly imply their strength in ceremony or discourse, and if (or when) they resorted to force, it was in the name of improving the victim's collective situation. In contrast, the colonizer's ends often include the annihilation of the marginal other. Both, of course, often end up in the same place despite claims to the contrary. Calling it colonizing rather than civilizing removes some of the self-produced absolution. Díaz's regime, and others like it, have yet to deserve this benefit of doubt.

The Presidential Expedition

The president felt he had earned the fashion and comfort appropriate to a head of state even in a venue of outdoors masculine endeavor. His well-insulated experience set him quite apart from that of the indigenous beaters and, in a sense, from his own Zapotec roots. For Díaz, one-quarter indigenous himself, directing the theater of hunt with undifferentiated indigenous beaters set him clearly in the role he so often claimed—the beneficent patron of his benighted nation. Perhaps echoing the imperial performance, Díaz also gave up the Mexican style of riding in favor of an English seat by at least 1883, much to the disgust of the American Consul.[106] His distance from the "indio" became that much more pronounced.

In an interview that would eventually help bring down the regime, Díaz spoke at length to an American reporter named James Creelman in 1908 about his reign. He imprudently mentioned that he might soon allow a fair election. While the text is well known by historians, the photos that accompanied it said a great deal about the president's ideal nation for foreign consumption. Taken from his offices or snapped by his son, the images included schools, city improvements, railways, heroes of history, and wedged right in the center, several pictures of Díaz out on an elite hunting expedition.

The hunting images, carefully selected, built a specific image of the presidential huntsman. In the first of his rough and tumble hunting photos, he posed with three companions, on foot, in what appears English hunting apparel. The caption speaks to what the photo might not: "President Díaz hunting in the mountains, at the age of seventy-five years. Mark the erectness and vigor of the figure, the strength and the bearing of the man, compared with his younger companions!"[107]

There is little to the caption left to the imagination of the gender historian. The following photograph gives the results of the hunt as he posed with twelve companions and sixteen dead deer hanging in a shed behind. Again, he took all credit in the caption, which reads "Behind him the deer killed by him, at the age of seventy-five, in two day's hard hunting."[108] It would seem that his companions came simply to carry, dress, and hang these carcasses. The seventy-five-year-old, as the captions keep insisting, did all the important killing.

FIGURE 7.2. Porfirio Díaz Jr., "President Diaz Hunting in the Mountains," in James Creelman, "President Díaz: Hero of the Americas," *Pearson's Magazine* (Mar. 1908): 240. Photograph.

The final photo presents my favorite of the tableau for its odd connections to food and indigeneity and the theater the elite portrayed. It shows, simply, six diners seated at a dinner table with nice white table clothes awaiting service. It reads: "President Díaz dining with his hunting companions in the forest." They remain, however, still in the middle of the woods where they are hunting. The servants were almost certainly indigenous men who had previously that day done the real work as beaters, and of carrying a table into the woods. Yet even washed up, they are kept off camera for fear of spoiling the portraiture. All we see are the hardy hunters taking their just meal after a tough day.[109] The animal made into meat disappears, a fetish removed from its production, into a dish carefully plated, and presented as if to royalty.

The virile hunt made political succession and legitimacy clear. The president's son gained accolades in the newspapers of the capital that had offered this note: "Enthusiastic applause for the young Porfirio Díaz, for his noteworthiness as a shooter. In the last hunt in Cuautla Morelos . . . he demonstrated his ability as a deer hunter. Good, young friend, good!"[110] The presumed heir took after the president, a man who used the show of the hunt as political propaganda and genuinely enjoyed the sport. The president felt he had earned the fashion and comfort appropriate to a head of state even in a venue of outdoors masculine endeavor. His well-insulated experience also set him quite apart from that of the indigenous beaters.

In the political and theatrical performance of the colonizers' hunt, the power that killed, owned. Díaz and hunters the world over tapped into ancient images and conceptualizations that converted the facade of the successful hunter into proof of his prowess, virility, and legitimate rule over the land and its denizens.[111] Empires and nations rely on such myths. The ritual elements and choice of photographed backdrops gave viewers easily read evidence of Díaz's power over all Mexico. The violent ends framed as a natural course of affairs blessed his authority and patriarchal place. The symbolism of the hanging carcasses of deer, in a land Díaz had rid of bandits by the thousands and whose cadavers then hung from telegraph poles, would escape few contemporary Mexican viewers.

Beyond his rare jaunts to the countryside, Díaz lived in an urban castle. Fortunately, the grounds and woods around Chapultepec remained semi-wild throughout his reign, and hunts for small game could be just a moment away.[112]This did risk stray bullets, given that the rest of the city lay easily within range, but this seems to have been of little concern. He also made use of some of his new parks, like

FIGURE 7.3. Porfirio Díaz Jr., "President Diaz Stands on the Right" in James Creelman, "President Díaz: Hero of the Americas," *Pearson's Magazine* (Mar. 1908): 241. Photograph.

FIGURE 7.4. Porfirio Díaz Jr., "President Diaz Dining with His Hunting Companions," in James Creelman, "President Díaz: Hero of the Americas," *Pearson's Magazine* (Mar. 1908): 242. Photograph.

the Desierto de Leones, and a private reserve along the shores of Lake Xochimilco. The latter seems to have been quite outside both the law and the sportsman's creed since Díaz' hunting parties were known to use armadas (batteries of multiple guns) to take down entire flocks of ducks at a time. According to one observer, one volley alone felled 1,500 birds.[113] Perhaps the modernity of the method trumped the lack of sport, or perhaps it was simply a double standard—after all, it was not the president who needed civilizing. At the same time of course, his regime enacted laws over wildlife that sought to divorce the indigene from his means of livelihood and sought to strip the "savage nature" that made him such a great guide in the first place. The hunt nonetheless had now returned to the edges of the city itself, to echo the gunfire within that controlled the dangerous strays and other beasts.

The presidential love of wildlife did go beyond the hunt. Since at least the times of Nezahualcoyotl of Texcoco, rulers in Mexico kept menageries of exotic animals.[114] Indeed, one of the most impressive was that of Mocteuzoma, the Aztec emperor, kept at Chapultepec. Not to be outdone, Díaz had one, too, built on remnants of the menagerie of Emperor Maximilian and those before.[115] The continuity of this menagerie is not well studied, but it is at least potentially the longest operated zoo in the Western world.[116]

Courting patronage, elites from across the country sent him animals so that he could build a veritable national collection. At one point, ocelots given him by a hacendado even escaped into the woods of Chapultepec, permitting him and his entourage a rare hunt, while at another, an escaped panther caused a great deal of concern.[117] It is important to note that the private menagerie was not properly a zoo. It presented a pure display of power over caged nature, a collection of national types, and a prestige item, but it was not at all open for public viewers.

With absolute control over contents and viewership, the zoo acted as a fetish object of power over human and animal alike.[118] One could not share in the ownership over tamed nature, the caged beast, unless the proprietor conceded permission. The animals of the patria thereby became the president's private domain. This political ecological complex of control implied a great deal about how humans tend to view animals. They became at best resources to be carefully and humanely used, and at worst, fetish objects existing for political theater and lethal entertainment.

FIGURE 7.5. Unknown, "En Chapultepec," *El Mundo Ilustrado*, Jan. 2, 1898, 1. Sketch.

Conclusions

The moral ecology of the indigenous hunter posed the killing of wildlife in alignment with subsistence and community needs. Reciprocities, complex foodways, and seasonal requirements informed a nuanced vision of the natural world, albeit one that might not be sustainable or scientific. Traditions and religion shaped a way of life. Again, the moral ecology reflects mores, not ethics or value-laden judgments. Foreigners acknowledged Mexico as a natural treasure house and advocated for conservation measures for it to remain so. They did so, nonetheless, in the expectation that this would facilitate future hunting expeditions for themselves. Their political ecology had little difference from that of the wealthiest Mexicans.

The imperial and foreign hunts proved the plainest sorts of the necropolitical where the powerful selected the populations that killed, or were killed, and yet here, too, twists appear. Conservation policies applied to the colonized far more stringently than to the powerful. The struggle to narrate and memorialize the mortality of the animal created a weird immortality. Death had been displaced to the farthest wilderness corners, and yet returned again to the outskirts of the city, and in taxidermic form, to the parlors of the wealthy urbanite.

The highest elite in Mexico, echoing European and American imperialist examples, performed the hunt as part of an orchestrated theater of power. In dress, in armament, in accessories, and in media coverage, they killed and fashioned a story from the experience. Their tales set them far above non-hunters, above fellow officials and politicians, and as distinct from less privileged local sportsmen. They reinforced the story they told with trophies taken and displayed in their mansions. Their excursions and displays also served to reinforce and establish a political vision founded on racial hierarchies. In their wilderness, the dispossessed natives became underpaid beaters for wealthy men's hunt.

In the stories hunters tell of who they were, truly and deep down, the profound experience of killing wildlife spoke volumes. Tales, from indigenous to foreign to elite, told the tales of how people related to animals, to the wilds, and how the non-human fit into a worldview.[119] Imperial pretense and native expertise constituted two ends of a spectrum within the same storyline. Ultimately, both formed cultural frames about nature and society. Repeated, passed along, and reframed, the tales about hunting became webs of significance that shaped social norms. The history of becoming Mexican appeared at the extreme edges of animal treatment.

Making a modern nation and modern city on the model of private game reserve had many implications. A dog chained in the yard was not the same as one in the streets. The urban indigene who could no longer legally hunt was no longer a *bárbaro*, a threat, a savage. Modern markets full of food replaced frontier forage. Scheduled theatrical hunts by approved men, with appropriate servants and licenses, replaced use of animals on the tables of the poor. Necropolitical control over animal populations, loosely construed by elites, extended the taming of the city frontiers across the entire terrain of the imagined nation.

Epilogue

The animal life culminates in fear.[1]

Reason distinguishes man from animal, [and] does not entitle domination of nature, but comprehension.[2]

From the great metropolis to the wilds of the sierras, conflicts between humans and animals made ideas about society evident. The permission to destroy, to kill, emphatically defined limits to that relationship. Many animals, over time, ceased to be fellow creatures and became instead commodities, fetishes, properties, and objects. Power applied in law and everyday practices changed animal personhoods and that of certain human animals as well. Can a bull, a cock, or a stag be Mexican? Can an indigenous hunter, or the urban poor? The nation brought together a composite of animals, non-human animals, and webs of complex relationships as social fields of power, and most appropriately, as arenas. In turn-of-the-century-Mexico, street dogs and vermin, cocks and bulls, activists and capitalists and scientists, came together in witness to repugnant spectacles.

Some social groups lumped roughly together in moral ecologies—sets of discourse and practice that collectively describe a relationship to nature—and established repertoires of culture. These people deployed ideas for contention or to preserve an equilibrium, and thus negotiated their place in society and against the natural world. Animals were tied to ideas about experienced changes, with urbanization and industrialization chief among these. Practically, animals represented food, aesthetics, well-being, entertainment, companionship, labor, and value.

Moral ecologies most often remained rooted in pragmatics. Their meanings could be situational and shifting, and influential as when sportsmen's culture became national laws. Most urban populations accepted the need for some measures of public health yet had little time for the politics of infection and had no preference for properly documented meats. What some termed *animal cruelty* in social practices of slaughter or sports, more often and no less negative, probably could be termed *public indifference* or *negligence*. And practical moral ecologies often propelled confrontations against what ordinary people deemed "malevolent laws" by deploying what authorities called disorderly habits.

Governmental, foreign, and scientific efforts roughly brought together the political ecology, biopower, and its inevitable necropolitics. This system allowed officials to attempt the management multiple populations and the exploitation of the public wealth, riqueza pública, that natural resources represented. For hungry humans, new laws fashioned class erasures through obstacles to their customary foodways. For hungry animals, cities both lured and killed. The practical and discursive seizure of the rights to kill represented a form of primitive accumulation and established security necessary for the nation to progress toward its emergent capitalism. It established control over a great proletariat, human, on one hand, but animal, too, and some of each now became detached from their previous places in society.

Necropolitical ecologies in the city regulated most effectively when elites discursively tied issues of public health to specific scientific advances. Despite the public's sentimental feelings toward strays and stubborn reliance on non-market sources of meat, officials made genuine gains in remedying urban shortcomings. Most urbanites' food came from the legal abattoirs, and more of it each year, and increasingly this decreased contaminations. Populations either gave up resisting and became consumers in a modern sense or they faced legal consequences (especially true for indigenous groups). From the same logics that incessantly spoke of "focuses of infection," the urban poor became legally animalized and suppressed. At the same time, the raucous, hypermasculine, and troubling cockfights thrived. Broad multi-class support and venerable traditions set a formidable barrier against unwanted interference. The cock thrived as a fetish symbolizing far more than an animal being. The state imposed the privilege of killing in markets or against vagrant animals, but the cockfight and bullfight also showed the limits to regulation, and these practices continued, or continue, to this day.

A necropolitics that set some creatures as expendable and Other underpinned all these elements.

Tentative Findings

In this context, animal deaths became a part of social fields of power. Who had the right or privilege to kill? Did execution rights belong to the patriarchy, to the rich, to the government, or to whom? Who, and what, are the "useful" populations? Who decides this?

The necropolitical permission to end lives, and to hide death from public visibility, had tremendous capacity to shape everyday existence. Elite choices and legislating made the killing of animals in the name of science and entertainment socially acceptable, and the popular classes largely concurred. Antonio Gramsci argues that class consciousness rises from both shared experiences and from normative practices inherited over time.[3] This dual consciousness certainly drew from the foodways, blood sports, and markets where Mexicans confronted the differences between collective assumptions and authorities' claims. In these everyday power relations, one sees the "marketplace as much an arena of class wars as factories and mines."[4] As such, the animal, and its place in society, especially at the extremes where its value came in unneeded death, represented a site of class struggle. Embedded traditions and continuities persevered against claims of backwardness, the unhygienic, or the cruel. The clashes in expectations between actors played out in debates, legislating, and, at times, destructive rioting. Violence represented a symptom of failed power, especially in the cases of prophylactic killings because it represented a last resort and an expensive one. Frequent clashes provide evidence of the stakes in making changes to the animal-human world.

Self-colonizing infuses each chapter as facets of an extended necropolitical ecology. The systemic death of the Other ties this work together. The demise of the "merely" animal became justified, hidden, arbitrary, celebrated, ritualized, commercialized, and romanticized, and all the while made into political theater. Humans stopped treating animals as subjects and saw them as fetishized objects whose meaning emerged from their use. Societal structures around public hygiene and wildlife conservation made decisions on a basis that removed a creature's individual value. Officials quarreled with locals over the visible contrast between informal slaughter and regulated sports. The industrial-entertainment complex fed the construction of a modern subject who cheered the death of the animal object, and cultivated senses of indifference to ritualized killing. The stories of the stalk told by a few privileged hunters became law, and in the alternative versions of the hunt its meanings shifted to race, empire, and power.

And through this all society reflected ideals that made some deaths the natural province of a changing nation increasingly attached to larger capitalist markets. The newly opened Palacio de Hierro department store and the new Peralvillo abattoirs drew on the same inspiration and sense of the meaning of becoming modern. The new consumer classes, carefully ordered and secure, emerged with a sense of identity and self-priority. The slender thread of creating the Other, the object, and relegated this to death came not as strange exception but normal, laudable, profitable, and Mexican. New structures emerged around behaviors.

The shifting between customary practices and the constraints of laws emerged in the hunt. Similar to the bullfighting complex, a moral ecology (of bullfight fans and mestizo sportsmen) facilitated the construction of a cultural set of norms that shaped broader ideas (those of bullfight promoters and conservationists). The animal as sacred prey became a national treasure, albeit one subject to ambush. Alien notions intervened in the hunter's world, too, particularly at the higher levels of foreign and elite expeditions. The expectations and customs from abroad represented colonial and imperial ideologies that kept the native animal, whether guide or game, in their respective places. These high-level hunters occasionally followed the laws and conservation practices, but at times chose to exercise their privileges instead. They also facilitated the dispossession and disentailment of indigenous and subsistence hunting peoples. The death of the Other underpinned new relations expressed in cultural modes.

Reading Tracks and Culture

At the heart of things, cultural stories reconciled the cost of killing the Other. Customs covered over distaste, placated human opponents, deflected senses of blame, and ultimately, allowed violence against animals to be forgiven. Across modernizing Mexico, the privileges or responsibilities around killing animals shifted legally to fall on the shoulders of the state, to acknowledged experts, to industrial processes, and largely, to adult men over any other citizens. Ideological rationales about animal deaths formed around excuses, through media and art, via collective participation, and in the contextual cultures of modern life and sciences. This resulting relationship to animal death evolved and transformed along with the emergence of the capitalist and secular state. The turn of the century introduced new tactics and tools, shaped evolving identities like fandoms or sportsmen, and drew on novel technological resources. In terms of quotidian practice, people excluded from power showed both resilience and adaptation in the face of these legal and discursive shifts. Animals had fewer options.

Relationships to animal deaths revealed progress and its discomforts. In displays of pageantry and the hiding of meat slaughter, society commercialized sports and food, created celebrities, and constructed gendered norms. The connection to animality framed a social experience, becoming part of other social identities, and illustrated part of modern life. Urban animality and nature represented the chaotic enemy of human progress and instigated a new necropolitics on the city street. Killing became either taboo and invisible, or blatantly orchestrated for public display, with little in between. Modern consumers became mass spectators. Capitalists exploited their fervor and built entertainment industries. The complexity of celebrity cultures highlighted traditional gender expectations and modern roles for the famous. Mestizo hunters appeared as self-made cultural constructs, and their narratives shaped laws and policies at highest levels and excluded indigenous and poor competitors. They, in turn, fell short of the luxurious hunting practices of the highest elite and foreigners on Mexican safari. Rituals and performances, present at all levels, reached new heights in the orchestrated trophy game hunts.

None of these drives and impulses come as entirely unique to Mexico, but the historical experience suggests broader relevance to our understandings of modernizing societies and animals in history. The choice to kill animals created identities through social conflicts and legal changes, and never in a straightforward process, and indeed this proved true also for other vastly different regions and even in different times. How humans interacted with the unnecessary deaths of animals can shed light on the formation of collective ideas, norms, and practices anywhere.

The relative social positions of humans, at times determined in their relation to the means of animal death, also reflects how society changed in terms of tastes, leisure, sociability, and status. The clash between indigenous hunters and conservationists, what José Martínez-Reyes terms a "nature industrial process in need of a post-conservationism," suggests that scholars need to take a healthy skepticism toward all the ecologies involved.[5] They are all local and cultural and at many times less than objective. For example, scholars need to take seriously a sense of complexity in considering climate change effects, not to dismiss them, but certainly to maintain skepticism toward "cultural capitalism" as providing a solution.[6]

Finally, the power of modern forms of society to enforce a necropolitical indifference, one that turns selected subjects into objects and Others, was always a feature of the biopolitics. It extended to animals, just as to the marginalized human. It explains the social acceptance of extinctions as simply another form of the genocidal impulse. This work should encourage scholars to read animal death differently, as with cases of capital punishment, and to see the human animal as performance rather than a given fact.

The animal world in the early twentieth century presents us with a vivid lived experience. Many people had a taste for game, felt wary of street dogs, and witnessed blood sports. Walking through towns and cities, Mexicans saw the gallero, the torero, and the cazador. They understood them in the context of their complex age.

Even the heads of the nation during the long dictatorship embodied the uncomfortable juxtaposition of Mexican ecologies. He, President Porfirio Díaz, everyone knew as a dedicated hunter, a fan of the bullfight, and a spectator at the cockfights. As chief executive of the country, the laws that regulated animal control, conservation, and public health ultimately came from his hand. At the same time, First Lady Carmen Romero Rubio sat both at her husband's side and at the head of the Mexican Society for the Protection and Care of Animals. Contrasting and conflicting views about animals' place in civilized society lived luxuriously together within the national palace of Chapultepec, high atop an urban wilderness.

Postscript

In a small city in central Mexico, residents and visitors celebrate an annual festival. Tequila flows, bands play music, the religious proceed in the streets, and decorations drape across the town facades. Many locals save for months to buy tickets for a proper, traditional, bullfight. Six bulls will fall, and children in the stands yell for the matador to take an ear as trophy. In other nearby venues, a well-organized cockfight fills a great barrel with dead competitors.

This festival, much of it recorded on cell phones, took place in 2022.[1]

The people participating and creating community in these cultural practices did so, ironically, to celebrate the feast of Saint Francis, the patron saint of animals.

And so, the power of the necropolitical to set some lives apart, to create and allow the killing of the Other, continues a century after the events of this book. Such, perhaps ironically, is life.

APPENDIX

Theoretical Interventions

On Necropolitics

A conception of power and death ties these disparate chapters together. The idea of necropolitics represents a society's capacity to seek the "generalized instrumentalization of human existence and the material destruction of human bodies and populations."[1] Here I suggest that it may also explain a great deal about relations to animals as well. Although originally applied in explanation for wars and pogroms of colonial circumstances, I do not equate these victimized human populations to "mere" animal status. The theory nonetheless may explain the connections between social fields of power, ideas about nature and about death, and the significant changes seen in the late nineteenth century.

The idea of necropolitics offers a valuable analytical tool for this era. Michel Foucault's biopolitics identified power as turning toward the statistical administration and governance of ways of living.[2] It works well in explaining the workings of power in institutions including policing, medicine, and prisons. Yet critical voices, many of them in postcolonial studies, noted the omission of attention to the ubiquitous violence in biopolitical systems that seemed designed to relegate some subjects to death. They also observed that the new governing powers of society required the exercising of this capacity as a fundamental and existential necessity for sovereignty. This power system they termed the *necropolitical*.

A nascent power structure, termed by Foucault as the liberal state, drew its claims to authority from imposing utilitarian systems rather than appealing to the duty owed to monarchs, religions, or traditions. It claimed to act for the common good where subjects obeyed and self-surveilled in rational ways. Of course, this only applied to those granted full inclusion as members of society. It required that those it excluded disappear.

The systemic necropolitics identified and eliminated the Other to create security. Foucault described this security as the disciplinary regimes enforced by various mechanisms that maintained order and social control. His wording of *secure* and *security* translated more closely to "fixed in place" rather than connoting safety or protected status. As a basis for security policies, necropolitics then deemed some subjects within the reach of the nation-state as expendable beings to be necessarily set aside and left to die, or encouraged to, for the sake of a grand idea of society. The necropolitical allowed no dissent, alternatives, or other "cancers" within the ideal societal body. The hostility that it showed toward those different from the acceptable social masses created what Achille Mbembe called "relations of enmity." Here, the majority participated in, or simply became inured and indifferent towards, the suffering, subordinating, or even killing of the groups excluded.

Systemic necropolitics arose as a function for defense of security and sovereignty against what the emerging liberal state labeled the Other. It created, intentionally or otherwise, a hegemonic society, if one replete with "relations of enmity," that imbued society with callous indifference to death.[3] More insidiously, this work tended to occur without obvious agents since policies appeared as the blameless side effect of benign bureaucratic protocols that seemed natural and rational. This arrangement with the world led minority subjects to experience annihilations and dread, as the "evil genies" so loosed redefined select populations within a nation as worthy or not.[4] The necropolitical inscribed this power upon bodies, whether human or not, and its effects stripped status from victims.

Animals also could embody and create subjectivities, since the sense of self is formed in relation to other things and beings; Mexican animals had long had a subject identity in the eyes (in particular) of the indigenous population.[5] But as Mbembe notes, "Can the Other, in light of all that is happening, still be regarded as a fellow creature?"[6] The formation of the subject, in this context, builds new forms of power that rejected certain groups as expendable and undesirable, and acted upon them as objects. Those excluded from a place in society became contingently accepted only if they demonstrated use value. More often they became second class or, worse, categorized as "born to die."

A modern secular capitalist society emerged with this basis. While a sense of shared humanity may sometimes have found a way through to social practices, the

Other becomes largely deprived of meaningful and authentic human encounters.[7] Those groups excepted by necropolitics and made eligible for state-empowered extermination first experienced the loss of their worth and any compassion in the eyes of the masses. The ideal of creating a cohesive and governable population next meant facilitating this new society as a political order. Governing bodies, social trends, and general authority therefore reconstituted into a form for organizing death.[8] In other words, a fundamental feature of this liberal state extended administrative management of the biopolitical to also label, manage, permit, and encourage the demise of those it considered dangerous alternatives to the social order.

I argue that this works broadly, far beyond the situations of racial and colonial violence where the notion began, to also describe animal contexts. As Frantz Fanon states, the necropolitical ignores "the inseparability of humans and other living creatures" as it mutely orders the execution of select groups.[9]

In this work the necropolitical logic ties together topics as disparate as animal control, home slaughter, and blood sport. The necropolitical system shaped the acceptability for death of the Other, whether this meant bandits, rebels, or minority groups or, in this book, the demise of animals. In each case, the liberal state attempted to stamp its claims to power on cadavers, and the necropolitical infused broad political ecologies with its own logics. Animals died at authorities' direct request, by license, and occasionally, in defiance of the laws. In each case, officials claimed the sole right to pronounce upon these and to hold the only legitimate opinion on who or what needed to die.

In this way, the necropolitical regime's controls over "repeopling" extended beyond humans to animals as well, since it sought dominion over all the living and devoured in a "bloody process" those it chooses.[10] The nation-state embraced a new place in a global capitalism and made cultural claims as a unique civilization. It displaced this violence against bodies from the sight of those who count, by moving violence to frontiers, to camps, to slums, and, perhaps, to industrial abattoirs. It disappeared intrinsic foes, what it deemed an "enemy by nature," through both open war and clandestine movements.[11] Necropolitical power also affected the larger population by instilling indifference and even cruelty by discursively cheapening lives, habituating losses, ritualizing executions, and justifying itself in the name of security and progress. This hid from view the underlying "fantasy of extermination."[12] The central and often nationalist discourse arranged power around questions of belonging, and if some humans could not make the cut, many animals would clearly be out of luck also.[13] The ultimate expression of sovereignty then extended not simply over the domain of life, but to dictating who shall die, and set the conditions for the "acceptability" of killing.[14] Those deemed Other, animal or not, became tamed and entered a life in suspension as they lost their subject status.[15] They became, by this emerging logic, objects for disposal in the name of the greater good.

The necropolitical impulse represented the underpinning of the political ecology and a facet of how power structures infiltrated relations between animals and "a society of enmity" shaped by a cold indifference to the Other. This, given definition through cultural norms including symbolic violence, shaped a changing element of an identity during a strangely important era.[16] The necropolitics, along with the moral ecology, help to explain the "joke" that we do not understand.

The Idea of the Moral Ecology

Moral ecological precepts connected the necropolitical impetus with community practices. Understanding the cultural constructs that shaped how humans related to the killing of animals requires leaving aside some sentimental judgments and seeking deeper insights into social history. Richard White argues that early environmental history proved weak on causation and that little attention had been given to cultural elements that would explain human practices.[17] A central concept of *Perilous Beasts* originates from E. P. Thompson's moral economic interpretation of early modern grain riots in England.[18] More recent studies have turned this focus toward nature into the moral ecology.[19] In the process, much of the value and significance has at times been twisted or ignored. Taking the idea of moral ecology back to its roots seems a worthwhile detour.

The classical Thompsonian moral economy made its clearest debut in 1971 to explain rural riots that acted against the participants' apparent interests. More broadly, the Marxist author attempted to explain the failure of these early movements to reach revolutionary potentials and tried to explain the failure of later European communists by implication. False consciousness rose from the intercession of a system of cultural norms and mores that he termed a *moral economy*. Rural communities found a collective voice for traditions, reciprocities, and relations on a local scale.

These could lead to riots to gain specific and often parochial short-term goals at the price of longer-term benefits. As Peter Linebaugh points out, a strong connection also existed to traditional Marxist notions that afforded the proletariat customary rights to nature.[20] The customs held in common defined a polity and its expectations against outside, often governmental, impositions. Their norms and demands became visible affective prompts and brought otherwise voiceless groups into the limelight.[21] Yet in this structuralist view and despite Thompson's intentions, man remained *homo economicus* or a being largely reactive to material determinants, even if culture interceded in how they expressed any discontent.[22]

Later scholars built on this in several ways, asserting, for example, that communities acted largely on stakes of subsistence and that they had a wider range of options to resist beyond riots. The cultures of the moral economy represent to James Scott a hidden transcript of unwritten framings that shaped subaltern behaviors.[23] Others show that religious and millenarian ideas could often seep into these community ideas, or how moral economies could become political cultures.[24] Some insist, mistakenly, that the moral economy fundamentally opposed a capitalist political economy, which misread the original notion.[25] Far too many interpretations insist on a moral aspect centering the idea on something ethical or about "goodness."[26]

In contrast to this, insightful studies pointed out that the moral economy does not prescribe a right or wrong value system.[27] Nor was the system necessarily anti-revolutionary or anti-capitalist—in fact, for Thompson that was precisely the point.[28] Taken as a risky shorthand for some unspecified community's value system, the moral economy can dismiss irrationalities and simplify rural politics in harmful ways. At the same time, if used with nuance, the idea can afford a way to explore understandings of the world found in the heart of practices and offer insights into less known actors.[29]

Here the proponents of moral ecology stepped in.[30] Communities have a culturally mediated set of relations and reciprocal expectations with the natural world around them. This has roots in traditions, memory, habitus, and practices.[31] It can be posed against an ideological complex imposed from without called a political ecology.[32] The latter can come from law, sciences, conservation, and international pressures, among other structural forces. Some scholars of the moral ecology continue, nonetheless, to misread Thompson as promoting an ethical judgment and now applied that to their ecological views.[33] A number of works deal with the idea but leave it relatively undeveloped in their analyses.[34] For a few though, the moral ecology presents a sharper way to understand deep ecologies, communities, the humanizing of nature, and complex social relations.[35] An intriguing article, for example, suggests that the moral ecology of northwestern indigenous groups focused on the Trickster Raven and social adaptation and suggested a reaction to combat climate changes.[36] Still, it seems that more consideration of the concept is needed to make it a proper tool of analysis.

The origins of the moral ecology suggest a variety of underexamined aspects, particularly in Marxist, especially Gramscian thought, that lead to different analyses.[37] Given Thompson's original connection to the enclosure movements in England and the rise of capitalist enterprises, the idea of primitive accumulation takes a central place.[38] For the moral ecology, instead of hoarding land, coin, or capital, one could look to raw nature. The powerful sought monopolies and ownership of animals, resources, and the rights to control nationalized biological matters in what some term *biopolitics* and, by extension, *necropolitics*. It unleashed powerful forces of dispossession against indigenous and rural populaces in Mexico. Yet the false consciousness of the elite moral ecological crowd pointed less to material determinants than to choosing short-term uses of nature in keeping with customs. This obstacle to deeper change could be just as obstinate or anti-revolutionary as any religious calling, and may indeed have had its own religious elements.

Revolutionary change came only slowly. The choices of the crowd, neither good nor evil but simply moral in the sense of mores, tended toward profound conservatism. Yet the moral ecology also provides a dialectical motor for history. As moral ecological practices (thesis) met political ecological challenges (antithesis), a transformed and synthesized result, both in culture and practice, resulted. Likewise, moral ecology does not leave out economic concerns but simply reprioritizes them. It turns *homo economicus* into *homo ecologicus*, perhaps, or simply acknowledges that humans make cultural choices about their relations to nature and then suit these to economic possibilities. For instance, spending their last coin on attending blood sports may not be rational, but makes sense within the moral ecological bounds. Classes, determined by people's relations to means of production, engage in constant struggle. In the moral ecology framework, the "thing produced" in terms of labor seems more purely cultural. It nonetheless positions different groups in a relative hierarchy of status and, through adversarial clashes, shaped hegemonies.

Not all elements of the original Marxist Thompsonian framework can work, nor should they all fit easily. The stakes for communities, the nature of exploitation, the position of the animals (who also inhabit "classes"), the place of the lumpenproletariat, and the role of intention all make differences.[39] Subsistence, in this case, is not necessarily at the root of matters.

A further caveat here is warranted. The moral ecology cannot capture all the complexity and paradoxes that any culture contains, nor can it delineate or concretely define a monolithic group of adherents. Importantly, the collectives addressed here transcend usual identity groups like race, class, gender, age, urbanity, region and so on. It is more complex. For instance, bullfights had a broad fandom from all classes, ages, and genders, and even if the experience varied for many, they generally shared a cultural perspective that deemed the sport appropriate. Similarly, hunters, cockfight spectators, and members of protection societies reveal a broad range of the usual identities that defies easy definition. This murkiness grows more pronounced due to considerable variation of ideas within these groups as well. Using the moral ecology as a shorthand can also risk reinforcing binaries (modern vs. locals, etc.) that oversimplify complex group dynamics and shifting loyalties.[40] That said, the idea still allows for (cautiously) tracking the cultural trends that shaped the nation over time, and it adds depth to how we examine social history in Mexico.

For *Perilous Beasts*, the moral ecological framework ties together various types of cultural practice and sets them in the context of an emergent capitalist society. For Mexico, elites increasingly drew on scientific discourses to facilitate controls over what they termed the "riqueza pública" or public wealth. Various outside forces aligned to combat blood sports including protection societies, foreigners, and government officials intent on biopolitical and the statistical control of populations and how they live, as a mechanism of administrating and governing. Although their efforts had good intent, often necropolitical consequences arose.[41] Broadly multi-classed audiences fought back. At times, in bullfighting rings, this led to actual full-throated rioting and arson. Public health officials attempted to make select animal deaths invisible in the city while also massacring vast numbers of stray dogs. Elite hunters took trophies and made laws while stripping indigenous hunters of their foodways and livelihoods. All these struggles had stakes in a long-term ecology. These fights determined animal rights, shaped the extents of national, scientific, and foreign influences on Mexico, and had an impact on wildlife populations. Animals of all kinds made a slow shift from fellow subjects to human property. The cultural constructions about nature forged a necropolitical human subjectivity in relations to the killing of critters.

NOTES

Introduction

1. Herzog, *Some We Love*, 2, 9–35.
2. Morris, *Story of Mexico*, 35; Gringo, *Life and Travels in Mexico*, 227; Bates, *Notes of a Tour in Mexico*, 26, 44–45.
3. Flandrau, *Viva México*, 113.
4. Flandrau, *Viva México*, 114.
5. Shukin, *Animal Capital*, 6–7.
6. Homi Bhabha cited in Shukin, *Animal Capital*, 10; Jacques Derrida cited in Shukin, 156.
7. Michel Foucault, *Security, Territory, and Population*, 4–13; on Mexican liberalism, see Hale, *Transformation of Liberalism*, 4.
8. As in other places, see von Hardenburg Matthew Kelly, and Claudia Leal eds., *Nature State*, 1–10; see also Andrew Arato and Eike Gebhart, "Introduction," in Arato and Gebhart, *Essential Frankfurt School Reader*, 8.
9. Herzog, *Some We Love*; on the conscience and guilt of hunters, see Serpell, *In the Company of Animals*, 169–195, and on killing for entertainment, 219–226.
10. For nuances on killing animals for food in modern cities, see Thrift, *Killer Cities*, 87–89; on early vegetarians, see Cartmill, *View to a Death*, 38–40; and on the changing nature of our relations, see Fagan, *Intimate Bond*, 265–268.
11. Herzog, *Some We Love*, 1, 57–58, 262.
12. Herzog, 39–41.
13. This is not to suggest a simple tradition-modern binary but, rather, a shifting and dynamic set of relations.
14. Mbembe, *Necropolitics*.
15. Norton, *Tame and the Wild*, 2–3.
16. Berman, *Modern Culture and Critical Theory*, 157.
17. See Pearson and Weisentel, "Does the Animal Exist?," 19–21.
18. Serpell, *In the Company of Animals*; Brantz, *Beastly Natures*, 2–4; Shapiro, "Human-Animal Studies."
19. Cronon, *Uncommon Ground*, 20, 25, 51, 79.
20. Among these, see Morton, *Ecology Without Nature*, 3–12; and Bourdieu, *Outline of a Theory in Practice*, 167.
21. The term often used, *Anthropocene*, has come under some fire by geologists and others as overly dismissive of fully understood epochal shifts through the millennia.

Nonetheless, it may apply from modern animal perspectives; Thrift, *Killer Cities*, 16–20; Alves, "Animal Question."
22. Thrift, *Killer Cities*, 5; Fudge, "Flourishing and Challenging Field"; Bonnell and Kheraj, *Traces of the Animal Past*.
23. Derby, "Bringing the Animals Back In"; Melville, *Plague of Sheep*; Conway, *Nineteenth-Century Spanish America*, 122–124; Neufeld, "Animal Perspectives."
24. Thrift, *Killer Cities*, 44–45.
25. Cf. Mikhail, *Animal in Ottoman Egypt*.
26. Reiger, *American Sportsmen*; Jacoby, *Crimes Against Nature*; Warren, *Hunter's Game*, 1–21; Knight, "Anonymity of the Hunt," 334–355; Eiss, *In the Name of El Pueblo*.
27. Vergara, "Bestiario latinoamericano," 187–208. All translations are my own, unless otherwise noted.
28. For more on these conceptual connections, see Pierotti and Fogg, "Neocolonial Thinking and Respect for Nature," 48–57; Castellanos, "Introduction," 771–781; Morano et al., *Coloniality at Large*.
29. Simonian, chapter 3 in *Defending the Land of the Jaguar*, 45–66; Vitz, *City on the Lake*, 19–50; Tenorio-Trillo, *I Speak of the City*; Soluri et al., *Living Past*, 8–13; Angelo, "From the City Lens."
30. Wakild, *Revolutionary Parks*; Wakild, "Parables of Chapultepec"; Vergara and Wakild, "Extinction and Its Interventions"; Boyer, *A Land Between Waters*.
31. Tortorici and Few, *Centering Animals in Latin American History*.
32. Pilcher, *Sausage Rebellion*.
33. Martínez-Reyes, *Moral Ecology of a Forest*; Sloan, *Death in the City*; Viquiera Albán, *Propriety and Permissiveness*; von Germeten, *Enlightened Patrolman*.
34. Schubert, *Death and Money in the Afternoon*.
35. Tenorio-Trillo, *I Speak of the City*.
36. Norton, *Tame and the Wild*.
37. Lomnitz, *Death and the Idea of Mexico*, 292–303.
38. In disclosure of my subject position, I grew up on farms, and I have hunted, regularly eaten meat, and spent considerable time working in the Canadian wilderness.
39. Darnton, *Great Cat Massacre*, 77–78.
40. This is an analogy that appears frequently in animal studies literature but is best formulated in Ginzburg, *Clues, Myths, and the Historical Method*, 96–126.
41. For a jargon-heavy example, see Grusin, *Nonhuman Turn*.
42. A note on the terminology used—*Ayuntamiento*, *City*, and *Council* are used as synonymous for Mexico City authorities at that level, while *pueblo*, *población*, *exurb*, and *suburb* describe the smaller municipalities, run by the Federal District governments, that surround the metropolis. Technically, exurbs are geographically distant, but this does not exclude those communities here on the other side of water. The categories are deliberately messy, which indeed was the case for them as well.
43. See works by Foucault: *Discipline and Punish*; *Birth of Biopolitics*; and *Security, Territory, Population*.

44. Intimacy can be found in human killings of animals. This is the inverse argument to Walker, "Animals and the Intimacy of History."
45. On this concept, see Agamben, *State of Exception*.
46. Imaz Baume, *Cacería*, 89–93; Cartmill, *View to a Death*, 72.
47. Morton, *Tame and the Wild*, 302–327.
48. On socially produced indifference to human death, see Scheper-Hughes, *Death Without Weeping*, 275.

Chapter One

1. Bourdieu and Wacquant, *Invitation to Reflexive Sociology*, 51.
2. Walter Benjamin, "One-Way Street," in Bullock and Jennings, *Walter Benjamin: Selected Writings*, 448.
3. Simonian, *Defending the Land of the Jaguar*, 45.
4. Thrift, *Killer Cities*, 92–95, and on incidental deaths from infrastructures including windows, rails, roads, planes, electricity, noise, and habitat, see 119–122; also of people, see Tenorio-Trillo, *I Speak of the City*, 311.
5. The elite's transformation of socio-spatial relations in a constructed cityscape built on powerful discourses that they intended to manage the inhabitants and their behaviors. On this idea, see Casey, "How to Get from Space to Place."
6. Walter Benjamin, "A Critique of Violence," in Bullock and Jennings, *Walter Benjamin: Selected Writings*, 252.
7. Benjamin, 237–238, 241.
8. Agostini, *Monuments of Progress*, 145n124.
9. Foucault, *Security, Territory, and Population*, 4–23.
10. On horses' adaptation, see Olsen, "Urban Horse", 57–87; Kalof, *Beastly Natures*, 227–228.
11. See the excellent Rojas Hernández, "Muerto el perro."
12. On dogs in Mexican history generally, see Lipsett-Rivera, "New Challenge."
13. Statistics from INEGI (National Institute of Statistics and Geography) cited in, Agostini, *Monuments of Progress*, 26.
14. On Mexico City in general, see Tenorio-Trillo, *I Speak of the City*, and on populations in 1800 and 1910, see 47.
15. Michael Johns, *City of Mexico in the Age of Díaz*; Lear, *Workers, Neighbors, and Citizens*, 258–259.
16. Blichfeldt, *Mexican Journey*, 61–62
17. Tenorio-Trillo, *I Speak of the City*, 11–15, 46.
18. Sherratt, *Mexican Vistas*, 69; Bates, *Notes of a Tour in Mexico*, 34.
19. Gringo, *Life and Travels in Mexico*, 6; Weiner et al., *América Pintoresca*, 267.
20. Speckman Guerra, *Historia de la vida cotidiana*, 17–18.

21. Speckman Guerra, 19–21, 26, and 77.
22. Harper, *Journey in Southeastern Mexico*, 3.
23. Agostini, *Monuments of Progress*, 4, 135; Vitz, *City on a Lake*, 8–10.
24. Consejo Superior de Gobierno del Distrito Obras Pubs, vol. 611, E55; also in Tenorio-Trillo, *I Speak of the City*, 97.
25. Consejo Superior de Gobierno del Distrito Obras Pubs, vol. 611, E12, Aug. 1, 1904.
26. AHDF, Policía: Salubridad 1870–1913, vol. 3688, E40, putrefección de zahurdas.
27. Ayunt. De Gob. del DF, vol. 3639, 1892–1896, E1027.
28. Consejo Superior de Gobierno del Distrito Obras Pubs, vol. 611, E41, 1908.
29. Ayunt. De Gob. de DF, vol. 3639, E1071; see also Agostini, *Monuments of Progress*, 130.
30. Ayunt. De Gob. De DF, Bando 1886 sobre aseo de las vías publicas and in Sanitary Code 1891.
31. Morris, *Story of Mexico*, 82.
32. Flandrau, *Viva México*, 32, 196.
33. Harper, *Journey in Southeastern Mexico*, 30.
34. Montano, *Electrifying Mexico*, 8–12, 24–27.
35. Von Germeten, *Enlightened Patrolman*, 29–30.
36. Schivelbusch, *Disenchanted Night*, 81.
37. Von Germeten, *Enlightened Patrolman*, 334.
38. Schivelbusch, *Disenchanted Night*, 83–85, 134.
39. Von Germeten, *Enlightened Patrolman*, 112–114; Picatto, *City of Suspects*; on the much older association of dogs with policing, see Cervantes, *Dialogue of Dogs*, 16–17.
40. *El Imparcial* (Aug. 26, 1897), 3.
41. Flack, "Dark Trails," 215–241.
42. Flack, 215.
43. Flack, 217.
44. Flack, 218.
45. Flack, 222; Curcio-Nagy, "Dangerous Souls."
46. Also in Washington, DC; see Tenorio-Trillo, 43–62.
47. Agostini, *Monuments of Progress*, 81.
48. Common in reports in newspapers of the era.
49. Max Horkheimer, "The End of Reason," in Arato and Gebhart, *Essential Frankfurt School Reader*, 30.
50. Agostini, *Monuments of Progress*, 145. Notably, the working class mocked these efforts in the penny press; see Buffington, *Sentimental Education*, 18.
51. Agostini, *Monuments of Progress*, 42.
52. Agostini, 69.
53. Tenorio-Trillo, *I Speak of the City*, 287.
54. Orvañas, *Sociedad Médico "Pedro Escobedo."*
55. Wasik and Murphy, *Rabid*.
56. México, *Colección de Leyes Federales*, 87–91.
57. México, *Memoria del Consejo Superior de Salubridad*.

58. Cited in Agostini, *Monuments of Progress*, 148n127.
59. James Serpell, *In the Company of Animals*, especially 147–168; Thrift, *Killer Cities*, 98–99.
60. Wasik and Murphy, *Rabid*, 93–94.
61. Morton, *Tame and the Wild*, 297–301.
62. So, too, special animals like the "guardian angel" dogs, strays who escort hikers at certain sites in Mexico of their own accord and in expectation of a snack at journey's end.
63. Strother, *Porte Crayon's Mexico*, 604.
64. Strother, 610–619.
65. Strother, 619, 623, 793–4.
66. AHDF, Gob. del DF, Policía, vol. 3662, *Matanza del Perros*, E32, letter from Luis Curiel to Ayuntamiento, on dog ownership and regulations; AHDF, Bandos 1900 and 1903, caja 71, E14, Bando 1907, caja 74, E69 (on public health and dogs).
67. Strother, *Porte Crayon's Mexico*, 864.
68. Gringo, *Life and Travels in Mexico*, 31
69. Agostini, *Monuments of Progress*, 88–91, 407.
70. On Pasteur, see Wasik and Murphy, *Rabid*, 119–148.
71. Canóvas y Pasqual, *Inoculaciónes Preventativas de la Rabia*.
72. Canóvas y Pasqual, 64–36.
73. A well-known figure in public health, Liceago directed the Mexican Red Cross, attended the International Congress in Moscow, and founded a philharmonic orchestra. He has a statue and a street in his name in Mexico City. "Eduardo Liceago," in *Diccionario Porrúa*, vol. 2.
74. E.g., see *El Universal* (Dec. 8, 1888), 1; *El Universal* (Feb. 19, 1890), 1; also articles in *El Imparcial*, 1899.
75. Licéaga, *Informe de Dr. Eduardo Licéaga*, 11.
76. Galinda y Villa, *Ciudad de México*, 47–49.
77. Galinda y Villa, 51.
78. Galinda y Villa, 53.
79. Galinda y Villa, 128.
80. PHO 1–28, Juan Olivera López interviewed by Eugenia Meyer on Nov 23 and Dec. 5, 1972, DF; this slogan was a sort of branded recognition as it was also the nickname for bullfighter Juan Silveti: see Heftye Etienne, *Corridos Taurinos*, 213–218.
81. PHO 1–8, Pedro Peréz Grovas interviewed by Eugenia Meyer on Sept. 13, 19, and 26, 1972; on typhus sciences, see Tenorio-Trillo, *I Speak of the City*, 312–331.
82. *El Diario* (Dec. 6, 1881), 1.
83. *El Imparcial* (July 23, 1891), 1.
84. *El Universal* (Aug. 26, 1888), 6; *El Universal* (Dec. 4, 1889), 1.
85. Also tests against tuberculosis; see *El Imparcial* (July 10, 1900), 2; *El Imparcial* (Feb. 15, 1901), 1.
86. On typhus in Mexico, see Tenorio-Trillo, *I Speak of the City*, 318–320; generally, see Herzog, *Some We Love*, 207–211.

87. AGN, Gobierno de distrito: Instrucción Pública, vol. 144, E5, 1905; AGN, Gobierno de distrito: Instrucción Públicas y Bellas Artes, vol. 144, E46, 1911.
88. Wasik and Murphy, *Rabid*, 91–118.
89. Gob. del DF: Policía: Matanzas de Perros, vol. 3662, E23, 1893; on the stink of it earlier in century, see *El Universal* (Apr. 7, 1851), 2.
90. Tenorio-Trillo, 331–333, 337.
91. Thrift, *Killer Cities*, 118; Agostini, *Monuments of Progress*, 145.
92. Official efforts made, at least on paper, in Gandara, *Destrucción de las ratas*.
93. Von Germeten, *Enlightened Patrolman*, 87–88.
94. For rabies laws, see México, *Colección de Leyes Federales*, 322–339.
95. Gob. del DF: Policía: Matanzas de Perros, vol. 3662, E28, Nov. 22, 1896.
96. Agostini, *Monuments of Progress*, 64. There are many reported bites in the papers; see *El Diario* (Apr. 25, 1884), 3; *El Diario* (Apr. 17, 1884), 3; *El Diario* (June 12, 1884), 3; *El Diario* (Aug. 6, 1884), 4; *El Diario* (Apr. 16, 1884), 4; *El Universal* (Sept. 16, 1888), 7; *El Diario* (Apr. 16, 1884), 2.
97. Wasik and Murphy, *Rabid*, 5.
98. Tenorio-Trillo, *I Speak of the City*, 288–293; Thrift, *Killer Cities*, 99–101.
99. Coren, *Pawprints of History*, xii.
100. Exbalin Oberto, "Perros asesinos y matanzas de perros."
101. For a partial record, see *El Diario* (Mar. 30, 1882), 1; *El Diario* (Feb. 9, 1882), 2; *El Diario* (Apr. 7, 1882), 3; *El Diario* (Mar. 7, 1884), 3; *El Diario* (Mar. 5, 1884), 3; *El Imparcial* (Aug. 15, 1902), 5; *El Imparcial* (June 17, 1899), 5; *El Imparcial* (Oct. 27, 1900), 5.
102. Frederick Schwatta, "A Peccary Chase in Central Sonora (1890)," in Carmony and Brown, *Mexican Game Trails*, 37.
103. Including Mazatlan, *El Diario* (Apr. 18, 1882), 3; Monterrey, *El Diario* (Jan. 6, 1882), 2; Ciudad Júarez, *El Imparcial* (Feb. 2, 1897), 3; Guadelajara, *El Universal* (Dec. 27, 1889), 2; and of course, Mexico City, *El Diario* (July 16, 1884), 4.
104. Coren, *Pawprints of History*, 154.
105. Coren, 170; Wang, "Dogs and the Making of the American State"; Shukin, *Animal Capital*, 158.
106. Coren, *Pawprints of History*, 173.
107. Thrift, *Killer Cities* 99–101n20.
108. Von Germeten, *Enlightened Patrolman*, 87–88.
109. Gob. del DF: Policía: Matanzas de Perros, vol. 3662, E32.
110. Gob. del DF: Policía: Matanzas de Perros, vol. 3662, E36, 37, 38.
111. Gob. del DF: Policía: Matanzas de Perros, vol. 3662, E29, Mar. 3, 1900.
112. Herzog, *Some We Love*, 262.
113. Von Germeten, *Enlightened Patrolman*, 88–89.
114. Harper, *Journey in Southeastern Mexico*, 43–44; Goodhue, *Mexican Memories*, 159; Sherratt, *Mexican Vistas*, 224.
115. Flippin, *Sketches from the Mountains of Mexico*, 5.

116. Rohlfes, "Police and Penal Correction" appendices; Santoni, "Policía de la Ciudad de México"; von Germeten, *Enlightened Patrolman*, 88.
117. *El Universal* (Feb. 25, 1905), 9.
118. Reportage on rabies was very common and appeared in all types of periodicals. E.g., see *El Universal* (Dec. 8, 1888); *Imparcial* (June 17, 1889, June 8, 1900, May 1902); *Diario del Hogar* (Apr. 5, 1894, Apr. 5, 1884).
119. Carlos Rivas México, *Colección de leyes*, Regulaciones para la portación de armas May 6, 1875.
120. *Universal*, Feb. 25, 1905.
121. Rolfes, "Police and Penal Correction," appendices; Santoni, "Policía de la Ciudad de México."
122. Flandrau, *Viva México*, 24
123. Sherratt, *Mexican Vistas*, 222; Flippin, *Sketches from the Mountains of Mexico*, 129–136; Harper, *Journey in Southeastern Mexico*, 43–44.
124. Ávila González, "Voces y ladridos."
125. Gob. del DF: Policía: Matanzas de Perros, vol. 3662, E1, 1703. This concern also applied to human dead, and the reforms saw many cemeteries moved outside cities.
126. Gob. del DF: Policía: Matanzas de Perros, vol. 3662, E2, 1778.
127. Gob. del DF: Policía: Matanzas de Perros, vol. 3662, E8, 1808.
128. Gob. del DFF: Policía: Matanzas de Perros, vol. 3662, E10, 1811.
129. Gob. del DF: Policía: Matanzas de Perros, vol. 3662, E13, 1820.
130. Gob. del DF: Policía: Matanzas de Perros, vol. 3662, E39–68.
131. Gob. del DF.: Policía: Matanzas de Perros, vol. 3662, E2, 1778–1779.
132. Gob. del DF: Policía: Matanza del Perros, vol. 3162, E16, 1866.
133. Gob. del DF: Policía: Matanzas de Perros, vol. 3662, E19, Apr.19, 1887.
134. Gob. del DF: Policía: Matanzas de Perros, vol. 3662, E20, May7, 1888.
135. Gob. del DF: Policía: Matanzas de Perros, vol. 3662, E22, 1890, José M González.
136. Gob. del DF: Policía: Matanzas de Perros, vol. 3662, E24, 1894.
137. Gob. del DF: Policía: Matanza del Perros, vol. 3662, E30, 1900.
138. Gob. del DF: Policía: Matanza del Perros, vol. 617, E36, F110, 1910; Gob. del DF: Policía: Matanza del Perros, vol. 68, E56, F9, 1911.
139. Gob. del DF: Policía: Matanzas de Perros, vol. 3662, E26, Apr 22, 1895.
140. Licenses had long been a requirement. In 1851, they ran for one peso per year; see *El Universal* (Oct. 16, 1853), 1.
141. "Luis de Carmen Curiel," in *Diccionario Porrúa*, vol. 1.
142. *El Diario* (Mar. 16, 1882), 1.
143. Gob. del DF: Policía: Matanzas de Perros, vol. 3662, E32.
144. Gob. del DF: Policía: Matanzas de Perros, vol. 3662, E33.
145. Gob. del DF: Policía: Matanzas de Perros, vol. 3662, E35.
146. Among many reports of dead animals, see *El Diario* (Apr. 13, 1884), 3; *El Diario* (Mar. 30, 1882), 3; *El Diario* (Apr. 13, 1884), 3; *El Imparcial* (Aug. 15, 1899), 1; *El Universal* (Oct. 29, 1850), 3. On animal cremation, see *El Imparcial* (Apr. 15, 1895), 2.

147. López, "Urgent Need for Hygiene."
148. Pitarch, "Almas y cuerpo."
149. Tortorici, "Animals and Archives"; see also Simonian, *Defending the Land of the Jaguar*, 20.
150. On the rich visions of indigenous groups, see Morton, *Tame and the Wild*, 223–247.
151. Von Germeten, *Enlightened Patrolman*, 88–89.
152. See AHDF, Consejo Superior de Gobierno del Distrito, vol. 611, E55, June 28, 1910; AHDF, Policía Salubridad, vols. 3668, 3670, E182, 197, vol. 3683, E1, F39–42 (sobre explotación de animales muertos); also in AHDF, Gob. del DF, Contratos, vol. 563 (1907–1910) for multiple contracts for "matanza de animales."
153. Strother, *Porte Crayon's Mexico*, 871; Policía y salubridad, vol. 3683, E1, 1863–1869.
154. Policía en general V3637 E847 f4 1882; Policía en general, vol. 3638, E989, F6, 1891; Thrift, *Killer Cities*, 102.
155. Shukin, *Animal Capital*, 20–24.
156. *El Imparcial* (Aug. 15, 1895), 2.
157. Coren, *Pawprints of History*, 151, 170, 173; Thrift, *Killer Cities* 80.
158. Ann Blum, *Domestic Economies*.
159. Wasik and Murphy, *Rabid*, 100.
160. Thrift, *Killer Cities* 9.
161. E.g., see Manuel Payno, *Bandidos del Rio Frio*, 1899.
162. Agostini, *Monuments of Progress*, 53, 65–71, 113.
163. See Vázquez Flores, *Discursos de la discriminación*, 15–25, 106–107, 184.
164. Donna Harraway, "Universal Donors in a Vampire Culture" in Cronon, *Uncommon Ground*, 321.
165. Buffington, *Criminal and Citizen*, especially 3–8.
166. Agostini, *Monuments of Progress*, 53, 65–71, 113.
167. Donna Harraway, "Universal Donors in a Vampire Culture," in Cronon, *Uncommon Ground*, 321; Spiegel, "Historical Understanding."
168. González Roa and Covarrubias, *Problema rural de México*, 5, 12.
169. This is an idea taken from Max Weber, as discussed in Andrew Arato, "Introduction to Part II," in Arato and Gebhart, *Essential Frankfurt School Reader*, 191–193.
170. *El Universal* (June 3, 1852), 3; *El Universal* (Apr. 9, 1850), 4.
171. *El Universal* (June 3, 1852), 3.
172. *El Universal* (Nov. 20, 1888), 1.
173. Harper, *Journey in Southeastern Mexico*, xii, 65; Edwards, *On the Mexican Highlands*, 61.
174. Sherratt, *Mexican Vistas*, 43.
175. Blichfeldt, *Mexican Journey*, 45; Goodhue, *Mexican Memories*, 95.
176. Weiner et al., *América Pintoresca*, 271.
177. Blichfeldt, *Mexican Journey*, 40.
178. Conkling, *Appleton's Guide*, 109.
179. Thrift, *Killer Cities*, 9; Serpell, 229.
180. Tenorio-Trillo, *I Speak of the City*, 17–18; Agostini, *Monuments of Progress*, 113.
181. Garner, *Porfirio Díaz*; Cosío Villegas et al., *Historia moderna de México*.

182. On barracks life and soldaderas, see Neufeld, *Blood Contingent*, especially 95–126.
183. *El Imparcial* (Aug. 10, 1897), 2.
184. *El Universal* (Dec. 19, 1888), 2.
185. *El Universal* (May 20, 1848), 4.
186. Regarding the "unthinkable," see Trouillot, *Silencing the Past*.
187. Mbembe, *Necropolitics*, 37.
188. Tenorio-Trillo, *I Speak of the City*, especially chapter 1.
189. Neufeld, *Blood Contingent*, 180.

Chapter Two

1. *El Diablito Rojo* (Sept. 1908). Cited in Buffington, *Sentimental Education*, 176.
2. Karl Marx cited in Taussig, *Devil and Commodity Fetishism*, 10.
3. Scheper-Hughes, *Death Without Weeping*, 275.
4. Shukin, *Animal Capital*, 62–63, 103.
5. Thrift, *Killer Cities*, 101–107; Pachirat, *Every Twelve Seconds*; Buillet, *Hunters, Herders, and Hamburgers*. The term "Great Separation" is Nigel Thrift's.
6. Thrift, *Killer Cities*, 107.
7. Berman, *Modern Culture and Critical Theory*, 88.
8. Walker, "Animals and the Intimacy of History."
9. Andrew Arato and Eike Gebhart, "Introduction," in Arato and Gebhart, *Essential Frankfurt School Reader*, 11.
10. Agostini, *Monuments of Progress*, 34, citing Julio Guerrero on crime and greenery.
11. Emily Wakild, "Naturalizing Modernity," 101–123; Wakild, "Parables of Chapultepec." On pulquerías, see Áurea Toxqui Garay, "'El Recreo de los Amigos'"; on this impulse elsewhere, see Cronon, *Nature's Metropolis*.
12. And total parks numbers went from 2 to 34, Simonian, *Defending the Land of the Jaguar*, 73. Parks increased from 2% up to 16% by 1910.
13. E.g., satellites in Knight, *Mexican Revolution*, 9. These municipalities included Atzcapotzalco, Tacuba, Guadalupe Hidalgo, Tacubaya, Cuajímalpa, San Angel, Mixcoac, Ixtapalapa, Coyoacan, Tlalpam, Xochimilco, and Milpa Alta.
14. Galinda y Villa, *Ciudad de México*, 15.
15. Agostini, *Monuments of Progress*, 15n66, on wandering animals in the era of the Revillagigedo, 1789–1794.
16. Loo, *States of Nature*, 40; Carolyn Merchant, "Reinventing Eden," in Cronon, *Uncommon Ground*, 150.
17. The *científicos* were the science-minded progressive elite faction within the government.
18. Matthews, *Civilizing Machine*, 103–142.
19. Neufeld, *Blood Contingent*, 170–172.
20. Cronon, *Uncommon Ground*, 81.

21. Consejo Superior de Gobierno del Distrito Obras Pubs, vol. 611, E20, Nov. 22, 1904.
22. González Roa and Covarrubias, *Problema rural de México*, 172.
23. Vega Amaya, "Gobierno de Ramón Corral," 102–110, 155.
24. Simonian, *Defending the Land of the Jaguar*, 14–15, 41.
25. Cartmill, *View to a Death*, 59–60; Darnton, *Great Cat Massacre*, 9–74.
26. On this historiography, see Sessions, "Deep Ecology Movement," 107.
27. For an example of this racial perspective, see Morris, *Story of Mexico*, 48.
28. Orvañas, *Sociedad Médico "Pedro Escobedo."*
29. AHDF, Ayuntamiento: Sección paseos y jardines, 1886–1893, vol. 3590, E365.
30. Andrés Lira, *Comunidades indígenas frente*.
31. Agostini, *Monuments of Progress*, 45–47, 18.
32. Tenorio-Trillo, *I Speak of the City*, 57.
33. Sherratt, *Mexican Vistas*, 166.
34. Thrift, *Killer Cities*, 6.
35. Flandrau, *Viva México*, 32.
36. Even at times, panthers or mountain lions; see *El Universal* (Dec. 25, 1889), 2; *El Universal* (Jan. 11, 1890), 2.
37. Quiroz, *Entre el lujo y la subsistencia*, 19.
38. Quiroz, 246, 253.
39. Quiroz, 17, 18.
40. Serpell, *In the Company of Animals*, 195–197; Thrift, *Killer Cities*, 102–106.
41. Shukin, *Animal Capital*, 225, 3–4.
42. Horowitz et al., "Meat for the Multitudes"
43. Quiroz, *Entre el lujo y la subsistencia*, 61.
44. Quiroz, 58.
45. Quiroz, 44.
46. Quiroz, 47.
47. Quiroz, 90.
48. Harper, *Journey in Southeastern Mexico*, 25, 82; Goodhue, *Mexican Memories*, 159.
49. Quiroz, 87.
50. Quiroz, 93, 81.
51. Vázquez Flores, *Discursos de la discriminación*, 170.
52. Quiroz, *Entre el lujo y la subsistencia*, 61–81; Eames and Goode, "Coping with Poverty," 379–381.
53. Vitz, "'Lands with Which We Shall Struggle,'" 42, 48, 52.
54. Gringo, *Life and Travels in Mexico*, 18.
55. Gringo, *Life and Travels in Mexico*, 20.
56. So much so that servants sometimes stole powder from employers; see Strother, *Porte Crayon's Mexico*, 604.
57. E.g., see collected laws on meat, streets, and food—México, *Colección de Leyes Federales*, 91–94, 96–98, 231–243.

58. Carlos Rivas México, *Colección de leyes*, Arts. 23 and 31.
59. Banda May 10, 1871.
60. Banda Apr., 11, 1871.
61. AHDF, Rastros y Mercados: Rastro San Luces, vol. 3774, E542, F2, 1898.
62. Agostini, *Monuments of Progress*, 66.
63. A certain degree of callousness struck visitors; see Morris, *Story of Mexico*, 34–45 on various blood sports; on Mexican perspectives, see Johns, *City of Mexico*, 80–88; Lomnitz, *Death and the Idea of Mexico*, 292–303.
64. Bates, *Notes of a Tour in Mexico*, 58.
65. Edwards, *On the Mexican Highlands*, 57.
66. Blichfeldt, *Mexican Journey*, 166.
67. Carlos Rivas México, *Colección de leyes*, "Prohibición para la caza en los calzados," July 23, 1878.
68. Sherratt, *Mexican Vistas*, 119.
69. Agostini, *Monuments of Progress*, 66–68; Kroll, "Environmental History of Roadkill."
70. *El Universal* (May 19, 1854), 3.
71. Alongside dinner tables, other animals appearing in markets included hummingbirds intended for love charms and exotic birds whose feathers adorned fine hats.
72. Pilcher, *Sausage Rebellion*, 152.
73. AHDF, vol. 3773, E448, Serrano et al. petition to city, June 26, 1890; see also Morris, *Story of Mexico*, 32.
74. Carl Lumholtz, "From the Tarascos to Porfirio Díaz," in Jürgen Buchenau, *Mexico Otherwise*, 122.
75. Gobierno de Distrito: Fomento: Bosques 1893–1916, caja 3, legajo 4 E69 (Yucatán); Gobierno de Distrito: Fomento: Bosques 1893–1916, legajo 5. E62; Gobierno de Distrito: Fomento: Bosques 1893–1916, caja 5, legajo 7, E113.
76. AHDF, Gobierno de DF: Sección Gob. Terranos, caja 12, E1072, July 12, 1905.
77. AHDF, Ayuntamiento: Serie policía, caja 378, E13, Apr. 27, 1919.
78. *El Imparcial*, June 20, 1902.
79. Flandrau, *Viva México*, 107.
80. *El Universal* (Feb. 25, 1905), 9.
81. Quiroz, *Entre el lujo y la subsistencia*, 90.
82. Pilcher, *Sausage Rebellion*.
83. Santoyo, "De cerdos y de civilidad urbana"; Horowitz et al., "Meat for the Multitudes."
84. Carlos Rivas México, *Colección de leyes*, regulaciones sobre el tránsito de cerdos por la ciudad, Apr. 25, 1883.
85. Pilcher, *Sausage Rebellion*.
86. Ayunt. De Gob. DF, vol. 3639, E1062, Nov. 27, 1884.
87. González Roa and José Covarrubias, *Problema rural de México*, 187.
88. Policía y salubridad, vol. 3670 E182, 1886 (market); E197, F7, 1893, prohibits meat "*sacrificado*."

89. AHDF, Gob. Del Distrito, vol. 1363, various expedientes, 1900.
90. AHDF, Sec. Grl. De Ayuntamiento, vol. 3917, E24, F1, 1917–1918.
91. Ayunt. De Gobierno de DF, vol. 3639, E1073.
92. AHDF, Policía: Salubridad 1870–1913, vol. 3688, E76, Oct. 27, 1881.
93. For general examples, see Corral de Consejo Animales Mostrencos, vols. 570–571, 1917–1919. Mules in Exp77, 1919.
94. Conkling, *Appleton's Guide*, 126.
95. Geertz, "Deep Play"; See also Herzog, *Some We Love*, 149–173, and on quasi-Freudian theories of cockfighting, 153; and Dundes, *Cockfight*.
96. See Ciudad de Chihuahua, *Reglamentos que debería usar los palenques de gallos*; see also Ciudad de Villahermosa, *Reglamentos para los palenques de gallos*.
97. Vargas, *Gallo de combate*, 184.
98. Vargas, 183.
99. Herzog, *Some We Love*, 166.
100. Ciudad de Chihuahua, *Reglamentos que debería usar los palenques de gallos*, Arts. VII, VIII; Ciudad de Villahermosa, *Reglamentos para los palenques de gallos*, Art. 28.
101. This was about the number reported at Tennessee fights by Hal Herzog for the 1970s; Herzog, *Some We Love*, 169–173.
102. AHDF, Fondo Municipales: Sección Tlalpan, Caja 92, 1908.
103. Sarabia, *Peleas de gallos*; López, *Reglas sobre cría*, xx–xxii.
104. Sarabia, *Peleas de gallos*, 69–79; under the Bourbons, 83–105.
105. Obregón González, *Gladiador emplumado*, 9.
106. Villa-Flores, *Dangerous Speech*.
107. AHDF, Justicia cédulas y reales ordenes, vol. 2977, E19, 1701.
108. Obregón González, *Gladiador emplumado*, 48.
109. Obregón González, *Gladiador emplumado*, 52.
110. AGN, Inquisición, vol. 1429, E7, F249–253, Jan. 31, 1805.
111. Obregón González, *Gladiador emplumado*, 168.
112. Obregón González, *Gladiador emplumado*, 212.
113. Mañas Perdano, *Gallo fino combatiente*, 9.
114. Carlos Rivas México, *Colección de leyes*, 155.
115. Luis Inclán (1816–1875) was a rancher and famed novelist of charro-themed works including his best-known novel, *Astucia*; see "Luis Inclán," in *Diccionario Porrúa*, vol. 2; Obregón González, *Gladiador emplumado*, 226–257.
116. Obregón González, *Gallos de pelea*, xii.
117. Authorities legalized cockfights in Queretaro in 1890, Campeche in 1892, Michoacan in 1893, Guanajuato 1894, San Luis Potosí in 1897, Chihuahua in 1902, and Tabasco, Baja, Coahuila, and Chiapas by 1908, as well as in limited form in Jalisco, with only DF banning it to the city's edge.
118. Ciudad de Villahermosa, *Reglamentos para los palenques de gallos*, Art. 23.

119. AHDF, Gob. de Distrito, vol. 1673, 1911–1912, E889.
120. AHDF, Gob. de Distrito, vol. 1673, 1911–1912, E834, 835, 879, 880.
121. E.g., a twenty-five-peso fine for illegal fights; see Ciudad de Villahermosa, *Reglamentos para los palenques de gallos*, Art. 26.
122. AHDF, Gobierno del Distrito, vol. 1673, E929, Nov. 8, 1911.
123. Neufeld, *Blood Contingent*, 221, 226.
124. Obregón González, *Gladiador emplumado*, 261.
125. Obregón González, *Gladiador emplumado*, 264–273; *El Palenque*, Tomo 3, nos. 80–81, Oct. 1953; Katz, *Life and Times of Pancho Villa*, 69.
126. AHDF, Personal del ayuntamiento de México, vol. 4075, E2130, F7, 1920, and vol. 4076, E2191, F14, 1920.
127. Mañas Perdano, *Gallo fino combatiente*, 114.
128. Mañas Perdano, 38.
129. Mañas Perdano; Vargas, *Gallo de combate*, 35, 157–160.
130. Buffington, *Sentimental Education*, 126.
131. Vargas, *Gallo de combate*, 21.
132. Santos, *Memorias*, 130–131.
133. Obregón González, *Gladiador emplumado*, vi.
134. Gutiérrez Flores, "Manual de crianza," 60.
135. On masculinity and animal sports, see Lipsett-Rivera, *Origins of Macho*.
136. For one discussion of examples, see Mitchell, *Blood Sport*, 120–145.
137. E.g., see, Ciudad de Villahermosa, *Reglamentos para los palenques de gallos*, Art. 7.
138. Ciudad de Villahermosa, *Reglamentos para los palenques de gallos*.
139. Gérardin, *Animales zoologico*, 229–230.
140. Morris, *Story of Mexico*, 96.
141. Edwards, *On the Mexican Highlands*, 116.
142. Gringo, *Life and Travels in Mexico*, 63.
143. Edwards, *On the Mexican Highlands*, 117.
144. Herzog, *Some We Love*, 161.
145. Gutiérrez Flores, "Manual de crianza," 30–45.
146. Herzog, *Some We Love*, 156.
147. Beezley, *Judas at the Jockey Club*, 5.
148. Sarabia, *Peleas de gallos*, 121–164; Knight, *Mexican Revolution*, 34.
149. Vargas, *Gallo de combate*, ii.
150. Camp, *Mexican Political Biographies*.
151. Olalde Vázquez, "Prohibición a las peleas de gallos," 194.
152. Thrift, *Killer Cities*, 107.

Chapter Three

1. Tragically Hip, "Cordelia."
2. Schubert, *Death and Money in the Afternoon*, 4.
3. Vargas Coto, *Gente taurina*, 63.
4. Bunker, *Creating Mexican Consumer Culture*, 162.
5. Schubert, *Death and Money in the Afternoon*, 163; somewhat more complicated in Mexico, see Francois, *Culture of Everyday Credit*, 92–100, 170–175, 260–267.
6. Schubert, *Death and Money in the Afternoon*, 130. Gambling tended to be on the performance of different bull-breeders, since outcome otherwise did not vary much.
7. Scott, *Moral Economy of the Peasant*.
8. The working class clearly kept their own culture; see Buffington, *Sentimental Education*, 14.
9. Schubert, *Death and Money in the Afternoon*, 133.
10. McDevitt, "Muscular Catholicism"; Marie Hart and Susan Birrell, "Introduction," in Hart and Birrell, *Sport in the Sociocultural Process*, x; Erving Goffman, "Fun in Games," in Hart and Birrell, *Sports in the Sociocultural Process*, 40–91,; Peter Donnelly, "Toward a Definition of Sport Subcultures," in Hart and Birrell, *Sports in the Sociocultural Process*, 565, 568–577; Mangan and DaCosta, *Sport in Latin American Society*; Thomas Carter, "Baseball Arguments: Aficionismo and Masculinity at the Core of Cubanidad," in Hart and Birrell, *Sport in Latin American Society*, 118, 121–122, 136.
11. Schubert, *Death and Money in the Afternoon*, 116.
12. Schubert, *Death and Money in the Afternoon*, 147.
13. Vargas Coto, *Gente taurina*, 68, 64.
14. Schubert, *Death and Money in the Afternoon*, 27–35.
15. James Grehan, "Smoking and 'Early Modern' Sociability."
16. Pierre Bourdieu argues that the habitus comes out of the unconscious strategies that construct individual and collective practices and that build group identities. These work as structuring mechanisms that further lead to dispositions of domination under power. See Bourdieu, *Outline of a Theory in Practice*, 72–73, 82–85; Bourdieu and Wacquant, *Invitation to Reflexive Sociology*, 18, 24.
17. Beezley, *Judas at the Jockey Club*, 4–7.
18. Schubert, *Death and Money in the Afternoon*, 138.
19. Schubert, *Death and Money in the Afternoon*, 134–135.
20. True in Spain, too; see Schubert, *Death and Money in the Afternoon*, 116–127.
21. Sloan, *Death in the City*, 61; Schubert, *Death and Money in the Afternoon*, 113; Bunker, *Creating Mexican Consumer Culture*, 68; Terry, *Terry's Guide*, 294.
22. Max Horkheimer, "The End of Reason," in Arato and Gebhart, *Essential Frankfurt Reader*, 31.
23. Taussig, *Devil and Commodity Fetishism*, 4; Andrew Arato, "Introduction to Part II," in Arato and Gebhart, in *Essential Frankfurt School Reader*, 190.

24. Russel Berman, *Modern Culture and Critical Theory*, 95–96; Theodor Adorno, "Subject and Object," in Arato and Gebhart, *Essential Frankfurt School Reader*, 499, 508.
25. Even today, one finds more steel fences than guiding ropes in event line-ups.
26. Nightclubs with bouncers, velvet ropes, and empty seats know this phenomenon well.
27. Edwards, *On the Mexican Highlands*, 66.
28. Edwards, 67.
29. Edwards, 68.
30. Edwards, 68.
31. Edwards, 68.
32. Bunker, *Creating Mexican Consumer Culture*, 68.
33. Bunker, 32–33.
34. Schubert, *Death and Money in the Afternoon*, 94; Sobaquillo, *Revistas taurinas de El Liberal*.
35. Bunker, *Creating Mexican Consumer Culture*, 28.
36. AHDF, Gobierno del Distrito, vol., 1673, E876, 1911.
37. AHDF, Gobierno del Distrito, vol., 1673, E887, 1911.
38. AHDF, Gobierno del Distrito, vol., 1675, E918, 1911.
39. Camacho Morfín, *Historietas de El Buen Tono*, 12–13.
40. Camacho Morfín, 51.
41. Schubert, *Death and Money in the Afternoon*, 77.
42. Schubert, 77.
43. Bunker, *Creating Mexican Consumer Culture*, 84–5, 92.
44. Relatively few minor thefts were charged in city, with many handled administratively with a night in jail or informal fines. See Piccato *City of Suspects*, 233, 236, 221.
45. AHDF, Diversiones publicas: Toros, vol., 857, E115, 1887.
46. *El Toreo*, no. 2, Nov. 25, 1895, 7.
47. AGN, Estado Mayor Presidencial, caja 98, Expediente de Samuel García Cuellar.
48. Neufeld, *Blood Contingent*, 231–233; AHDF, Diversiones publicas: Toros, vol., 857, E195.
49. Rosell, *Plazas de toros de México*, 48, 152.
50. AHDF, Diversiones publicas: Toros, vol. 857, E142.
51. Schubert, *Death and Money in the Afternoon*, 62. Spain had lost about 259 matadors in this era.
52. AHDF, Diversiones publicas: Toros, vol., 857 E184, 1898
53. AHDF, Diversiones publicas: Toros, vol., 857 E153, 1895.
54. Schubert, *Death and Money in the Afternoon*, 140–143.
55. This appears in numerous articles found in Sobaquillo, *Revistas taurinas de El Liberal*.
56. Alyce Taylor Cheska, "Sports Spectacular: The Social Ritual of Power," in Hart and Birrell, *Sport in the Sociocultural Process*, 374–377; Thomas Carter, "Baseball Arguments: Aficionismo and Masculinity at the Core of Cubanidad," in Hart and Birrell, *Sport in Latin American Society*, 131.
57. Schubert, *Death and Money in the Afternoon*, 93, and on Darwinism, 93n12.
58. Schubert, 133.

59. Schubert, 143.
60. These were prominently cited and had consistently long runs. On periodical circulations, see Kabalen de Bichara, "Late 19th-Century Periodical Print Culture."
61. Somewhat similarly to sharing by penny press audiences, see Buffington, *Sentimental Education*.
62. *El Toreo*, Nov 18, 1895, 2.
63. *El Toreo*, no. 10, Jan. 13, 1896, 2.
64. *El Toreo*, no. 11, Feb. 3, 1896, 2.
65. *Ratas y Mamarrachas*, no. 10, year 1, Dec. 13, 1903, 5.
66. Bunker, *Creating Mexican Consumer Culture*, 44.
67. *Ratas y Mamarrachas*, no. 30, year 2, June, 1904, 3.
68. *Ratas y Mamarrachas*, no. 13, year 2, Jan. 3, 1904, 56. This conflict is discussed in the next chapter.
69. Not so different from kayfabe in the modern US professional wrestling industry.
70. *El Toreo*, Nov. 18, 1895, 1–2.
71. *Ratas y Mamarrachas*, no. 1, year 1, Oct. 11, 1903, 1–3.
72. *El Toreo*, no. 19, Apr. 20, 1896, 4.
73. Roughly, a clown, fools, idiots, wise monkeys, and baggage.
74. *Ratas y Mamarrachas*, no. 1, year 1, Oct. 11, 1903, 7.
75. "No mames" roughly means don't be an idiot; *Ratas y Mamarrachas*, no. 13, year 2, Jan. 3, 1904, 2; on albur as language, see Buffington, *Sentimental Education*.
76. *El Toreo*, no. 9, Jan. 20, 1896, 2.
77. "Las Novilladas," *El Toreo*, no. 17, Mar. 16, 1896, 2.
78. *El Toreo*, no. 18, Apr. 6, 1896, 1–2.
79. *El Toreo*, no. 3, Dec. 2, 1895, 7.
80. "Recuerdos y suplicas a Don Ponciano," *El Toreo*, no. 4, Dec. 9, 1895, 1.
81. "La Venida del Mesias," *El Toreo*, no. 7, Jan. 6, 1896, 1.
82. *El Toreo*, year 3, no. 1, Jan. 15, 1897, 2.
83. "Tauromachias," *El Toreo*, no. 6, Dec. 23, 1895, 6.
84. Goodhue, *Mexican Memories*, 120, 127; Bates, *Notes of a Tour in Mexico*, 77.
85. Edwards, *On the Mexican Highlands*, 66.
86. *El Toreo*, year 3, no. 3, Nov. 16, 1897, 2.
87. *Ratas y Mamarrachas*, no. 3, year 1, Oct. 25, 1903, 4.
88. *Ratas y Mamarrachas*, no. 19, year 2, Feb. 14, 1904, 2.
89. *El Toreo*, year 3, no. 4, Dec. 13, 1897, 3.
90. Louis A. Zucher Jr. and Arnold Meadow, "On Bullfights and Baseball: An Example of Interaction of Social Institutions," in Hart and Birrell, *Sport in the Sociocultural Process*, 645–675.
91. Buffington, *Sentimental Education*, 6–7.
92. Leal et al., *Multiplicación de los cines en la provincia*, vol. 15, 157–258.
93. Neufeld and Matthews, *Mexico in Verse*, 10–12.
94. Heftye Etienne, *Corridos Taurinos Mexicanos*.

95. Mendoza, *Corrido Mexicano*, 278–285; Heftye Etienne, *Corridos Taurinos*, 63.
96. Heftye Etienne, *Corridos Taurinos*, 63.
97. Heftye Etienne, *Corridos Taurinos*, 73.
98. Heftye Etienne, *Corridos Taurinos*, 81.
99. Mendoza, *Corrido Mexicano*, 369–372; Moreno, *Charro*.
100. Heftye Etienne, *Corridos Taurinos*, 85.
101. Heftye Etienne, 83.
102. Heftye Etienne, 94.
103. Heftye Etienne, 115.
104. Heftye Etienne, 143.
105. Heftye Etienne, 138–147.
106. Mendoza, *Corrido Mexicano*, 372–376, 376–379, 379–382.
107. Heftye Etienne, *Corridos Taurinos*, 162.
108. About eight inches; Heftye Etienne, *Corridos Taurinos*, 180.
109. Heftye Etienne, *Corridos Taurinos*, 164. See chapter 5 for details on this case.
110. Heftye Etienne, 299.
111. Heftye Etienne, 301.
112. Heftye Etienne, 306.
113. Mendoza, *Corrido Mexicano*, 367–368.
114. Heftye Etienne, *Corridos Taurinos*, 69.
115. Heftye Etienne, 339–340.
116. Campos, *Homegrown*, 150–160.
117. *El Toreo*, no. 4, Dec. 9, 1895, 1
118. *El Toreo*, year 3, no. 2, Jan. 29, 1897, 1
119. *Diario del Hogar*, Mar. 9, 1904.
120. *El Toreo*, year 2, no. 8, Nov. 23, 1896, 3
121. Schubert, *Death and Money in the Afternoon*, 129–130
122. Schubert, 128.
123. Heftye Etienne, *Corridos Taurinos*, 303.
124. AHDF, Diversiones publicas: Toros, vol. 857, E173; Alexander, *City on Fire*, 3, 23–24, 150.
125. *El Toreo*, no. 3, Dec. 2, 1895, 1
126. Moliné y Roca, *Cháchara taurina*, 71.
127. *New York Times*, "Bullfight Stopped, Crowd Burns Arena" (June 6, 1904), 1.
128. *Ratas y Mamarrachas*, no. 32, year 2, July 1904, 2.
129. *Ratas y Mamarrachas*, no. 14, year 2, Jan. 10, 1904, 1.
130. Sobaquillo, *Revistas taurinas de El Liberal*, 87.
131. *Ratas y Mamarrachas*, no. 47, year 2, Oct. 23, 1904, 2.
132. "Viajes del recreo," *El Toreo*, no. 6, Dec. 23 1895, 1.
133. *Ratas y Mamarrachas*, no. 13, year 2, Jan. 3, 1904, 5.
134. *Ratas y Mamarrachas*, no. 12, year 1, Dec. 27, 1903, 1.
135. *Ratas y Mamarrachas*, no. 16, year 2, Jan. 24, 1904, 5.

136. *Ratas y Mamarrachas*, no. 18, year 2, Feb. 7, 1904, 3.
137. *Ratas y Mamarrachas*, no. 3, year 1, Oct. 25, 1903, 5.
138. Erving Goffman, "Fun in Games," in Hart and Birrell, *Sport in the Sociocultural Process*, 59.
139. Allen, *History of Boxing in Mexico*, 13–27.

Chapter Four

1. Schubert, *Death and Money in the Afternoon*, 52, citing a Spanish bureaucrat in 1868.
2. On slaughterhouse as origin, see Morton, *Tame and the Wild*, 59.
3. Schubert, *Death and Money in the Afternoon*, 19.
4. Schubert, 24.
5. Rosell, *Plazas de toros de México*.
6. Townsend, *Fifth Sun*.
7. Curcio-Nagy, *Great Festivals of Colonial Mexico City*, 74–92.
8. Schubert, *Death and Money in the Afternoon*, 194.
9. Rosell, *Plazas de toros de México*, foreword.
10. Viqueira Albán, *Propriety and Permissiveness*, 15–18.
11. Viqueira Albán, *Propriety and Permissiveness*, 10–27.
12. AHDF, Diversiones públicas, tomo 8, vol. 803, Fondo Municipal, E406, 1868.
13. Carlos Rivas México, *Colección de leyes*.
14. AHDF, Diversiones publicas: Toros, vol. 801, E610, 1874.
15. *El Toreo*, year 3, no. 6, Dec. 27, 1897, 3.
16. Normally, but one in the seventeenth century had 1,350 in attendance.
17. AHDF, Diversiones públicas, tomo 8, vol. 803, Fondo Municipal, E725, 1885; on the potential political repercussions of puppetry and theater, see Beezley, *Mexican National Identity*.
18. AHDF, Diversiones públicas, tomo 8, vol. 803, Fondo Municipal, E719, 1885.
19. AHDF, Diversiones públicas, tomo 8, vol. 803, Fondo Municipal, E725, 1885.
20. AHDF, Diversiones públicas, tomo 8, vol. 803, Fondo Municipal, E780, 1886, 1895.
21. Schubert, *Death and Money in the Afternoon*, 27–28.
22. AHDF, Diversiones publicas: vol. 857, E160, Dec. 12, 1896.
23. Schubert, *Death and Money in the Afternoon*, 36–39.
24. Schubert, 39n100.
25. Rosell, *Plazas de toros de México, 59*.
26. Rosell, 77.
27. Rosell, 85; on his charro styling, see Moreno, *Charro*.
28. Rosell, *Plazas de toros de México*, 177.
29. Rosell, 59, 128.
30. AHDF, Diversiones publicas: Toros vol. 857, E195, 196, 1899.
31. AHDF, Diversiones publicas: Toros vol. 596, E1, 1903.

32. Ramírez Rancaño, "Rodolfo de Gaona," 35.
33. Rosell, *Plazas de toros de México*, 63, 93, 128.
34. AHDF, Diversiones publicas: Toros, vol. 596, E5, 1905.
35. AHDF, Diversiones publicas: Toros, vol. 596, E12, 1908.
36. AHDF, Diversiones publicas: Toros, vol. 857, E130.
37. AHDF, Diversiones publicas: Toros, vol. 857, E139, 140, 141.
38. Price was listed in vara squared, with a vara measuring 33.3 inches.
39. The US and British investors did not seem to be involved in this; see Garner, *British Lions and Mexican Eagles*.
40. Schubert, *Death and Money in the Afternoon*, 59–61.
41. AHDF, Diversiones publicas: Toros, vol. 857, E136, 1894.
42. (A.k.a. Iñigo) Laso (1853–1920) was a Spanish mine owner with six haciendas, a paper factory, and a small railway. A decorated war hero against the United States in Cuba, he was close with Porfirio Díaz and hated by the surgeon Aureliano Urrutia, who had him sent into exile in United States during the Revolution. "Iñigo Noriego Laso," in *Diccionario Porrúa*, in vol. 2.
43. AHDF, Diversiones publicas: Toros, vol., 857, E142.
44. AHDF, Diversiones publicas: Toros, vol., 857, E105, 1887.
45. AHDF, Diversiones publicas: Toros, vol., 857, E119, 1887.
46. Schubert, 42. Usually, each bull killed two to three horses.
47. AHDF, Diversiones publicas: Toros, vol. 857, E104, 1887.
48. AHDF, Diversiones publicas: Toros, vol. 857, E122, 121, 138, 1888.
49. AHDF, Diversiones publicas: Toros, vol. 857, E138.
50. In contrast, the Spanish press had most criticism directed at the bullfighters' agents. Schubert, *Death and Money in the Afternoon*, 49–50.
51. *El Toreo*, no. 1, Nov. 18, 1895, 1–2.
52. *El Toreo*, no. 1, Nov. 18, 1895, 7.
53. *El Toreo*, no. 2, Nov. 25, 1895, 7.
54. "Tauromachias," *El Toreo*, no. 6, Dec. 23, 1895, 6.
55. *El Toreo*, no. 11, Feb. 3, 1896, 3.
56. "Tauromachias," *El Toreo*, no. 6, Dec. 23, 1895, 6.
57. *El Toreo*, year 3, no. 9, Jan. 17, 1898, cover.
58. "Consideraciones," *Ratas y Mamarrachas*, no. 23, year 2, Mar. 13, 1904, 2.
59. *Ratas y Mamarrachas*, no. 26, year 2, Apr. 17, 1904, 1.
60. *Ratas y Mamarrachas*, no. 39, year 2, Aug. 1904, 1.
61. *Ratas y Mamarrachas*, no. 40, year 2, Aug. 1904, 1.
62. *Ratas y Mamarrachas*, no. 42, year 2, Sept. 18, 1904, 1, 2.
63. *El Toreo*, year 2, no. 9, Nov. 30, 1896, 2.
64. "Díceres y calumnias," *Ratas y Mamarrachas*, no. 60, year 3, Feb. 5, 1905, 2.
65. E.g., "Últimos abusos," *Ratas y Mamarrachas*, no. 62, year 3, Mar 5, 1905, 1–2.
66. *Ratas y Mamarrachas*, no. 63, year 3, Apr. 3, 1905, 2.
67. *Ratas y Mamarrachas*, no. 13, year 2, Jan. 3, 1904, 2.

68. *El Toreo*, year 2, no. 3, Oct. 19, 1896, 2.
69. *El Toreo*, year 2, no. 4, Oct. 26, 1896, 3.
70. "Estafemo Taurino," *El Toreo*, year 2, no. 5, Nov. 2, 1896, 2.
71. *El Toreo*, no. 17, Mar. 16, 1896, 1.
72. *Ratas y Mamarrachas*, no. 21, year 2, Feb. 28, 1904, 2, 3.
73. *El Toreo*, year 3, no. 9, Jan. 17, 1898, 2.
74. *El Toreo*, no. 6, Dec. 23, 1895, 5.
75. *Ratas y Mamarrachas*, no. 10, year 1, Dec. 13, 1903, 2.
76. *Ratas y Mamarrachas*, no. 20, year 2, Feb. 21, 1904, 2; revisited in *Ratas y Mamarrachas*, no. 23, year 2, Mar. 13, 1904, 3.
77. *Diario del Hogar*, Mar. 9, 1904.
78. *Ratas y Mamarrachas*, no. 24, year 2, Apr. 2, 1904, 1, 2.
79. Heftye Etienne, *Corridos Taurinos*, 81.
80. *El Toreo*, no. 19, Apr. 20, 1896, 1.
81. *El Toreo*, year 2, no. 8, Nov. 23, 1896, 2.
82. *Ratas y Mamarrachas*, no. 39, year 2, Aug. 1904, 2.
83. PHO 1–144, Victor Velasquez, interviewed by Eugenia Meyer, Feb. 6, 1975. In Ygnacio's personal life, he may have been less traditional, as some claim he had been released without arrest from the police raid on the Famous 41 cross-dresser's ball.
84. *El Toreo*, year 3, no. 2, Jan. 29, 1897, 2.
85. *El Toreo*, year 2, no. 2, Oct. 12, 1896, 3.
86. *El Toreo*, year 2, no. 6, Nov. 9, 1896, 1–2.
87. *El Toreo*, year 2, no. 2, Oct. 12, 1896, 7.
88. *El Toreo*, year 2, no. 11, Jan. 4, 1897, 2.
89. *Ratas y Mamarrachas*, no. 10, year 1, Dec. 13, 1903, 1, 2.
90. *El Toreo*, no. 15, Mar. 2, 1896, 2–3.
91. *Ratas y Mamarrachas*, no. 18, year 2, Feb. 7, 1904, 6.
92. *Ratas y Mamarrachas*, no. 22, year 2, Mar. 3, 1904, 2.
93. Sobaquillo, *Revistas taurinas de El Liberal 89*.
94. AHDF, Diversiones publicas: Toros, vol. 857, E198, 1900.
95. Ads in *El Universal*, June 11, 1851; May 22, July 12, and Oct. 19, 1852; May 5, 1854.
96. Sobaquillo, *Revistas taurinas de El Liberal*, 94.
97. Eric Larson, *Devil in the White City*, 222–223.
98. PHO 2–48, Raúl de Anda interviewed by Ximena Sepulveda Otaira, Nov. 27 and 28, 1975.
99. See the next chapter for details on these ladies.
100. Coello and Lerdo, *Multiplicación de los cines*, vol. 14, 187.
101. Schubert, *Death and Money in the Afternoon*, 56.
102. Coello and Lerdo, *Multiplicación de los cines*, vol. 14, 183–260.
103. AHDF, Diversiones públicas: vol. 857, E121, 1880.
104. Schubert, *Death and Money in the Afternoon*, 136.

105. AHDF, Consejo Superior de Gobierno del DF vol. 611, exp. E22, F11, 1904, statutes in Feb. 17 in English and Spanish.
106. AHDF, Consejo Superior de Gobierno del DF, vol. 611, E23, 1904.
107. Gramsci, *Prison Notebooks*, 238.
108. "A los impugnadores de las corridas de Toros," *Ratas y Mamarrachas*, no. 66, year 3, Apr. 10, 1905, 2–3.
109. "A los impugnadores de las corridas de Toros," *Ratas y Mamarrachas*, no. 66, year 3, Apr. 10, 1905, 3.
110. *Ratas y Mamarrachas*, no. 67, year 3, Apr. 17, 1905, 1–3.
111. *Ratas y Mamarrachas*, no. 68, year 3, May 1, 1905, 2–3.
112. Sherratt, *Mexican Vistas*, 85–86.
113. Gringo, *Life and Travels in Mexico*, 112.
114. Schubert, *Death and Money in the Afternoon*, 12–13.
115. Including Mazzantini; Moliné y Roca, *Cháchara taurina*, 62–63, 149.
116. On setting water out versus rabies, see *El Diario* (Apr. 25, 1884), 2.
117. Gob. del DF: Policía: Matanzas de Perros, vol. 3662, E16, 1863–1866; Gob. Del DF: Policía: Matanzas de Perros, vol. 611, E22, 1904; also, in the colonial era, see von Germeten, *Enlightened Patrolman*, 87.
118. Schubert, *Death and Money in the Afternoon*, 165.
119. AHDF, Diversiones publicas: Toros, vol. 857, E107; AHDF, Diversiones publicas: Toros, vol. 857, E109, 1887; AHDF, Diversiones publicas: Toros vol. 857, E116.
120. Agostini, *Monuments of Progress*, 141.
121. AHDF, Diversiones publicas: Toros, vol. 857, E136, 1894.
122. AHDF, Diversiones publicas: Toros, vol. 857, E116.
123. AHDF, Diversiones publicas: Toros, vol. 857, E117, 1887.
124. AHDF, Diversiones publicas: Toros, vol. 857, E131.
125. Lafevor *Prizefighting and Civilization*, 29, 35.
126. AHDF, Gobierno de Distrito, vol. 1673, E888, July 15, 1911, signed by I. and B. Romero Aug. 12, 1910.
127. Schubert, *Death and Money in the Afternoon*, 165.
128. AHDF, Diversiones publicas: Toros, vol. 800, E128.
129. AHDF, Diversiones públicas: Toros, vol. 857, E151.
130. *Ratas y Mamarrachas*, no. 73, year 3, Aug. 1905, 2.
131. *El Toreo*, year 2, no. 10, Dec. 9, 1896, 2, 4–5.
132. AHDF, Ayunt. de DF, vol. 800, E384, 1866.
133. Olalde Vázquez, "Prohibición a las peleas de gallos."
134. Ortega y Gasset, *Caza y los toros*, 161.
135. Agostini, *Monuments of Progress*, 148; Alan Knight, "Revolutionary Project, Recalcitrant People: Mexico 1910–1940," in Rodriguez, *Revolutionary Process in Mexico*, 213–244
136. AHDF, Diversiones públicas, tomo 8, vol. 803, Fondo Municipal, E720, 1885.
137. *Mexican Herald*, Oct. 2, 1895.

138. Goodhue, *Mexican Memories*, 8.
139. Blichfeldt, *Mexican Journey*, 143.
140. Bates, *Notes of a Tour in Mexico*, 77; Gringo, *Life and Travels in Mexico*, 56.
141. Sherratt, *Mexican Vistas*, 86.
142. Sherratt, *Mexican Vistas*, 137.
143. Conkling, *Appleton's Guide*, 125.
144. E.g., see Blichfeldt, *Mexican Journey*, 248–249; Bates, *Notes of a Tour in Mexico*, 77–78; Edwards, *On the Mexican Highlands*, 73–74.
145. Goodhue, *Mexican Memories*, 121–126; Gringo, *Life and Travels in Mexico*, 58, 61.
146. Conkling, *Appleton's Guide*, 126.
147. Conkling, 125.
148. Goodhue, *Mexican Memories*, 121–126.
149. Gringo, *Life and Travels in Mexico*, 59.
150. Edwards, *On the Mexican Highlands*, 69.
151. Edwards, 74.
152. Blichfeldt, *Mexican Journey*, 248–249.
153. Goodhue, *Mexican Memories*, 128.
154. Bates, *Notes of a Tour in Mexico*, 84.
155. Flippin, *Sketches from the Mountains of Mexico*, 263; Gringo, *Life and Travels in Mexico*, 56, 60.
156. Bates, *Notes of a Tour in Mexico*, 79.
157. Goodhue, *Mexican Memories*, 128.
158. Edwards, *On the Mexican Highlands*, 68.
159. Edwards, 75.
160. Flippin, *Sketches from the Mountains of Mexico*, 264.
161. Gringo, *Life and Travels in Mexico*, 57.
162. For just one example, see Goodhue, *Mexican Memories*, 128.
163. Blichfeldt, *Mexican Journey*, 249.

Chapter Five

1. On the fight by Luis Mazzantini, see Edwards, *On the Mexican Highlands*, 74.
2. Sloan, *Death in the City*; and Sloan, *Runaway Daughters*.
3. Heftye Etienne, *Corridos Taurinos*, 316–317.
4. Heftye Etienne, 316–317.
5. Gaona, *Mis 20 años de torero*, iii, 5, 11.
6. Rosell, *Plazas de toros de México*, 177.
7. Gaona, *Mis 20 años de torero*, 144; Sloan, *Death in the City*, 86.
8. Mbembe, *Necropolitics*, 16.
9. Schubert, *Death and Money in the Afternoon*, 93; Shepard, *Others*; Beezley, *Judas at the Jockey Club*, 14–16.

10. Schubert, *Death and Money in the Afternoon*, 94–95.
11. As depicted, e.g., in the novel *Santa*. These habits are also featured in Schubert, *Death and Money in the Afternoon*, 82–87.
12. Sloan, *Death in the City*, 61.
13. Ramírez Rancaño, "Rodolfo de Gaona" 32–34
14. Rodolfo Gaona, *Mis 20 años de torero*, 16.
15. Pica Pica, *Gaona*, 5–6.
16. Ramírez Rancaño, "Rodolfo de Gaona," 34.
17. Gaona, *Mis 20 años de torero*, 30, 32.
18. Pica Pica, *Gaona*, 10; Gaona, *Mis 20 años de torero*, 32.
19. Gaona, *Mis 20 años de torero*, 81, 84.
20. Gaona, *Mis 20 años de torero*, 16, 322–29, 330–332. He makes no mention of his elaborate toasts, nor of meeting with Francisco Madero, Venustiano Carranza, or Alvaro Obregón.
21. Ramírez Rancaño, "Rodolfo de Gaona" 34.
22. Pica Pica, *Gaona*, 4.
23. Aureliano Urrutia (1872–1975) also served as a medic with Huerta's 3rd Battalion in Quintana Roo, was made Minister of Gobernación in 1913, and later exiled to San Antonio, United States. "Aureliano Urretia," in *Diccionario Porrúa*, vol. 3; Heftye Etienne, *Corridos Taurinos*, 339n54. According to this book, Urrutia stood accused of cutting out a rival senator's tongue (one Serapio Rendón).
24. Ramírez Rancaño, "Rodolfo de Gaona" 35.
25. Schubert, *Death and Money in the Afternoon*, 80.
26. Ramírez Rancaño, "Rodolfo de Gaona"37.
27. Ramírez Rancaño, 37.
28. Ramírez Rancaño, 38.
29. Ramírez Rancaño, 39; Gaona, *Mis 20 años de torero*, 98, 198.
30. Gaona, *Mis 20 años de torero*, 204–205.
31. Ramírez Rancaño, "Rodolfo de Gaona,"40.
32. Ramírez Rancaño, 41.
33. Ramírez Rancaño, 42–44.
34. Gaona, *Mis 20 años de torero*, 90.
35. The press generally worked to shape ideas of honor and status; see Piccato, *Tyranny of Opinion*.
36. Gaona, *Mis 20 años de torero*, 86–88.
37. Gaona, 92.
38. Sloan, *Death in the City*, 63.
39. Gaona, *Mis 20 años de torero*, 98.
40. Sloan, *Death in the City*, 58–64.
41. México, Inspección de policía, E1718, Juzgado Quinto de Instrucción, Dec. 5, 1909 (etc.), on Rapto charge.
42. Gaona, *Mis 20 años de torero*, 88–90.

43. Sloan, *Death in the City*, 61.
44. Gaona, *Mis 20 años de torero*, 92.
45. Schubert, *Death and Money in the Afternoon*, 90–114.
46. Heftye Etienne, *Corridos Taurinos*, 315.
47. Heftye Etienne, 318.
48. Heftye Etienne, 164, 193–936.
49. Heftye Etienne, 196.
50. Heftye Etienne, 328. Conde Koma was a famed Japanese jujitsu fighter who taught at the Military College and would later go on to found Gracie jujitsu in Brazil.
51. Heftye Etienne, *Corridos Taurinos*, 316–317.
52. Sloan, *Runaway Daughters*, 43–45.
53. French, *Heart in a Glass Jar*, 196–211.
54. French, "Prostitutes and Guardian Angels," 529–531.
55. Gamboa, *Santa*; *Santa* quickly sold 6,000 copies, Ramírez Rancaño, "Rodolfo de Gaona," 2.
56. Agostini, *Monuments of Progress*, 136–137.
57. Rosell, *Plazas de toros de México*, 170.
58. Also the case in Guatemala; see Kirkpatrick, "Consumer Culture in Guatemala City."
59. Schubert, *Death and Money in the Afternoon*, 74–76, 211.
60. Schubert, 211.
61. The people or the mafia of the ponytail. This proved the case in Spain, too; see Moliné y Roca, *Cháchara taurina*, 98–99.
62. Mendoza, *Corrido Mexicano*, 382–386.
63. Heftye Etienne, *Corridos Taurinos*, 213–218; and see the discussion in chapter 1.
64. *Ratas y Mamarrachas*, no. 17, year 2, Jan. 3, 1904, 2.
65. Moliné y Roca, *Cháchara taurina*, 18.
66. *El Toreo*, Nov. 18, 1895, 2.
67. *El Toreo*, no. 10, Jan. 13, 1896, 2.
68. *Ratas y Mamarrachas*, no. 3, year 1, Oct. 25, 1903, 3, 4.
69. *Ratas y Mamarrachas*, no. 27, year 2, May 1, 1904, 2.
70. *El Toreo*, no. 8, Jan. 13, 1896, 1.
71. *Ratas y Mamarrachas*, no. 1, year 1, Oct. 11, 1903, 6.
72. Moliné y Roca, *Cháchara taurina*, 47.
73. Moliné y Roca.
74. Higueras, *Intimidades taurinas*, 27.
75. Higueras, *Intimidades taurinas*, 27, 41, 43, 48.
76. Higueras, 45.
77. Heftye Etienne, *Corridos Taurinos*, 198.
78. Vargas Coto, *Gente taurina*.
79. Vargas Coto, 2–7.
80. Vargas Coto, 12–14.

81. Louis A. Zucher Jr. and Arnold Meadow, "On Bullfights and Baseball: An Example of Interaction of Social Institutions," in Hart and Birrell, *Sport in the Sociocultural Process*, 673.
82. Blichfeldt, *Mexican Journey*, 11.
83. Edwards, *On the Mexican Highlands*, 66.
84. Bates, *Notes of a Tour in Mexico*, 82–83.
85. Edwards, *On the Mexican Highlands*, 71.
86. Edwards, 75.
87. Goodhue, *Mexican Memories*, 127.
88. Higueras, *Intimidades taurinas*, 24–25.
89. AHDF, Diversiones publicas: Toros, vol. 857, E184, 1898.
90. AHDF, Diversiones publicas: Toros, vol. 857, E112.
91. Schubert, *Death and Money in the Afternoon*, 56.
92. Schubert, 86–87.
93. Rosell, *Plazas de toros de México*, 158.
94. Schubert, *Death and Money in the Afternoon*, 82.
95. Schubert, 85.
96. Francois, *Culture of Everyday Credit*, 170–173.
97. Rosell, *Plazas de Toros de México*, 88.
98. Vinciane Despret, "From Secret Agents to Interagency," 29–44. To Vinciane Despret's mind, the animal's reactions to stimuli cannot be dissociated from deliberate subjective thought and must be considered a form of conscious agency. Where he goes too far into a non-falsifiable fantasy, the bulls certainly did have "selfhood" beyond that of, say, a sea sponge.
99. Heftye Etienne, *Corridos Taurinos*, 173–174.
100. Moliné y Roca, *Cháchara taurina*, 39
101. Images in newspapers: e.g., *El Toreo*, year 3, no. 11, Jan. 31, 1898; *El Hijo de Ahuizote*, Feb. 27, 1898; Beezley, *Judas at the Jockey Club*, 126–127.
102. Schubert, *Death and Money in the Afternoon*, 93.
103. AHDF, Diversiones publicas: Toros, vol. 857, E172.
104. AHDF, Diversiones publicas: Toros, vol. 857, E172.
105. Schubert, *Death and Money in the Afternoon*, 92.
106. AHDF, Diversiones publicas: Toros, vol. 857, E179, 1898.
107. *El Toreo*, year 3, no. 11, Jan. 31, 1898, 3, 6.
108. *El Toreo*, year 3, no. 12, Feb. 28, 1898.
109. *El Toreo*, year 3, no. 13, Mar. 7, 1898.
110. Schubert, *Death and Money in the Afternoon*, 99–101.
111. Sherratt, *Mexican Vistas*, 86.
112. Schubert, *Death and Money in the Afternoon*, 104.
113. Matthews, *Civilizing Machine*, 95–97.
114. Schubert, *Death and Money in the Afternoon*, 104–109.

115. Beezley, *Judas at the Jockey Club*, 5–7, 14–17.
116. Schubert, *Death and Money in the Afternoon*, 181.
117. Louis A Zucher Jr. and Arnold Meadow, "On Bullfights and Baseball: An Example of Interaction of Social Institutions," in Hart and Birrell, *Sport in the Sociocultural Process*, 657–658.
118. Cf Beezley, *Judas at the Jockey Club*, 14.
119. Beezley, 15–17.
120. Beezley, 17.
121. Berman, *Modern Culture and Critical Theory*, 95–96.
122. Shepard, *Others*, 81–100.
123. *Ratas y Mamarrachas*, no. 85, year 3, Oct. 30, 1905, 6.
124. Schubert, *Death and Money in the Afternoon*, 64–70.
125. Gérardin, *Animales zoologico*, 310–314.
126. Bourdieu, *Outline of a Theory in Practice*, 17, 164; Bourdieu and Wacqant, *Invitation to Reflexive Sociology*, 7, 18–24.

Chapter Six

1. Cited in Cartmill, *View to a Death*, 12.
2. Berman, *Modern Culture and Critical Theory*, 4, 5, 7.
3. To critique some underlying logics of conservation is not to "throw the baby out with the bathwater." As others have noted while covering their own butts, this is not a call to abolish conservation. See Jacoby, *Crimes Against Nature*, 202–203; and Martinez-Reyes, *Moral Ecology*, 5–7.
4. Cartmill, *View to a Death*, 230–240.
5. José Ortega y Gasset (1883–1955) was a prominent Spanish writer and philosopher known best for his 1930 work, *The Revolution of the Masses*. A libertarian socialist who took the republican side of the Spanish Civil War, he was often associated with conservative pessimism. His greatest philosophical contribution was to reconsider the Cartesian ontology and *cognito ergo sum*, saying instead that "I am I and my circumstances." He was also an avid essayist on bullfights and hunting.
6. Ortega y Gasset, *Caza y los toros*, 11.
7. Cartmill, *View to a Death*, 27, 226.
8. Ortega y Gasset, *Caza y los toros*, 14.
9. Ortega y Gasset, 55.
10. Rebella, *Caza mayor*, 14.
11. Ortega y Gasset, *Caza y los toros*, 104.
12. Ortega y Gasset, 90.
13. Cartmill, *View to a Death*, 232–240.
14. Cartmill, 231–236.

15. Cartmill, 243–244.
16. Ortega y Gasset, *Caza y los toros*, 90.
17. Ortega y Gasset, 64–65.
18. Morton, *Tame and the Wild*, 41–42.
19. Ortega y Gasset, *Caza y los toros*, 70–71.
20. Ortega y Gasset, 34, 35.
21. Ortega y Gasset, 30.
22. Ortega y Gasset, 72.
23. Ortega y Gasset, 80–81.
24. "Pedro Blazquez," in *Diccionario Porrúa*, vol. 1.
25. Blazquez, *Cazador Mexicano*, iv.
26. Blazquez, vii
27. Blazquez, v.
28. Blazquez, 8.
29. Blazquez, 10.
30. Blazquez, 13–14.
31. Blazquez, 18.
32. Blazquez, 20
33. Blazquez, 21–26.
34. Blazquez, 19–20.
35. Blazquez, 35.
36. Blazquez, 44–46.
37. Blazquez, 64–65; Cartmill, *View to a Death*, 148–160. This is also a theme in the popular novel *Santa*.
38. Blazquez, *El Cazador Mexicano*, 65.
39. Blazquez, 96, 385.
40. Blazquez, 151.
41. Blazquez, 224–228.
42. Blazquez, 363–375.
43. Blazquez, 335
44. Blazquez, 291.
45. Blazquez, 30.
46. Blazquez, 106.
47. Blazquez, 111.
48. Blazquez, 114–115.
49. Blazquez, 390.
50. Blazquez, 212; also discussed in Carpenter, *Hunting Big Game*, 20; and Cartmill, *View to a Death*, 231.
51. Serpell, *In the Company of Animals*, 169–195.
52. Theodor Adorno, "The Sociology of Knowledge and Its Consciousness," in Arato and Gebhart, *Essential Frankfurt School Reader*, 462.
53. Blazquez, *El Cazador Mexicano*, 339.

54. Blazquez, 347–349.
55. Blazquez, 354
56. Blazquez, 297–299.
57. Blazquez, 94
58. Blazquez, 264.
59. Galinda y Villa, *Ciudad de México*, 27.
60. López and López, *Caza Mexicana*.
61. Lopez and Lopez, xi–xv.
62. López and López, 40–42.
63. López and López, ix.
64. Terry, *Terry's Mexico*, lxxvii–lxxix.
65. Lopez and Lopez, *Caza Mexicana*, xiv
66. Lopez and Lopez, 589.
67. López and López, x.
68. López and López, 3, 5.
69. López and López, 52–54. In theory, this eventually extended to some foreigners, as with the Club Cazadores Mexicanos founded in early 1940s for hunters coming from the United States.
70. López and López, *Caza Mexicana*, 46.
71. López and López, 247.
72. López and López, 33, 38.
73. PHO 1-8, Pedro Pérez Grovas.
74. Frederic Remington, "The Blue Quail of the Cactus (1896)," in Carmony and Brown, *Mexican Game Trails*, 41–48.
75. López and López, *Caza Mexicana*, 21.
76. Also as regards the United States case, see Jacoby, *Crimes Against Nature*, 92.
77. Barbara Tenenbaum, "Streetwise History," in Beezley et al., *Rituals of Rule, Rituals of Resistance*, 127–150; Rebecca Earle, *Return of the Native*, 161–183.
78. López and López, *Caza Mexicana*, 594.
79. López and López, 471, 145, 337.
80. López and López, 591. They seemed, nonetheless, unaware of how exclusive and regulated those clubs were and how unlikely that any of them could earn a jäger license by the same standards.
81. Morton, *Tame and the Wild*, 3.
82. Holden, *Mexico and the Survey*, 7, 9, 22–24, 113.
83. Knight, *Mexican Revolution*, 94
84. Knight, 36, 155–167.
85. Morton, *Tame and the Wild*, 95–104.
86. Washbrook, *Producing Modernity in Mexico*, 155, 278.
87. Knight, *Mexican Revolution*, 92–93, 95–97, 102–105.
88. Imaz Baume, *Cacería*, 13–16.
89. Imaz Baume, 128, 599.

90. Imaz Baume, 124.
91. Imaz Baume, 126.
92. Imaz Baume, 98.
93. Imaz Baume, 191, 193.
94. Imaz Baume, 101.
95. Imaz Baume, 289.
96. Imaz Baume, 29, 40, 54.
97. Imaz Baume, 198, 201–202.
98. Imaz Baume, 162.
99. Imaz Baume, 215.
100. Imaz Baume, 605.
101. Imaz Baume, 514.
102. Imaz Baume, 327, 208.
103. Imaz Baume, 417.
104. Imaz Baume, 431.
105. Imaz Baume, 75–77.
106. Imaz Baume, 28.
107. Imaz Baume, 298, 397.
108. Imaz Baume, 480, 498.
109. Imaz Baume, 257–267.
110. Imaz Baume, 214.
111. Imaz Baume, 143
112. Jacoby, *Crimes Against Nature*, 151, 194–198.
113. Loo, *States of Nature*, xiii.
114. Loo, *States of Nature*, 9, 23, 24, 37, 41, 47.
115. See also Carolyn Merchant, "Reinventing Eden," in Cronon, *Uncommon Ground*, 132–170.
116. Loo, *States of Nature*, 13.
117. Louis Warren, *Hunter's Game*; Jacoby, *Crimes Against Nature*, 1–23.
118. Warren, *Hunter's Game*, 3.
119. Warren, 5–9; Jacoby, *Crimes Against Nature*, 23.
120. Warren, *The Hunters Game*, 19, 29, 93–95; Jacoby, *Crimes Against Nature*, on Adirondacks, 58–59.
121. Warren, *Hunter's Game*, 129. See also on Mexico, Wakild, *Revolutionary Parks*; Cartmill, *View to a Death*, 153–156.
122. López and López, *Caza Mexicana*, 590.
123. Jacoby, *Crimes Against Nature*, 169.
124. Herrera, *Catálogo de la colección*.
125. Robles Fernández, *Memorias y proyectos de leyes*, 13.
126. Herrejon, *Vida silvestre mexicana*, 11.
127. Quiroz, *Entre el lujo y la subsistencia*, 28.
128. Robles Fernández, *Memorias y proyectos de leyes*, 15.
129. Robles Fernández, 17, 18.

130. Herrejon, *Vida silvestre mexicana*, 14.
131. Herrejon, 16–17.
132. In Simonian, *Defending the Land of the Jaguar*, 31: *Novísima recopilación de las leyes de España*, tomo 3: 639–642, 651–652.
133. Beltrán, *Instituto México de recursos naturales*,34, 237–238; Simonian, *Defending the Land of the Jaguar*, 65.
134. México, *Disposiciones de caza vigentes*.
135. Robles Fernández, *Memorias y proyectos de leyes*, 63.
136. Robles Fernández, 33; on the United States, see Warren, *Hunter's Game*; and Jacoby, *Crimes Against Nature*.
137. Simonian, *Defending the Land of the Jaguar*, 3; *Novísima recopilación de las Leyes de España*, tomo 3: 639–642, 651–652.
138. Much as elsewhere, see Loo, *States of Nature*, 14, 70–90.
139. López and López, 629, also in Blázquez, *El Cazador Mexicano o el arte de la caza en México*, 1884 ed.
140. Loo, *States of Nature*, 13, 14.
141. Terry, *Terry's Mexico*, 412.
142. Loo, *States of Nature*, 26.
143. Morris, *Story of Mexico*, 91.
144. Simonian, *Defending the Land of the Jaguar*, 65.
145. Loo, *States of Nature*, 25.
146. Simonian, *Defending the Land of the Jaguar*,65, 66.
147. See Ochoa, *Feeding Mexico*; Pilcher, *Que vivan los tamales*. Natives were also a part of nonconsumptive use of wildlife; see Loo, *States of Nature*, xvi.
148. Loo, *States of Nature*, 151.
149. Warren, *Hunter's Game*, 63.
150. Beltrán, *Instituto México de recursos naturales*, 57–68.
151. Beltrán, 72–75.
152. Beltrán, 52–54.
153. Treviño Jr., *Relatos de cacería en México*, 35.
154. Herrejon, *Vida silvestre mexicana*, 35.
155. Herrejon, 182.
156. Robles Fernández, *Memorias y proyectos de leyes*, 65, 112.
157. Beltrán, *Instituto México de recursos naturales*, 16.
158. Beltrán, 16.
159. Beltrán, 35–41.
160. Herrejon, *Vida silvestre mexicana*, 36–38.
161. Morris, *Story of Mexico*, 32.
162. México, *Disposiciones de caza vigentes*, Art. 74. This charity is not unique to 1918 Mexico, as rural communities in Canada continue to make poached meat informally and unofficially available to poor people "off the books."
163. México, *Disposiciones de caza vigentes*, Sept.11, 1918, explotación de esquilmos en los lagos.

164. México, *Disposiciones de caza vigentes*.
165. México, *Disposiciones de caza vigentes*, Quail 1926.
166. Robles Fernández, *Memorias y proyectos de leyes*, 28.
167. Herrejon, *Vida silvestre mexicana*, 39, 40.
168. Robles Fernández, *Memorias y proyectos de leyes*, 30.
169. Beltrán, *Instituto México de recursos naturales*, 24.
170. Beltrán, 9–11.
171. Beltrán, 12.
172. México, *Disposiciones de caza vigentes*, Arts. 50–51.
173. México, *Disposiciones de caza vigentes*, 1909 Prohibición para caza del berrendo, 1909 Prohibición para caza del borrejo salvaje.
174. México, *Disposiciones de caza vigentes*, Veda venado 1924.
175. Herrejon, *Vida silvestre mexicana*, 214–218.
176. México, *Disposiciones de caza vigentes*, Art. 49.
177. Robles Fernández, *Memorias y proyectos de leyes*, 66.
178. Robles Fernández, 111.
179. Robles Fernández, 145, guides 151.
180. Simonian, *Defending the Land of the Jaguar*, 61.
181. Robles Fernández, *Memorias y proyectos de leyes*, 20–23.
182. Treviño, *Relatos de cacería en México*, 44.
183. Treviño, 11.
184. Beltrán, *Instituto México de recursos naturales*, 19.
185. Villa, *Venados en México*, 12–15.
186. Villa, *Venados en México*, 16.
187. "Carlos Sanchez Mejarada," in *Diccionario Porrúa*, vol. 2.
188. Beltrán, *Instituto México de recursos naturales*, 28.
189. Beltrán, 1–7.
190. Neil Carmony and David Brown, "Epilogue," in Carmony and Brown, *Mexican Game Trails*, 249.
191. Jacoby, *Crimes Against Nature*, 194–198.

Chapter Seven

1. Baruch Spinoza cited in Fiasso, *Hombre contra el animal*, 6.
2. Cartmill, *View to a Death*, 28–29.
3. Berman, *Modern Culture and Critical Theory*, 161.
4. Taussig, *Devil and Commodity Fetishism*, 3–8.
5. PHO 1–33, Jesús José de Arrias Villaseñor interviewed by América Briseño Ramírez, Mar. 1, 8, and 15, 1973.
6. PHO 1–33, Andrés Aula Barrera interviewed by Laura Espejel, May 15, 1973.

7. Morris, *Story of Mexico*, 32; O'Connor, "We Shot the Tamales (1937)," in Carmony and Brown, *Mexican Game Trails*, 96–100; Warren, *Hunter's Game*, 86; González Roa and Covarrubias, *Problema rural de México*, 179.
8. Martinez-Reyes, *Moral Ecology of a Forest*, 106–107, 141; Jacoby, *Crimes Against Nature*, 185.
9. Eiss, *In the Name of El Pueblo*, 218–243.
10. For an excellent discussion of this, see Morton, *Tame and the Wild*, 107–129.
11. Vázquez Flores, *Discursos de la discriminación*, 5.
12. Vázquez Flores, 79.
13. Neufeld, *Blood Contingent*, 283–291.
14. Vázquez Flores, *Discursos de la discriminación*, 184–186.
15. Vázquez Flores, 204.
16. Cronon, *Uncommon Ground*, 144.
17. Beltrán, *Instituto México de recursos naturales*, 26–27.
18. William H. Bergtold, "An Indian of the Sierra Madre (1904)," in Carmony and Brown, *Mexican Game Trails*, 191; Frederick Schwatka, "A Peccary Chase in Central Sonora (1890)," in Carmony and Brown, *Mexican Game Trails*, 37.
19. Edwards, *On the Mexican Highlands*, 78.
20. Moisés et al., *Yaqui Life*, 3, 170.
21. Morton, *Tame and the Wild*, 4–5, 157–185.
22. Jacoby, *Crimes Against Nature*, 194.
23. Morton, *Tame and the Wild*, 331; Martínez-Reyes, *Moral Ecology of a Forest*, 152–166.
24. James Mestaz, *Strength from the Waters*, 216–218.
25. Thornton and Thornton, "Mutable, the Mythical, and the Managerial," 68.
26. Martínez-Reyes, *Moral Ecology of a Forest*. They also had their own "environmental imaginaries" and connections to the wilds and to animals; Grim, *Indigenous Traditions and Ecology*, xli.
27. Martínez-Reyes, *Moral Ecology of a Forest*, 140.
28. Martínez-Reyes, 128.
29. Martínez-Reyes, 143–151.
30. See the discussion in chapter 6.
31. Flandrau, *Viva México*, 124–125.
32. Carpenter, *Hunting Big Game*, 16; the author "cavorts like a Navajo" when he makes a kill.
33. Sharon Wilcox Adams, "On the Trail of the Devil Cat: Hunting for the Jaguar in U.S. and Mexico," in Kalof and Montgomery, *Making Animal Meaning*, 94.
34. Conkling, *Appleton's Guide*, 86.
35. Harper, *Journey in Southeastern Mexico*, 34–35.
36. Gringo, *Life and Travels in Mexico*, 203.
37. Weiner et al., *América Pintoresca*, 321; also in Harper, *Journey in Southeastern Mexico*, 45.
38. Weiner et al., *América Pintoresca*, 321.
39. Harper, *Journey in Southeastern Mexico*, 94–95.
40. Thomas, *Hunting Big Game with a Gun*, 133.
41. Blichfeldt, *Mexican Journey*, 204.

42. Ortega y Gasset, *Caza y los toros*, 10.
43. Thomas, *Hunting Big Game with a Gun*, 133.
44. Thomas, *Hunting Big Game with a Gun*, 125, 133.
45. Carpenter, *Hunting Big Game*; Conkling, *Appleton's Guide to Mexico*. Coincidentally, Ulysses S. Grant created the first National Park in the US system.
46. Carpenter, *Hunting Big Game*, 10.
47. Carpenter, 10, 35, 38, 42.
48. Carpenter, 18, 30, 48.
49. Carpenter, 40.
50. Thomas, *Hunting Big Game with a Gun*, 130.
51. Lew Wallace, "A Buffalo Hunt in Northern Mexico (1866)," in Carmony and Brown, *Mexican Game Trails*, 14–28.
52. Bishop, *Old Mexico and Her Lost Provinces*.
53. Wallace, "A Buffalo Hunt in Northern Mexico (1866)," in Carmony and Brown, *Mexican Game Trails*, 28.
54. Knight, *The Mexican Revolution*, 121; Wasserman, *Persistent Oligarchs*.
55. Carpenter, *Hunting Big Game*, 13, 44.
56. Frederick Schwatka, "A Peccary Chase in Central Sonora (1890)," in Carmony and Brown, *Mexican Game Trails*, 38.
57. William H. Bergtold, "An Indian of the Sierra Madre (1904)," in Carmony and Brown, *Mexican Game Trails*, 189.
58. Frederick Remington, "The Blue Quail of the Cactus (1896)," in Carmony and Brown, *Mexican Game Trails*, 41–48.
59. William Humphrey, "Hunting Bighorn Sheep and Pronghorn Antelope in Baja California (1909)," in Carmony and Brown, *Mexican Game Trails*.
60. Ben Burbridge, "Bear and Lion (1908)," in Carmony and Brown, *Mexican Game Trails*, 199.
61. Carpenter, *Hunting Big Game*, 17–18.
62. Harper, *Journey in Southeastern Mexico*, 82.
63. Harper, *Journey in Southeastern Mexico*, 83–87.
64. Kermit Roosevelt, "The Sheep of the Desert (1911)," in Carmony and Brown, *Mexican Game Trails*, 83.
65. Emmet R. Blake, "Among the Clouds for Rare Birds (1934)," in Carmony and Brown, *Mexican Game Trails*; Dale Lee, "First Jaguars in Sinaloa (1935)," in Carmony and Brown, *Mexican Game Trails*, 227.
66. See MacKenzie, *Empire of Nature*, 6–24, 49–51.
67. Even the US Consul took part in this, deer hunting in Cuautla with hounds; Strother, *Porte Crayon's Mexico*, 694; on manners and masculinity, see Macías-González and Rubenstein, *Masculinity and Sexuality in Modern Mexico*, especially 1–53, 157–196.
68. *El Universal* (Feb. 10, 1905).
69. See Stephen Neufeld, "Behaving Badly in Mexico City," in Rugeley and Fallaw, *Forced Marches*, 84–86.
70. Loo, *States of Nature*, 32.

71. Mackenzie, *Empire of Nature*, 29–34.
72. Shukin, *Animal Capital*, 130; Loo, *States of Nature*, 35.
73. On Porfiriato generally, see Garner, *Porfirio Díaz*; Cosío Villegas ed. *Historia moderna de México*.
74. Cota Soto, *Historia militar de México*, 87–90.
75. See Alonso, *Thread of Blood*; Hu-deHart, *Yaqui Resistance and Survival*.
76. Macias-González, "Curtseying in the Shadow of Dictators," 83–87.
77. Cartmill, *View to a Death*, 29–30, 135–138; Loo, *States of Nature*, 33.
78. "El gran cacería," *El Universal* (Feb. 18, 1900).
79. MacKenzie, *Empire of Nature*.
80. Bergtold, "An Indian of the Sierra Madre (1904)," in Carmony and Brian, *Mexican Game Trails*, 189–195.
81. Many works examine this idea in postcolonial studies; for an overview, see Mackenzie, *Empire of Nature*. For a take on Mexico, see Matthews, *Civilizing Machine*, 252–253.
82. López and López, *Caza Mexicana*, 41.
83. Morton, *Tame and the Wild*, 25–29.
84. Morton, 87–88.
85. Hussain, "Sports-hunting, Fairness, and Colonial Identity," 115.
86. Poliquin, *Breathless Zoo*, 22, 83.
87. Poliquin, *Breathless Zoo*, 142; photos in Mexico, Chapultepec palace.
88. Poliquin, 2–3.
89. Poliquin, 6–7.
90. Poliquin, 7; and see chapter 4.
91. Hussain, "Sports-hunting, Fairness, and Colonial Identity," 122.
92. Poliquin, *Breathless Zoo*, 154.
93. Poliquin, 5.
94. Poliquin, 80–81; Hussain, "Sports-hunting, Fairness, and Colonial Identity," 113–114.
95. Poliquin, *Breathless Zoo*, 81.
96. Poliquin, 90–91.
97. Cartmill, *View to a Death*, 72–83; Poliquin, *Breathless Zoo*, 70, 151–152.
98. Hussain, "Sports-hunting, Fairness, and Colonial Identity," 119.
99. Hussain, 117.
100. Hussain, 113.
101. Drawn from Dove and Kannen, cited in Hussain, "Sports-hunting, Fairness, and Colonial Identity," 114.
102. Hussain, 114.
103. Hussain, 116.
104. Hussain, 117; Jacoby, *Crimes Against Nature*, 151; Cartmill, *View to a Death*, 135–138.
105. Tying these notions to liberal ideology, see Hale, *Transformation of Liberalism*, 206–213, 219–225, 235–240, 253.

106. Strother, *Porte Crayon's Mexico*, 277.
107. Creelman, "President Díaz," 240.
108. Creelman, 241.
109. Creelman, 242.
110. On Porfirito's hunting, the press exclaimed in *El Tiempo*, "calurosos aplausos del joven Porfirio Díaz, por su notabilidad como tirador. En la última cacería de Cuautla Morelos…demostró su habilidad como cazador de venados. Bien, joven amigo, bien!"
111. Bourdieu, *Outline of a Theory in Practice*, 196.
112. Warren, *Hunter's Game*, 76–77.
113. Morris, *Story of Mexico*, 92.
114. Simonian, *Defending the Land of the Jaguar*, 25.
115. Some mentions in Díaz del Castillo, *Discovery and Conquest of Mexico*.
116. Duarte, "Zoológico del porvenir."
117. *El Imparcial* (Feb. 24, 1900), 3; *El Universal* (Dec. 25, 1889), 2 and *El Universal* (Jan. 11, 1890), 2.
118. Oliver Hochadel, "Darwin in the Monkey Cage," in Brantz, *Beastly Natures*, 81–107.
119. Cartmill, *View to a Death*, 28–30.

Epilogue

1. Ortega y Gasset, *Caza y los toros*, 62.
2. Max Horkheimer, "The End of Reason," in Arato and Gebhart, *Essential Frankfurt School Reader*, 47.
3. Bolton and Laaser, "Work, Employment and Society," 514–515.
4. Thompson cited in Genovese, "Many Faces of the Moral Economy," 162.
5. Martínez-Reyes, *Moral Ecology*, 127–129.
6. The notions of cultural capital (from Pierre Bourdieu) extended into the structures of capitalism as features (filled with contradictions) in the works of Slavoj Žižek. For many left-leaning thinkers, the attempt to inculcate mass consumers to the basic premises of capitalism, often an effort cynically created at corporate levels, creates a new avenue of false consciousness and makes exploitation seem a natural and acceptable part of modern life; see Shukin, *Animal Capital*, 199–200.

Postscript

1. Alyssa Rodríguez, communication with author, Mar. 2024.

Appendix

1. Mbembe, *Necropolitics*, 69.
2. Foucault, *Security, Territory, and Population*, 4–13.
3. Mbembe, *Necropolitics*, 2.
4. Mbembe, 2.
5. Morton, *Tame and the Wild*, 13–14.
6. Mbembe, *Necropolitics*, 2–3.
7. Mbembe, 6.
8. Mbembe, 4, 6–7.
9. Mbembe, 7.
10. Mbembe, 14.
11. Mbembe, 25.
12. Mbembe, 43.
13. Mbembe, 63.
14. Mbembe, *Necropolitics*, 63–66.
15. Mbembe, 160.
16. Bourdieu, *Outline of a Theory in Practice*, 196.
17. White, "Environmental History, Ecology, and Meaning," 113.
18. While he was not the first, his work popularized the term. Thompson, "Moral Economy of the English Crowd"; Thompson, *Customs in Common*; with precursors in Thompson, *Making of the English Working Class*. See, too, Genovese, "Many Faces of the Moral Economy"; Frevert, "Moral Economies, Present and Past," 15, 26–28; Bolton and Laaser, "Work, Employment, and Society," 508–509.
19. Notably, for the United States, see Jacoby, *Crimes Against Nature*; and for the Maya, Martínez-Reyes, *Moral Ecology of a Forest*.
20. Linebaugh, "Karl Marx, the Theft of Wood," 140–142, 157.
21. Tortolero Villaseñor, *Notarios y agricultores*; Tortolero Villaseñor, "Canales de riego y canales navegables"; Adams and Raisborough, "What Can Sociology Say About Fair Trade?," 1173–1178.
22. Bolton and Laaser, "Work, Employment, and Society," 513–516.
23. Scott, *Domination and the Arts of Resistance*; Scott, *Moral Economy of the Peasant*.
24. Kevin Gosner, *Soldiers of the Virgin*, 6–9, 163; Jimenez, *Making an Urban Public*, 9.
25. E.g., Diquattro, "Labor Theory of Value,", 455–483.
26. The popularity of this notion, not incidentally, caters to those calling for cultural capitalism, or "capitalism with a human face," as the proponents at Davos conferences and elsewhere have championed and thinkers like Slavoj Žižek have criticized.
27. Frevert, "Moral Economies, Present and Past," 36–38; Genovese, "Many Faces of the Moral Economy," 162.
28. Thompson, "Moral Economy of the English Crowd," 90–93.
29. Bolton and Laaser, "Work, Employment, and Society," 515.

30. See, especially, Martínez-Reyes, *Moral Ecology of a Forest*.
31. Setten, "Habitus, the Rule," 399, 406–408.
32. Hinchliffe, *Geographies of Nature*.
33. Farrell, "Introducing American Studies."
34. Somewhat undeveloped in Jacoby, *Crimes Against Nature*; political ecology only in Vitz, *City on a Lake*, 12–13.
35. E.g., George Sessions, "Deep Ecology Movement."
36. Thornton and Thornton, "Mutable, the Mythical, and the Managerial," 68.
37. Sundararajan, "From Marxian Ecology to Ecological Marxism"; Frevert, "Moral Economies, Present and Past," 18–21; Bolton and Laaser, "Work, Employment, and Society," 514; Antonio Gramsci, *Selections from the Prison Notebooks*.
38. Genovese, Many Faces of the Moral Economy," 164.
39. Hribal, "'Animals Are Part of the Working Class'" 435–453.
40. For a critique made of Martínez-Reyes, see Gallagher, Review of *Moral Ecology of a Forest*, 174.
41. On some of the implications of this, see the excellent overview by Whitehead, "Loving, Being, Killing Animals."

BIBLIOGRAPHY

Abbreviations used in the notes

AGN (Archivo General de la Nación, Mexico City)
AHDF (Biblioteca del Archivo Histórico del Distrito Federal, Mexico City)
Ayunt. (Ayuntamiento del Distrito Federal)
E (Expedientes)
F (Folios)
Gob. del DF (Gobierno del Distrito Federal)
PHO (Instituto Mora, INAH, Instituto Nacional de Antropología y Historia, Proyecto de Historia Oral)

Archives and Libraries

Archivo General de la Nación, Mexico City
    Folletería Mexicana
    Ramo Gobernación
Biblioteca del Archivo Histórico del Distrito Federal, Mexico City, BAHDF
Biblioteca Miguel Lerdo de Tejada, Mexico City
Centro de Estúdios de Historia de México, Carso Mexico City
Instituto de Investigaciones Dr. José María Luis Mora, Mexico City
Instituto Nacional de Antropología e Historia (INAH)
    PHO-INAH Proyecto de Historia Oral
    Sistema Nacional de Fototecas S I N A F O
Los Angeles Public Library
Universidad Autónoma de México, Mexico City
    Biblioteca de la Facultad de Veterinaria y Zootecnia
    Hemeroteca Nacional
University of Texas, Austin
    BLAC, Nettie Lee Benson Latin American Collection

Periodicals

Arte de Lidia
Boletín de Instrucción Pública
El Chisme
El Combate
Diario del Hogar
Excélsior (Mexico City)
El Gráfico (Mexico City)
The Graphic (London, UK)
El Hijo de Ahuizote
Juventud Literaria
El Imparcial
México Gráico
El Nacional (Mexico City)
New York Times
El Observador
El País
La Patria
Ratas y Mamarrachas
Regeneración
La Revista Moderna
Revistas Taurinas de El Liberal, 1887–1894
El Tiempo
El Toreo
El Universal (Mexico City)
El Universal Gráfico (Mexico City)

Books, Dissertations, Theses, Articles

Adams, Matthew, and Jayne Raisborough. "What Can Sociology Say About Fair Trade? Class, Reflexivity and Ethical Consumption." *Sociology* 42, no. 6 (Dec. 2008): 1165–1182.

Agamben, Giorgio. *State of Exception*. Translated by Kevin Attell. University of Chicago Press, 2005.

Agostini, Claudia. *Monuments of Progress: Modernization and Public Health in Mexico City, 1876–1910*. University of Calgary Press, 2003.

Alexander, Anna Rose. *City on Fire: Technology, Social Change, and the Hazards of Progress in Mexico City, 1860–1910*. University of Pittsburgh Press, 2016.

Allen, Stephen. *A History of Boxing in Mexico: Masculinity, Modernity, and Nationalism*. University of New Mexico Press, 2017.

Alonso, Ana María. *Thread of Blood: Colonialism, Revolution, and Gender on Mexico's Northern Frontier*. University of Arizona Press, 1995.

Alves, Abel A. "The Animal Question: The Anthropocene's Hidden Foundational Debate." *História, Ciências, Saúde-Manguinhos* 28, supl. (Dec. 2021): 123–140.

Anderson, Virginia DeJohn. *Creatures of Empires: How Domestic Animals Transformed Early America*. Oxford University Press, 2004.

Angelo, Hillary. "From the City Lens Toward Urbanisation as a Way of Seeing." *Urban Studies* 54, no. 1 (Jan. 2017): 158–178.

Arato, Andrew, and Eike Gebhart, eds. *The Essential Frankfurt School Reader*. Continuum, 2002.

Ávila González, Jesús Salvador. "Voces y ladridos: Ensayo sobre los perros de la Ciudad de México, siglos xviii y xix." PhD diss., Universidad Iberoamericana, 2007.

Ballantyne, T., and A. Burton, eds. *Bodies in Contact: Rethinking Colonial Encounters in World History*. Duke University Press, 2005.

Bates, J. H. *Notes of a Tour in Mexico and California*. Burr Publishing House, 1887.

Beatty, Edward. *Technology and the Search for Progress in Modern Mexico*. University of California Press, 2015.

Beezley, William. *Judas at the Jockey Club and Other Episodes of Porfirian Mexico*. University of Nebraska Press, 1987.

Beezley, William. *Mexican National Identity: Memory, Innuendo, and Popular Culture*. University of Arizona Press, 2007.

Beezley, William, Cheryl E. Martin, and William E. Frencheds. *Rituals of Rule, Rituals of Resistance: Public Celebrations and Popular Culture in Mexico.* Scholarly Resources, 1994.

Beltrán, Enrique, ed. *Instituto México de recursos naturales y renovables: Mesas redondas sobre problemas de caza y pesca deportivas en México.* Ed. IMRNR, 1966.

Berman, Russel. *Modern Culture and Critical Theory: Art, Politics, and the Legacy of the Frankfurt School.* University of Wisconsin Press, 1989.

Bianet Castellanos, M. "Introduction: Settler Colonialism in Latin America." American Quarterly 69, no. 4 (Dec. 2017): 777–781.

Bishop, W. H. *Old Mexico and Her Lost Provinces.* Harper's, 1883.

Blazquez, Pedro. *El Cazador Mexicano o el arte de la caza en México.* Tipo. de Pedro Alarcón, 1884.

Blazquez, Pedro. *El Cazador Mexicano o arte de la caza en México y en sus relaciones con la Historia Natural.* 2013 ed. Tipografía de Pedro Alarcón, 1868.

Blichfeldt, Emil Harry. *A Mexican Journey.* Thomas Crowell, 1912.

Blum, Ann. *Domestic Economies: Family, Work, and Welfare in Mexico City, 1884–1943.* University of Nebraska Press, 2009.

Bolton, Sharon, and Knut Laaser. "Work, Employment, and Society Through the Lens of the Moral Economy" *Work, Employment and Society* 27, no. 3 (June 2013): 508–525.

Bonnell, Jennifer, and Sean Kheraj. *Traces of the Animal Past: Methodological Challenges in Animal History.* University of Calgary Press, 2022.

Bourdieu, Pierre. *Outline of a Theory in Practice.* Cambridge University Press, 1977.

Bourdieu, Pierre, and Loïc Wacquant. *An Invitation to Reflexive Sociology.* University of Chicago Press, 1992.

Boyer, Chris, ed. *A Land Between Waters: Environmental Histories of Modern Mexico.* University of Arizona Press, 2012.

Brantz, Dorothee, ed. *Beastly Natures: Animals, Humans, and the Study of History.* University of Virginia Press, 2010.

Brunk, Samuel, ed. *Heroes and Hero Cults in Latin America.* University of Texas Press, 2006.

Buchenau, Jürgen, ed. *Mexico Otherwise: Modern Mexico in the Eyes of Foreign Observers.* University of New Mexico Press, 2005.

Buffington, Robert. *Criminal and Citizen in Modern Mexico.* University of Nebraska Press, 2000.

Buffington, Robert. *A Sentimental Education for the Working Man: The Mexico City Penny Press, 1900–1910*. Duke University Press, 2015.

Buillet, R. W. *Hunters, Herders, and Hamburgers: The Past and Future of Human-Animal Relationships*. University of Columbia Press, 2005.

Bullock, Marcus, and Michael Jennings, eds. *Walter Benjamin: Selected Writings*. Vol. 1: *1913–1926*. Belknap Press, 1996.

Bunker, Steven. *Creating Mexican Consumer Culture in the Age of Porfirio Díaz*. University of New Mexico Press, 2012.

Burton, Antoinette, and Renisa Mawani, eds. *Animalia: An Anti-Imperial Bestiary for Our Times*. Duke University Press, 2020.

Camacho Morfín, Thelma. *Las historietas de El Buen Tono (1904–1922): La litografía al servicio de la industria*. UNAM, 2013.

Camp, Roderic Ai. *Mexican Political Biographies, 1884–1934*. University of Texas Press, 1991.

Campos, Isaac. *Homegrown: Marijuana and the Origins of Mexico's War on Drugs*. University of North Carolina Press, 2014.

Canóvas y Pasqual, Sebastien. *Inoculaciones preventativas de la rabia en México, Tesis Medical por Escuela Nacional de Medicina*. Imprenta de Gobierno Federal, 1891.

Casey, Edward S. "How to Get from Space to Place." In *Senses of Place*, edited by Steven Feld and Keith Russo, 15–52. SAR, 1996.

Cartmill, Matt. *A View to a Death in the Morning: Hunting and Nature Through History*. Harvard University Press, 1996.

Carmony, Neil, and David Brown, eds. *Mexican Game Trails: Americans Afield in Old Mexico*. University of Oklahoma Press, 1991.

Carpenter, Donald. A. *Hunting Big Game in the Sierra of Chihuahua*. Melville Pollack, 1906.

Cervantes, Miguel de. *The Dialogue of Dogs*. Translated by David Kipen. Melville Press, 2008. First published in 1613.

Chakrabarty, Dipesh. *Provincializing Europe: Postcolonial Thought and Historical Difference*. Princeton University Press, 2000.

Ciudad de Chihuahua. *Reglamentos que debería usar los palenques de gallos*. Chihuahua, June 1902.

Ciudad de Villahermosa. *Reglamentos para los palenques de gallos*. 1st ed. Villahermosa, Tabasco, 1908. The second edition was published in 1913.

Coello, José Francisco, and Juan Felipe Lerdo. *La multiplicación de los cines en la provincia: Anales del cine en México, 1895–1911.* Vol. 14. Voyeur, 2016.

Coleman, Jon T. *Vicious: Wolves and Men in America.* Yale University Press, 2004.

Conkling, Alfred Ronald. *Appleton's Guide to Mexico, Including a Chapter on Guatemala and on English-Mexican Vocabulary.* D. Appleton, 1886.

Conway, Christopher. *Nineteenth-Century Spanish America: A Cultural History.* Vanderbilt University Press, 2015.

Coren, Stanley. *The Pawprints of History: Dogs and the Course of Human Events.* Free Press, 2002.

Cosío Villegas, Daniel, ed. *Historia moderna de México.* Editorial Hermes, 1955.

Cota Soto, Guillermo. *Historia militar de México.* N.p., 1947.

Creelman, James. "President Díaz: Hero of the Americas." *Pearson's Magazine* 19 no. 3 (Mar. 1908): 231–277.

Cronon, William. *Nature's Metropolis: Chicago and the Great West.* Norton, 1992.

Cronon, William. *Uncommon Ground: Rethinking the Human Place in Nature.* Norton, 1996.

Curcio-Nagy, Linda. "Dangerous Souls: Duendes, Almas from Purgatory, and Popular Religion in 17th-Century Mexico." Paper presented at the Rocky Mountain Council for Latin American Studies annual conference in Santa Fe, NM, April 2023.

Curcio-Nagy, Linda. *The Great Festivals of Colonial Mexico City: Performing Power and Identity.* University of New Mexico Press, 2004.

Darnton, Robert. *The Great Cat Massacre and Other Episodes in French Cultural History.* Perseus, 1984.

Dean, Joanna, Darcy Ingram, and Christabelle Sethna., eds. *Animal Metropolis: Histories of Human-Animal Relations in Urban Canada.* University of Calgary Press, 2017.

De los Reyes, Aurelio, ed. *Historia de la vida cotidiana en México: Tomo V, Vol. 1. Campo y Ciudad.* Fondo de Cultura económica, 2006.

Derby, Lauren. "Bringing the Animals Back In: Writing Quadrupeds into the Environmental History of Latin America and the Caribbean." *History Compass* 9–8 (2011): 602–621.

Despret, Vinciane. "From Secret Agents to Interagency." *History and Theory*, theme issue 52 (Dec. 2013): 29–44.

Dopico Black, Georgina. "The Ban and the Bull: Cultural Studies, Animal Studies, and Spain." *Journal of Spanish Cultural Studies* 11, nos. 3–4 (2010): 235–249.

Dove, Michael R. *Bitter Shade: The Ecological Challenge of Human Consciousness*. Yale University Press, 2021.

Dove, Michael R., and Daniel M. Kannen. *Science, Society, and the Environment: Applying Anthropology and Physics to Sustainability*. Routledge, 2015.

Díaz del Castillo, Bernal. *The Discovery and Conquest of Mexico*. New York: Perseus, 2003.

Diccionario Porrúa de historia, biografía y geografía de México. Vols. 1–3. 5th ed. Editorial Porrúa, 1986.

Diquattro, Arthur. "The Labor Theory of Value and Simple Commodity Production." *Science and Society* 71, no. 4 (Oct. 2007): 455–483.

Duarte, Regina Horta. "El zoológico del porvenir: Narrativas y memorias de nación sobre el zoológico de Chapultepec, Ciudad de Mexico, siglo XX." *Histórica Crítica*, no. 72 (2019): 99–113.

Dundes, A. *The Cockfight: A Casebook*. Madison: University of Wisconsin Press, 1994.

Eames, Edwin, and Judith Goode. "Coping with Poverty." In *Urban Life: Readings in Urban Anthropology*, edited by Petra Kuppinger and George Gmelch, 379–381. Waveland Press, 1996.

Earle, Rebecca. *The Return of the Native: Indians and Mythmaking in Spanish America, 1810–1930*. Duke University Press, 2007.

Edwards, William Seymour. *On the Mexican Highlands with a Passing Glimpse of Cuba*. Jennings and Graham, 1906.

Eiss, Paul K. *In the Name of El Pueblo: Place, Community, and the Politics of History in Yucatán*. Duke University Press, 2010.

Esposito, Matthew. *Funerals, Festival, and Cultural Politics in Porfirian Mexico*. University of New Mexico Press, 2010.

Exbalin Oberto, Arnaud. "Perros asesinos y matanzas de perros en la ciudad de México (siglos xxi–xviii)." *Relaciones* 137 (Winter 2014): 91–111.

Fagan, Brian. *The Intimate Bond: How Animals Shaped Human History*. Bloomsbury Press, 2015.

Fanon, Franz. *Black Skin, White Masks*. Rev. ed. Grove Press, 2008.

Farrell, James J. "Introducing American Studies: The Moral Ecology of Everyday Life." *American Studies* 33, no. 1 (Spring 1992): 83–102.

Feld, Steven, and Keith Russo, eds. *Senses of Place*. SAR, 1996.

Few, Martha, and Zeb Tortorici, eds. *Centering Animals in Latin American History.* Duke University Press, 2013.

Fiasso, Raymond. *El hombre contra el animal.* Prensa Universitario de France, 1971.

Flack, Andrew. "Dark Trails: Animal History Beyond the Light of Day." *Environmental History* 27, no. 2 (Apr. 2022): 215–241.

Flandrau, Charles Macomb. *Viva México.* Barranca, 2012. First published in 1908.

Flippin, J. R. *Sketches from the Mountains of Mexico.* Standard Pub., 1889.

Flynn, Clifton P. *Social Creatures: A Human and Animal Studies Reader.* Lantern Books, 2008.

Foucault, Michel. *The Birth of Biopolitics: Lectures at the College De France, 1978–79.* Palgrave McMillan, 2008.

Foucault, Michel. *Discipline and Punish: The Birth of the Prison.* Translated by Alan Sheridan. Vintage Books, 1977.

Foucault, Michel. *Security, Territory, Population: Lectures at the Collège de France, 1977–1978.* Picador, 2009.

Francois, Marie Eileen. *A Culture of Everyday Credit: Housekeeping, Pawnbroking, and Governance in Mexico City, 1750–1920.* University of Nebraska Press, 2006.

French, William. *The Heart in the Glass Jar: Love Letters, Bodies, and the Law in Mexico.* University of Nebraska Press, 2015.

French, William. "Prostitutes and Guardian Angels." *Hispanic American Historical Review* 72, no. 4 (Nov. 1992): 529–531.

French, William, and Katherine Bliss. *Gender, Sexuality, and Power in Latin America Since Independence.* Rowman and Littlefield, 2007.

Frevert, Ute. "Moral Economies, Present and Past: Social Practices and Intellectual Controversies." *Geschichte und Gesselschaft Sonderheft* 26 (2019): 13–43.

Fudge, Erica. "The Flourishing and Challenging Field of Animal-Human History." *Society and Animals* 27 (2019): 645–652.

Fudge, Erica. "Milking Other Men's Beasts." *History and Theory*, theme Issue 52 (Dec. 2013): 13–28.

Gamboa, Federico. *Santa.* Editorial Dracena, 2013. First published in 1903.

Gaona, Rodolfo. *Mis 20 años de torero: El libro intimó de Rodolfo Gaona.* 3rd ed. Biblioteca El Popular, 1925.

Gallagher, Patrick. Review of *Moral Ecology of a Forest* by José Martínez-Reyes. *Environment and Society* 9 (2018): 173–174.

Galinda y Villa, Jesús. *Ciudad de México.* Sec. Instrucción Pública y Bellas Artes, 1906.

Gandara, Guillermo. *La destrucción de las ratas*. Imprenta de Sec. de Fomento, 1912.

Garner, Paul H. *British Lions and Mexican Eagles: Business, Politics, and Empire in the Career of Weetman Pearson in Mexico, 1889–1919*. Stanford University Press, 2011.

Garner, Paul H. *Porfirio Díaz, Profiles in Power*. Longman, 2001.

Geertz, Clifford. "Deep Play: Notes on the Balinese Cockfight." Special issue "50 Years." *Daedalus* 134, no. 4, (Fall 2005): 56–86.

Genovese, Elizabeth Fox. "The Many Faces of the Moral Economy." *Past and Present* 58 (Feb. 1973): 161–168.

Gérardin, Léon. *Los animales zoológico*. Lin. de Bouret, 1884.

Gil, Bonafacio. *Muertes de toreros según el romancero popular*. Taurus Ediciones, 1964.

Ginzburg, Carlo. *Clues, Myths, and the Historical Method*. Translated by John and Anne Tedeschi. Johns Hopkins University Press, 1989.

Gómez de Bedoya, Fernando. *Historia del Toreo*. Extramuros Edición, 2008. First published in 1850.

González Roa, Fernando, and José Covarrubias. *El problema rural de México*. SRA-CEHAM: 1981. First published in 1914.

Goodhue, Bertram Grosvenor. *Mexican Memories: The Record of a Slight Sojourn Below the Yellow Rio Grande*. Geo. M. Allen, 1892.

Gosner, Kevin. *Soldiers of the Virgin: The Moral Economy of a Colonial Maya Rebellion*. University of Arizona Press, 1992.

Graf von Hardenburg, Wilko, M. Kelly, C. Leal, and E. Wakild, eds. *The Nature State: Rethinking the History of Conservation*. Routledge, 2017.

Gramsci, Antonio. *Selections from the Prison Notebooks*. Lawrence and Wishart, 1971.

Gray, John. *Straw Dogs: Thoughts on Humans and Other Animals*. Farrar, Straus and Giroux, 2002.

Grehan, James. "Smoking and 'Early Modern' Sociability: The Great Tobacco Debate in the Ottoman Middle East (Seventeenth to Eighteenth Centuries)." *American Historical Review* 111, no. 5 (Dec. 2006): 1352–1377.

Grim, John A., ed. *Indigenous Traditions and Ecology*. Harvard University Press, 2001.

Gringo, A. *Life and Travels in Mexico: Through the Land of the Aztecs*. Spottiswoode, 1892.

Grusin, Richard, ed. *The Nonhuman Turn*. University of Minnesota Press, 2015.

Gutiérrez Flores, Murillo. "Manual de crianza, raza, entrenamiento y reglamento del gallo de combate." PhD diss., Universidad Nacional de Agricultura, Nicaragua, 2012.

Hale, Charles. *The Transformation of Liberalism in the Late Nineteenth-Century.* Princeton University Press, 1989.

Harper, Henry H. *A Journey in Southeastern Mexico: A Narrative of Experiences and Observations on Agricultural and Industrial Conditions.* De Vinne Press, 1910.

Harraway, Donna. *When Species Meet.* University of Minnesota Press, 2008.

Hart, Marie, and Susan Birrell, eds. *Sport in the Sociocultural Process.* Brown, 1981.

Heftye Etienne, Eduardo E. *Corridos Taurinos Mexicanos.* Bibliófilos Taurinos de México, 2012.

Herrejon, Morelos. *La vida silvestre mexicana: Apuntes de un cazador.* SEP, 1963.

Herrera, Alfonso. *Catálogo de la colección de mamíferos del Museo Nacional.* Imprenta del Museo Nacional, 1895.

Hertzke, Allen D. "The Theory of Moral Ecology." *Review of Politics* 60, no. 4 (Autumn 1998): 629–659.

Herzog, Hal. *Some We Love, Some We Hate, Some We Eat: Why It's So Hard to Think Straight About Animals.* HarperPerennial Press, 2010.

Higueras, Dalmacio. *Intimidades taurinas y el arte de torear.* Imprenta Artística Española, 1910.

Hinchliffe, Steve. *Geographies of Nature: Societies, Environments, Ecologies.* Sage, 2007.

Hoage, R. J. and William A. Deiss, eds. *New Worlds, New Animals: From Menagerie to Zoological Park in the Nineteenth Century.* Johns Hopkins University Press, 1996.

Holden, Robert H. *Mexico and the Survey of Public Lands: The Management of Modernization, 1876–1911.* Northern Illinois Press, 1994.

Horowitz, Roger, Jeffrey M. Pilcher, and Sydney Watts. "Meat for the Multitudes: Market Culture in Paris, New York City, and Mexico City over the Long Nineteenth Century." *American Historical Review* 109, no. 4 (Oct. 2004): 1054–1083.

Hribal, Jason. "'Animals Are Part of the Working Class': A Challenge to Labor History." *Labor History* 44, no. 4 (2003): 435–453.

Hu-deHart, Evelyn. *Yaqui Resistance and Survival: The Struggle for Land and Autonomy, 1821–1910.* University of Wisconsin Press, 1984.

Hussain, Shafqat. "Sports-Hunting, Fairness, and Colonial Identity: Collaboration and Subversion in the Northwestern Frontier Region of the British Indian Empire." *Conservation and Society* 8, no. 2 (2010): 112–126.

Imaz Baume, Arturo. *Cacería.* 2nd ed. Secretaría de Educación Pública, 1949.

Irwin, Robert McKee, Edward McCaughan, and Michelle Rocío Nasser, eds. *The Famous 41: Sexuality and Social Control in Mexico, 1901*. Palgrave, 2003.

Jacoby, Karl. *Crimes Against Nature: Squatters Poachers, Thieves, and the Hidden History of American Conservation*. University of California Press, 2003.

Jimenez, Christina M. *Making an Urban Public: Popular Claims to the City in Mexico, 1879–1932*. University of Pittsburgh Press, 2019.

Johns, Michael. *The City of Mexico in the Age of Díaz*. University of Texas Press, 1997.

Kabalen de Bichara, Donna M. "Late 19th-Century Periodical Print Culture in the US–Mexico Border Region." In *The Oxford Research Encyclopedia of Latin American History*, ed. Stephen Webre. Oxford University Press, 2022. https://doi.org/10.1093/acrefore/9780190201098.013.1162.

Kalof, Linda, Amy Fitzgerald, Jennifer Lerner, and Jessica Temeles. "Animal Studies: A Bibliography." *Human Ecology Review* 11, no. 1 (Spring 2004): 75–99.

Kalof, Linda, and Georgina Montgomery, eds. *Making Animal Meaning*. Michigan State University Press, 2011.

Katz, Friedrich. *The Life and Times of Pancho Villa*. Stanford University Press, 1998.

Kirkpatrick, Michael D. "Consumer Culture in Guatemala City During the 'Season of Mazzantini,' 1905: The Political Economy of Working-Class Consumption." *Journal of Latin American Studies* 52, no. 4 (2020): 735–758.

Knight, Alan. *The Mexican Revolution*. Vol. 1: *Porfirians, Liberals, and Peasants*. University of Nebraska Press, 1986.

Knight, John. "The Anonymity of the Hunt: A Critique of Hunting as Sharing." *Current Anthropology* 53, no. 3 (June 2012): 334–355.

Kroll, Gary. "An Environmental History of Roadkill: Road Ecology and the Making of the Impermeable Highway." *Environmental History* 20, no. 1 (Jan. 2015): 4–28.

Lafevor, David C. *Prizefighting and Civilization: A Cultural History of Boxing, Race, and Masculinity in Mexico and Cuba, 1840–1940*. University of New Mexico Press, 2020.

Larson, Eric. *Devil in the White City: Murder, Magic, and Madness at the Fair That Changed America*. Vintage Books, 2003.

Lawrence, D. H. *Mornings in Mexico*. Amsterdam: Fredonia Books, 2003. First published in 1934.

Leal, Juan Felipe, José Francisco Coello, and Eduardo Barraza. *La multiplicación de los cines en la provincia: Anales del cine en México, 1895–1911*. Vol. 15. Voyeur, 2016. First published in 1908.

Lear, John. *Workers, Neighbors, and Citizens: The Revolution in Mexico City.* University of Nebraska Press, 2001.

Leopold, Aldo Starker. *Wildlife of Mexico: The Game Birds and Mammals.* University of California Press, 1972.

Licéaga, Eduardo. *Informe de Dr. Eduardo Licéaga a gobierno del estado.* Imprenta del Estado, 1895.

Linebaugh, Peter. "Karl Marx, the Theft of Wood, and Working-Class Composition: A Contribution to the Current Debate." *Social Justice* 40, nos. 1–2 (2014): 137–161.

Lipsett-Rivera, Sonya. "A New Challenge: Social History and Dogs in the Era of Post-Humanism." *Sociedad indiana*, posted online on August 12, 2015, http://socindiana.hypotheses.org/320.

Lipsett-Rivera, Sonya. *The Origins of Macho: Men and Masculinity in Colonial Mexico.* University of New Mexico Press, 2019.

Lira, Andrés. *Las comunidades indígenas frente a la Ciudad de México.* El Colegio de México, 1983.

Lizardi, José Joaquín Fernández de. *El periquillo sarniento.* Porrúa, 2012.

Lomnitz, Claudio. *Death and the Idea of Mexico.* Zone, 2005.

Loo, Tina. *States of Nature: Conserving Canada's Wildlife in the Twentieth Century.* University of British Columbia Press, 2006.

Lópes, María-Aparecida. "Struggles over an 'Old, Nasty, and Inconvenient Monopoly': Municipal Slaughterhouses and the Meat Industry in Rio de Janeiro, 1880–1920s." *Journal of Latin American Studies* 47, no. 2 (May 2015): 349–376.

López, Amanda M. "An Urgent Need for Hygiene: Cremation, Class, and Public Health in Mexico City, 1879–1920." *Estudios Mexicanos/Mexican Studies* 31, no. 1 (2015): 88–124.

López, Carlos M., and Carlos López. *Caza Mexicana: Obra escrita con la colaboración de varios cazadores del país e ilustrado con retratos y con fotografías tomadas de animales, también del país.* Librería de la Viuda de C. Bouret, 1911.

López, Paulino. *Reglas sobre cría, educación, y preparación de gallos de combate.* Mexico City: A. Pola Ed., 1908.

Lumholtz, Carl. "From the Tarascos to Porfirio Díaz." In *Mexico Otherwise: Modern Mexico in the Eyes of Foreign Observers*, edited by Jürgen Buchenau, 115–125. University of New Mexico Press, 2005.

Macías-González, Víctor. "Curtseying in the Shadow of Dictators." In *Heroes and Hero Cults in Latin America*, edited by S. Brunk, 83–109. University of Texas Press, 2006.

Macías-González, Víctor, and Anne Rubenstein, eds. *Masculinity and Sexuality in Modern Mexico*. University of New Mexico Press, 2012.
MacKenzie, John M. *The Empire of Nature: Hunting, Conservation, and British Imperialism*. University of Manchester Press, 1988.
Mañas Perdano, Rafael. *El gallo fino combatiente*. Albatros, 1993.
Mangan, J. A., and Lamartine DaCosta, eds. *Sport in Latin American Society: Past and Present*. Frank Cass, 2002.
Martínez-Reyes, José. *Moral Ecology of a Forest: The Nature Industry and Maya Post-Conservation*. University of Arizona Press, 2016.
Matthews, Andrew. *Instituting Nature: Authority, Expertise, and Power in Mexican Forests*. MIT Press, 2011.
Matthews, Michael. *The Civilizing Machine: A Cultural History of Mexican Railroads, 1876–1910*. University of Nebraska Press, 2013.
Matthews, Michael. *Sex and Love in Porfirian Mexico City: A Social History of Working-Class Courtship*. University of Florida Press, 2025.
McCrea, Heather. *Diseased Relations: Epidemics, Public Health, and State-Building in Yucatán, Mexico, 1847–1924*. University of New Mexico Press, 2010.
McDevitt, Patrick F. "Muscular Catholicism: Nationalism, Masculinity, and Gaelic Team Sports, 1884–1916." In *Bodies in Contact: Rethinking Colonial Encounters in World History*, edited by T. Ballantyne and A. Burton, 201–218. Duke University Press, 2005.
Melville, Elinor. *A Plague of Sheep*. Cambridge University Press, 1997.
Mendoza, Vicente. *El Corrido Mexicano*. Fondo de Cultura Económica, 1954.
Merchant, Carolyn. "Reinventing Eden: Western Culture as Recovery Narrative." In *Uncommon Ground: Rethinking the Human Place in Nature*, edited by William Cronon, 132–170 Norton, 1996.
Mestaz, James. *Strength from the Waters: A History of Indigenous Mobilization in Northwestern Mexico*. University of Nebraska Press, 2022.
México, Carlos Rivas, Secretaría de Gobernación, México. *Colección de leyes y disposiciones gubernativos municipales y de policía vigentes en el D.F. Pub*. Ireneo Paz:, 1884.
México. *Colección de Leyes Federales, Código Sanitario, 1902–1903*. N.p., n.d.
México. *Memoria del Consejo Superior de Salubridad, 1901*. Imprenta de Eduardo Dublán, 1901.
México. Secretaría de estado y del despacho de fomento y colonización e industria. *Disposiciones de caza vigentes*. N.p., 1929.

Mikhail, Alan. *The Animal in Ottoman Egypt*. New York: Oxford University Press, 2014.
Miller, Shawn W. *An Environmental History of Latin America*. Cambridge University Press, 2007.
Mitchell, Timothy. *Blood Sport: A Social History of Spanish Bullfighting*. University of Pennsylvania Press, 1991.
Moisés, Rosalio, J. Kelley, and W. Holden. *A Yaqui Life: The Personal Chronicle of a Yaqui Indian*. University of Nebraska Press, 1971.
Moliné y Roca, Miguel. *Cháchara taurina: Colección de anécdotas, sucedidos, chascarrillos y dicharachos, de toreros y aficionados*. Ed. Iberoamericana, 1906.
Monbiot, George. *Feral: Rewilding the Land, the Sea, and Human Life*. University of Chicago Press, 2014.
Montano, Diana. *Electrifying Mexico: Technology and the Transformation of a Modern City*. University of Texas Press, 2021.
Moreno, Gary. "Charro: The Transnational History of a Cultural Icon." PhD diss, University of Oklahoma, 2015.
Morris, Charles. *The Story of Mexico: A Land of Conquest and Revolution Giving a Comprehensive History of This Romantic and Beautiful Land from the Days of Montezuma and the Empire of the Aztecs to the Present Time*. Ulan Press, 2006. First published in 1923.
Mullin, Molly H. "Mirrors and Windows: Sociocultural Studies of Human-Animal Relationships." *Annual Review of Anthropology* 28 (1999): 201–224.
Nance, Susan, ed. *The Historical Animal*. Syracuse University Press, 2015.
Neufeld, Stephen. "Animal Perspectives: Non-Human Creatures' Roles in Modern Latin America." In *The Oxford Research Encyclopedia of Latin American History*, edited by Stephen Webre. Oxford University Press, 2022.
Neufeld, Stephen. *The Blood Contingent: The Military in the Making of Modern Mexico, 1876–1911*. University of New Mexico Press, 2017.
Neufeld, Stephen, and Michael Matthews, eds. *Mexico in Verse: A History of Music, Rhyme, and Power*. University of Arizona Press, 2015.
Norton, Marcy. *The Tame and the Wild: People and Animals After 1492*. Harvard University Press, 2024.
Ochoa, Enrique. *Feeding Mexico: The Political Uses of Food Since 1910*. SR Books, 2000.
Obregón González, Alberto. *Gallos de pelea: Secretos para el entrenamiento*. Morfri, 2010.
Obregón González, Alberto. *El gladiador emplumado de México: Historia de las peleas de gallos en México*. Edinova, 1995.

Olalde Vázquez, Brenda Yesenia. "Prohibición a las peleas de gallos. Comentario sobre la sentencia del amparo en revisión 163/2018 de la Suprema Corte de Justicia de la Nación (México)." *dA. Derecho Animal* (Forum of Animal Law Studies) 10, no. 1 (2019): 185–195.

Olsen, Sherry. "The Urban Horse and the Shaping of Montreal, 1840–1914." In *Animal Metropolis: Histories of Human-Animal Relations in Urban Canada*, edited by Joanna Dean Darcy Ingram, and Christabelle Sethna, 57–87. University of Calgary Press, 2017.

Orlove, Benjamin S. "Meat and Strength: The Moral Economy of a Chilean Food Riot." *Cultural Anthropology* 12, no. 2 (May 1997): 234–268.

Ortega y Gasset, José. *La caza y los toros*. Ed. Espasa-Calpe, 1962.

Orvañas, D. Domingo. *Sociedad Médico "Pedro Escobedo", Discurso at Concurso científico, 1895*. Sec. Fomento, 1895.

Pearson, Susan, and Mary Weisentel. "Does the Animal Exist: Towards a Social Life with Animals." In *Beastly Natures: Animals, Humans, and the Study of History*, edited by Dorothee Brantz, 17–37. University of Virginia Press, 2010.

Pierotti, Raymond, and Brandy Raelene Fogg. "Neocolonial Thinking and Respect for Nature." *Ethnobiology Letters* 11, no. 1 (2020): 48–57.

Pica Pica (pen name). *Gaona: Su biografía*. N.p., 1911.

Piccato, Pablo. *City of Suspects: Crime in Mexico City, 1900–1931*. Durham, NC: Duke University Press, 2001.

Piccato, Pablo. *The Tyranny of Opinion: Honor in the Construction of the Mexican Public Sphere*. Duke University Press, 2010.

Pilcher, Jeffrey, ed. *The Human Tradition in Mexico*. Scholarly Resources, 2003.

Pilcher, Jeffrey. *Que vivan los tamales! Food and the Making of Mexican Identity*. University of New Mexico Press, 1998.

Pilcher, Jeffrey. *The Sausage Rebellion: Public Health, Private Enterprise, and Meat in Mexico City, 1890–1917*. University of New Mexico Press, 2006.

Pitarch, Pedro. "Almas y cuerpo en una tradición indígena tzeltal." *Archives de sciences sociales des religions*, 45e Année, no. 112 (Oct.–Dec. 2000): 31–47.

Poliquin, Rachel. *The Breathless Zoo: Taxidermy and the Cultures of Longing*. Pennsylvania State University Press, 2012.

Pratt, Mary Louise. *Imperial Eyes: Travel Writing and Transculturation*. 2nd ed. Routledge, 2007.

Quiroz, Enriqueta. *Entre el lujo y la subsistencia: mercado, abastecimiento y precios de la carne en la Ciudad de México, 1750–1812*. Colegio de México, 2005.
Ramírez Rancaño, Mario. "Rodolfo Gaona: El célebre matador y su relación con cuatro presidentes (1907–1925)." MA thesis, Universidad Nacional Autónoma de México, 2008.
Ramos, Mario Arturo. *Cien corridos: Alma de la canción mexicana*. Mexico City: Océano, 2002.
Rebella, Carlos. *Caza mayor*. Ed. Albatros, 1989.
Reiger, John F. *American Sportsmen and the Origins of Conservation*. Oregon State University Press, 1975.
Robles Fernández, Miguel Alessio. *Memorias y proyectos de leyes sobre la conservación de la fauna silvestre y el ejercicio de la caza en México*. Sec. Hacienda y Crédito Pública, 1959.
Rodríguez, Jaime. *The Revolutionary Process in Mexico*. UCLA Latin American Center Publications, University of California, 1990.
Rohlfes, Laurence J. "Police and Penal Correction in Mexico City, 1876–1911: A Study of Order and Progress in Porfirian Mexico." PhD diss., Tulane University, 1983.
Rojas Hernández, Laura. "Muerto el perro, se acabó la rabia. Perros callejeros, vacuna antirrábica y salud pública en la ciudad de México, 1880–1915." MA thesis, Universidad Nacional Autónoma de México, 2011.
Rosell, Lauro E. *Plazas de toros de México: historia de cada una de las que han existido en la capital desde 1521 hasta 1936*. Talleres Gráficos de Excelsior, 1945.
Rugeley, Terry, and B. Fallaw, eds. *Forced Marches: Soldiers and Military Caciques in Modern Mexico*. University of Arizona Press, 2012.
Russel, Edmund. *Evolutionary History: Uniting History and Biology to Understand Life on Earth*. Cambridge University Press, 2011.
Said, Edward. *Orientalism*. Vintage Press, 1979.
Sandstrom, Alan P. "Ethnic Identity and Its Attributes in a Contemporary Mexican Indian Village." In *The Indian in Latin American History: Resistance, Resilience, and Acculturation*, edited by John Kicza, 269–283. Scholarly Resources, 2000.
Santoni, Pedro. "La policía de la Ciudad de México durante el Porfiriato: Los primeros años (1876–1884)." *Historia Mexicana* 33, no. 1 (July–Sept., 1983): 97–129.
Santos, Gonzalo N. *Memorias*. Ed. Grivaljo, n.d.

Santoyo, Antonio. "De cerdos y de civilidad urbana. La descalificación de las actividades de la explotación porcina en la ciudad de México durante el último tercio del siglo xix." *Historia Mexicana* 47, no. 1 (July–Sept., 1997): 69–102.
Sarabia, María Justina. *Las peleas de gallos*. Noriega, 2001.
Schivelbusch, Wolfgang. *Disenchanted Night: The Industrialization of Light in the Nineteenth Century*. Translated by Angela Davies. University of California Press, 1995.
Schwartz, Marion. *A History of Dogs in the Early Americas*. Yale University Press, 1997.
Scheper-Hughes, Nancy. *Death Without Weeping: The Violence of Everyday Life in Brazil*. University of California Press, 1992.
Schubert, Adrian. *Death and Money in the Afternoon: A History of the Spanish Bullfight*. Oxford University Press, 1999.
Scott, James. *Domination and the Arts of Resistance: Hidden Transcripts*. Yale University Press, 1990.
Scott, James. *The Moral Economy of the Peasant: Rebellion and Subsistence in Southeast Asia*. Yale University Press, 1976.
Serpell, James. *In the Company of Animals: A Study of Animal-Human Relationships*. Cambridge University Press, 1996.
Sessions, George. "The Deep Ecology Movement: A Review." *Environmental Review* 11, no. 2 (Summer 1987): 105–125.
Setten, Gunhild. "The Habitus, the Rule, and the Moral Landscape." *Cultural Geographies* 11, no. 4 (Oct. 2004): 389–415.
Shapiro, Kenneth. "Human-Animal Studies: Remembering the Past, Celebrating the Present, Troubling the Future." *Society and Animals* 28 no. 7 (2020): 797–833.
Shaw, David Gary. "A Way with Animals." *History and Theory* 52, no. 4 (Dec. 2013): 1–12.
Shepard, Paul. *The Others: How Animals Made Us Human*. Washington, DC: Island Press, 1996.
Shepard, Paul. *The Tender Carnivore and the Sacred Game*. Georgia University Press, 1998.
Sherratt, Harriot Wight. *Mexican Vistas Seen from Highways and By-ways of Travel*. Rand McNally, 1899.
Shukin, Nicole. *Animal Capital: Rendering Life in Biopolitical Times*. University of Minnesota Press, 2009.
Simonian, Lane. *Defending the Land of the Jaguar: A History of Conservation in Mexico*. University of Texas Press, 1995.

Sloan, Kathryn. *Death in the City: Suicide and the Social Imaginary in Modern Mexico.* University of California Press, 2017.
Sloan, Kathryn. *Runaway Daughters: Seduction, Elopement, and Honor in Nineteenth Century Mexico.* University of New Mexico Press, 2008.
Sobaquillo. *Revistas taurinas de El Liberal, 1887–1894.* F. Bueno y Co., n.d.
Soluri, John, Claudia Leal, and José Augusto Pádua, eds. *A Living Past: Environmental Histories of Modern Latin America.* Berghahn, 2018.
Speckman Guerra, Elisa. *Historia de la vida cotidiana en México, siglo XX.* Tomo. V, vol. 1. Edited by Aurelio de la Reyes. Fondo Cultura y Económica, 2014.
Spiegel, Marjorie. "An Historical Understanding." In *Social Creatures: A Human and Animal Studies Reader*, edited by Clifton Flynn, 233–244. Lantern Books, 2008.
Strother, David Hunter. *Porte Crayon's Mexico: David Hunter Strother's Diaries in the Early Porfirian Era, 1879–1885.* Edited by John E. Sealey III. Kent State University Press, 2006.
Sundararajan, P. T. Saroja. "From Marxian Ecology to Ecological Marxism." *Science and Society* 60, no. 3 (Fall 1996): 360–379.
Swabe, Joanna. *Animals, Disease and Human Society: Human-Animal Relations and the Rise of Veterinary Medicine.* Routledge, 2014.
Taussig, Michael T. *The Devil and Commodity Fetishism in South America.* University of North Carolina Press, 1980.
Tenorio-Trillo, Mauricio. *Mexico at the World's Fairs: Crafting a Modern Nation.* University of California Press, 1996.
Tenorio-Trillo, Mauricio. *I Speak of the City.* University of Chicago Press, 2012.
Terry, T. Philip. *Terry's Mexico: Handbook for Travelers.* Houghton Mifflin, 1909.
Thrift, Nigel. *Killer Cities.* Sage, 2021.
Thomas, William S. *Hunting Big Game with a Gun and with a Kodak: A Record of Personal Experiences in the United States, Canada, and Mexico.* Knickerbocker Press, 1906.
Thompson, Edward P. *Customs in Common: Studies in Traditional Popular Culture.* New Press, 1993.
Thompson, Edward P. *The Making of the English Working Class.* Vintage Books, 1966.
Thompson, Edward P. "The Moral Economy of the English Crowd in the Eighteenth Century." *Past and Present* 50 (Feb. 1971): 76–136.
Thompson, Edward P. *Whigs and Hunters: The Origin of the Black Act.* Allen Lane, 1975.

Thornton, Thomas F., and Patricia Thornton. "The Mutable, the Mythical, and the Managerial: Raven Narratives and the Anthropocene." *Environment and Society* 6 (2015): 66–86.

Tortolero Villaseñor, Alejandro. "Canales de riego y canales navegables en la Cuenca de México: Economía, patrimonio y paisaje en el México porfirista." *Historia Caribe* 10, no. 26 (Jan.–June 2015): 75–105.

Tortolero Villaseñor, Alejandro. *Notarios y agricultores: Crecimiento y atraso en el campo mexicano, 1780–1920*. Universidad Autónoma Metropolitana, 2008.

Townsend, Camilla. *Fifth Sun: A New History of the Aztecs*. Oxford University Press, 2019.

Toxqui Garay, Áurea. "'El Recreo de los Amigos': Mexico City's Pulquerías During the Liberal Republic, 1856–1911." PhD diss., University of Arizona, 2008.

Tragically Hip, The. "Cordelia." Track 6 on *Road Apples*. MCA, 1991, CD.

Treviño Jr., Tomas. *Relatos de cacería en México*. Tomo 2. Ed. Castillo: 1995.

Tucker, Catherine M. Nature, *Science, and Religion: Intersections Shaping Society and the Environment*. SAR Press, 2012.

Uribe Mendoza, Blanca. "La intervención de los animales: Una historia de la veterinaria mexicana, siglo XIX." *Historia, Ciências, Saúde-Manghuinos* 22, no. 4 (2015): 1391–1409.

Vargas, Domínguez. *El gallo de combate*. Diana, 1983.

Vargas Coto, Joaquín. *Gente taurina: El arte en decadencia*. Tipolit. De Samuel Romillo, 1910.

Vázquez Flores, Erika Julieta. *Discursos de la discriminación: El indígena en la prensatapatía*. Universidad de Guanajuato, 2012.

Veblen, Thorstein. *The Theory of the Leisure Class*. N.p., 1899.

Vega Amaya, María Patricia. "El gobierno de Ramón Corral en el Distrito Federal (1900–1903): Su impacto en la Ciudad de México visto a través de la obra pública." MA thesis, Instituto Mora, 2004.

Vergara, Germán. "Bestiario latinoamericano: Los animales en la historiografía deAmérica Latina." *História, Ciências, Saúde-Manguinhos* 28, supl. (Dec. 2021): 187–208.

Vergara, Germán, and Emily Wakild. "Extinction and Its Interventions in the Americas." Special Forum. *Environmental History* 27 (Apr. 2022): 294–307.

Villa, Bernardo. *Los venados en México*. Dept. de caza, 1950.

Villa-Flores, Javier. *Dangerous Speech: A Social History of Blasphemy in Colonial Mexico*. University of Arizona Press, 2006.

Viquiera Albán, Juan Pedro. *Propriety and Permissiveness in Bourbon Mexico*. Translated by S. Lipsett-Rivera and Sergio Rivera Ayala. SR Books, 2004.

Vitz, Matthew. "'The Lands with Which We Shall Struggle': Land Reclamation, Revolution, and Development in Mexico's Lake Texcoco Basin, 1910–1950." *Hispanic American Historical Review* 92, no. 1 (Feb. 2012): 41–71.

Vitz, Matthew. *A City on the Lake: Urban Political Ecology and the Growth of Mexico City*. Duke University Press, 2018.

von Germeten, Nicole. *The Enlightened Patrolman: Early Law Enforcement in Mexico City*. University of Nebraska Press, 2022.

Wakild, Emily. "Naturalizing Modernity: Urban Parks, Public Gardens and Drainage Projects in Porfirian Mexico City." *Mexican Studies/Estudios Mexicanos* 23, no. 1 (Winter 2007): 101–123.

Wakild, Emily. "Parables of Chapultepec: Urban Parks, National Landscapes, and Contradictory Conservation in Modern Mexico." In *A Land Between Waters: Environmental Histories of Modern Mexico*, edited by Chris Boyer, 192–218. University of Arizona Press, 2012.

Wakild, Emily. *Revolutionary Parks: Conservation, Social Justice, and Mexico's National Parks, 1910–1940*. University of Arizona Press, 2011.

Wakild, Emily. "Saving the Vicuña: The Political, Biophysical, and Cultural History of Wild Animal Conservation in Peru, 1964–2000." *American Historical Review* 125, no. 1 (Feb. 2020): 54–88.

Walker, Brett L. "Animals and the Intimacy of History." *History and Theory*, theme issue 52 (Dec. 2013): 45–67.

Wang, Jessica. "Dogs and the Making of the American State: Voluntary Association, State Power, and the Politics of Animal Control in New York City, 1850–1920." *Journal of American History* 98 (Mar. 2012): 998–1024.

Warren, Louis. *The Hunter's Game: Poachers and Conservationists in Twentieth Century America*. Yale University Press, 1997.

Washbrook, Sarah. *Producing Modernity in Mexico: Labor, Race, and the State in Chiapas, 1876–1914*. Oxford University Press, 2012.

Wasik, Bill, and Monica Murphy. *Rabid: A Cultural History of the World's Most Diabolical Virus*. Penguin, 2012.

Wasserman, Mark. *Persistent Oligarchs: Elites and Politics in Chihuahua, Mexico, 1910–1940*. Duke University Press, 1993.

Weiner, Carlos, Jules Crevaux, D. Charney, and André Edouard. *América Pintoresca: Descripción de viajes al nuevo continente por los más modernos exploradores*. Mantanery Simon, 1894.

Wolfe, Cary. *Animal Rites: American Culture, the Discourse of Species, and Posthumanist Theory*. University of Chicago Press, 2003.

Worster, Donald. *The Wealth of Nature: Environmental History and the Ecological Imagination*. Oxford University Press, 1994.

White, Richard. "Environmental History, Ecology, and Meaning." *Journal of American History* 76, no. 4 (Mar. 1990): 1111–1116.

Whitehead, Neil. "Loving, Being, Killing Animals." In *Centering Animals in Latin American History*, edited by Zeb Tortorici and Martha Few, 329–345. University of Arizona Press, 2013.

INDEX

Note: Page numbers in italic text indicate figures.

A. Cerdan and Company, 145
Abogado Cristiano, 160
Acevedo, Benito, 67
Acevedo, Victoriano, 67
activism (in bullfighting): bans, 140–47; and foreigners' memories, 148–50; reformers, 140–47
advertising, 1; and bullfight audience, 87–88, 93–94; and *corrida* industry, 127, 129–30; in specialty papers, 100–101. *See also* newspapers
afición taurino (bullfighting fandom), 102–5. *See also* fandom (of bullfighting)
afueras (outsides), 57, 61–62, 70
agencement (agency), bulls and, 174–75
agents. See *apoderas*
Aguilar, Luis, 133
Alamán (family name), 129
Alameda Park, 110
Albán, Juan Pedro Viqueira, 124
alcohol, hunting and, 196–97
Alfaro, Gonzalo, 133
Alfonso XIII (king), 159
alrededores (surrounds), 57
alternativa (promotion), 108, 172
amarradores (handlers), 73, 77–78. See also *pelea de gallos*
American Society for the Protection and Care of Animals (ASPCA), 34, 45
Anda, Raúl de, 139
Angelita, Lolita Guerrera y, 140
Angelita (matadora), 177–78
animal deaths: anecdotes, 1–3; big questions regarding, 3–7; bullfight audience, 87–120; bullfighter expectations, 152–82; capitalism and activism, 121–51; hunter performances and, 213–38; methods and situation in literature, 8–11; in neighboring municipalities, 54–83; overview of studying, 11–16; reading tracks and culture, 242–44; role of game hunters in, 185–212; street dogs, 19–53; tentative findings regarding, 241–42
animal rights, class-based notions of, 62–65, 67
antathropes, 19–20
Anthropocene, term, 253n21
Anti-Rabies Institute (Instituto Anti-Rábico Mexicano), 29
apoderas (agents), 172. *See also* management (of matador); matador
arena, animal deaths in, 1–3; activism, 121–51; bullfight audience, 87–120; capitalism, 121–51; gender and social roles, 152–82. See also *corrida*
Armengel, Don Mariano, 177
Arte de Lidia Imparcial, 99
asadero (barbeque), 63
Asilo Colón, 146
ASPCA. *See* American Society for the Protection and Care of Animals
assistants. See *cuadrillas*, matador and
Atenco, 136
audience (of bullfighting): *broncas*, 112–19, *113, 115, 117*; bullfight as experience, 93–99; bullfighting fandom in papers, 102–5; creating fans, 89–92; human factors shaping experience in negative ways, 97–98; marketing toward, 93–94; merchandise, 94; modern audiences, 98–99; nostalgic fandom, 106–7; other entertainment, 96–97; overview, 87–89, 119–20; prefight experience, 93; promoters, 95–96; "rain checks," 95; reacting to fight changes, 97; scalpers, 95; singing to fans, 107–10; specialty papers, 99–101. See also *corrida*

311

INDEX

"authenticities," mingling of traditional practices and, 122–23
Ayuntamiento, 69, 103, 114, 131, 134, 141, 177, 254n42

Baja California, 209, 222
Bando of 1856, 43
bans, 13, 150, 177, 179; boxing fans, 145–46; bull as Othered object, 140–41; cockfights and, 80–81; different approaches, 144–45; "social good" argument, 146–47; SPCMA role in, 141–44; temporary bans, 77, 103, 140, 150
barbeque. See *asadero*
bats, 57, 62
beaters, use of, 194
Beezley, William, 179
Benjamin, Walter, 20
Bergh, Henry, 34
Bergtold, William, 222
Berjoin (animal lover), 142–43
Bernáldez (doctor), 28
biopolitics, 3, 244, 246, 248, 251–52; and culling of street animals, 20–22, 35, 44; and hunting, 186, 214; and killing of food animals, 55–56, 63. See also necropolitics
birds. See *pelea de gallos*
Blake, Emmet R., 222
Blazquez, Pedro, 189–92
Blichfeldt, Emil, 149
blinds, using, 194
Bombito (bullfighter), 101
bond. See *fiador*
Bourdieu, Pierre, 91, 181
boxing, 73, 110, 120, 143, 145–46, 199
breeders. See *ganaderos*
Bringas, Carlos, 133
Britain, 45
broncas (riots), *113*, *115*, *117*; applause and, 116, 118; blame for, 118; circumstances of, 112, 114; and entitlement, 116; foreign plazas and, 114, 116; papers on, 118–19; press discussing, 114. See also *corrida*
Brown, David, 221

Bucareli Plaza, 94, 103–4, 108, 112, 126–27, 132, 138, 171, 177
"buck fever" (*fiebre del ciervo*), 192
Buen Tono, El, 93–94, 127, *195*
Buffalo Bill Show, 139
bullfight. See *corrida*
bullfighter, 92, 98, 119; career progression, 171–73; celebrity politics, 157–59; compensating, 133–34; core criteria of, 170; cowardice of, 112, 118; *diestros*, 166–69, *168*; foreigners and, 148–50; Gaona story, 154–56, *155*; Gaona trial, 160–65, *161*, *164*; goring, 101; guilds of, 140; leaving France, 144; new fandom in papers, 102–5; nostalgia and, 106–7; overview, 152–54, 181–82; personal section in papers, 101; pitching *toreras*, 176–78; reputations, 169–71; singing tales of, 107–10; societal tastes, 179–81. See also *corrida*
bullfight events. See *festejos taurinos*
bullfighting arts. See *tauromachia*
bullfighting fandom. See *afición taurino*
bulls, 4, 12–13, 79, 89, 92, 121–23; arguments regarding, 143; breeding, 136–39; and *broncas*, 112–19; and bullfight as experience, 97–101; and *corrida* industry, 130–35; gender of matador fighting, 152–82; making modern celebrities of, 126; memories of, 149; as Othered object, 140–41; in papers, 102–7; and social good, 146–47; in songs, 107–9; as stars, 174–76; and *toreras*, 176–78; and the weird, 139–40. See also *corrida*
Bunker, Steve, 94
Burbridge, Ben, 222
butcher, indigenous person as, 197

cadavers, 2, 232, 248; burning, 39–40, 109; proper use of, 29–30, 42–43; removal of, 64, 68; selling off, 40; as spectacle, 44–46; stealing, 35
Califa, El. See Gaona, Rodolfo
Calles, Plutarco Elías, 159
cambio de rodillas (veronica on one knee), 106
Camp, Roderic Ai, 80
Campos, Juan, 30

Canada, 191, 202, 282n162
capitalism (in bullfighting): bans, 140–47; breeders, 136–39, *137*; brief history of bullfighting, 123–25; creating mass spectacle of leisure, 125–27; and foreigners' memories, 148–50; overview, 121–23, 151; reformers, 140–47; selling the weird, 139–40; venue construction, 127–35. See also *corrida*
Cardos, Olivera, 125
career (of matador), progression of, 171–73
Careta, La, 99, 135
Carmony, Neil, 221
carp, selling, 65
Carpenter, Donald, 220–22
Carranza, Venustiano, 77, 158–59
carrederas (walkways), 129
Carrodegiias, Domingo, 133
Castro, Casimiro, *58*
catrin banquetero (city dandy), 204
celebrity politics, matador and, 157–59
Centering Animals in Latin American History (Tortorici and Few), 9
cerrado punta de capote (closed cape), 106
"Chapultepec, En," *236*
Chapultepec Forest, 60
Chapultepec Plaza, 1, 24, 60, 127, 130, 133, 135, 138, 139, 232, 235, *236*, 244
Chihuahua, 209
cigarettes, advertising, 93–94, 169, 178, *195*, 199
cities, animal deaths in: neighboring municipalities, 54–83; street dogs, 19–53. See also Mexico City
"Ciudad de México desde un Globo, Le" (Castro), *58*
Ciudad Porfirio Díaz, 30
Civil Code of the Federation, 204
clandestine meat, 67–69
class, forming around cuisine choices, 62–65, 67
Club Atlético Internacional, 145
Club Cazadores Mexicanos, 280n69
Coahuila, 209, 264n117
cockfight. See *pelea de gallos*
Código Civil (1870), 204
Código Sanitario (Sanitary Code), 28, 30, 69
Coliseo, 127

Colón, 127
Colón Asylum, 132
Colonia Españoles, 136
Commission of Veterinary Subjects, 30
compadrazgo (godparenthood), 172–73
concealment, 62–63
Condesa, 127, 129–30
conservation, 7, 9, 13, 15, 65, 185–87, 198; adjusting limits on firearms, 209–10; and economic value of hunting, 209; good intentions of laws of, 204–5; and great wealth in wild animal populations, 210–10; hunting laws in Mexico, 201–3; initial laws of, 204; killing wrong animals, 208; long roots of, 204; official policies on, 205–6; poachers and, 208–9; reimagining hunting, 206–7; and rural population, 207–8
Constitution of 1917, 204
consumer, creating, 89–92
contractors: arguing about capturing dogs, 41; hiring, 38–39; identifying other issues, 42–43; setting demands, 39–41; warnings against employing, 43
Cook, Karl, 41
Coren, Stanley, 34
corpses, cremating, 44
Corral, Ramón, 157
corral de mostrenco (missing animals lost and found), 70
corrida (bullfight), 77, 79; activism in business of, 121–23; anecdote, 1; audiences of, 87–120; bans and reformers, 140–47; brief history of, 123–25; *broncas* at, 112–19, *113*, *115*, *117*; capitalism in business of, 121–23; constructing venues for, 127–35; creating fans of, 89–92; as experience, 93–99; foreigners witnessing, 148–50; *ganaderos* and, 136–39, *137*; Gaona story, 154–56, *155*; gender and social roles, 152–82; making stars in, 171–76; new fandom in papers for, 102–5; nostalgic fandom of, 106–7; selling the weird at, 139–40; singing to fans of, 107–10; "social good" argument, 146–47; specialty papers for, 99–101; and tastes of society, 179–81; *toreras* in, 176–78

"Corrido a la despedida de Rodolfo Gaona" (song) 169
corrido (folksong), 156, 175, 182; *broncas* at, 112–19, *113*, *115*, *117*; Noecker affair and, 163; singing for fans, 107–10
"Corrido relativo a La Gran destrucción y terrible incendiado de la plaza . . ." (song), 114
Cortés, Hernan, 136
Cortés, León, 123, 134
Coto, Joaquín Vargas, 169
Coyoacán, Mexico, 22
coyotes, 22, 57, 62, 191, 197, 201, 203
Creel, Enrique, 220
Creelman, James, 230, *231*, *233*, *234*
Criminal Code (in 1871), 124–25
Cronon, William, 8
cuadrillas, matador and, 171–73
Cuatrodedos, Diego Prieto Barrera, 126, 127, 130, 166
Cuellar, Samuel de, 96
cuisine, forming class identities around, 63
culture: constructing, 3–7; reading, 242–44
curanderos (folk healers), 30
Curcio-Nagy, Linda, 124

Darnton, Robert, 10
death, Mexican meanings of, 10
Death in the City (Noecker), 154
Department of Hacienda (Mexico City), 67
Department of Public Works (Mexico City), 70
Desierto de Leones, 235
Despret, Vinciane, 174
DF. *See* Mexico City
Diario del Hogar, 135
Díaz, Braulio, 156
Díaz, Ponciano, 104, 107–8, 126–27, 130, 132–33, 139, 153, 166, 167
Díaz, Porfirio, 77, 136, 157, 215, 223–25, 244; huntsman image of, 230–36, *231*, *233*, *234*, *236*
Díaz, Porfirio, Jr., *231*, *233*, *234*, *236*
diestros (expert bullfighters), 98, 103, 107–8, 118, 127, 131, 135; managing, 171–73; and matadors, 166–67; reputations, 169–71

Directorate of Forestry, Hunting, and Fishing, 204
Director Taurino, 134–35
disorders (at bullfight). *See broncas*
displacement (of death): killing of swine, 67–69; presenting meat, 62–65, 67
Dockery, Alexander M., 114, 116
"doctor sapientísimo, el." *See* Gaona, Rodolfo
dogfights. *See pelea de gallos*
Dog Massacres. *See* street dogs
dogs, culling of. *See* street dogs
domestic, term, 201–2
Don Chepito (character), 110
Dulzaras, La, 177
Duque de Veragua, 138

"Ecijano," Juan Jiménez, 126–27, 132
Edwards, William, 93
Egypt, 191
elite hunters, 223–25
England, 148
"en-soulment," 44
entrada (entry way), 93. *See also corrdia*
Escobar, Antonio, 100, 167
Escobedo, Pedro, 60
Esguia, Luis Mazzantini y, 94, 104, 110, 149, 166
Espinosa, Fermín, 153
Espinosa, Luis, 142
expectations (of bullfighter). *See* gender, bullfighter and
expert bullfighter. See *diestros*

Fabla, Octaviano González, 31
Faico, El (bullfighter), 101
fanáticos. See fans, creating
fandom (of bullfighting), 12, 88; creating members, 89–92; and nostalgia, 106–7; in papers, 102–5; songs for, 107–10. See also *corrdia*
fans, creating, 89–92
farol (cape at side, one hand high one low), 106
female bullfighters. See *toreras*
female fans, catering to, 126. *See also* fandom (of bullfighting)

INDEX

Fernández, Ignacia, 178
Ferrar, Lorenzo R., 145
festejos taurinos (bullfight events), 130
fiador (bond), 70
Fierro, Rodolfo, 77
fighting bulls. See *toros bravos*
"figurina parisién" (Parisian figurine). See matador: critiques of
firearms, adjusting limits on, 209–10
first-time hunter, bane of, 192
fish, 65, 82, 194
folk healers. See *curanderos*
folksong. See *corrido*
Fonssament, Manuel, 31
foreigners, ineffable memories of, 148–50
foreign hunters, 219–23
forests, reserving, 59–60
Foucault, Michel, 20, 246
France, 63, 75, 107, 144, 148, 190
Francisco, Bao Juan, 41
French Intervention, 39, 144
frente por detrás (front from back), 106
Frutos, Saturnino, 156

galleros (cockfighters), 72, 76–77, 79, 167. See also *pelea de gallos*
gallos, science of, 77. See also *pelea de gallos*
game, killing. See hunting, philosophies of
game, term, 201–2
ganaderos (breeders), 136–39, *137*
Gaona, Rodolfo, 10, 107, 109, 152, 153, 180; and celebrity politics, 157–59; overview of, 154–56, *155*; trial of, 160–65, *161*, *164*
García Bravo, Ignacio, 38
Garita de Belén, 127
Gaviño, Bernardo, 107–8, 166
gender, bullfighter and: career progression, 171–73; celebrity politics, 157–59; *diestros*, 166–68, *168*; Gaona story, 154–56, *155*; Gaona trial, 160–65, *161*, *164*; overview, 152–54, 181–82; pitching *toreras*, 176–78; reputations, 169–71; societal tastes, 179–81. See also bullfighter; *corrdia*; matador
glanders. See *muermo*

"glee of killing," 149
godparenthood. See *compadrazgo*
Gómez, Enriqueta, 159
Gomez, Octavio S., 78
González, Rafael, 167
"good hunter," philosophy of, 190–92
Gramsci, Antonio, 241
Gran Desagüe (Great Drain), 129
Grant, Ulysses S., 220
Great Drain (Gran Desagüe), 59
Great Separation, 55, 63, 70, 82, 261n5
greenery, maintaining, 56–60
gritón (announcers), 73. See also *pelea de gallos*
Guadalajara, 63, 213
"guardian angel" dogs, 257n62
Guaymas, Sonora, 34
Gutiérrez, Fernando, 119

Harper, Henry, 223
Harper's Magazine, 222
Heraldo, El, 160
Heraldo Taurino, 99
Hidalgo, Miguel, 75
Hidalgo, Tino, 147
hidrofobios. See rabies
Higueras, Dalmacio, 169
home-slaughtered meat, estimates of, 65
homo economicus, 250–51
Hondius, Hendrik, *71*
Horkheimer, Max, 27
"How to Make a Good Fan" (Neira), 104–5
Huerta, Adolfo de la, 159
Huerta, Victoriano, 157–59, *158*
Humphrey, William, 222
hunt, forms of, 194. See also sportsman's creed
hunter, performance of: elite hunters, 223–25; foreign hunters, 219–23; hunting in colonized nation, 225–29, *227*; indigenous hunters, 215–18; overview, 213–15, 237–38; presidential expedition, 230–36, *231*, *233*, *234*, *236*
hunter-authors. See hunting, philosophies of
hunter-native guide hierarchy, 225–26
hunter's law, 198

hunting, philosophies of: historical trajectory of conservation, 204–11; hunting laws, 201–3; intimate kill, 187–89; necessity of hunting, 187–88; non-subsistence hunters, 188; overview, 185–87, 211–12; Romantic view, 188–89; sportsman's creed, 189–201, *193*, *195*, *200*
hunting, "subtle ritual" of, 213–14
Hunting Big Game in the Sierras of Chihuahua (Carpenter), 220–21
hunting laws, 186, 199, 201–4, 211, 216

Ibañez and Company, 171
ideological rationales (about animal deaths), framing, 3–7
idiot hunters, 190–91
Imaz Baume, Arturo, 189, 198–99, *200*, 201
Imparcial, El, *32*, 146, 160, 167
imperial hunts, 225–29, *227*
Independiente, El, *158*
India, 229
indigenous hunters, 215–18
indigenous people: as hunters, 215–18; sportsman and, 197–98
Instituto Anti-Rábico Mexicano. *See* Anti-Rabies Institute
intimacy, finding, 255n44
intimate kill, philosophy of, 185–87
I Speak of the City (Tenorio-Trilllo), 10
Iturbide, Agustín, 124
Ixtapalapa, 67

J. J. Orrin Brothers, 125–26
Jacoby, Karl, 202
Juárez, Benito, 28–29, 124
juez (judge), 73. See also *pelea de gallos*
Junto Central de Bosques, 59

KCn. *See* potassium cyanide
kill, fetishization of. *See* mounting, practices of
"kill" (cultural artifact), 214
killing, reconciling psychological cost of, 3–7
kills, "harvesting," 205

Lacerdo (doctor), 31
Lake Xochimilco, 235
Laso, Yñigo Noriego, 131
Latin America, 8–10, 178
laws, 4, 6, 12–15, 240, 242–44, 248, 252; bullfighting and, 95, 129, 180; and conservation, 204–13; and customs, 218; and foreign hunters, 219–23; and imperial drive, 226; and indigenous hunts, 216–18; international laws, 201–3; moving slaughtered animals, 64, 69, 76; and philosophy of intimate kill, 185–7; and sportsman's creed, 196–99; street dogs and, 21, 28, 34, 36, 42, 45–46, 53
League of Protection for Animals, 144
Lecumberri, 1
Lee, Dale, 223
leisure, creating mass spectacle of, 125–27
Licéaga, Eduardo, 29–30, 257n73
Limantour, José Yves, 59, 145, 170
Linebaugh, Peter, 250
literature, methods and situation in, 8–11
Lizardi, José de, 31
Lolita (matadora), 177
Lomnitz, Claudio, 10
López, Carlos, 189, 194–98, *227*
López, Carlos M., 189, 194–98, *227*
López, Juan Olivera, 30
López, Luz Cosío de, 146
López, P., 80
López, Ramón, 101, 126, 129–30, 133–35, 142
Lopez, Amanda, 44
Luisa, María, 162, 180
"Luis el Tumbón" (poem), 105
lumbreras (luminaries), 104

Machaquito, Machaco (matador), 118, 133, 167
Madero, Francisco, 158
Malthus, Thomas, 45
mamarracha, term, 102–3
management (of matador), 171–73
Manifest Destiny, 5
Maragas, Carmen Ruiz de, 159

Martínez, Enrique, 145
Martínez-Reyes, José E., 217, 243
matador, 6, 13, 30, 87, 112, 116, 118; birth of bullfight audience, 87, 93, 97, 99–101; capitalism and activism, 122, 124, 126–27, 130, 132–33, 138, 140, 147, 150; career progression, 171–73; celebrity politics, 157–59; creating modern celebrity matador, 126–27; critiques of, 169–71; *diestros*, 166–68, *168*; fandom in papers, 102–35; Gaona story, 154–56, *155*; Gaona trial, 160–65, *161*, *164*; and nostalgic fandom, 106–7; overview, 152–54, 181–82; pitching *toreras*, 176–78; reputations, 169–71; societal tastes, 179–81; songs about, 107–10
Maximilian (emperor), 29, 59, 235
Maya, 215, 224
Mayo, 217, 220, 224
Mbembe, Achille, 5, 52, 247
meat, moving, 62–65, 67
Medical Institute of Toluca, 30
Medina, Antonio, 177
Mejarada, Carlos Sánchez, 210–11
Mendoza, Antonio de, 124
mercado volador (thieves' market), *37*
Mexican Game Trails (Carmony and Brown), 221
Mexican Herald, 143
Mexican Mosquito, 166
Mexican Red Cross, 257n73
Mexican Revolution, 4, 21, 31, 80, 90, 146, 157, 159, 179, 198–99, 208–10, 215
Mexican Society for the Protection and Care of Animals (SPCMA), 80, 141–44, 150, 244
Mexico, 239–40; animal death anecdotes in, 1–3; bans in, 140–47; big question regarding animal deaths in, 3–7; brief history of bullfighting in, 123–25; bullfight audience in, 87–120; bullfighter expectations in, 152–82; capitalism and activism in bullfight business in, 121–51; cock fetish of, 79; controlling municipalities, 54–83; foreigners in, 148–50; *ganaderos* in, 136–39, *137*; great wealth in wild animal populations in, 210–11; hunter performances, 213–38; hunting laws in, 201–3; methods and situation in literature, 8–11; modernization in, 21; *pelea de gallos* in, 72–81; public health in, 27–32; public health pioneers in, 30–31; reading tracks and culture, 242–44; reformers in, 140–47; role of game hunters in, 185–212; sausage maker autonomy in, 68; street dogs in, 33–38; tentative findings regarding, 241–4; urban ecology as sensory experience in, 22–26; war against typhus, 31. *See also* animal deaths

Mexico City, 1, *66*; animals thriving in darkness in, 25; artificial urban lighting in, 25; bans in, 140–47; brief history of bullfighting in, 123–25; bullfighting fans in, 91–92; bullfighting venue construction in, 127–35; calls for assistance in "saneamiento" in, 24; canine scavengers in, 34; contract dog killers in, 38–43; creating mass spectacle of leisure in, 125–27; displacing death in, 62–65, 67; drive for better public health and hygiene in, 27–32; efficient dealers in death in, 25–26; feces and water issues in, 24; increase of parks in, 56–60; moving clandestine meat in, 67–69; obvious death as taboo in, 26; overview, 19–22; *pelea de gallos* in, 72–81; rapid urbanization in, 22, 24; reformers in, 140–47; sensory world of, 24–25; street dogs in, 19–53; terminology of, 254n42; urban ecology as sensory experience in, 22–26; weather in, 95. *See also* animal deaths

Military Hospital, 30
Ministry of Development (Mexico), 204
missing animals lost and found. See *corral de mostrenco*
mixed city, 1, 54, 56–57, 62, 64, 81–82
modes of interaction, 5–6

Mondragón (family name), 129
Montes, Antonio, 101, 108–9, 138, 166
moral ecology, 5–7, 11–12, 14; in bullfighting, 88, 99, 106, 116, 120, 123, 140, 148, 151, 153, 174–76, 179–81; and cockfighting crowds, 56, 61, 79, 81; food and subsistence, 81–82; hunters and, 214–15, 217, 228–29, 237; idea of, 249–52; rendering meanings to other communities, 46; resistance to outside interference, 54–55; sportsman and, 186, 189, 198, 201
moral economy, 249–50
moral law, 198
Moreno, Fernando, 30
mortality, visibility of, 62–65, 67
mounting, practices of, 225–29, *227*
muermo (glanders), 70
Mundo Ilustrado, El, *115*, *193*, *195*
municipalities, animal deaths in: displacing death, 62–65, 67; green boulevards and busy outskirts, 56–60; missing animals lost and found, 70; official limits on visibly killing food animals, 55–56; overview, 54–56, 81–83; *pelea de gallos*, 72–81; slaughter displacement, 67–69; suburban *afueras*, 61–62
Murguia, Pedro, 41
music, bullfight audience and, 107–10

National Autonomous University of Mexico (UNAM), 76
national patrimony, preserving and conserving, 194
native hunters. *See* indigenous hunters
nature as natural wealth. *See riqueza pública*
navajas, 73, 76–77
Navarro, Eduardo, 30
necropolitics, 12, 14, 16, 52–53, 240, 251; biopolitics and, 35–36; constitution of, 35; consumer moral ecology and, 120; in *corrida*, 122, 151, 154, 166, 181; and death of the lesser, 63; defining, 4–5; and discourse of public health and hygiene, 27–28; extending logic of, 10–11; food animals and, 55; hunters and, 216, 219, 237–38; and imprint of power, 82–83; indifference to death, 89; influencing benign policies and institutions, 27; and liberal-capitalist state, 20; manifestation of, 21–22; and notions of the acceptable, 56; opposition to, 45; political ecology shaped by, 6–7; tentative findings, 241–44; theoretical intervention, 246–49; wild animals and, 185–86, 206, 212
Neira, José Sanchez de, 104–5
newspapers: bullfighting fandom in, 102–5; reporting on *broncas*, 112–19, *113*, *115*, *117*; reporting on venue construction, 132–35; specialty papers, 99–101
New York Times, 116
Niño, Fernando Gutiérrez el, 126
Noecker, María Luisa, 92, 109, 152, 154, 159, 160, 163
Norris, Richard, 116
Norton, Marcy, 6, 10
Novísima recopilación de las Leyes de España, 204–5
Nuñez, Augustin Alfredo, 118–19

Obregón, Alvaro, 159
ocelots, 62, 222, 235
O'Farril, Gonzalo Bautista, 207
operas. *See zarzuelas*
Opinión Nacional, La, 39
Ortega y Gasset, José, 187, 189, 278n5
Other, the, 7, 20, 36, 56, 120, 122, 212, 241–42, 245, 247–48
outsiders, ineffable memories of, 148–50
outskirts, business of, 56–60. See also *afueras*

Pagés. Angela. *See* Angelita (matadora)
País, El, 160, 167
pajuelas, 95
Palacio, Luis, 35
paladins of humanity, 143
palenques. *See* arena, animal deaths in
Parangueo, 136
Paris Exposition, 144
parks, increase of, 59
partridges, 65, 208

INDEX

Paseo, 127
Paseo de la Reforma, 29
Paseo Nuevo, 124
paso en redondo (round step), 106
paso en rodillas (turn from the knees), 106
Pasteur Institute, 29, 31
Pavón, González, 138
pelea de gallos (cockfight), 55; ban on, 76–77; basis for rules of, 76; and bullfighting, 143; as common part of life, 72; crowd behavior at, 79; dodging bans of, 80–81; endurance of, 72; first recorded fight, 73, 75; gambling at heart of, 78–79; integration into Mexican culture, 77–78; nationalism and, 78; necropolitical assumptions, 83; new regulations for, 75–76; opportunity for, 76–77; outside observers of, 80; photograph of, *74*; science of, 77; simplicity of, 73; venue for, 73. See also *corrida*
Peralvillo, Mexico, 1, 22, 24
Pérez, Cirilio, 160, 162, 165
Pérez Grovas, Pedro, 30–31, 196
Perez, Ramón, 33
Periá, Julio, 119, 135
Periquillo Sarniento, 31
perros callejeros. See street dogs
pheasants, 65, 216
Pickett, Will, 139
Piedras Negras, 136, 138
pigs, displacing slaughter of, 67–69
Pilcher, Jeffrey, 68–69
Pimiento (matador), 156
Plaza Bucareli, 108, 127, 132
Plaza Chapultepec, 130
Plaza de Toros, 114, 127, 129–30, 130, 133
Plaza Mexico (Condesa), 127
Plaza Nuevo, 139
poblaciónes (populations), 57
"poblaciones," removal of hunting from, 194, 196
political ecology, 6–7, 13–14, 181, 211, 237, 240, 249–50; city ordinances as, 36; conservationist efforts representing, 212; demonstrating workings of, 20–22; displacing slaughter, 69; drive for better public health and hygiene, 27; and elite mestizo huntsmen, 201; foreign hunters and, 219, 223; hunting laws abroad, 203; indigenous hunting and, 217–18; legalist scientific political ecology, 185–87; moral ecology coaligning with, 180; "nature state" and, 212; people shaping their foodways and choices, 55; *riqueza pública* management, 205; setting hunting against broader socio-legal structures of, 226; society shaping, 203
politics, matador and, 157–59
"pontífice de la torería" (pontiff of bullfighting). See Gaona, Rodolfo
poor (class), 8, 14, 53; and bullfighting, 80, 82, 124; claims regarding food of, 64; comparing to street dogs, 46, 48, 50, 52; dogs as enemies of, 39; and Great Separation, 55; and hunting, 190, 198, 203, 206, 211, 215, 238; liberal-capitalist state affecting, 20; menu of, 65; at parks, 60; policing, 25; and slaughter displacement, 68; targeting, 27–28
populations. See parks, increase of; *poblaciónes*
Porfirian era, 4
Porfirian Persuasion, 91
Porfirians, 96
Porfiriato, 21, 48, 88, 179, 205
Posada, José Guadalupe, *49*, 110, *111*, *128*, *155*, *168*
possums, 1, 62, 205
potassium cyanide (KCn), 43
Prensa Ilustrado, 43
preservation, practices of, 225–29, *227*
president, huntsman image of, 230–36, *231*, *233*, *234*, *236*
Pretel, Lolita. See Lolita (matadora)
promoters (of bullfighting), 17, 89, 91–92, 104, 120–21, 242; bans and reformers, 145–47; bullfight as experience, 95–98; and bullfighting industry, 130–32; bulls as stars, 174–76; and female matadors, 176–78; and foreigners, 150–51; and mass spectacles, 126–27; matador management, 171–73; and societal tastes, 178–82; and the weird, 139–40

public figure, matador as, 169–71
public health and hygiene: banning animals from households, 28; dogs as test subjects, 31; empowering discourse of, 27–28; pets and, 28–29; public health pioneers in, 30–31; reserving forests for, 59; securing streets, 29–30; sterilization, 28–29; and urban ecology as sensory experience, 22–26; war against rabies in, 29–30; war against typhus, 31
public indifference, term, 240

quite galleado (cape behind back), 106

rabies, 10–11, 28–31, 33, 35–36, 38–42, 44, 46, 56, 62, 144, 201
racism, double standards of. *See* indigenous hunters
Ramírez, Arcadio, 166
Ratas y Mamarrachas, 99, 101, 133–35, 160, 167; and new fandom in papers, 102–5; and nostalgic fandom, 106; reporting on *broncas*, 118
ratoneros, 77
rats, 1, 4, 25, 33, 57, 61, 102
rebajimiento de afición (lowering of the fans), 167
"Recuerdos y suplicas a Don Ponciano," 104
reformers: boxing fans, 145–46; bull as Othered object, 140–41; different approaches, 144–45; "social good" argument, 146–47; SPCMA role in, 141–44
Regidor de Policía, 40–41
"relations of enmity," 247
religion, coding bulls with, 175–76
Remington, Frederick, 196–97, 222
"repeopling," control over, 248–49
reputation (of matadors), 169–71
Reverte Mexicano, 156, 166
Revueltas, Victor, 35
riots (at bullfight), 112–19, *113*, *115*, *117*
riqueza pública (nature as natural wealth), 186
ritual alternativa (ritual), 172

Robles Gil (family name), 129
Rodríguez, Juan, 30
Romero Rubio, Carmen, 80, 142, 244
Roosevelt, Kermit, 223
Royal Society for the Protection and Care of Animals (RSPCA), 34, 45
Runaway Daughters (Noecker), 154

Salieri, Juan Romero, 167
Salm-Salm, Agnes (princess), 28
salto de la garrocha (pole-vaulting bull using spear), 106
salubridad. *See* public health and hygiene
Sánchez de Neira, 103
San Diego de los Padres, 136
Sandoval, Aureliano Urrutia, 157
"saneamiento" (making healthy), assistance in, 24
San Hipólito's Day, 123
Sanitary Code. *See* Código Sanitario
Sanitary Code of 1891, 30
Sanitary Code of 1902, 28
Sanitary Service. *See* Servicio Sanitario
San Lázaro, 1
San Nicolás Peralta, 136
San Rafael, 127
Santa Ana, Antonio López de, 75
Santa Cruz Acatlán, 35
Santa (novel), 165
Santiago, Benito José Agustin de la Peña y, 39
Santiago Gil, 156
Santín, 136
Santo Domingo, dogs in, 45
satellites, term, 57
scalpers, bullfighting and, 95–96
Schubert, Adrian, 10, 162
Schwatta, Frederick, 222
Scott, James, 90, 250
Scribner's Magazine, 221
Second Empire, 75
sensory experience, urban ecology as, 22–26
Serpell, James, 62
Servicio Sanitario (Sanitary Service), 30
Sierra Madre Occidental, 222

Sierro, Justo, 31
Silveti, Juan, 107, 166
Sinclair, Upton, 68
singing, bullfight audience and, 107–10
skunks, 62, 219
slaughter, displacing, 67–69
Sloan, Kathryn, 154
society, tastes of, 179–81
"Society de marras." *See* Society for the Protection and Care of Mexican Animals
Sol, El, 160
Soledad, A. José, 124
soltadores (releasers), 73. See also *pelea de gallos*
Sol y Sombra, 104–5
Soto, Gabriel, 35
Spain, 10, 46, 130, 135, 146, 153, 156, 158–59, 172, 175; breeding stock from, 136–39, *137*; brief history of bullfighting in, 123–25; folksongs, 107–9; precedent of the weird in, 139–41; spectators in, 112, 114; *toreras* in, 106, 153, 176–78
SPCMA. *See* Mexican Society for the Protection and Care of Animals
Special Committee of Ladies, 141
sportsman, idealization of, 196
sportsman's creed: Baume and, 198–99, 201; Blazquez and, 190–92; López and M. López with best articulation for, 194–98; "new age" of hunting, 189
stalking, superiority of, 191, 194
stars, making: bulls, 174–76; matadors, 171–73
stray dogs, poor selling meat of, 65
street animals, culling of. *See* street dogs
street dogs: and arrival of influential foreigners, 50; baseline for sentiments about, 28–29; cadavers as spectacle, 44–46; *callejero* as description, 52; contract dog killers, 38–43; countering intuitions about "man's best friend," 35–36; and drive for public health and hygiene, 27–32; finding social equals in other urban venues, 50, 52; as gradually ubiquitous presence, 33–34; meaning of term, 48, 50; mitigating dangers of, 36; in other cities, 34–35; overview, 19–22, 52–53; racist discourses overlapping with, 46, 48; reports of killings of, 36, 38; urban ecology as sensory experience, 22–26; in war against typhus, 31

Strother, David, 28–29
suburbs, term, 57
Sunday hunters, 190–91
Superior Health Council, 30
surrounds. See *alrededores*
swine, displacing slaughter of, 67–69
synanthropes, 19, 62

Tacubaya, 67, 132
tame, term, 201–2
tauromachia (bullfighting arts), 89. See also *corrida*
taxidermy, hunting and, 225–29, *227*
Tempesta, Antonio, 70
Tenorio-Trilllo, Mauricio, 10, 61
Tepeyahualco, 136, 138
Thomas, William, 220
Thompson, E. P., 249–501
Thrift, Nigel, 55, 63
Tiburón Island, 222
Tiempo, El, 287n110
tió de coleta, lifestyle of, 169
tipos degenerados, 30
Toreo, El (building), 126, 156, 158
Toreo, El (paper), 99–101, *117*, 127, 129, 131, 133, *137*, 138, 160
toreras (female bullfighters), 176–78
toreros. See bullfighter
Tornal, Luis G., 98
toros bravos (fighting bulls), 103, 136
Torre, Ignacio de la, 129, 136
Torreón Plaza, 101
Torres, Juan, 40
tracks, reading, 242–44
traps, using, 191, 194, 196–97, 201, 206, 209
travelers, ineffable memories of, 148–50

Trepiedig Company, 41
trophies. *See* mounting, practices of
true Indian hunting. *See* indigenous hunters
"Two Roosters Fighting" (Hondius and Tempesta), *71*
typhus, war against, 31

UNAM. *See* National Autonomous University of Mexico
United States, 5, 34, 45, 80, 148, 191, 202
urban critters, categories of, 61–62
urban ecology, sensory experience of, 22–26
urbanization, animosity toward, 190. *See also* Blazquez, Pedro
urban-rural boundaries, blurring, 56–60
Urbina, Tomás, 77
Urrutia, Aureliano, 30, 157–58

Valentine (hunting guide), 220–21
Vámanos con Pancho Villa (film), 140
van dos, term, 109
Vasquez, Jesús, 40
veladores (watchmen), 109
venues, constructing: appointments based on patronage or favoritism, 134–35; building spree, 127–29, *128*; commercial investment, 129–30; construction complexity, 129; general policy regulation, 131–32; matador businessmen, 130–31; newspapers reporting on new plazas, 132–34; setting hygiene regulations, 131. See also *corrdia*
Vera Cruz, Mexico, 22, *23*, 81
vermin, term, 201–2
Viga Canal, *66*
Villasana, J. M., *47*, *51*
vultures, 22, *23*, 41, 61, 67, 223

walkways. See *carrederas*
Warren, Louis, 202
water fountain, installing, 141–42
Weiner, Carlos, 48
weird, selling, 139–40
White, Richard, 249
wild, term, 201–2
wild animals, killing: historical trajectory of conservation, 204–11; hunting laws, 201–3; intimate kill, 187–89; overview, 185–87, 211–12; sportsman's creed, 189–201, *193*, *195*, *200*
Wildlife Code of 1894, 205–7
wilds, animal deaths in: historical trajectory of conservation, 204–11; hunter performances, 213–38; hunting laws, 201–3; intimate kill, 187–89; overview, 185–87, 211–12; sportsman's creed, 189–201, *193*, *195*, *200*
Wild West Show, 139
Woods of Death, 191
working class, taming of, 60
World's Fair, 114
World War I, 31

Xochimilco, Mexico, 22

Yaqui, constructing as Other, 199, 216–17, 220, 222, 224
Yeaza, Jesús de, 129
Yucatán, travelers, 219

Zamora, Lino, 156
Zapata, Emiliano, 77
zarzuelas (operas), 94
Zayas, Alberto, 138
Žižek, Slavoj, 288n26

www.ingramcontent.com/pod-product-compliance
Lightning Source LLC
Chambersburg PA
CBHW020637230426
43665CB00008B/207